River of the Golden Ibis

A Florida Sand Dollar Book

River of the

Illustrated by
Ben F. Stahl, Jr.

Golden Ibis

Gloria Jahoda

University Press of Florida

Gainesville · Tallahassee · Tampa · Boca Raton
Pensacola · Orlando · Miami · Jacksonville

Other Books in the Florida Sand Dollar Series

Nine Florida Stories by Marjory Stoneman Douglas, edited by Kevin M. McCarthy (1990)

Flagler: Rockefeller Partner and Florida Baron, by Edward N. Akin (1992)

St. Petersburg and the Florida Dream, 1888–1950, by Raymond Arsenault (1996)

Southwest Florida's Wetland Wilderness: Big Cypress Swamp and the Ten Thousand Islands,
     by Jeff Ripple (1996)

Some Kind of Paradise, by Mark Derr (1998)

The Immigrant World of Ybor City: Italians and Their Latin Neighbors in Tampa, 1885–1985,
     by Gary R. Mormino and George E. Pozzetta (1998)

Surrounded on Three Sides, by John Keasler (1999)

Palmetto Leaves, by Harriet Beecher Stowe (1999)

Sunshine States: Wild Times and Extraordinary Lives in the Land of Gators, Guns, and Grapefruit,
     by Patrick Carr (1999)

Contemplations of a Primal Mind, by Gabriel Horn (2000)

River of the Golden Ibis, by Gloria Jahoda (2000)

Going to Miami: Exiles, Tourists and Refugees in the New America, by David Rieff (2000)

Copyright 1973 by Gloria Jahoda

This 2000 paperback edition reprinted by arrangement with Henry Holt and Company, LLC
Printed in the United States of America on acid-free paper
All rights reserved

05 04 03 02 01 00   6 5 4 3 2 1

Library of Congress Cataloging-in-Publication Data

Jahoda, Gloria.
River of the Golden Ibis / Gloria Jahoda.
p.cm. – (Florida sand dollar series)
Originally published: New York: Holt, Rinehart & Winston, 1973.
Includes bibliographical references and index.
ISBN 0-8130-1789-0 (paper)
1. Hillsborough County (Fla.)—History. 2. Tampa Bay region (Fla.)—History. I. Title.
II. Series.
F317.H6 J33 2000
975.9'65—dc21   99-058807

The University Press of Florida is the scholarly publishing agency for the State University
System of Florida, comprising Florida A&M University, Florida Atlantic University, Florida
International University, Florida State University, University of Central Florida, University
of Florida, University of North Florida, University of South Florida, and University of West
Florida.

University Press of Florida
15 Northwest 15th Street
Gainesville, FL 32611-2079
http://www.upf.com

For
Nigel Coxe,
  in token of a gift of music;
Ella Grainger,
  in token of a gift of memory;
Stewart Manville and Ralph Stang,
  in token of a gift of faith.

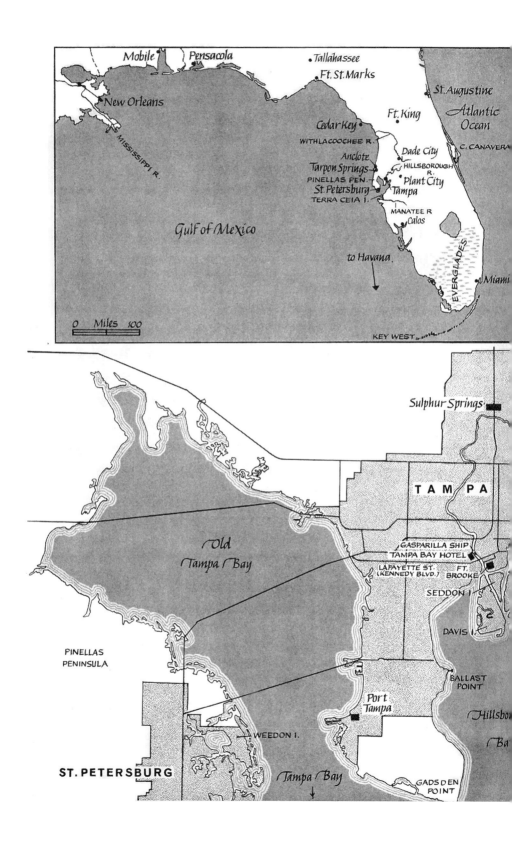

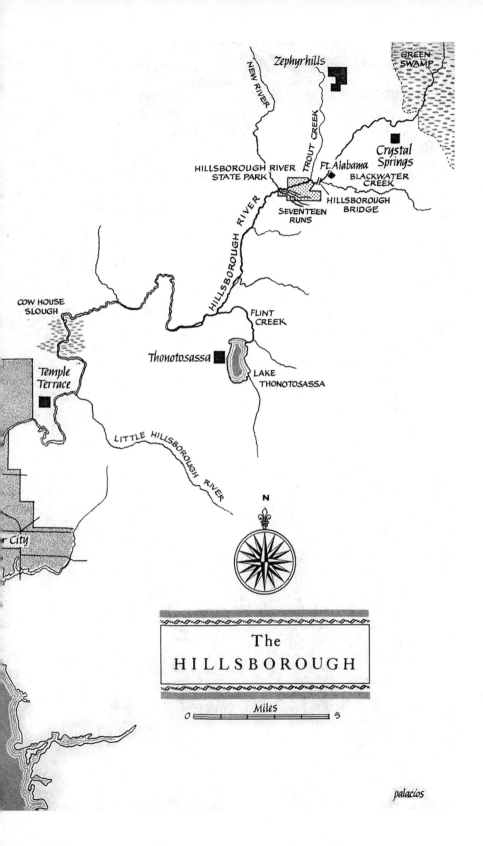

GREEN SWAMP

Zephyrhills

NEW RIVER

TROUT CREEK

Crystal Springs

HILLSBOROUGH RIVER STATE PARK

Ft. Alabama

BLACKWATER CREEK

HILLSBOROUGH BRIDGE

SEVENTEEN RUNS

HILLSBOROUGH RIVER

COW HOUSE SLOUGH

FLINT CREEK

Thonotosassa

LAKE THONOTOSASSA

Temple Terrace

LITTLE HILLSBOROUGH RIVER

City

N

The
HILLSBOROUGH

Miles

0   5

palacios

Contents

ACKNOWLEDGMENTS   Grateful acknowledgment is made to the following copyright holders for material quoted: ASCAP and the Estate of Elmer Schoebel for lines from "The Senior Citizen" by Elmer Schoebel; Chiquita Brands, Inc., for "The Chiquita Banana Song"; Devin-Adair Co. for material from *José Martí* by Jorge Manach; Exposition Press for material from *The Bell(e)s of St. Petersburg* by Milton Paul Magly; Farrar, Straus & Giroux and the Sterling Lord Agency for material from *Big Sur* by Jack Kerouac, © 1962 by Jack Kerouac; the University of Florida Press for quotations from *Frank M. Chapman in Florida* by Elizabeth Austin; Harcourt Brace Jovanovich for extracts from *The Town and the City* by Jack Kerouac; Little Brown and Co. for material from *The Little War of Private Post* by Charles Johnson Post; McGraw-Hill and Co. for extracts from *Billy Graham* by John Pollock; Ye Mystic Krewe of Gasparilla, Tampa, Fla., for lines from *The Life . . . of Gasparilla* by Edwin Dart Lambright and for quotations from the Gasparilla Festival Program of 1971; New Directions Publishing Corporation for lines from "Elegaic Feelings American (For the Dear Memory of John Kerouac)" by Gregory Corso, © 1970 by Gregory Corso; University of Oklahoma Press for extracts from *The Seminoles* by Edwin McReynolds; Mrs. Grace Sell, Naples, Fla., for material from *The Hysteria of Flour Dough* by William Sell; the Skidmore Music Co. for lines from "Yes! We Have No Bananas" by Frank Silver and Irving Cohn, copyright 1923 by Skidmore Music Co., 666 Fifth Avenue, New York, N.Y. 10019, copyright renewed and assigned to Skidmore Music Co., Inc.; the Viking Press for an excerpt from *On the Road* by Jack Kerouac, © 1955, 1957 by Jack Kerouac.

I am indebted to the following people and organizations for valuable information, insights, and generous cooperation: Miss Margaret Chapman of the library of the University of South Florida, Tampa, Fla.; Mr. Nigel Coxe, Amherst, Mass.; Mr. T. E. Culbreath of the Hav-a-Tampa Cigar Co., Tampa, Fla.; the Marchioness of Downshire, London; the late Karl Grismer whose histories of Tampa and St. Petersburg are exhaustive; the Hillsborough River State Park; my husband, Gerald Jahoda; "Joe," who introduced me to the River of the Golden Ibis; Mr. Frank Laumer of Dade

City, Fla., who has written the definitive account of the Dade Massacre; Dr. Durward Long of the University of Wisconsin who shared his manuscripts on Tampa with me most graciously; Mr. Anthony P. Pizzo of Tampa, Fla., first Alcade of Ybor City; the St. Petersburg Chamber of Commerce; Mr. Charles Salter of the Florida Forest Service, Tallahassee, Fla.; Miss Bonnie Sharp of the Division of Parks and Recreation, Tallahassee, Fla.; Miss Mary Nic Shenk, St. Petersburg, Fla.; Mr. James Stevenson of the Division of Parks and Recreation, Tallahassee, Fla.; the Tampa Chamber of Commerce; Miss Mary Rae Thompson of the Hillsborough County Historical Commission; Captain John D. Ware, Tampa, Fla.; Mrs. Harry Weedon of the Tampa Public Library; Mr. Harold Werner, Dade City, Fla.; and Mr. Esteban Valdes, Ybor City, Tampa, Fla.

GLORIA JAHODA

Tallahassee, Florida
July 1972

CARL CARMER

Foreword

A few years ago when my wife and I bade a cherished guest farewell after he had spent a week of Florida sunshine with us, we discovered that he had carelessly left behind a book entitled *The Other Florida*.

Because my major interest has for many years been the investigation of the quirks, the vagaries, the whimsicalities of unique areas of the United States I looked upon this volume as possibly valuable to me and not necessarily to be returned to its legal owner without my perusal. Since I have been the editor of the Rivers of America Series for more than a decade I looked upon the contents of the volume as material that somehow could be composed into the kind of music that other writers have patterned from their affectionate memories of waters that once enchanted their respective childhoods, and from the documented truths of history.

No sooner had I completed my reading of *The Other Florida* than I recommended to my publisher-employers that they communicate to the author their desire for her to choose the river that she loved best and write a manuscript telling the sources of her emotion to all readers who might wish to know. The answers she sent Holt, Rinehart and Winston were quick and decisive and the staff immediately found itself committed to present them to its national audience.

The word "discovery" must be used with meticulous exactitude when a fellow writer attempts to communicate enthusiasm in a foreword for a new book such as this. A former reader of Gloria Jahoda's work might well speak out in sharp criticism of anyone claiming to be her discoverer by announcing, "I've been reading this author for years." Such statements leave the writer of this Introduction searching his mind and memory for those facts, those qualities, and those savors with which she has enriched her previous writings.

The introducer of *this* author to her prospective audience, then, must take into consideration the size of her already won enthusiastic following and the possibility of increasing it. That was attained as soon as Mrs. Jahoda began to write for publication. No sooner had she done so than the circle of readers from her Florida locale began its certain enlargement.

Suddenly, to a publisher's offices where great books are sometimes born, came the realization that from this manuscript emanated not only the essence of an American stream but the comprehensive soul of America itself. An understanding of a vast people with all its history and traditions had asserted itself in the musical prose of a woman whose knowledge of her native country was prodigious. Here was an author whose eagerness to celebrate the land and its waters was implicit in her every syllable.

Ignoring the requisites of the Rivers Series she had chosen to write what was in her own judgment a work of art, regardless of its demands upon her creative abilities. Her talents proved so limitless that it was no longer a question of a book about a river. Her volume had transcended the details of the Hillsborough and it could not in all fairness be restricted to the Rivers of America Series. The country as a whole will find itself under the spell of a major writer who has chosen to entitle this book *River of the Golden Ibis.*

River of
the Ibises

The Hillsborough begins in the Green Swamp, nine hundred square miles of central Florida wilderness where white ibises drift in the shadows over willow-bordered pools. From high water oaks grey Spanish moss trails softly. The stillness is broken by the songs of Carolina wrens in the thickets, by the insistent voices of leopard frogs, by the calling of rain crows on slow summer afternoons. The smells are acrid: tannin-stained sloughs and the sourness of the hydrogen sulfide and methane gases that rise when the mud is turned by the foot of some wild creature, by a rare canoe, by a storm. Pileated woodpeckers rap high in the pines in the drier places, where the ground rises a foot or two and bare sand shows under pinestraw that glistens rusty in a fitful swampland sun. The Green Swamp is a trackless place. Its milky clusters of crinum lilies spend their beauty unseen by men, and bobcats prowl the tangles unafraid. The world of the white ibises is, as yet, inviolate. When the light strikes their feathers through the canopy above, they shimmer in a blaze of gold.

The Green Swamp is the southernmost large mixed hardwood swamp in Florida. South of it stretch the flats of the great Kissimmee Prairie, until these merge into the heat-flickering saw-grass distances of the Everglades. The Everglades are storied; they are also accessible these days, crossed by two major highways and studded with nature sanctuaries operated by the National Park system. No one has made an official wildlife refuge of the Green Swamp. Roads skirt it but never quite penetrate it. Long ago the Seminole Indians who now people the Everglades left the Green Swamp to white men who settled on its fringes but never hacked through to tame its interior. No Everglades airboats can conquer columns of cypress and sweet gum towering above matted shrubs tangled in turn with smilax and wild grape and thorn. Boggy muck underfoot, thick growth overhead and on every side are features the Green Swamp shares with other southeastern swamps. But the Green Swamp is special. It has been touched by the tropics. Wild orchids festoon the rough trunks of its temperate-zone trees as well as its palms, and leathery-leaved bromeliads shine in its morning dews. It is never true tropics, with such exotics as mahogany and gumbo-limbo. Rather, it is a humid woodland unique because its familiar species are interspersed with harbingers of Central America but never overpowered by them. The orchids of the Green Swamp are never commonplaces; they are fragile reminders that another world of nature is about to begin but has not begun yet, that the Green Swamp magnolias and ashes are almost the last of their kind on a southward pilgrimage which must end in steel-tough saw grass and, eventually, coral islands. And last things, too, are fragile, not commonplace, in the imagination of man.

From the Green Swamp flow five rivers: the Kissimmee and Peace southward, the Oklawaha toward the north, the Withlacoochee northwest to Inglis and Yankeetown and the Gulf of Mexico, and the Hillsborough southwest to the city of Tampa and Hillsborough Bay and then greater Tampa Bay, where Anna Maria Island and Egmont Key are the first Gulf landmarks met by oceangoing ships inbound for the largest harbor in the United States between Norfolk and New Orleans. During the summer rainy season, the Withlacoochee and the Hillsborough are one within the swamp, though their currents can be seen running in opposite directions in the same pool. Where the Hillsborough begins is wherever its current may first be distinguished; the place changes with the rising and lowering of the Green Swamp's water table. At Crystal Springs, on the swamp's edge, I have cupped the river's fresh sweet water in my hands and drunk.

In the cities, Tampa and St. Petersburg, the Hillsborough and Tampa Bay are eloquent of civilization. Too much so, conservation purists say. The river winds through downtown Tampa past high alabaster buildings,

The Green Swamp

a stunning Florida sun gleaming back from their shiny pallor. It coils its way beneath the smoky blue boughs of blooming jacaranda trees on streamside banks until, freighted with fragments of water hyacinth, it flows under bridges burdened with ceaseless traffic out to glassy stretches of salt water. In summer some of Tampa Bay's mangrove clusters are thick with rookeries of shy roseate spoonbills. Both river and bay have their paradoxes. In St. Petersburg you can watch the spoonbills from a superhighway. Everywhere there the atmosphere is a special luminous whiteness thrown up to the horizon from water on every side.

The river and the bay have all the Florida glamour of tourist postcards. Along the Hillsborough's central curve lies a state park, where raccoons file past woodland cottage doors in the morning and the evening. In the Port of Tampa loaded banana wharves crowd phosphate piers, foreign freighters loom proud bows, and the city night-lights strung along causeways flicker like star sapphires. Nearby Bird Island shelters an Audubon sanctuary where brown pelicans roost. Mixtures dazzle: pollution and crystalline beauty, solitudes and crowds, the wispy rustles of casuarina trees along the beaches and the clang of commerce at the docks. For the Hillsborough and Tampa Bay are an ever-changing pageant. They are a part of Florida's urbanized, publicized Suncoast. Yet they also contain primeval fastnesses in the outer islands of tangled mangrove roots and, in the interior, forests where ironwoods and hackberries are so dense that sunlight in them is an occasional shock of yellow on brown earth rich with leaf mold.

The Suncoast is only occasionally the domain of the homespun Florida Cracker. For the most part he has moved northward into the Deep South. Suncoast people are vacationers, middle-American retirees, transplanted northern businessmen and—according to rumor—the Mafia. The Suncoast's native Floridians aren't apt to be rural by inclination or by heritage. Since I live in north Florida, I too am a tourist on the Suncoast. But so is, or was originally, nearly everyone else. Tourism has written the history of the river and the bay as surely as it has written that of Miami Beach.

I had known the bay even before my husband and I moved to Florida in 1963. As northern vacationers before that we had several times crossed the arching Sunshine Skyway from St. Petersburg to Terra Ceia Island and thereafter a Florida of coconut palms and flame trees. My first sight of the river itself came after we had come to Florida to stay.

One afternoon I stood on the balcony of a downtown Tampa motel over the Kennedy Boulevard Bridge. I saw the slow river and the brilliant bay beyond; I also saw the Arabian Nights. On the opposite bank silver-topped minarets were glittering above dark magnolia trees. A red brick Moorish castle sprawled in heroic dimensions that were astounding and yet strangely familiar. Railroad tycoon Henry B. Plant's Tampa Bay Hotel, now the University of Tampa, is a surprising spectacle of turn-of-the-century fantasy gone wild. But I knew I had seen it before, and soon I remembered where.

It had been in Chicago, in my grandmother's house, an old brownstone full of mementoes of her career as a singer. Beyond its golden-oak-framed windows a January snow had been falling softly. I had been poring over her collection of postcards. When Victorian convention had decreed her retirement at marriage, she had begun saving messages from friends who still traveled. The collection had grown huge, and as a child I loved dreaming of seeing all its places myself some day, when I would escape the world of cornfields, grey Depression cities, and antiseptic suburbs that was Illinois for me. Stockholm, Paris, Berlin, London, San Francisco—and Florida. Especially Florida. Plant's Arabian pile graced most of the postcards from Tampa, and there were many. The Tampa Bay Hotel had cachet.

After that afternoon on the balcony in Tampa I unearthed the postcards I had long since inherited. Quickly I found the one that had, for me, been special. "Lafayette Street Bridge, Tampa Bay Hotel in Background. Beautiful Florida Series. C. T. American Art Colored. Courtesy of the Tourist Information Bureau of the Tampa (Fla.) Board of Trade. This bridge was erected at a cost of approximately three hundred and fifty thousand dollars. It is of the cantilever type." The cost of the hotel had been left to the imagination.

"Dear Mrs. Peterson," someone named E. B. Mintline had written my grandmother, "the weather is beautiful. Just like June in January! My, but you'd love it down here. Hard to believe it isn't balmy and green in Chicago. We wish you were with us to enjoy it." Nineteen twenty-eight: Henry Plant's minarets were there, but also two biplanes and two monoplanes in the sky to betoken Progress, decorous pedestrians in cloche hats and derbies, electric broughams and touring cars with fabric tops. The card is a painting, not a photograph. Trolleys are colored an Aztec gold, the waters of the Hillsborough a violent turquoise. At the foot of the bridge—for Lafayette Street became Kennedy Boulevard only in 1963—rocks a white sailing sloop. June in January indeed! The triteness of the sentiments escaped me. I had never seen June in January then. I had never, in my sober childhood world, seen anything like Henry Plant's hotel. I had never seen a turquoise river or a magnolia or four airplanes in the sky at once. I had never been in a sailboat. How marvelous must be Tampa, Florida, with its three hundred and fifty thousand dollar cantilever bridge! When I grew up I would go there. And I did, though I had forgotten the postcard until I stood on a motel balcony overlooking the reality.

The next time I saw the Hillsborough it was the wilderness river northeast of the cities. For me this was a voyage of discovery. For Joe, my companion and guide, it was a voyage of farewell. He had lived all his life on the river; now he had been drafted, though he had not yet finished a graduate degree in biology. Joe knew the river as no one else did, Florida Park Board officials had told me. He was writing a dissertation on the birds of Florida swamps. Joe had a red canoe and a cheerful willingness to paddle while a writer asked questions and took notes. He was twenty-two. We would glide downstream all the way from the Green Swamp into Tampa's outskirts. He hoped I knew how to shoot rapids and to portage. I did, I assured him, though I was astonished. Rapids? In Florida, where rivers are level and lazy? But the Hillsborough, perhaps uniquely, has several sets, each swifter than the last; the river falls three feet per mile on its course toward Tampa Bay. Not only were there rapids—eight sets by my count—where I had to kneel in the boat as Joe maneuvered it furiously and we careened over rock beds, but also portages formidable indeed in midsummer heat.

"I hope you use waterproof ink, ma'am?" Joe murmured. Water hyacinths had collected in huge masses, and we waded in muck up to our knees, through dense lavender blooms gorgeous to the eye but agonizing to the foot. Balance was precarious. At the end of the afternoon I knew that Joe might be twenty-two but I was not. We were covered with mud, our faces streaked. At the suburban Tampa fish camp where we tied up, people stared at our dishevelment. Undaunted, Joe discussed contamination and salinity and Tampa sewage operations that had made the urban river to the west a place unsafe to swim in, let alone drink. We had come only about thirty miles as the crow flies, but we had passed through different worlds.

There had been the Green Swamp in early morning mist, its eternities formless. Then the sun had broken through, and the wings of the drifting ibises had caught its light. High plumes of dog fennel had waved on the banks like conquistadores' feathers. Young pine trunks grew stockade-thick wherever the ground rose. All morning we glided between the mossy ribbons of the banks, among myrtle bushes and swamp lilies and yellow clumps of coreopsis. We passed rocky outcrops that were forty million years old, Joe said, dating back to the Oligocene geological era. We met nobody. In the river bottom lay tiny apple snails, and at the bends the water beetles shimmered. Tricks and flashes of the light on crusted trunks were mesmerizing. Wild butterfly orchids hung purple-brown from the treetops; ferns interwove their blue-green fronds high overhead. Once a prothonotary warbler followed our canoe, a panoply of orange head and yellow back and dim blue wings, testimony of how few men ever invaded his domain. Mullets leaped. I heard the gentle thump, thump of the creeks flowing in, and after we had shot the last set of rapids we unwrapped our lunch sandwiches on a bank near an abandoned pioneer fort enduring only in two protruding logs at the bank's edge. Joe talked of his life then, of how he had brought his schoolbooks to the river's edge year after year, of how he had known and named all the alligators, of how he had painstakingly recorded the wildlife he feared would soon pass away forever. Tampa and St. Petersburg would grow; the Southwest Water Management District wanted to flood a stretch of the river called Seventeen Runs, a maze of tiny creeks. Only a few inches, the officials had said, but those few inches could mean life or death for the trees there. The Army Corps of Engineers were to do the work. The story is a sadly familiar one in the annals of Florida conservation.

We paddled on, into Seventeen Runs' dark tangles where ivory-billed woodpeckers had once called harshly. Now an occasional red-shouldered hawk screamed. Mosquitoes assaulted us and so did the afternoon heat. Time after time we struggled through solid walls of elephant ears and hyacinths, and to cheer me up Joe told me about his river experiences: of the day, for instance, when he had been canoeing with his girl and they had come on a group of teenage boys stark naked with axes in their hands.

"What did you do?" I laughed.

"Well, ma'am, I tied up and then I told those boys just exactly

what axing did to trees!" And his girl hadn't been surprised or embarrassed, for she was conservation-minded too.

The saddest thing about the contemporary ecology crusade was that
it had cheapened the word, Joe said. People would tire of conservation;
they would move on to other craze-causes, leaving the same small band
of naturalists to fight a losing war. As we floated on, the canopy overhead parted and we began to see patches of dead spatterdock weeds.
Phosphate lines ran into the river here, and with them pollution. The
myrtle stands thinned. Our idyll was nearly over. At the Tampa sewage
plant the stench was oppressive. No more birds, no more butterfly
orchids or shoestring ferns or pronged pineapplelike *Tillandsia fasci-
culata* plants nestled in tree crooks. But what I did not tell Joe was
that the Hillsborough in Tampa, and Tampa Bay, have their own
fascinations for me, that I thrill too at the sound of foghorns on ocean
liners, and that the echoes of Tampa wharves where black dockworkers
chant as they toil are, for me, a symphony of peculiar compulsion. So
are the clattering wind-bent African oil palms on St. Petersburg shores,
and the breezy white beaches where pensioners in straw hats fish and
bikini-clad girls play tag in the sand. From the time of the landing of
the conquistadores on Tampa Bay's shores, the Hillsborough and its
harbor have been the reason for the entire area's development. Hillsborough County, with Tampa, and Pinellas County, with St. Petersburg,
draw not only their water supply but their lives from the Hillsborough
as surely as do the shady reaches of the sloughs upstream where brown
limpkins forage for snails. From the Green Swamp to Egmont Key
in the Gulf is an aeon in time and more or less a day's trip in fact, but
the length of the river and the width of the bay are out of all proportion
to the influence they have had on Florida's history. And their drama
is not only one of nature but of human aspiration too.

Today the Suncoast is prime retirement territory. "In St. Petersburg,"
one of my friends once sighed to me, "every time I see the canes and
walkers on the streets I feel so *mortal*." St. Petersburg is a young town
too; it has its discotheques and boutiques, and southern football madness prevails; but it is the older citizens who have come seeking heaven
on earth. Elderly Tampans have searched out the same Utopia: a paradise of sun and warmth and cheap living and spectacular Gulf beach
landscapes. To numbers of Americans far from Florida, Hillsborough
River and Tampa Bay country are also heaven: a heaven to be strived

for, a distant goal. As heaven, the river and the bay bear an awesome responsibility. They draw a wide American cross-section, and so they affect much more of America than their mileage or even their winter fruits and vegetables which America savors would indicate. The story of river and bay is the story of what heaven is really like, how it got that way, and whether it has lived up to its reputation—if, indeed, a landscape must bear the onus of human dreams. On the banks of the Hillsborough and on the shores of the bay many men and women walk with the slow gait of people who have nowhere to go. They have reached the ultimate, and it must be enough.

To the first-time Suncoast visitor what assaults is the brightness. Florida whites are everywhere: in elderberry blossoms and wild mallows and puffy clouds and roadside egrets, in bridge rails and flowering arrowhead plants and billboards, even in washing machines on whitewashed shack porches and the tennis shoes of aged black women trudging home from cleaning jobs in St. Petersburg's stylish Maximo Moorings or Tampa's Davis Islands. Lawn furniture is white, as are shuffleboard courts and small neighborhood Baptist churches with picket fences. Highways glare in the timeless violence of the sun, and in gardens white crape myrtles open snowy racemes. The remembered world of the North is strangely dark when viewed from the Suncoast. Even in the shadowy expanses of the Green Swamp, white water hemlocks crowd along the banks and white ibises, turned briefly golden in the open places, are eternal seekers in the swamp's slow waters.

They have been for millions of years. Yet, once, they were not there. There was no swamp and no river and no bay. There was only the rain falling on the cooling compound of earth's elements for centuries of deluge, a grey and changeless sheet.

PART I
Invaders

1

The Landscape
Born

When the clouds and the rains finally passed, strong sunlight fell upon the seas of earth and warmed them. At last they bore life. If North America's biological history were to be depicted on a giant screen unrolling before us, we would see man only for the last seconds of the pageant. For a little longer, we would see the Hillsborough and Tampa Bay, though man did not come to them until years after his Old World evolution. Before mammals and birds had developed from saltwater ancestors, the world was a quiet place, its vast fish-filled oceans glittering through millennia of sunlight. Beneath the Atlantic, at the southeastern tip of North America, Florida lay submerged. When parts of it began to rise, southern Florida became an islanded arc of volcanic mountains. Continuous erosion and deposition buried them again, more deeply in some places than in others. A large trench separated the old mountain arc from the mainland. When the mountains sank down into it, it turned into a shallow sea that washed over the minerals beneath that were to become, in part, the Suncoast. The oldest fossil ever found in Florida is a partial turtle skeleton dating from the Cretaceous period of one hundred and twenty million years ago—the screen of North America's time not quite halfway unrolled. The fossil was discovered during drilling operations by the Amerada Petroleum Corporation near Lake Okeechobee in the summer of 1955, and it came from a core bored more than nine thousand feet into the ground. Possibly, scientists say, Cretaceous dinosaur remains

3

might be recovered under similar conditions, but this is not likely. Dinosaurs were land animals, and during much of prehistory Florida was beneath the Atlantic. By the time it had emerged dinosaurs were extinct.

Fossils found in Florida are almost always petrified—that is, the original animal bones and teeth have been replaced by mineral substances carried in solution through water over the entombed animal. Its body must be covered with sand immediately after death or the process cannot begin. The fossils of the river and the bay are occasional miracles, but few as they are they are our only key to a sea and, later, a land no reasoning being ever saw. The great quakes and upheavals that rocked from time to time were heeded only by fishes and amphibians and reptiles, most of them finally to be conquered by the mammal. The Suncoast remained sea until mammals had been dominant on earth for nearly fifty million years. Zeuglodon, a forty-foot-long, sharp-toothed whale with a thin body well adapted for speed, swam through the warm waters that churned where St. Petersburg, Tampa, and even the Green Swamp lie today. Only north Florida and the central ridge of the state which is now a sea of orange trees were then exposed. On their shores, as on tropical shores throughout the world, were born the earth's only salt-water trees, the mangroves. These, too, were to create Suncoast earth. Today mangroves are thick in the bay, as thick as in Cuba where Christopher Columbus exclaimed in disgust, "A cat couldn't get ashore!"

The world of the mangroves is a mysterious one. It is perpetually dim; waters rank with tannic acid swirl among exposed roots. The seeds of most mangroves germinate while they are attached to the parent branch; then they fall, to grow more breathing roots of their own encrusted with the coral, shells, and marine skeletons which become additional soil. The primary builder of the bay's shores through the ages has been the red mangrove, which grows always at the water's edge. Slightly farther inland are the black mangroves, which are distant relatives of teak though their wood is useless except for the smudge fires Floridians have long burned against gnats and mosquitoes in mangrove latitudes. The white mangrove is exceptional; it bears no living seeds and it sends up no breathing roots, but it is a mangrove nonetheless. Scientists have given it the tongue-twisting name of *Laguncularia racemosa*; Floridians call it the buttonwood, and tourists often mistake it for a type of willow.

The Suncoast's mangrove islands have never been eternal. They are made first through accretion, and the mangrove branches become rookeries for hundreds of water birds—big wood ibises known on the Suncoast as flintheads, herons and egrets and cormorants. As the birds so gracefully and movingly adorn the mangrove branches they destroy them; the guano the birds drop is so concentrated that it burns living mangrove tissue. The trees are hardy; their salt-crystal-coated leaves contain special glands made to concentrate and give off salt. But guano continues its work of scorching until the mangrove is killed, the tides sweep farther inland, and the skeletons themselves are prey to the merciless fury of hurricanes that make of mangrove islands what one witness has called "sun-bleached graveyards." And then new seedlings float in to clutch the shoreline sand, and the cycle begins once more. The shorelines shift and change. The map of Tampa Bay fifty years ago is never quite the map of now. When the mangroves of Florida's ancient shores decayed they became the peat that is one of modern Florida's buried resources.

About forty million years ago—for we have unrolled our North American time screen more than three fourths of the way—Florida's seas formed the substance eventually to be known as Tampa limestone, the second oldest formation in the state. Today it underlies the river and the bay, though it is seldom exposed except on the river's upper banks where Joe had pointed it out to me as Oligocene rock on our canoe trip. Most of the riverbanks' surface sands are of a later era. The period of the Tampa limestone was also a marine epoch on what is now the Suncoast, and so far it has yielded no mammal fossils. Nevertheless, Tampans have found other fossils of the time and for years they made marketable treasures of them. At Ballast Point on the bay, and several miles upriver at the first set of rapids, lie the Tampa Silex Beds composed of prehistoric mollusks.

Here the limestone has mingled with clay, marl, and chert, residual sands and fuller's earth. Near high water the stratum crops out with fossilized silica shells of unusual and striking beauty. They are forms exquisitely reproduced in mineral, some translucent, some varying shades of brown and peach. Their interior walls are coated with brilliant crystals in hues of brown, red, blue, and yellow. As curios they were sold to nineteenth century tourists. The most characteristic mollusk fossil at Ballast Point is the orthaulax, though there are others: whorled drillas now found in Africa, tiny slender olivellas, and the delicate conical-ridged shell oceanographers have christened *Potamides hillsboroensis* in the river's honor. There was, too, a circular snail scalloped into graceful arcs; there were strange little castles of whelk ancestors and large heart-

Wood ibis

shaped shells. Some of the mollusks were phosphorescent on ancient nights, reminiscent of the shells the Roman historian Pliny was later to describe in his *Natural History*:

> It is the property of these . . . to shine brightly in the dark, when all other lights are removed, and the more moisture they have the brighter is the light they emit. In the mouth, even, when they are being eaten, they give forth their light and the same too when in the hands; the very drops, in fact, that fall from them on the ground or on the clothes, are of the same nature. Hence it is beyond a doubt that it is liquid that possesses this peculiar property, which even in a solid body would be ground for considerable surprise.

No human eye ever saw the luminous orthaulax shells at Ballast Point, though since their discovery Floridians have made a legend of the shimmering spectacle they must have made there. Other shells glow now in the darkness which echoes the swish of Tampa Bay's waves and is fragrant, in spring, with orange blossoms.

Twenty million years ago the Suncoast was finally thrust above sea level. The surrounding water became cooler. Whales and porpoises and dolphins and blackfish swam offshore. On land, tiny brown bats flew into reddish twilight skies and by day prey-hunting meat eaters roamed: wolves and foxes, dogs and a doglike creature with long muzzle and immense ears. Badgers, skunks, and weasels foraged too, the horses *Parahippus* and *Merychippus*, camels and rhinoceroses and piglike animals, all of them moving across the mossy earth where agate and chalcedony were forming under their feet. Phosphate pits not far from Tampa have yielded other relics: the fossil bones of a giant sloth and those of hyenas and bearlike carnivores. Phosphate, silt and clay continued to sweep down from northern rivers to create the phosphate beds. Today Florida is the world's largest phosphate producer. The material is used in everything from pharmaceuticals to detergents, and most of it is shipped from the Port of Tampa.

The great glaciers of the ice age a million years ago never reached Florida. When they advanced in the North, Florida knew cool rains which gradually formed the Green Swamp and the meandering Hillsborough. As rivers go, it is young. Forked Tampa Bay came into being as the lower portions of the Hillsborough and another, now-vanished, river sank beneath the ocean in one of the Ice Age's last fluctuations of land level. Tides rushed inland to erode the earth until the estuary had deepened. As the ocean waters rose and fell a series of terraces were laid down. One of them, the Pamlico, borders both shores of Tampa Bay, all of Old Tampa Bay, and Hillsborough Bay, where the river's once-exposed floodplain now lies twenty to thirty feet underwater to form a ship channel.

Between the rainiest periods during which the northern glaciers advanced, the Green Swamp turned into a vast prairie tangy in the warm winds which combed it. The interglacial periods when the faraway ice sheets were retreating farther still were drier in Florida than the modern postglacial. But during them the Hillsborough still flowed, and on its banks gathered the most profuse assemblage of animals any part of America has ever known. It was then, too, that the ibises came.

Mostly their land was tranquil but not always. Rising breezes made low music in the trees. Occasionally a mastodon or mammoth trumpeted and the echo shook riverbank woodlands. Saber-toothed tigers snarled beneath tall branches on clumps of grass over the carcasses of their quarry. Giant armadillos, glyptodonts, cumbersomely moved their armored bodies across the sandy soil. Capybaras, large rodents, scurried in the ever-pressing search for food. From the mouths of limestone caves the cave bear, Tremarctos, watched them. Margays, pumas, jaguars, and bobcats stepped softly under a blinding sky where great auks flew and oversized vultures circled slowly in the warm uplifting wind currents. Kites and falcons soared over them higher still. In the underbrush on late afternoons when the sun sank low the feathers of a now-extinct wild turkey glinted darkly. Snowy egrets followed the herds to their water hole at Crystal Springs, in the Hillsborough's upper basin, which even in the driest years discharged millions of gallons a day as it does now. At twilight the heron and ibis flocks came in to roost as they do still, and alligators bellowed. Occasionally the shrill barking of dire wolves pierced the blue velvet of night. In the hammocks, islands of rich woodland soil within the grasslands, wild plumbagos opened their blue blooms on the mornings which followed, and mayflies flashed gauzy wings. It was a paradise man can only, now, imagine from the fossil traces it left for his curiosity.

Sometimes there were fires, their flames forking hot orange tongues up to the boughs of sand pines where seeds were sealed tight in their cones. The intensity of the heat unlocked them, and when they dropped and germinated the pine forests spread farther into the prairie. Fire, as well as water, was a sculptor of life along the river and the bay. From time to time hurricanes lashed in from the Caribbean and the bay's mangroves turned to twisted relics while inland trees fell crashing to the ground. Rains roared across the land then, leaving a swath of death soon burgeoning with brake ferns and fresh life.

It lasted hundreds of thousands of years, this time of nature's uncontested dominance on the river. As earth's history is reckoned the period is short. When it was over, almost two thirds of the mammals had gradually vanished—the camels and horses and tapirs and peccaries. Some went down over the land bridge to South America where modern forms still persist. Others disappeared entirely: the saber-toothed tiger and, finally, the mammoth and mastodon. Rains became more frequent, and grasslands slowly turned to the thick woods and moss-festooned swamps through which the river flows down to the bay today. Florida became the Florida seen now in wildernesses like the Green Swamp.

The passing of the Ice Age herds is still a mystery. Climate may have had something to do with it, for camels and horses are not jungle animals. Survival of the fittest undoubtedly had something to do with it too; when a sabertooth's prey had gone he starved, unable to adjust his heavy bulk to the swift running a panther could do in pursuit of the deer still at hand. Perhaps, though, the course of the history of animals like the mastodon changed some glistening morning thousands of years ago when the forest echoed strange footfalls and stranger sounds. Tall red-brown bodies shone with sweat as heavy-knuckled hands swished stone axes through the brush. Perhaps these new inhabitants had come to Florida directly from the north, perhaps from the north indirectly via the south. Exactly when they came no one knows. But one day men saw the river and the bay for the first time. They stood on the river's banks and exclaimed at the crowded tracks of prey. They shaded their eyes as they scanned the bay's shores, and when they peered into its shallows they saw myriad fish. Life would be good here, the red men told each other in the first speech the landscape ever knew. As they stayed on they wondered at the mildness of winters still rich with game. They discovered oysters and the tender flesh of brown limpkins and the starchy roots of the zamia plant from which they began to make a bread. They picked muscadine grapes from the tough green mats of vines coiling and hanging from riverbank trees and shrubs. The Hillsborough's oldest name is lost, but probably it was not unlike the word sixteenth century conquistadores were to hear from its Indians, *hibita*. Simply, The River.

2

The Landscape
Found

For at least ten thousand years men have lived on the Hillsborough River and Tampa Bay. When the Indians came, perhaps glyptodonts and fanged wolves were still crackling through pine forests and storks, now extinct, were beating huge wings in the sky. Fish darted thickly together at Crystal Springs, and in the bay shrimps burrowed and oysters bedded among silvery fingerlings. The earliest men who found the Suncoast, the Paleo-Indians, probably had traditions of winter if not a direct memory of ice and snow. If their journey from Siberia across the Bering Strait and down into continental North America had been by roundabout way of Mexico, still there were tales of bitter cold and howling winds for evening campfires under the pines and palms, and perhaps, too, fables of dry deserts baking under a white-hot sun. In fertile Florida, cool winds blew in steadily from the Gulf and shining rains fell daily in summer to break the heat. Winter was never rigor but only change, a time of mysterious orange moons and morning fogs and crisp leaves underfoot. Always there were the seafood and the game; no man need starve.

The Paleo-Indians were not farmers. They gathered shellfish, which they supplemented with turtles, bass, mullet, redfish, alligators, and rattlesnakes and deer. They also savored pine nuts and a variety of roots. The means by which they took their food were simple: fish weirs, hooks, reed baskets, stone knives, nets of native grasses weighted down with shells, and large arrowheads on arrows propelled by spear-throwers, *atlatls*. Under primitive palm-thatched shelters they lived on middens, high piles of their discarded seashells which they found drier than surrounding land during the rainy season. Even for the Indians at the Gulf's edge a trip upriver yielded plentiful firewood. Along the river course and on the bay's shores they built small self-contained settlements. They heaped small mounds of sandy earth for their dead, though they left in them no burial offerings. The Paleo-Indians made no pottery; it was later tribes who were to acquire the skill and develop their vessels and plates in increasing stylistic complexity, intricately punched and stamped and colored with vegetable dyes.

From the beginning, the Hillsborough marked a boundary. North of it one tradition of pottery making and tool manufacture developed, and south of it another. When the southern Indians sent war parties to capture northern villages the attacked northerners fought back vigorously. River and bay were a perpetual battleground. In the darkness long war canoes stealthily made their way through tangles of shore mangroves and inland myrtle. Life was governed by wind, sun, tide, food, and a longing for ever more land.

Change came to the Paleo-Indians from the north, as modern change usually comes to the Suncoast. A mortuary cult centering on the erection of larger burial mounds gradually spread down to the river. Villages of kindred tribes worked for the dead together to build them, and the offerings they placed within were some of their finest artifacts: shell pendants, the incised bowls and plates they had begun making, conch hammers and drinking cups, varicolored shell bracelets destined to glow in no sunlight, and strands of shell beads. On Weedon Island, which is not an island but a peninsula jutting from modern Pinellas County into the bay, these burial mounds still stand, many of them excavated but others intact. Time covered them long ago with green zamia tufts, needle palms and saw palmettos and pungent beach rosemary. Black-legged egrets delicately stalk their borders, and brackish water laps at the mangroves now as it lapped in the time of the burial-mound builders, though industry has come to Weedon Island. American folklore has tried to make them a separate race of vanished supermen, but they were Indians nonetheless. Later white settlers discovering their pottery and implements found them tasteful. Therefore, they reasoned, no savages could have possessed such talent. Modern archaeologists have proved otherwise, while modern laymen are less sure of what a savage really is.

By 1500 A.D. the Indians of the river and the bay were building still another kind of mound, higher and flat topped, on which they raised temples to the sun. North of the river, though not south of it, there came a day when the Indians saw their first corn, brought perhaps by a northern trader, and planted its kernels until they sent up tender green shoots. Agriculture changed the lives of the Timucua Indians north of the river forever. Their political and social organization proliferated; villages banded together in confederations under chiefs and subchiefs. War was no longer a series of sporadic raids and defenses but a formal strategy closely involved with civil and religious privileges. The earlier burial mounds were abandoned, and the temple mounds replacing them stood proudly dominating village squares. In the main plaza near the temple lived the chief. Traders from as far away as Mexico and Louisiana and Ohio were welcomed, and many of their ideas were adopted as farming had been: styles of metalwork, totemic bird effigies, and the ritual drinking of a juice made from the dahoon holly, *Ilex cassine*. This was called the Black Drink, and in the temples a formal ceremony accompanied its use.

The village chief, splendid in tattoos and egret feathers, presided. Special wooden benches were allocated to high village officials, their chests hung with shell pendants. Lesser men, women, and children squatted on the ground. The holly leaves were first parched in a pot, then cooked in a cauldron over an open fire until they softened. Heavy, acrid smoke filled the temple during the cooking. Timucua eyes watered, and Timucua throats coughed. When the liquid had cooled, the chief poured a portion of it on the ground and then drank. Slowly the cup passed to each of the village headmen. All day the commoners sat smoking tobacco and watching; they were forbidden the sacred drink, which exalted only the rank of the already powerful. As darkness fell, the Indians took the cauldron in which the Black Drink had been cooked and stretched a deerskin over it. Rhythmically they beat on it with gourd rattles while moss-skirted women chanted and danced around it until midnight came and everyone left reluctantly for his palm shelter and sleep under a pallid moon traced with black palmetto fronds.

South of the river temples rose too, though the southern Indians, the Calusa, never practiced agriculture. Seafood and game were enough for them. The temples of the corn-growing Timucua with their statues of gilded fowls were to amaze the conquistadores. Down into the Everglades stretched the empire of the Calusa, whom the conquistadores were

to find more terrifying than the Timucua. Calusa worship centered around
the totem figure of a buzzard; death dominated their lives, and along
the Hillsborough's ferny banks and Tampa Bay's mangrove beaches many
a warm subtropic night echoed the screams of Timucua who had been
surprised by Calusa raiders, buzzard-cult jewelry rattling on their brown
bodies. When Timucua armies marched, they marched to the graceful
music of reed flutes. Eventually the Timucua towns had to be fortified
against the Calusa with wooden stockades. At the head of Hillsborough
Bay, not far from the spot where Henry Plant's hotel later rose so
garishly, stood the Timucua town called Mocoso. The Hillsborough became the Mocoso River, the earliest designation it ever had. Westward
stood Tocobaga, on Old Tampa Bay, and Ucita lay west and south on a
Tampa Bay island. The bay was christened by the Timucua the Bay of
Culata.

They were a genial people, fond of ornament and pomp. The men
decked themselves in feather cloaks and the women were proud of their
long hair and the iridescent fish bladders they had fashioned into earrings
to catch the sunlight as they moved. Laughing Timucua girls jangled
tiny metal bells as they flirted with handsome breechclouted boys, for
copper came by trade from the Appalachian Mountains and a few pieces
of silver and gold from Mexico. Timucua boys played a boisterous ball
game before enthusiastic audiences. A Spanish missionary's description of
it has survived:

> They arrange themselves twenty on a side and play the game in a
> brisk, athletic manner. The ball carrier handles it smartly and he plays
> such an effective game with his sure shots that we can state he scores on
> each shot. They erect goal posts made from pine trees about seven feet
> tall and on the top of this goal they place a figure. Suddenly the forty
> players dash to the field, commence playing, and the game has begun
> with a rush. It is a rough game which many times proves to be costly to
> some unfortunate player who gets seriously injured.

Elements of Timucua life linger on the Suncoast today. A prominent
temple, or church, stands near a civil headquarters, or courthouse. Modern
pensioners buy a spring tonic called Syrup of Black Draught in Suncoast
drugstores, and everybody is crazy about footfall which can also "seriously injure" its heroes. There were even prehistoric tourists from Ohio.

The Timucua were tall. Their strong faces survive in the drawings

made of them by artists who accompanied early conquerors: Jacques
LeMoyne de Morgue, who visited Timucua villages on Florida's east
coast with a party of French, and John White, an Englishman becalmed
offshore in sight of a Timucua settlement. From Cedar Key on the west
coast and modern Jacksonville on the east, Florida was Timucua country
as far south as Mocoso and Ucita and Tocobaga and, on the east coast,
the northern limit of the long saltwater lagoon known today as the
Indian River.

Village days began early for the Timucua. As the sun climbed in a
rosy sky, stirring dark-eyed babies cried. In their oblong huts, *bohios,*
women began to grind the daily corn ration on stone slabs. By midmorning, in spring, they were in outlying fields, some making holes in the
earth with long sticks while others dropped corn and bean seeds after
them. Later the harvested beans and corn were stored in a public granary
where village men carried them upriver in dugout palmetto canoes.
Timucua families shared their bounty; each was trusted to take only what
it needed.

While the women planted, their men fished and hunted. Sometimes
an exultant cry reverberated: a baleen whale had swum into the shallow
waters of the bay and a Timucua brave was calling his tribesmen. A party
of them rowed out to it; the first hunter on the spot grabbed a stake and
mallet from the canoe's floor and leapt out on top of the whale, which
was unable to dive deeply and escape. When the whale turned, the
hunter drove his stake into its breathing hole. The animal finally suffo-
cated and foamy waves washed its dead body ashore. The whole village
gathered then; they cut up its meat and dried it; afterwards they celebrated with a feast.

Alligator hunters spent their mornings waiting in brush blinds for
the 'gators to seek the sun. When a 'gator opened his jagged jaws for
fish, the Indians sprang at him and rammed a rough-barked pole down his
gullet, heaved him over, and pierced his belly. 'Gator meat tasted especially delicious on the picnics Timucua families loved. At noon, their
grinding and sowing and hunting chores finished, mother and father
and children often crossed the bay flats out to offshore islands. The father
carried his bow and arrows, ever on guard for roving war parties. Older
children frolicked alongside him in coruscating green water. The mother
carried her youngest baby and a reed basket full of provisions: meat,
fruits, fish, and herbs. On the beaches the family feasted together while

Early settler

raccoons hunted for oysters in the mangrove roots and nearby herons stabbed for a meal of their own.

In the afternoon there might be a town gathering. Each spring the Festival of the Stag took place. Village men removed from storage the skin of the largest stag they had caught that winter and stuffed it with savory roots. On the stag's horns, neck, and body they festooned garlands of fruit. A singing procession carried the stag to an open place where they hung it on a post, its head and breast pointed toward the sun. The Timucua prayed for plenty, while the chief stood below the stag with his shaman, a sorcerer. He and the shaman intoned a chant which the worshippers answered in soft murmurs. When the prayers were finished, boys hurried to archery contests, girls to pinewoods fires where they helped their mothers cook corn cereal. Sometimes, at dusk, the chief and his wife went walking along the bank of the Mocoso River, he dressed in a deerskin dyed in many colors and a belt of tinkling silver bells, she in her skirt of moss. Beside them two boys fanned them with palmetto fans. A third held up the chief's deerskin train, and behind him handmaidens of the chief's wife played reed flutes. Always there were harmonies, some of them thanks that Timucua lands had been fruitful, some prayers for continuing prosperity, and some pure joy in living. Everywhere Timucua life was dominated by the Florida sun they worshipped and hymned.

In war they could be fierce enough. In full paint and egret plumes the village headmen would gather in a circle; then the chief let out a blood-curdling yell and seized a pot filled with water. Facing the sun with it, he asked for victory: "May the blood of the enemy be scattered as the water from this bowl!" He emptied it on the ground. A second pot of water he poured over the fire burning in front of him and admonished his warriors: "So may you be able to extinguish your enemies and bring back their scalps!" Afterward the men rose and went to battle. With them went the shaman; when the party made its first camp he stationed himself in its midst, drawing a circle and standing in it to talk with unseen gods. Then he contorted himself into twisted postures while he shouted in ecstasy until, suddenly, he calmed, stepped out of the circle, and announced matter-of-factly to the chief how many were the enemy and where they would fight. The chief, his body stained a vivid red, gravely nodded. Through the shaman the gods had spoken, and they were usually right.

Everybody had his place in Timucua society; rituals prescribed how the smallest task should be performed. The slaughter of battle had its special rites. The enemy were scalped with sharp-edged reed knives and their scalps were dried over battlefield fires. Fallen warriors had their arms and legs cut off; the bones were also dried on the spot. Every brave shot a final arrow into his victim's heart; after this he was free to rest. Villagers welcomed their victorious by helping them to tie the scalps and bones to pine poles. The villagers assembled in a circle in front of the poles, where the shaman started a low-voiced curse to the enemy whose image he held in his hand. Three men knelt opposite, one of them pounding on a flat stone with a club in hard, hypnotic beats, the other two rattling hollow pumpkins filled with seeds while they chanted in answer to the shaman's mutterings. Not always were these directed toward the dreaded Calusa; the Timucua had their family quarrels too.

A special day was set aside for the widows of slain warriors to see the chief. Approaching him with loud wails they crouched and hid their faces in calloused hands, begging him to avenge their husbands' murders, provide for themselves during the period of mourning, and grant permission for their remarriage at the interval's end. When the chief agreed they went home still sobbing and moaning to show respect for the dead. A few days later they carried their husbands' weapons and the utensils they had used in day-to-day life to the village burial ground, where the widows cut off their long hair over the graves. Not until their hair had grown back enough to cover their shoulders could they take other mates.

In common with many North American tribes, the Timucua had the berdache, an accepted institutionalized role for homosexuals. Berdaches carried provisions into battle, and they tended the village sick, laying them face downward on a stretcher of poles to inhale a purgative smoke. When the invalid could sit up, he was given a pipe and told to breathe in the tobacco. If he died, berdaches bore him to his grave on a stretcher covered with deerskins.

Timucua clans took the names of the creatures they knew around them: panthers, raccoons, wildcats, skunks, alligators, and otters. River springs they venerated as the abodes of gods. Who knew what mysteries lurked on the Mocoso at Crystal Springs, its long ribbons of eelgrass undulating in the clear water, its ethereal strands of green-brown angel-hair algae waving silkily in the sun? White lilies and yellow pondweeds bloomed in perpetual profusion. Mosses on the submerged rocks made patterns of their own. The dwelling places of the gods were enchanted, and the men who lived close to them wove myths now vanished in time. The river sustained them; it carried their canoes. The gushes of its rapids, the rainbows of its late summer afternoons when the final thunder of cloudbursts rumbled and the sun broke through a silver gap in the sky, the spangled scales of its fish, the fresh scent of its water hemlocks— all were the stuff of which Timucua lives were made.

The Calusa tribal name may have derived from a Calusa word for trout. Speckled trout abounded in the Gulf then as now. An early Spanish explorer translated Calos, the name of the chief Calusa town, differently. "Village cruel" was the name he gave it. Later the British corrupted it to Charlotte Harbor. Some Calusa chiefs controlled over seventy towns with a rigid autocracy that demanded unquestioning allegiance. Most of these towns were well below Tampa Bay, but the Calusa forever roamed northward. They not only did no farming, but little or no cooking. The sea and its fresh plenty were enough to keep them strong. They were expert divers, their ruddy bodies splashing in bright Gulf waters as they collected oysters, shrimps, conchs, and fish. In the forests and swamps of the interior they gathered berries and roots. A man's rank in Calusa society often determined what he ate; only the powerful were allowed seals, for instance. Calusa fishermen, like the Timucua, made nets for Gulf mullets. Their weights and floats were of shell and wood, for there are few stones in Florida south of the Hillsborough River. But with shell and wood they managed ingeniously to make not only the tools and utensils they needed but delicate religious effigies and statues which in places like Marco Island on Florida's southwest coast were to be preserved by total immersion in mangrove swamps. Calusa houses were built on pilings at the water's edge; their furniture consisted of carved stools, rush pillows and rugs, finely woven baskets and pottery with characteristic Calusa designs: scrolls and disklike cuts. For their children they made toy canoes; always the Gulf, not inland rivers and fields, was the center of their existence.

Calusa religion was concerned not with crop growing and sun worship, as Timucua religion was, but with war and death to a far stronger degree. Their Buzzard Cult had unique emblems: vultures' heads, magic circles, symbols for human hands and eyes, crosses, large shell gorgets depicting the figures of warriors clad in eagle feathers. They practiced human sacrifices to an idol who was said to eat human eyes. Their temples witnessed masked dances on nights when the spume of waves spiced the air and raucous Calusa chants echoed and faded and rose once more. The spirits of their dead warriors, not gods, were the oracles they consulted before they made important decisions.

A Calusa chief's wives were drawn from subordinate towns owing him tribute; sometimes, too, he married his full sister. He reigned absolute; below him were nobles, a chief shaman whose esoteric knowledge must be shared with him, a class of inferior shamans, the bulk of the common people, and slaves. The chief wore an ornament of shining gold on his forehead and beaded bands on his legs. When he died his slaves were sacrificed with him; his overlordship went beyond the grave. Human life was cheap; when his son died all the latter's friends were killed too. The Calusa were famous archers and dart throwers. When they killed a man they not only scalped him but cut off his head and paraded it on a spike in a shuffling ritual dance. Military campaigns were formally organized not only for the purpose of conquering land but to obtain more victims for cult sacrifices.

They were supreme artists, these austere Indians. They painted wooden tablets with calendrical designs and with figures of crested birds each of which had its own symbolism. They polychromed ritual masks and carved furry raccoons and feathered kingfishers and crocodiles complete with scales. Painstakingly they chiseled shell daggers. Calusa warriors shattered the air with sharp conch trumpets. Never were these men conquered or converted; it was disease that would destroy them in the end. Unfortunately no artist like Jacques LeMoyne or John White ever penetrated into the interior of Calusa country. Theirs was a maze of mangrove channels where a man in a canoe might be lost forever if he forgot a single turning. Even today the thick mangrove wilderness of southwest Florida is forbidding. The Everglades were Calusa country too, the great prairie with bleached daggers of saw grass, hammock tangles of strangler fig and mahogany and gumbo-limbo, arching orchids along banks quiet but for the splash of the crocodiles and the fluttering of ducks. Calusas knew the cypress swamps where parrakeets flashed green-gold in long shafts of sunlight: the Big Cypress, Fahkahatchee, nameless slow waters choked with lettuce where wild yellow cannas sent up flags of flame and pileated and ivory-billed woodpeckers hammered. Thousands of herons and cranes and ibises filled Calusa skies every morning on their way to feeding grounds. At sunset, when they flew back, the golden sky darkened with them. Sometimes it darkened too with grey and white clouds which exploded in a tumult of thunder as jagged forks of lightning streaked down to sear high cypresses. It was a torrid, humid world—changeless, its people thought.

But even while the Calusa dreamed of marching once more against the Timucua at their towns of Tocobaga and Ucita and Mocoso, Christopher Columbus landed in the West Indies and with him the Spanish hunger for gold. Before Juan Ponce de León's ships ever touched the Florida coast and named it, Spanish caravels and brigantines were tossing in Florida seas. Soon the first wind-swelled sails appeared on the Calusas' Gulf. Some of the ships, carrying Cuban and Caribbean Indians enslaved by the Spanish, were wrecked on Gulf reefs. Several of the slaves, tougher and better swimmers than their captors, fought wind and wave and breasted their way to shore, where they told the Calusa what they themselves had endured at the hands of white men. Spanish treasure ships were wrecked too, and the gold and silver ornaments from Mexico and Peru they bore were salvaged by Calusa divers who took them home. However it happened that the Calusa were forewarned, they were ready to defend themselves when the Spanish set foot on their shores at last.

There were also shipwrecks in Timucua waters; the Timucua heard a few tales of Cuban and Caribbean horrors of slavery and beating and shackling. When the first Spanish helmet gleamed before them in the sun they gaped at it from the brush where they were hiding; curiously they stared at the massive Andalusian horses, and they pondered the brown-robed figures kneeling in the sand before crossed sticks. Thousands of years before, Ice Age herds had yielded to the pressures of Indian hunters. Now the hunters were different, but the cycle of extinction had begun once more.

3

"The Sport of Killing Indians"

Juan Ponce de León, Governor of Puerto Rico, was a vigorous campaigner who had maneuvered a rival out of office by 1509, seventeen years after Columbus had first set foot on West Indian soil. Any Puerto Rican Indians who refused to acknowledge Ponce's rule of the island he promptly enslaved; he captured them by hunting them down with the bloodthirstiest of greyhounds. His favorite dog was Bexerillo, who according to an observer

> made wonderful havoc among those people, and knew which of them were in war and which in peace, like a man; for which reason the Indians were more afraid of ten Spaniards with the dog, than of one hundred without him, and therefore he had one share and a half of all that was taken allowed him, as was done to one that carried a crossbow, as well as gold and slaves and other things, which his master received. Very extraordinary things were reported of this dog.

What Bexerillo did with his gold and slaves his admirers never revealed, but his place in history as the New World's first pampered pet seems assured.

Among Puerto Rican palms and flame vines Ponce began to build a fortified city, San Juan. His family had accompanied him from Spain; the Ponces all envisioned a San Juan future glinting with gold and silver and echoing perpetually with the deferential homage of sun-burnished captives on their patios. Puerto Rico would be the Ponces' and their descendants' domain forever, rich with tropical blooms and fruits and the distillations of sugarcane Puerto Ricans were beginning to call *ron*. Not that Juan Ponce de León cared much about blooms and fruits and rum. He wanted power and a fortune, and both lay within his grasp.

He was sure of them until King Charles of Spain began to have second thoughts about the rights of other West Indian conquistadores. When Charles quixotically took the governorship of Puerto Rico away from Ponce, he was left with money and property in San Juan but nothing to do. He was not a man to sit idly by while his peers flourished. He longed for an island of his own subjects and sent urgent letters to his friends at court in Spain to plead his case. King Charles had third thoughts and granted him a patent to capture the island of Bimini. Just as Ponce was about to set sail, Charles vacillated once more. Ponce was needed to control Puerto Rico's Indians, the king proclaimed. Not until 1513 was Ponce able to embark from San Juan with Anton de Alaminas, his pilot, in search of Bimini and glory.

March was a stormy month. Alaminas was forced to change his course west-northwest because of heaving grey seas and stinging rains. When the storms finally subsided during Easter week, the lead ship came into harbor near an unknown and sparkling lagoon and a cape of land. Canaveral, mapmakers would name it later. Much later, Kennedy. Ponce knew it was not Bimini but he decided he had found another island. In honor of the religious season, though not of botany, he named it Pascua Florida, Easter of the Flowers. Yet what he saw were not flowers but darkly thick stands of pines, mica-studded coral sands, and live oaks spreading massive branches fringed with moss as grey as the beards of Castilian grandfathers. On his way to the beach in his longboat, Ponce unfurled the royal banner of Castile and León and plunged the flagpole, ashore, into softly yielding ground. Only the breath of wind and the gentle rustle of the live oaks and his own prayers broke the piney stillness as he claimed Florida for Spain and a share of its treasures, whatever they might be, for himself. Then he scanned the horizon for signs of settlement. There were none. On Friday, April 8, he set sail again in search of Indians to subjugate and by the twentieth he had found a cluster of huts on Florida's lower southeast coast, the land of Mayami. Two of his ships anchored; the third, a brigantine, couldn't withstand the powerful currents of cobalt Gulf Stream waters and it was blown out to sea.

On shore a party of Indians gathered, making signs to him to come to them. Expecting a guileless welcome from heathen who, he thought, knew nothing of Spanish soldiers of fortune, he went. Instead of greeting him as a brother the Indians aimed bone darts at him and his followers when they came close. Two Spaniards were severely wounded, and not until darkness was Ponce able to collect his dazed band and row out to the safety of his ships. By May he had cruised past the Florida Keys, which he named The Martyrs "because the high rocks look at a distance like men suffering." At their tip he shifted his course northward. Near the end of the month he sighted the Bay of Culata and stopped briefly on an island at its mouth. Then, searching for straits, he continued north and west probably as far as Pensacola. When he failed to find any straits he turned back until he had anchored south of the Bay of Culata in the Bay of Calos where the pile dwellings of the Calusa were spread out against an uncertain and summer-misted horizon. The Calusa congregating at the tideline beckoned him to land. He was warier now, however, and stayed on his caravel until long palmetto-log Calusa canoes were ploughing toward him through the waves. With their arrows the Calusa attacked; in the fray, Ponce sent a longboat ashore and its crew seized four Indian women and broke up two canoes. "When there was no falling out, as finding no opportunity" after a display of Spanish guns, the Indians traded a few deer hides. One of them understood Spanish; he had encountered a shipwrecked Spaniard years before. The Chief of Calos had much gold, this warrior told Ponce; if he would wait in the bay, messages would be sent to the chief and he would bring gold in person. Ponce waited eagerly if innocently and not until twenty canoes full of Calusa warriors were approaching his caravel did he realize the trap which had been set for him. The Indians were making for his cables, trying to cut his anchor. A Spanish longboat crew handily killed Indian warriors with crossbows; the Indians in the canoes retreated until they could send still more canoes against the caravel, this time eighty of them. Spanish guns reverberated once more and Spanish crossbows and arquebuses beat them back. Ponce, however, had had enough of the Calusa and retired to the Bahamas. The warriors of Calos had saved not only themselves but their northern neighbors on the Bay of Culata, the Timucua, to whom Ponce might have turned had he not been discouraged from further exploration by Calusa ferocity. Later Spanish historians found the whole expedition rather inglorious, and to make the tale of

Ponce de León more picturesque they endowed him with a desire to find a Fountain of Youth.

In 1517, four years after Ponce's failure to conquer Florida, Francisco Hernandez de Cordova set out from Cuba with a fleet of caravels; one of them was captained by Ponce's former pilot, Anton de Alaminas. A fierce Atlantic storm blew them off course and drove them to the Bay of Calos, where Cordova was mortally wounded in the throat by Calusa warriors as he attempted to land. In 1519 Alonzo Alvarez de Pineda led a caravel up Florida's Gulf coast past the bays of Calos and Culata to survey the coast's extent. Alvarez de Pineda, like Ponce, found no straits in northern Florida, and it was he who determined Florida was not an island at all but part of a greater mainland. There were splendid wonders in Florida, he announced. The natives wore golden ornaments in their noses and ears, and there was one race of giants eleven hands high and another of pygmies only five.

By 1521 an exiled Ponce de León had determined to try Florida once more. To his king he wrote: "Among my services I discovered at my own cost and charge the Island of Florida and others in its district. Now I return to that Island, if it please God's will, to settle it." Unaware of Alonzo Alvarez de Pineda's discovery that Florida was no island, he sailed up the west coast until he reached what was probably Apalachee Bay in north Florida where the local Indians set upon him with sharp arrows of stone and gave him the wound from which he died in Cuba a few days later. His body was sent to San Juan for burial. On his tombstone was placed an epitaph: "Here rest the bones of a LION, mightier in deeds than in name." The dog Bexerillo's grave went unmarked, though his fable persisted as immortally as that of the Fountain of Youth.

The next lion was made of even sterner stuff than Ponce. Huge, red-bearded Pánfilo de Narváez had a voice "of a great volume, like that of one speaking in a cave." In Mexico he had tilted with Cortez in a jurisdictional dispute and Cortez's lieutenants had put out one of his eyes. The socket gaped hollow and terrible from his ruddy face. A rich man, he supplied his sailors with the most meager of provisions. He was stingy, pigheaded, impulsive, undauntable, and determined to succeed where Ponce had failed.

In the spring of 1528, armed with a royal proclamation to be read to Florida's Indians, Narváez left Havana with a fleet of three caravels and one brigantine. In them went four hundred men and eighty Andalusian horses. Diego Miruelo, the chief pilot, shepherded them all through two tropical storms to the sight of Florida land. Along it he coasted north and west until he saw a large bay and on it a cluster of palm-covered Indian huts. They were Timucuan, and the bay was the Bay of Culata. Here on the Gulf the ocean was calmer than on the Atlantic. Gentle Gulf waves lapped at mangrove-lined shores. Narváez squinted his good eye at the huts and decided to send a messenger to them. When the messenger returned, he brought Timucua venison as a gift to his commander. Bahía de la Cruz, Narváez christened the harbor: Bay of the Cross. Brown-robed Father Suárez, a Franciscan monk aboard Narváez's ship, said a solemn prayer over the venison, and the high sheriff of the expedition, Alvar Núñez Cabeza de Vaca, remembered that the day was Holy Thursday. On Good Friday Cabeza de Vaca went ashore with his commander in a small skiff that held only a few handpicked crewmen. They would go to the chief (they called him the cacique) who had made them the present of venison. Spring breezes ruffled the palmettos. Cabeza marveled at the grace of egrets and the height of the live oaks. Along the beach miniature purple flowers bloomed, and sea-grape leaves rattled. The jade-colored water danced with light. Narváez's men rowed into the bay until they reached the Timucua village they had seen.

They found it deserted. As they wandered through it they stared at a village temple they estimated could hold three hundred people. Near it fishing nets were piled in a heap, and in one of them crewmen exclaimed over a golden rattle. Where had the Indians gone? The Spaniards moved on through the Indians' houses and found them all empty. But gold! Where was more gold? They saw none as they ransacked hut after hut. Only the tantalizing rattle was theirs. Probably it was Father Suárez who reminded Narváez what he had to do to make his possession of Bahía de la Cruz legal. Among the abandoned huts, to a wilderness apparently empty of red men, Narváez roared out his formal proclamation:

> In behalf of the Catholic Caesarean Majesty of Don Carlos, King of the Romans, and Emperor ever Augustus, and Doña Juana his mother, Sovereigns of León and Castile, Defenders of the Church, ever victors, never vanquished, and rulers of barbarous nations, I, Pánfilo de Narváez, his servant, messenger, and captain, notify and cause you to know in the best manner I can that God, our Lord, one and eternal, created the heaven and earth, and one man and one woman of whom we and you and all men in the world have come . . . All these nations our Lord gave in

charge to one person, called St. Peter, that he might be master and superior over mankind, to be obeyed and head of all the human race, wheresoever they might live and be . . . Him they call Papa, which means admirable, greatest, father, and preserver. Thus St. Peter was obeyed and taken for King. One of the Popes who succeeded him in that seat made a gift of these islands and the main of the Ocean Sea to the said Emperor and Queen . . . Wherefore, as best you can, I entreat and require you to understand this well which I have told you . . . and that you recognize the Church as Mistress and Superior of the Universe, and the High Pontiff, called Papa, in its name, the Queen and King, our Masters in their place as Lords, Superiors, and Sovereigns of these islands and the main . . . You shall not be required to become Christians except when, informed of the truth, you desire to be converted to our Holy Catholic Faith, as nearly all the inhabitants of the other islands have done . . . when his Highness will confer on you numerous privileges and instruction, with many favors.

Narváez paused for breath. Then his voice boomed louder still:

If you do not do this, and of malice you be dilatory, I will enter with force, making war upon you from all directions and in every manner that I may be able. I will take the persons of yourselves, your wives and your children to make slaves, sell and dispose of you, as their Majesties shall think fit, and I will take your goods, doing you all the evil and injury that I may be able . . . and I declare to you that the deaths and damages that arise therefrom, will be your fault and not that of his Majesty, nor mine, nor of these cavaliers who came with me.

When the last threat had died on the April air, the Spaniards prepared to make camp. They had done their duty. Now, nervously, they took turns at watch during the long night that followed, their arquebuses gleaming in the firelight. Nerves strained at the smallest sounds: the foraging of a raccoon in the brush, the shrill scream of a distant panther, the hoot of a barred owl, the unexpected liquid outpouring of a mockingbird under a white moon. Where were the people of this land? No human footstep echoed—only, toward dawn, the soft footfalls of deer on their way to low branches tender with new green willow leaves. The sun came up, hazy at first, then a piercing ball of gold in a sapphire sky.

When the red men came they strode noisily through the brush and made threatening gestures: clenched fists, taut hands on their quivers of arrows. They began to shout Timucuan curses no one but themselves

understood. When Narváez bellowed back about Catholic Caesarean
Majesty and the High Pontiff called Papa they only stared menacingly
at him. All Narváez could understand was that they wanted him to leave
—quickly. Their venison had been diplomacy, nothing more. When
they retreated into a cluster of palmettos after the last angry shout,
Narváez joylessly resolved to go inland to explore. The country did not
look promising; but where there was one golden rattle, there had to be
others.

With forty men and six horsemen he began knifing his way through
spiky mats of saw palmetto and prickly pear until, from his Bahía de la
Cruz, he came to a second large bay, the modern Hillsborough Bay. It
was the fork that would lead to the Mocoso River, though he never followed the shoreline long enough to find the Hillsborough's mouth. After
a night of restless camp among pungent clumps of wild savory and pepper-
vine, a night during which the Spaniards' dogs growled at the stealthy
prowlings of possums and skunks, Narváez led his party back again to
the wide waters of Bahía de la Cruz. Here he directed the pilot of the
brigantine to try to find a port up the coast which Diego Miruelo said
he had heard existed and would be easier to defend than Bahía de la
Cruz in case of attack. Narváez himself would go inland again, this time
with more men. For four Spanish leagues—about ten and a half miles—
the party followed the shore of Bahía de la Cruz until they were surprised
in a batch of brush by a party of four tattooed and painted Indians.
Quickly the Spaniards surrounded them and then seized their arrows.
Narváez showed them an ear of corn; did they know what it was? he
tried to ask by signs. Cowed, in awe of the horses and armor and Spanish
crossbows, the captured Timucua nodded and began leading the expedition back to their village of Ucita, the cacique Hirrihigua's town. Here an
astonished Narváez and his high sheriff Alvar Núñez Cabeza de Vaca
found several crates they recognized as being of Castilian manufacture.
Either there had been a shipwreck in nearby waters, or the boxes had
been traded from other tribes. In each lay a rotting corpse covered with
multicolored deer hides. Idolatry! cried one of the Spaniards, crossing
himself. Immediately he struck his tinderbox and set fire to every coffin,
and, when the Indians protested at this violation of their dead, Narváez
seized Hirrihigua, slashed off half his nose and lips to a mass of pulp, and
killed a wailing old woman making signs that she was Hirrihigua's
mother. The Timucua who watched this butchery stripped of their

weapons were helpless. While Narváez's men turned bohios upside down for gold, their owners stared numbly at the bleeding and mangled face of their chief, at the huge-muscled horses stomping in the sand, at the snarling greyhounds, then at the glaring breastplates of the soldiers.

Triumphantly one of the Spaniards emerged from a hut clutching a few gold trinkets. Narváez began barking out questions supplemented by sign language. Where had the gold come from? The Indians tried to understand him. Several of them watching as he pored over the trinkets began to think desperately of a way to get rid of him. If Red-Beard were sent on a long search for what he appeared to want, there might be peace at least in this village. . . . "Apalachen! Apalachen!" the Indians exclaimed. They motioned north. There, they tried to make clear, was all the gold Red-Beard might desire. It was a strategy that would perhaps be hard on their Apalachee neighbors, but many things might happen to Red-Beard and his monstrous horses and dogs before he reached the Apalachees' territory.

Narváez, hearing the tale, determined to set out immediately with Indian guides. What treasure Cortez had found in Mexico, he would yet find in Florida. The fleet could follow him on the coast while he penetrated the inland forests. The Indian guides would know the way to this golden Apalachen, toward which they and Spanish pride pointed so tantalizingly.

Alvar Núñez Cabeza de Vaca, the high sheriff, thought the plan was lunatic and he said so. The Spanish should at least command their port certainly; who knew what war parties might lurk to surprise the ships at anchor in the bay or cruising the coast? Horses could never survive in the thick interior jungles of gallberry and gum and water oak the men could already see before them. There wasn't a single Indian who understood Spanish; there was no interpreter. What density of swamps and forests lay ahead and who lived in them? Where would the Spaniards get food and water? They couldn't possibly take all the supplies they needed if they went on foot.

Narváez's sutler disagreed. He was all for fresh adventure; the ships would follow along the coast as agreed and the inland party could rendezvous with them in Apalachen itself if they met at no river-mouth harbor beforehand.

"I beg of you, in the name of his Majesty, do not forsake the vessels until they are in safe port," Cabeza de Vaca pleaded.

"You have no authority for making such a demand!" Narváez countered, the blood throbbing in his temples. "If you are afraid to proceed inland, you yourself may take charge of the ships."

Cabeza was furious at his sneer. He was no coward and Narváez knew it; how did Narváez dare to imply it? Tempers flared.

"You are utterly unprepared," Cabeza told Narváez contemptuously. Then he lowered his voice. "But I prefer to share the risk with you and your people, and suffer what you will have to suffer, than to place my honor in jeopardy."

Sunday, May 1, was a golden day of bright butterworts along stream banks, of yellow pond lilies and flowering St. Johnswort and saffron plums. The three hundred Spaniards who left Hirrihigua's stockaded village of Ucita included not only Narváez and Cabeza de Vaca but Father Suárez, three other priests, a monk, officers, and forty mounted men. Their provisions consisted of biscuits and of bacon which began rapidly to turn rancid in the heat of noon. These they supplemented with the young leaves of the saw palmetto, which reminded Cabeza of the palmettos of Andalusia. Would he ever see them again? He doubted it. He felt he was marching to oblivion and Narváez with him. For fifteen days the Spaniards saw nothing. Not a soul stood in their path. They found no villages, only the hopeless underbrush of holly and hemlock which skirted the depths of what later explorers would know and fear as the Green Swamp. Hawks rasped and black vultures circled slowly overhead, around and around, until the grotesqueness of the omen they were sent shudders down weary Spanish spines. At the banks of the Withlacoochee the party had to pause to hack down palmettos. The river was high; shortly after they had crossed it on makeshift rafts bound with grapevines they were confronted by two hundred Indians near a village where the famished Spanish saw fields of harvest-ready corn. Narváez followed his usual tactic of brandishing crossbows, releasing dogs, and seizing hostages. When the hostages led him reluctantly into their town he ravaged its cornfields for two days while a party of scouts went down the Withlacoochee toward the Gulf in search of Diego Miruelo's harbor and the Spanish fleet. They found neither, and returned. Then they all marched out of the stripped village, this time to the Suwannee River where they were met by a party of Indians playing flutes. The absurdity of it was ironic. Where was the gold? Where was Apalachen? Northward, the Indians motioned. Always northward. It began to look as if what conquistadores considered "the sport of killing Indians" might be delayed.

Pánfilo de Narváez and his party passed from Bahía de la Cruz in an odyssey that for most of them would lead to drowning on a storm-tossed Gulf in boats they had fashioned of wilderness wood and the hides of their slaughtered horses. They never found their fleet again, and its caravels returned to Cuba. Spanish dogs ended as food fiercely fought over. When Narváez directed his exhausted followers to build the tiny craft in which they would escape an Apalachen where there turned out to be no gold but only murderous Indians, his followers obeyed as if in trances. All were to perish but Cabeza de Vaca and his lieutenant Lope de Oviedo. Somewhere off the Texas coast Cabeza and Lope were finally cast ashore. For years they wandered through tribes of southwestern Indians, some docile, some hostile. Cabeza tried to cure Indian sick with herb remedies, and he tried to escape slavery in their towns. With a haggard Lope, living on grasses and berries and cactus fruits, he climbed central Texas's dry pebbled mountains and the forbidding cliffs of Mexico's Sierra Madre until the two wanderers stumbled at last into Mexico City and the palace of the Spanish viceroy. On July 24, 1536, eight years after they had started from Bahía de la Cruz with hot-tempered Narváez in search of Apalachen's gold, they heard their native Castilian once more. Years later, Cabeza became an emaciated ghost in Spanish councils, a grim reminder of what lay in store for conquistadores who unlike Cortez found no gold and knew nothing of the path lying before them in a cruel country which alternated between rank jungle and parched brown desert.

It was not that the Spaniards in Cuba hadn't wondered what had become of Pánfilo de Narváez when his caravels returned without him. Shortly afterward they sent a young boy named Juan Ortiz in a pinnace, a light sailing ship, to search for him. Juan had been on board a caravel with part of the Narváez party but had returned to Cuba when the caravel had failed to find its roaming commander in chief. Bewildered and heartsick, Narváez's wife listened to Juan's tale of loss. In tears she begged Juan to return to Bahía de la Cruz, and full of daring and compassion he consented.

He knew the way. He even recognized Hirrihigua's village when his pinnace anchored. As he peered to land, he also thought he saw something else: a piece of white stuck on a stick. A message from Narváez! Surely that was what it was. In an instant he was clambering toward a rowboat on deck. The crew begged him to wait, but he brushed them aside. With another teenager as adventurous as himself he lowered the rowboat on its creaking winches, snaked down the ship's ropes, and jumped in. Furiously they began to row ashore. Uncertainly they heard the sailors' warnings dying on the wind—that the natives were known to be fierce, that two Spanish boys would stand no chance of survival in Hirrihigua's town. But all they both could think of was the thrill of discovery surging in their veins. Juan Ortiz was just eighteen, and he longed to be as gallant among the conquistadores as his erstwhile commander Narváez and men like Ponce and the pilot Anton de Alaminas had been. He was, he thought, rowing toward his own immortality.

He was also—and he knew this too, but he believed in miracles—rowing directly toward the place where Narváez had cut off Hirrihigua's nose and lips and thrown his mother to greyhounds. When the Timucua saw Juan they swept down on him and his companion innocent of miracles with all the pent-up fury of the revenge they had been dreaming of. Hirrihigua relished the prospect of killing the boys—but slowly. His outrage at the hands of Red-Beard had smoldered in him without hope of satisfaction. Now, suddenly, it blazed before him. The Spanish boys would die by torture on the same Bay of Culata where Red-Beard had tortured Hirrihigua's mother and burned Timucua dead in their coffins. Grimly Hirrihigua pondered his plans for execution.

Juan's companion he decided to kill by ordering his warriors to shoot their arrows into the boy's flesh—but only a few arrows at a time, to prolong the suffering. The youngster screamed in agony far into a black night when high Ucita council fires crackled and a bound Juan Ortiz watched in terror, the Catholic prayers dying on his lips. When the torture was over and his friend's heart had been pierced, Juan knew his own turn had come. Roughly he was seized by strong Timucua arms and dragged into the clearing. But then in his shackles as he stood there he saw an Indian woman suddenly rush up to Hirrihigua accompanied by three girls. Vehemently she shouted while she made signs in Juan's direction, and the girls in their shiny fish-bladder earrings and their skirts of moss fell to their knees.

"He is too young!" Hirrihigua's wife and daughters were begging, though the youth of the other boy had left them unmoved. Juan was handsomer. He had not come ashore with Red-Beard, they argued; he was innocent; he had committed no crime. Fingering his scars, Hirrihigua listened. He loved his wife and his children, as he had loved his mother.

Finally he muttered appeasingly that the boy might live as a Timucua slave—for a while. Privately he planned to torture him anyway, but the women would at least be satisfied that his life had been spared.

As the sweltering weeks passed Juan came to wish he had died with his companion. His back ached from burdens of firewood and water pots. He missed meal after meal, tormented by the smell of roasting oysters and steaming beans. Whenever he fell asleep it was only for the briefest of respites, for the Indians always woke him up again by slapping him and lashing him until ugly welts had scarred his browning flesh. On feast days he was whipped publicly, and all the angry protests of Hirrihigua's wife and the tears of Hirrihigua's daughters were powerless to spare him. He yearned to kill himself. But he couldn't, he was a Catholic, and so day after day he begged heaven for the very gift of freedom in which he had lost faith. Continually Hirrihigua thought of fresh ordeals. One sunrise Juan saw, through the blinding tears of pain and fatigue, the deformed face of his tormentor laughing as he ordered him by signs to run all day in the village plaza without once stopping. Should Juan pause, Hirrihigua made it plain he would be stabbed to death by the arrows of burly braves on every side of him. The race began as the sun ascended above the glinting green tops of the surrounding pines and it did not end until the sun had sunk in the west behind masses of needles now dark against its fire. When blackness made them vanish at last, Juan staggered to the ground more dead than alive. His lungs were bursting and his legs were stabbed with hot knives of pain. Yet even while he lay temporarily abandoned and Hirrihigua's rage at his survival increased, Hirrihigua's wife and oldest daughter Ulele stole softly out to him bringing ointments for his gashes and fresh spring water for his thirst. He almost wished they would leave him alone.

When Hirrihigua found out about his wife's nursing of Juan he decided once for all to put an end to him. He called a feast day, and ordered his warriors to build a gigantic pyre in the village square. Over it they stretched a grill; here Juan would be roasted alive in the torture Spaniards called *barbacoa* and feared more than any other death. Hirrihigua's henchmen kindled the wood; flames leapt high. Juan was bound on his side, and when blisters the size of oranges began to form on his skin he could not help screaming just as his companion who had been shot to death with Timucua arrows had screamed. Then he fell into a daze. Surely now death would come soon. . . . He did not see Ulele rush up to the pyre and in open defiance of her father begin to untie his thongs. Dimly he realized something was happening, that he was not to die yet, but what? Later, he understood he was in Hirrihigua's own hut being tended by the girl herself. She had once again prevailed against her father. Under Hirrihigua's very roof Juan felt her sure hands as she gently rubbed herb juices into his burns. After several days he could walk again. Hirrihigua came and went in the bohio and appeared hardly to notice him. Juan, listening to the Indians' speech, slowly began to understand it. Finally Hirrihigua summoned him and Juan was able to comprehend the cacique's orders. Juan's duty from now on would be to guard Timucua corpses in a section of the pine forest several leagues inland from town. The bodies lay in wooden chests which were sealed with board coverings weighted down by rocks. Since the chests had no hinges, panthers often tore them apart and carried away their contents. Juan was to stand sentry. He was given a quiver of darts and sent on his way across the bay. He must not sleep in that forest, he knew.

The dark of his exile was never silent. Twigs snapped, frogs croaked in woodland pools, crickets chirped loudly. Juan's campfire was often reflected in strange eyes: the ruby red of 'gators and possums, the green of bobcats. Nighthawks flapped above him, and everywhere glowed fireflies. Whenever the moon was bright mockingbirds sang their daytime songs. Chuck-will's-widows called low and throatily. Even as he heard the sounds Juan did not recognize them. At first he feared them; later they were almost company. Owls hooted in wind-stirred swamp maples at the edge of a nearby hammock. A night came when he couldn't hold up his head; toward dawn, he slept at last, only to be awakened by the crashing footfalls of a panther. He heard the rip of boards. Horrified, he saw the massive cat carrying off the body of an infant girl who had only been placed in her grave two days before. In an instant he was on his feet, muttering prayers as he sprinted after the panther. The animal swiftly disappeared into a hammock. The undergrowth on its edge was impassable. Hopelessly Juan wandered for a while in the dark forest until he came to an open, faintly moonlit trail. Escape! But escape to where, to what? Just as he decided to begin running, he heard grunts of satisfaction and a sound of gnawing. The panther . . . He groped his way through mats of smilax and muscadine, and when he saw the panther eating its prize he aimed his dart by moonlight. With a shrill cry the panther fled deeper into the brush. Juan knew he could never follow him; it was still too dark.

The wait until dawn was interminable to him now, though already the eastern sky was lavender at the horizon. Not until the sun came up was he able to make out the dead carcass of the panther with his arrow in its side. Quickly he snatched up the child's body and returned with it to the cemetery. Then he dragged the panther over a trail of pine needles and thorns and all the way through the shallow bay to the village plaza at Ucita. When Hirrihigua came out of his bohio he stared first at the soaked panther, then at Juan. His look was still a look of hatred, but in it Juan now saw respect.

To Hirrihigua, Juan's bravery was indeed admirable; it was also Juan's undoing. Such courage in an enemy could not be allowed to exist. Once again Hirrihigua set a death date; Juan would be shot with arrows, not burned, in deference to his heroism. This was Hirrihigua's only concession. He also summoned his wife and daughters and told them they had saved Juan for the last time.

Quickly Ulele stole away to Juan where he was chopping firewood in a secluded spot. He understood just enough of her whisperings to realize that she was offering to help him flee. In the forest he was to meet an Indian who would guide him to the town of Mocoso, on an inland river. The cacique of Mocoso would protect him because he loved her. Later that night Juan slipped quietly out of Hirrihigua's house, over the water, and into the waiting forest unheard. The guide stood ready, and motioned him ahead. All night they followed a narrow forest trace until they came to the Mocoso River, its ripples broken under a faint moon. At dawn two armed Indians came threateningly up to him and his guide, but the guide calmed them. Soon afterwards the cacique, whose personal name was that of his village and his river, welcomed Juan and promised him asylum. To Juan's amazement Mocoso even embraced him and gave him a kiss of peace. Then he understood the reason; Mocoso hated Hirrihigua, his rival, as much as he loved Hirrihigua's daughter. Mocoso appointed Juan as one of his warriors, and when Juan told him how he had killed a panther with a single dart Mocoso made Juan understand he regarded him as a brother in bravery. Perhaps too he regarded him as something of a curiosity.

Hirrihigua made several attempts to recapture Juan. When Mocoso was deaf to the orders of his envoy, Hirrihigua began intriguing with Urribarracuxi, the husband of Mocoso's sister. Mocoso turned Urribarracuxi away with a curt refusal. The longer Juan stayed in Mocoso the more the cacique grew fond of him. Juan learned the language; they both declared themselves eternally bound in friendship. This decision on Mocoso's part eventually cost him not only the hand of Hirrihigua's daughter in marriage but also the alliance of Urribarracuxi in times of war. But Mocoso never wavered in his loyalty to Juan, who settled into Timucua life as a warrior and hunter. He had his place in the council house where he drank the Black Drink. Soft-eyed girls cast him bashful glances, and he responded. Years passed: steaming summers, autumns full of the tenuous rain of falling leaves in grey mists, winters fragrant with the blooms of early jasmine, springs with memories for Juan of the boy he had been, rowing into his existence as a Timucua because he thought he saw a message from Narváez. Had it been? He would never know. Sometimes he dreamed of Spain with its tiled red roofs and beige plains, sometimes of Cuba and early dew shining on cascades of bloom there. But mostly he was content. He lived a free man among friends. After what he had endured, it was sufficient.

4

De Soto

Hernando de Soto, a native of the Spanish village of Barracota, had impressive ancestors on both sides of his family. His bearded good looks were patrician. He rode magnificently, and by his mid-thirties he had already proven himself against the Incas in Spain's conquest of South America. The gold and jewels he had seized from Inca villages were not enough to satisfy him, however. Conquistadores were seldom satisfied. Always he was obsessed by Florida, the land where Ponce had met death and where Narváez had disappeared. Cabeza de Vaca, in 1537, was on his way back to Spain from Mexico even as de Soto laid his plans, but rumors of Cabeza's survival had not yet reached the Spanish court when de Soto was pleading his case there for Florida's governorship. Why should he be refused? He was rich, distinguished, a known hero. He was sure he could succeed where Ponce and Narváez had failed. King Charles agreed and gave him a commission to "conquer and pacify" and colonize Florida. For himself de Soto would earn twelve leagues square of the territory he captured "provided it should not include a seaport or the chief town of the territory." Half the gold, silver, pearls and other jewels in Florida were to be retained by the king. The rest belonged to de Soto and his men. In high spirits, he began making preparations to sail.

Then the news of Cabeza de Vaca's arrival home began to spread like wildfire. One rumor piled upon another. Cabeza had seen "the richest Countrie in all the world"; he had heard of de Soto's plans and had advised all his relatives to go to Florida; he had seen huge gold and silver mines. The trouble, of course, was that Cabeza himself said nothing at all before he saw the king who must hear his story first. Greedy imaginations were free to conjure up the usual visions of El Dorado, and de Soto's followers had imaginations as picturesque as those of any of the followers of Ponce and Narváez. When de Soto learned of Cabeza's coming he sent messages to him announcing his planned conquest of Florida. Would Cabeza accompany him? His experience would be invaluable. At first Cabeza was tempted. Then he remembered how Narváez's bullheadedness had led an army into tragedy, and he replied to de Soto: "I am loath to go under the command of another." Eventually he was appointed to an official post in Paraguay. Without him de Soto gathered his forces: nine ships, "six hundred lancers, targeteers, crossbowmen, and arquebusiers, all suitably armed," two hundred and thirteen horses, and enough greyhounds to tear stubborn Indians to pieces when necessary. De Soto's ships stank with the swine he was taking to feed his men. The decks teemed with activity. Priests and Dominican and Franciscan friars carried aboard their vestments and the paraphernalia of the Mass and crosses to plant in Florida sands. Portable forges were hauled over the ships' sides; they would be needed for making armor and captives' chains. Doctors and coopers and caulkers jostled each other, while in the Spanish sea below bumboats bobbed full of additional supplies. Ropes creaked and winches grated. De Soto paced restlessly back and forth, checking, supervising, determined to forget nothing. He had no intention of following Narváez into eternity.

In Florida, May came to the village of Mocoso that year of 1539 as it had come in other years. The laughing gulls came back to the river and the bay from the south. Frigate birds soared above, and by night the bay was phosphorescent. The Indians feasted and drank and hunted and tended their sick and buried their dead as usual. Juan Ortiz was one of them now. He no longer remembered much Spanish. His body was painted like Timucua bodies, and his skill at moving noiselessly in pine forest and hammock was as great as theirs. The skin of his face was weathered and swarthy. He still prayed sometimes, without forming the Castilian words he had once known; Jesus and the Blessed Virgin had preserved him and had given him the warm friendship of Mocoso. Juan never dared to wander far. Always, he knew, Hirrihigua would be waiting for a chance to recapture him. Juan had explored little of Florida beyond Ucita, where he had had his baptism of horror, and Mocoso and its river, where he had found peace and life.

In 1539 Pentecost fell on May 25. Hirrihigua's subjects at Ucita were unaware of it; they only knew that on the horizon ships like those of Narváez appeared. Miles from shore, the ships anchored. Then their sailors began taking cautious soundings, edging closer and closer to Ucita with each tide. De Soto, a religious man, named the bay Espíritu Santo because he had first seen it on the festival of the Holy Spirit. Eagerly he stood at the rail. He could hardly wait to get ashore. As governor of Florida, adelantado, he longed to be one of the first to set foot on its soil. His army were well equipped to deal with unruly savages. His confidence was boundless.

Hirrihigua remembered only too well what the last Spanish fleet had brought. Spaniards had mutilated him for life and murdered his mother. Quickly he ordered a high fire to be built in the plaza in front of his house. He must send smoke signals to other towns. Even Mocoso, his enemy, deserved a warning against the most terrible enemy of all, the Christian. By these signals news of the catastrophe of de Soto's arrival spread, to Tocobaga and to tiny Timucua fishing settlements like Pohoy across Tampa Bay, to Weedon Island and to the mouth of the Mocoso River. Flee! Hirrihigua warned his fellow Indians; then, from the forest, attack with all your strength; forest and swamp are the only places where you will be safe; leave the beaches.

De Soto, too, saw the signals. He guessed what they meant. Narváez had come this way, and Narváez had been a peppery warrior ready to kill at sight. But de Soto was not afraid; he only meant to be wary. By Friday, May 30, he was close to Ucita and for the first time he saw its palm-thatched timber huts, its high temple mound, its broad plaza. He could wait no longer. Commanding a brigantine he ordered its pilot to steer for shore. His men protested and so did his secretary, Ranjel; the adelantado must not risk a foolhardy landing. Who knew what the savages would do? But de Soto, heedless of the danger, barked to Ranjel that the señor should confine himself to his duties and stop predicting disaster. Soon de Soto was on the beach supervising the landing of his two hundred and thirteen horses and a few handpicked lieutenants. His Captain-General Porcallo he ordered to take seven horsemen with him and make a reconnaissance of Ucita, which now appeared to be empty. Porcallo galloped away in a cloud of sand. He was almost immediately attacked by six Indians brandishing arrows. The Spanish horsemen killed two of them; the others fled into a shrubby thicket. Porcallo tried to follow them, but his horse bogged down time after time in nearby ponds and their riders were too tired from the long sea voyage to be able to control them efficiently. When Porcallo at last returned to the beach he gave an account of what had happened. De Soto listened; he would march on Ucita with troops and any Indians around would see the numbers in his vanguard, battalion, and rear guard, and, he hoped, be impressed.

Ucita lay indeed deserted. With exclamations of wonder de Soto's soldiers inspected its temple, topped by the wooden fowl with staring gilded eyes. Inside they found a few pearls. De Soto marched into Hirrihigua's empty house and proceeded to unpack a few personal belongings. The company's provisions were stored in another Indian house. All the rest of the buildings, including the temple, de Soto ordered destroyed. Broad Spanish axes hacked them down under a fiery sun; then the soldiers built themselves closed cabins with the wood. De Soto, seeing the marshes and mangrove and shrub thickets on every side of him, ordered the thickets felled the distance of a crossbow shot around his camp. This way he would have the advantage if the Indians attacked at night.

What he needed, he knew, was an interpreter. In two directions he sent his personal assistants, a few horses, and some foot soldiers to try to find and capture a savage. One of the groups traveled as far as it could through gnarled mangrove country until they came to a creek on whose bank were clustered a few huts. As the Spaniards approached, the people in them dived into the water; the soldiers managed to capture four women, but were soon attacked by Timucua warriors and had to beat a hasty retreat to camp. One of the soldiers, an arrow in his side, fell dead from his mount. The second group of Spaniards rode until they came to an open field; here they found ten Indians who astonished them by not charging with their arrows. Curiously the Spanish stared at the tattooed and painted bodies. The Indians stared back. Their passivity was too much for the horsemen, who began to charge. Three of the Indians were wounded; the rest fled into a palmetto clump. One of the horsemen followed them and drew his lance. Just as he was about to use it on a hapless Indian he got the shock of his life.

"Do not kill me, Cavalier!" the Indian cried. "I am a Christian! Do not slay these people; they have given me my life! My name is Juan Ortiz, and I come from Seville." Juan shouted to the other Indians, who came forward. He would protect them, he said. Then he explained in halting Spanish strangely accented with Timucuan that he and his companions had come from the village of Mocoso. The cacique Mocoso, seeing the signal fires, had summoned Juan and told him of the Spanish ships. At first Juan had laughed, thinking it was a joke. Sadly, Mocoso had said it was not. If Juan felt he must join the Christians once again Mocoso would be sorrowful but he would understand.

In triumph de Soto's soldiers mounted Juan and his friends and they all rode back to Ucita together. The Indians' wounds were not serious. Mocoso's Indians were only too happy to cooperate with friends of Juan; he had hunted and fought and lived with them a decade. They were also anxious to plot against Hirrihigua. Of the Indians of Ucita there was no sign. De Soto gave a huge banquet that night: dried fish and roast pig and unripe grapes which some of his men had found growing wild. Juan would have his own horse, and armor. He would become a valued member of the expedition. Juan had to admit he knew little of the country, and when he tried on Spanish clothes they were so uncomfortable that for days he could only wear a loose, long linen shirt. De Soto's men crowded around him, gaping at his adventures, fingering curiously the scars of his torture in the village of Hirrihigua. To Mocoso's Indians de Soto explained that he merely wanted provisions. He would pass through their town to go inland and explore. "Florida is so wide it cannot fail to have rich country," he explained. Riches were what he sought; the beaches and woods roundabout did not have them. A message was sent to Mocoso, and while Juan relearned his Spanish and once more prayed familiar Catholic prayers with the troops, de Soto waited.

Mocoso soon arrived with his retinue, all splendid in feathers and deerskins and bells. De Soto greeted him as an equal, and through Juan the cacique gave his reply: "I appear before you in the full confidence of receiving your favor, as much so as though I deserved it, not in requital of the trifling service I rendered in setting free the Christian when he was in my power, which I did not do for the sake of my honor and my promise but because I hold that great men should be liberal. The favor I hope for, great lord, is that you will hold me to be your own, calling on me freely to do whatever may be your wish."

It was a dangerous game Mocoso was playing; but he was ready to risk much for a chance to humiliate Hirrihigua. The Spaniards said they only meant to march through his town, not rule it; very well, he would take them at their word. The wisest thing he could do would be to pass them on to the cacique Urribarracuxi. Urribarracuxi, he told them, had much gold, though he himself had none. Further ceremonious speeches were made by both sides. Then Mocoso feasted with the Spaniards. For two days the gathering celebrated Juan Ortiz's arrival until increasingly fulsome orations were rudely interrupted by the arrival of Mocoso's mother. The old woman was in a high state of agitation. When her son had left the village she had been away. Then she had returned to the news that he had gone to put himself into the hands of the Spanish.

"Give him back to me!" she cried, through Juan, to de Soto. "Do not do to him what Red-Beard did to Hirrihigua! If you think of such a deed set my son free and do your will upon me, not him. I am old, and I am willing to bear the pain for both."

De Soto reassured her that he meant her son no harm. He was not Red-Beard. He came in peace, he said, looking only for gold and silver. Wouldn't she join him at the banquet table? Warily, her sharp eyes taking in every detail of the men and animals and arms around her, she sat down. At first she refused food. Did she dare to accept it, she asked Juan? De Soto and his men found it all very funny and laughed heartily, but Juan knew what she feared and tried to comfort her. He would first taste all her food himself, he promised.

"Madam, you have just offered your life for your son," a Spanish soldier teased her. "Why do you now worry about dying?"

With dignity she answered, "I do not hate life. I love it as much as anybody, but I am willing to die for Mocoso because I love him more than life itself. I cannot bring myself to trust you. Let me have my son, and we will leave."

But Mocoso was enjoying himself too much to go. After he and Juan and de Soto had reasoned with his mother, she reluctantly went to the door. Then, turning, she told Juan loudly that the least he could do was liberate Mocoso since Mocoso had liberated him. At this the soldiers laughed more hilariously than before, and Mocoso laughed with them. Mothers! Once again he promised her he would soon return, and realizing she could warn him no more she left.

During all this time, Hirrihigua did not appear. Doubtless he had fled inland, where the swamps were so dense he could safely hide and ambush the conquerors when they came that way. But the Spanish were relying on their guns and crossbows. They were also relying on Juan

Ortiz to curry favor with the chiefs through whose territory they would pass. De Soto was anxious to get started. He had promised King Charles all "seaports and chief towns in the territory." Why stay in an Ucita he could never own?

From the Bay of Espíritu Santo—Tampa—the Spaniards proceeded on the march to Urribarracuxi's village, leaving behind a small garrison to hold Ucita for the Crown. In this the garrison were to fail, and many died of fever and starvation. One, Juan Muñoz, was captured and enslaved by Hirrihigua's Timucua, who soon began living at Ucita the life they had always lived. Juan Muñoz had to wait nearly a decade for release and the sight of Spanish countrymen.

Near the Gulf, de Soto found, the country was open. Afterwards Juan Ortiz led them all down an oak-shaded Indian trace he knew. He had never traveled it any distance, but he was sure it led through hammocks and pine forests to Urribarracuxi, of whom he had no fear since de Soto's men were beside him. When the troops arrived at a small swamp they met a canoe containing thirty Indians. Quickly Juan Ortiz spoke to them. Then he gave back their message: "King Urribarracuxi, lord of this province, whose vassals we are, sends us to ask of you what it is you seek in his country." Peace, friendship, and gold, the Spanish answered. The Indians in their long dugout led them through watery tangles to Urribarracuxi, who greeted them with formal courtesy. Mocoso was mistaken, Urribarracuxi said; he had no gold or silver whatever. However—and he raised a tattooed arm, pointing vaguely toward the sun—there was much gold in the country of the Ocali. There was so much gold there that all the Indians wore golden helmets in battle. Urribarracuxi must have been amused when his visitors rose to the bait. Politely he offered to give them provisions for the march ahead. Ocali was the place to go. He, and his ally Hirrihigua, had nothing. De Soto's Captain General, Porcallo, was disgusted. Another march, through the Blessed Virgin only knew what bogs and pits and jungles! "Hurri, harri, hurri, higa, burra coja, hurri harri!" he swore out loud. "The devil take a land whose names are so vile and infamous! I swear to God, a man can get no good from such princes, nor good events from such omens. Let him labor who must to eat. As for me, I have enough property for this life as well as the one to come." So saying, he announced his intention to go back to the waiting fleet in the bay of Espíritu Santo and take a ship to Cuba. He divided his arms and horses among members of the expedition. Then he rode west toward the Gulf with his Negro and West Indian servants, away from the adventure of crossing a continent and into a sensible old age in balmy Havana.

Three leagues beyond Urribarracuxi's town the Spanish found the Green Swamp. Its cypresses towered over rusty water. Snakes lay sunning themselves on half-submerged logs. Something was droning, but the Spanish did not know what the jarfly was. Everywhere the vines swung and looped in lofty sweet gums and hickories. Whole trees had their limbs covered with vultures. The water was coated with pale green duckweed the Spanish thought was slime. Rain crows called back and forth, and tree frogs were croaking. To the Spanish the sounds were sinister. Juan Ortiz admitted he had never been through this swamp. He did not know the way out. From it flowed many rivers, but few men knew its interior. The leaves of red maples glinted in the sun. In places the muck would be waist-deep. How could horses ever plod through such treacherous country? Every so often the harsh call of an ivory-billed woodpecker cut through the air. Maidenhair ferns waved delicate fronds in low winds. When the Spanish made camp on the swamp's edge twilight began to fall. One moment the sky was blue; the next it faded to a pallid pearl. From high perches black-crowned night herons slowly flapped their wings toward their feeding grounds. The moon came up, scrimmed by ragged July clouds. The night was redolent of the smell of swamp honeysuckle and wild phlox. To the Spanish, the very sweetness of it all was sinister. Katydids chirped. Raccoons sniffed at the army's provisions, and sentries stirred nervously until they realized the noise came from animals, not Indians. Had Hirrihigua escaped into this swamp? What other Indians waited in it? What chance would a man have of emerging alive? Hernando de Soto, lying in his bed of grasses, wondered these things too. Beyond the swamp lay Ocali. He would risk anything for its golden treasures. But he wondered what savages were ready for him along the way, and what perils lay in the depths of the swamp. His wife Isabel had come out with him from Spain, but he had left her in Cuba, knowing there would be wildernesses like this vast wet world ahead. He had loved Isabel from childhood. For years they had waited to marry; he had had a gallant ancestry, true, but he had had to go to Peru for the gold to support her. They had been able to wed only when both were middle-aged. Isabel had understood why he had had to become adelantado of Florida. In Cuba he had made her his Florida regent, because he had known there would be obstacles. She understood his ambition, his lust for excitement. But on the edge of morasses such as the Green Swamp, a man could not help wondering what his destiny might be and what Jesus and the Blessed Virgin had planned for the rest of his earthly life.

For eight days de Soto's scouts plodded back and forth in the swamp, wading in its lettuce-choked rivers, hearing the slide of its turtles into the water as they approached, seeing the shiny skins of water moccasins as they hung on low willow branches, marveling at the fragile blooms of butterfly and green-fly orchids high in the trees. At last they found a current which ran through a relatively open stretch. They followed it, and came out on the swamp's other side. Then, to their consternation, they realized the entire army could not follow them. The streams running from the swamp had created sticky marshes everywhere beyond it. Back through the Green Swamp they hacked their way to de Soto. The swamp could be crossed, they told him, "because of the great amount of water flowing over it from the channel of a river." But in the marshes outside, the water was not deep. Supplies could not be floated. Horses would stumble. Rafts of pigs could not move in the marsh grass. Impatiently de Soto resolved to explore the swamp himself. If you wanted something done, he thought, you could seldom depend on others. For three days he reconnoitered the swamp; unfamiliar noises jarred him, from the frogs to thumping marsh rabbits. One day a volley of Indian arrows suddenly zinged at him from the trees. His men attacked and captured a few Indians who offered to guide them for a price. But the guides began leading them into muddy creeks where more Indian arrows rushed at them. Angered, the Spanish set their greyhounds at the guides and watched while the hungry dogs tore all but one Indian to pieces. The survivor offered, in fear now of his life, to guide the Spaniards correctly. De Soto followed him out of the swamp to a wide trail. For four leagues he marched along it until the guide turned once again toward the swamp and showed him a passage without mud along which his men and horses and rafts could pass. For about a hundred feet the water was too deep to ford, but here the Indians had built a rude log bridge. Elated, de Soto sent messengers back to the main camp. They were to give his lieutenants the news, and they were to bring back cheese and biscuits, for he was famished. When they returned, he "greeted them most cordially and praised them with magnificent words," one of them afterwards reported. The biscuits tasted splendid.

At last the expedition with its baggage was able to cross the Green Swamp. Not an Indian was in sight now, and de Soto's men thanked

God for their good luck as they thanked God also for the Indian cornfield
they found at the swamp's edge. They were so hungry they stripped the
tall stalks and ate the corn raw. It was a labor of Hercules to get the heavy
forges, the armor, the chains and barrels and chests through the swamp's
mazes, to say nothing of the pigs which had to be loaded onto vine-lashed
logs and floated under cypresses whose pale needles were barely moving
in the windless heat. Once beyond the swamp, Juan Ortiz calculated, they
would be entering the province of the cacique Acuera, which must be
crossed before they reached Ocali where all the gold was. When Acuera
and his people saw the Spanish emerging from the Green Swamp they
fled to a dense pine forest beyond—all but an unlucky handful who stayed
behind to watch the spectacle of invasion and were captured by Spanish
soldiers. De Soto promised them their freedom if they would go back to
Acuera with the message that the Spanish were his "friends and brothers."
There were the usual elaborations on the power of King Charles, his
mother Doña Juana, and the High Pontiff called Papa; there was also
the classic postscript. Should Acuera fail to feel brotherly, "my men
can cause much damage to your vassals and your lands. . . . Our principal
purpose is to reduce by peaceful and friendly means all the provinces and
nations of this great kingdom to the obedience and service of Our Lord
and the mighty Emperor and King of Castile."

When the Indians reappeared from Acuera's sanctuary they brought
his reply:

> I have long since learned who you Christians are. . . . I already know
> very well what your customs and behavior are like. To me you are pro-
> fessional vagabonds who wander from place to place, gaining your
> livelihood by robbing, sacking, and murdering people who have given
> you no offense. I want no manner of friendship or peace with people
> such as you. . . . I promise to maintain war upon you so long as you wish
> to remain in my province, not by fighting in the open, although I could
> do so, but by ambushing and waylaying you whenever you are off guard.
> . . . I have commanded my vassals to bring me two Christian heads
> weekly, this number and no more. I shall be content only to behead two
> of you each week since I can thus slay all of you within a few years, for
> even though you may colonize and settle you cannot perpetuate your-
> selves because you have not brought women to produce children and
> pass your generation forward. I am king in my land and it is unneces-
> sary for me to become the subject of a person who has no more vassals
> than I. I regard those men as vile and contemptible who subject them-
> selves to the yoke of someone else when they can live as free men. . . . I

and all my people have vowed to die a hundred deaths to maintain the freedom of our land.

The experience of the Green Swamp had exhausted his followers, de Soto knew. For twenty days the army camped in Acuera to recover. Fourteen were never to leave it. Acuera's stealthy warriors were unable to restrain themselves to two heads a week. Instead they killed at once any man who strayed so much as a hundred yards from the camp. De Soto always ordered Christian burials for such victims, but at night the Indians would come to dig up the headless bodies and cut them into pieces which they hung in the trees where the Spanish could see them. It hardly built morale. Other Spanish soldiers kept their heads but suffered the sharp wounds of bone arrows. Fifty Indians who roamed too far from their forest were first mutilated as Hirrihigua had been and then killed. The rest shouted Timucua words which Juan Ortiz understood only too well: "Advance, thieves and traitors! Here and further on you will be treated as you deserve. All of you will be quartered and cut into pieces and hung on the largest trees along the road." The Timucua of Mocoso's village had been Juan's friends for so long. He could sympathize too with the feelings of Acuera. But Juan was a Christian, and he had no choice but to follow de Soto. Otherwise his soul would be damned eternally.

Juan Ortiz, Hernando de Soto, and the rest of their troupe left the country of Gulf and bay and river and swamp goaded by dreams. At Ocali they were to find no gold, only the promise that there was gold in Apalachen. At Apalachen it was the same story. Westward they marched, then north to the Appalachian foothills, then south once more. Always they heard heady promises; never did they find their treasure. Juan eventually caught a fever and, weakened by it, drowned crossing a river. De Soto perished on the banks of the Mississippi where his men weighted down his corpse and sank it deep. A few tattered survivors—none of them clergy—finally made their way to Tampico in Mexico and told the tragic details of the expedition's failure. When Isabel de Soto learned of her husband's end, she sickened and died of grief in Cuba. She never saw Spain again. De Soto's secretary Ranjel and two other members of the party published their adventures, and another gave an account to the half-Spanish, half-Inca writer Garcilaso de la Vega, who embellished the drama with vivid details of his own. An avid reader of the earliest chronicles was Captain John Smith, of England, who was so enchanted with the tale of Juan Ortiz being saved by Hirrihigua's daughter that he borrowed it for the second, though not the first, edition of his own adventures in Virginia. Pocahontas had her archetype in Ulele.

The prophecies of the cacique Acuera had been only too correct, the de Soto survivors realized. Once again, Spain had set out from Tampa Bay to conquer Florida and had failed completely. In 1545 a treasure-loaded galleon on its way from Cartagena, in South America, was wrecked offshore from a Calusa village in southwest Florida. Of its two hundred crew and passengers, only a handful lived to suffer Calusa slavery. Among them was a bright thirteen-year-old boy named Hernando de Escalante Fotaneda who danced a jig for the chief of Calos that made him laugh. Seventeen years later Escalante escaped and made his way to a French settlement just begun on the upper east coast. Of his time among the Calusa he wrote a stirring narrative, and his descriptions of them and their daily lives has survived. "These Indians have no gold, less silver, and less clothing," he said truthfully. "They go naked, except only some breechclouts woven of palm. . . . The women do the like with certain grass that grows on trees." Why, the Calusa asked him, wouldn't their Spanish captives do as they were told? The Indians were incredulous when Escalante replied it was because the Spanish hadn't been as quick as himself to learn the Calusa language. He listened carefully to Calusa accounts of their northern neighbors. There were Timucua at Tocobaga, to whom the Calusa traded tiny oyster pearls. There was Mocoso on its river. There was also another village on a great Bay the Calusa called Tanpa. It is one of the few Calusa words which has come down to us. What had been the Bay of Culata to the Timucua, the Bay of the Cross to Narváez, and the Bay of the Holy Spirit to De Soto, was finally to take its modern name, made more pronounceable as Tampa, from Hernando de Escalante Fontaneda's report to the nobility and king of Spain on what he had found in Florida. Florida's subjugation, he told them, "is befitting His Majesty for the security of his armadas that go to Peru, New Spain, and other parts of the Indies. . . . This much should be done, and another thing also—to go in search of pearls, for there is no other wealth in that country." It was sound advice. Oysters were tangible. But there were men in Spain and the Indies and South America who dreamed of wealth of another kind in Florida. They were the priests and monks of the Catholic Church, and where the conquistadores had sought impossible gold they sought the souls of the Indians who had failed to have it.

5

The Martyrs

In the minds of New World adventurers and Madrid officials alike, the conquest of the Spanish Main was cherished from the outset as a gigantic rape. They all professed concern for the spiritual destinies of the natives. Avaricious explorers like Narváez piously read proclamations when they landed on unknown soil. Soldiers of fortune always included priests and monks in their retinues. Masses were duly offered on wilderness shores. Indians who made no resistance were to be tolerated—except when the tempers of Spanish military men became short. All these things the priests and monks who served the conquistadores witnessed. Most of the clergy were dedicated men bent on redeeming heathen from the wrath of Satan, and occasional clerical voices of protest against Spanish cruelties and Spanish enslavement of the Indians were raised. How could the natives be converted if they considered Christians thieves and killers? What missionary, for instance, now dared risk Tampa Bay, where Narváez and de Soto had robbed and murdered?

The most eloquent apologist for the New World's Indians was Bartolomé de las Casás, who had labored among them as a Dominican priest since the early 1500s and who was consecrated Bishop of Chiapas, Mexico, in 1542. Before he assumed his episcopal duties Las Casás made a trip home to Spain, and there he penned for Prince Philip, the heir of King Charles, a vivid account of what he had seen of Spain's treatment of red men. Las Casás had been pleading for mercy since 1514; his sermons had for decades fallen on deaf ears. Prince Philip, he hoped, would intervene on the Indians' behalf. Spanish adventurers were creating a "black legend" in Las Casás's future dominions across the Atlantic that were making missionary labors impossible.

His *Short Relation of the Destruction of the Indies* is a catalogue of horrors. In Hispaniola, for instance,

> the Christians, with their horses and swords and lances, began to slaughter and practice strange cruelties. . . . They made bets as to who would slit a man in two, or cut off his head at one blow; or they opened up his bowels. They tore the babes from their mothers' breasts by the feet and dashed their heads against the rocks. Others they seized by the shoulders and threw into the rivers, laughing and joking. . . . They made a gallows just high enough for the feet to nearly touch the ground, and by thirteens, in honor and reverence of our Redeemer and the twelve Apostles, they put wood underneath and, with fire, they burned the Indians alive.

In Florida there had been de Soto, "the chief tyrant," who had wrought his vengeance on "friendly, intelligent, politic, and orderly" Indians all the way from Tampa Bay to Apalachen and beyond. Bartolomé de las Casás had heard tales from the lips of the expedition's veterans. Not a priest or friar had lived, but ordinary soldiers were free in their admissions even outside the confessional. In the Green Swamp and beyond, de Soto's men had

> tormented and killed [the Indians], leading them like animals. When one became tired or fainted, they cut off his head at the neck, in order not to free those in front from the chain that bound them, and the body fell to one side and the head to the other. . . . It is said that the chief tyrant had the faces of many Indians cut, so that they were shorn of nostrils and lips, down to the beard; and in particular of a group of two hundred whom he either summoned or who came voluntarily from a certain town. Thus he dispatched these mutilated, suffering creatures dripping with blood, to carry the news of the deeds and miracles done by those baptized Christians, preachers of the Holy Catholic Faith. It may be judged in what state those people must be, how they must love the Christians, and how they will believe that their God is good and just.

Prince Philip pondered; the New World conquerors protested; Bartolomé de las Casás's passionate voice continued to ring out in vain from his pulpit. And no missionary wanted to go to Tampa Bay. Who knew what had really happened there? There were such conflicting stories.

Fray Luis Cancer de Barbastro was a saintly Dominican who began the study of Indian languages under Las Casás himself. From Las Casás he heard the "black legend" of the conquistadores as well as Indian grammar. In Mexico, where he worked among what was left of the Aztecs, he heard of the arrival of Cabeza de Vaca in Mexico City, of the coming of the de Soto expedition's last handful to Tampico, of the fierceness of the natives on Florida's Gulf Coast. He began longing to go to Florida. Among the Mexican Indians he had been able to make himself beloved; he had made many converts. Why could he not succeed in Florida? With a friend, Dominican friar Gregorio de Beteta, he started to plan a strategy. They would land, in Florida, not at Tampa Bay but at a place where no Spanish soldiers had been. They would be men of peace, unarmed; the Indians would respect this, and would slowly be won over to the Holy Faith by the example of love and self-sacrifice set by its priests. Word would spread from tribe to tribe of the Dominicans' coming. Slowly, Florida would be Christianized, and even the Indians of Tampa Bay would eventually come to understand, as they heard of the friars, that there were many kinds of Christians, and that some of them were good. The plan was pitiful in its naïveté, but saints are seldom men of sophistication.

In 1549, having won the permission of their Spanish superiors in the Dominican order, Fray Luis and Fray Gregorio embarked for Florida from the Mexican port of Vera Cruz. With them in the caravel *Santa María de la Encina* sailed Fray Juan García, an old colleague of Fray Gregorio's, a Basque named Fray Diego de Tolosa, and Brother Fuentes, a Dominican oblate. The May wind was gentle on the blue Mexican Gulf. Coconut palms rustled dreamily along the shore. Fray Luis and Fray Gregorio both had a little knowledge of Timucuan, but they decided they needed a native in their group. Accordingly the *Santa María* put in an unscheduled stop at Havana, where the priests were soon congratulating themselves at their luck in finding a native Floridian convert named Magdalena. She spoke and understood Timucuan well, and knew other Florida dialects. Before the ship set sail again Fray Luis gave Juan de Arana, its captain, his instructions. He was not to land in any port where the conquistadores had gone in search of gold and slaves. Otherwise, he was free to choose the best landing place he could find.

On Ascension Day, Arana sighted Florida's west coast. Eagerly the four priests and Brother Fuentes hurried to the taffrail. They saw thick mangrove canals and shell-strewn sands. Palmetto fronds arched gracefully above tiny clumps of lavender goatsfoot. Florida! Its pristine beauty was dreamlike, and it filled the priests with fresh hope. Perhaps they would find unspoiled children of nature who would welcome them and be eager to learn. On the following day, after a moonlit night during which the Gulf's waves barely rocked the caravel, a boatload of sailors went ashore in search of a port. Soon they sighted a Calusa canoe; the Indians in it made hostile gestures, and quickly the sailors hurried back to report to Arana. He then sailed farther north. As the water close to shore became shallower he was forced to stay six leagues from an island he spotted at the entrance of what looked like a large harbor. Again a party of sailors set out to explore. This time Fray Luis and Fray Juan García went with them, unable to restrain their eagerness. The little boat cut its way quickly through the calm water and soon the party stepped onto dry land. Almost immediately a group of Indians emerged from the brush and began shaking their fists. But then they disappeared. Fray Luis had seen Indians in Mexico do this, after all, and he had won them in the end to his way. He was not unduly disturbed. The Indians were naturally afraid of strangers. He had trusted Arana to follow his directions. Surely this was not a bay where Spanish soldiers had been; it could not be. Arana knew enough navigation to avoid places like the Bay of Calos. He had; but unknown to him or to his passengers, he had steered his caravel oblivious of latitude straight to Tampa Bay's northern shore and had landed Fray Luis and Fray Juan on what was the worst location they could possibly have been in. Ucita, Tocobaga, Pohoy . . . they were Timucua villages which had indeed known Christians before.

The sailors and the priests passed a starry night on the island without incident. This further encouraged Fray Luis. But all the soundings the sailors made told them the water was too shallow for a port. The party returned to the caravel and Arana steered back toward the bay's southern shore. Everywhere it looked the same: mangroves, distant pines, glittering sands. When Arana found some empty Indian huts on an inlet, he himself went ashore with Fray Luis, Fray Diego de Tolosa, Brother Fuentes, and the Indian woman Magdalena. Fray Diego climbed a tree to scan the country. Slowly, small groups of Indians began emerging from the coastal forest. They stared. By instinct Fray Luis fell to his knees and prayed while they watched him. Then he rose, and, smiling, reached inside his habit. From it he drew trinkets he had brought them: rosaries, exquisitely wrought handled knives from Spain. "Deeds are love," he told himself, "and gifts shatter rocks." Smiling still he presented them to the dark spectators, who silently took them. Then Fray Luis and Fray Diego knelt to pray again, and with them Brother Fuentes and Magdalena. Fray Luis began reciting litanies. For a while the Indians appeared baffled. Then, uncertainly, they too began to kneel and squat until they grew impatient. Fray Luis tried to conceal his excitement. He left a last litany half unsaid and followed the Indians to a hut toward which they were beckoning him. Here, they gestured toward the ship, was a harbor. How friendly they were now! God in His grace was already working a miracle! After Fray Luis had spoken, through Magdalena, with his hosts he went back to the boat for more presents. Fray Diego, Fuentes, and Magdalena wanted to remain on shore while the caravel came into port. A tiny doubt stabbed at Fray Luis, but the three were insistent and he consented, trying to stifle his misgivings.

When the caravel, with Fray Luis and Fray Juan and Fray Gregorio on board, approached the harbor where the Indians had prayed with Fray Luis no Fray Diego or Fuentes or Magdalena appeared. An Indian emerged from a palmetto thicket and beckoned; one of the sailors rowed in to see what he wanted, and soon the sailor too had disappeared. By the following day Fray Luis and Fray Gregorio and Fray Juan were more worried than they dared to admit. Where were their companions? Where was the sailor? Where were all the friendly natives? The landing of the caravel was a slow business. Every few feet fresh depth readings had to be taken. For sixteen days the *Santa María de la Encina,* with Juan de Arana at the helm, cruised the south shore of Tampa Bay trying to find the best approach to the harbor the Indians had indicated. In the distance columns of smoke began to rise. Not until Corpus Christi were the priests able to say Mass on the beach. Their sonorous Latin cadences echoed alien among the plaints of gulls. Afterwards an Indian appeared carrying a staff topped with a bunch of palmetto fronds. A companion who followed him astonished Fray Luis by starting to call out in broken Spanish: "Friends, friends! Good. Good. Come here. Sword no, sword no!"

"We are good men!" Fray Luis called out in Timucuan.

"We are good men!" the two Indians echoed him.

Slowly Fray Luis went up to them. They handed him the staff. Where, he asked them, were his companions Brother Fuentes, the sailor, Fray Diego de Tolosa, and Magdalena? He wished to see them again. The Indians nodded, and Fray Luis managed to understand their promise that all four would be reunited with their party—but on the next day. There was nothing to do but wait and pray.

When the remaining friars, Luis, Gregorio, and Juan, came ashore the next morning Indians began wading out to their longboat holding gifts of fish. They motioned then to Fray Luis's habit, and he knew they wanted more trinkets. He took a tiny wooden cross, kissed it slowly, and handed it to an Indian who also kissed it and began passing it from hand to hand among his tribesmen who kissed it each in turn. "Oh!" exclaimed Fray Luis, "I am the happiest man in all the world!" Soon he recognized Magdalena wading out to the longboat, but even as the Indians continued to pass the cross to one another he noticed her worried expression.

Brother Fuentes, the Spanish sailor, and Fray Diego were in the house of the cacique, she told him. But all the Indian villages roundabout had been aroused; another Spanish fleet had come, was the message the fires had carried along the shore. Now there were at least sixty Indians gathered nearby, and in spite of their ritual politeness over the cross—for it was not reverence, Magdalena knew—they were planning to exterminate the invaders. When Fray Luis and Fray Gregorio and Fray Juan had returned, deeply troubled, to the caravel, they received further news. A small canoe soon pulled up alongside the ship. From it an Indian clambered up the rope ladder to the caravel's deck. Breathlessly, he clamored to talk to Fray Luis. At once Fray Luis realized it was no Indian. The man was Juan Muñoz, a captive of the Timucua. He had come with the de Soto expedition a decade before. Like his predecessor Juan Ortiz, he had almost forgotten his Castilian Spanish, but he stammered in a mixture of Spanish and Timucuan that Brother Fuentes and the sailor and Fray Diego de Tolosa were not in the house of the cacique alive. They had been murdered.

Slowly, Fray Luis began to understand the danger he was in. Supplies aboard ship were rotting now, he knew. He needed drinking water but it was no longer safe to go ashore for it. None of the sailors on the caravel would take a longboat inland after they learned of the fates of the three Spaniards. What was to be done? Only one thing, Fray Gregorio and Fray Juan told Fray Luis. They themselves would go ashore on the morrow and try to learn whether Juan Muñoz had indeed spoken the truth. They would supplicate as humbly as they could for the supplies they needed. When they got them they would promise the Indians to leave for Havana or Mexico, whichever was the closer, and this was what they must do.

Fray Luis shook his head. "Our work among the Indians cannot be accomplished without the spilling of blood. I shall remain here."

But he could not! Fray Juan and Fray Gregorio pleaded with him. It was no use, Fray Luis replied. God in His wisdom would dispose of His servants. They must bow to His will. Fray Luis retired to his cabin and began putting his diary in order. Whatever happened, he wanted to leave a record. The next day was grey and stormy. Sharp ribbons of rain slashed at the Spaniards' faces whenever they went on deck; wind moaned in the caravel's rigging. "It is the interposition of God!" breathed Juan Muñoz; it showed He did not mean Fray Luis to land. Fray Luis only answered calmly that he would land when the weather cleared. On Wednesday, June 26, the weather was still foul, but Fray Luis ordered the longboat, and its tiny crew—Juan Muñoz among them because he was a Christian, and Fray Gregorio and Fray Juan—rowed hard through swelling waves to take him to the beach. There were Indians watching in the trees, Fray Luis saw. There were Indians half-hidden in the thickets. All of them were armed with arrows and clubs. The rain pierced on, and wind mourned in the beach grasses.

"Is the slave there?" an Indian shouted from his post in a sand pine.

"I am he whom you seek," Juan Muñoz shouted back from the longboat. "But you will not kill us. We know what you have done!"

Fray Luis silenced him. "Do not provoke them, Juan."

"No people in the world could be more enraged than these Indians are!" Fray Gregorio exclaimed to Fray Luis. "For the love of God, wait a little!"

Fray Luis knew he could not. The magnet will of God was drawing him with irrevocable compulsion. He climbed over the longboat's side and began wading in the shallow water toward shore, the rain whipping at his cheeks. Then he realized he had forgotten his favorite crucifix.

"Father, for mercy's sake, will not your reverence come back for it?" begged Fray Gregorio. The sailors would not take it to him; they were afraid to. Fray Luis knew he would miss his crucifix, yet he could not return. He had to go on into the midst of people he would save by love and courage. Slowly, he began walking toward a tiny hillock tufted with fronds of green zamia. An Indian came up to him and astonished him by embracing him. But a second Indian followed the first, and then all Fray Luis knew was that a club was being raised above his tonsured head. He began to try to form words. The Indians never let him finish. As they beat him to death he cried out once, and he fell down to the rain-pocked sand, his rosary tinkling impotently in the stormwind.

When the Indians had finished with him they began shooting arrows

Fray Luis and the Indians

into the longboat. Swiftly the crew rowed back toward the caravel, wondering with every stroke if the Indians would follow in their canoes. But the waves were too high for canoes, and the sailors and the remaining two friars regained the caravel chilled and soaked and stunned at the loss of Fray Luis.

Fray Gregorio knew he now wore Fray Luis's mantle. After prayer he conferred with the pilot, Juan de Arana. They must go on in Fray Luis's name. Arana must find another Florida port, and Fray Gregorio and Fray Juan would carry on the work of Fray Luis among the natives there. Arana laughed outright. The ship was leaking. They would be lucky to make Mexico alive. The vision of Fray Luis Cancer de Barbastro to win Florida for his creed ended finally on the moonlit night of July 9, 1549, when the *Santa María de la Encina* limped into the Mexican port of San Juan de Ulloa. The Gulf waves had subsided. Faint tropical perfumes, cestrums and gardenias, hung vaguely in the air. Fray Gregorio and Fray Juan knew they both would always remember the martyrdom of Fray Luis: the single cry, the falling to the sand. . . . When they arrived in Chiapas to report to Bishop Bartolomé de las Casás, all prayed together. "Holy Fray Luis," whispered Las Casás. "Blessed Fray Luis."

Nothing marks Luis Cancer de Barbastro's grave on Tampa Bay; no one knows where it is. His church has never canonized him. What remains are the beach grasses humming in trade winds, mangrove branches heavy with snowy egrets and roseate spoonbills and herons, palms sighing their own litanies above blue Florida lagoons. Fray Luis's killers have passed into legend along with him; the only monument he has is beauty. For simplicity such as his, nothing less would be enough.

6

Menéndez
and Missions

For seventeen years the Hillsborough and Tampa Bay knew an uneasy interlude—uneasy because the constant shipwrecks of Spanish galleons offshore and the subsequent capture of their passengers by Calusa and Timucua warriors told the Indians Spain was maintaining a firm foothold elsewhere in the New World. When would the Spaniards come again, they wondered? How could they be tricked into leaving? Restlessly the Calusa and Timucua pondered their strategy; they also maintained communication with Timucua tribes in the interior who would tell them if and when any Spanish expeditions came into their own country. In 1565, couriers from these tribes finally arrived on the Gulf Coast to tell a disturbing tale. A peaceable race of whites called Frenchmen had established a settlement in the territory of the Timucua cacique Saturiba, on the peninsula's upper east coast. The French had built a fort to protect themselves against conquistadores who might happen their way, and conquistadores finally had. The leader, terrible with hard eyes, a harder jaw, and a stiffly erect posture full of the authority of command, had come with brigantines full of troops and had proceeded to murder Frenchmen wherever he found them.

The new conqueror, Pedro Menéndez de Avilés, was hard-bitten from forays in the Indies, and he carried a commission from the king of Spain to be adelantado of Florida as Narváez and de Soto had carried commissions before him. He, too, was a zealot. When he learned the French

58

who had begun to colonize Florida were Huguenot refugees he saw no reason to spare them. "Not as Frenchmen, but as Lutherans!" was his thunderous justification for the slaughter he ordered. He had equipped his fleet and troops largely with his own money; by now the Spanish court had become skeptical about the chances of conquering the Land of Flowers. But he was more shrewdly calculating than Narváez or de Soto had been. He also had a personal motive for conquest. Years before, his son had been lost on a voyage from South America to the Bahamas. Menéndez was impelled by a father's hope, admittedly frail, that the lad might have been shipwrecked off the Florida coast and captured by savages. There was always a chance that Menéndez, as victorious adelantado, might find him. Intently Menéndez studied the accounts of previous expeditions to determine the greatest, and the smallest, reasons for their failure. In Florida he meant to build a permanent colony whose treasures would replenish his coffers in due course. By 1565 he had begun an east coast city which he christened St. Augustine, far from Tampa Bay and the bitter memories of Indians there. Assiduously he courted the favor of the natives around him; the caciques he treated with pomp; he fed their avarice with a constant stream of gifts; his troops displayed prominent weapons; the fort he built at St. Augustine was strong, and over it the red and white banner of Castile fluttered triumphantly day after day in smart trade winds. Without the impulsiveness of Narváez and de Soto or the naïveté of Fray Luis Cancer de Barbastro, Menéndez, entrenched, stayed. His strategy with the Indians was a judicious balance of military display, diplomacy, and bribery.

In 1566, having secured his St. Augustine base, he began planning to explore Florida's west coast in search of gold and his son. Rumor had reached him of Spanish captives there. The warlike chief of Calos beheaded a few each year as sacrifices to Death Cult deities, he was told by east coast Indians; the rest of the Christians survived as slaves who went about as naked as the Calusa themselves, and their lives were made miserable by heavy labor as well as by suspense over which of them would be next to be dismembered. Menéndez began fitting out an expedition. As religious insurance he had his priests say several Masses to St. Anthony, asking the saint's intercession in order that Menéndez might find a safe harbor and, if God willed, his boy. By February, on a darkly cloudy morning, his ships reached the Bay of Calos. It stretched before him steely and cream-flecked in the subdued light of an approaching northeaster.

Soon he sighted a canoe; when it pulled up to his brigantine one of its crew quickly climbed onto the Spanish deck.

"Spaniards, brothers, Christians, be welcome! We have been expecting you for eight days, for God and Holy Mary told us that you were coming. The Christian men and women who are alive here have ordered me to come and await you with this boat." Passionately the weathered Spaniard, clad only in a loincloth, pleaded with Menéndez not to pass the harbor. Menéndez replied by telling him to carry a message to the cacique of Calos that he had brought him and his wives many splendid gifts, and that he desired to present them personally.

The cacique came the next morning accompanied by three hundred archers. On board the brigantine Menéndez set up a platform, and here he seated the cacique with many bows. Thirty Spanish arquebusiers stood nearby, their fuses lighted just in case. The cacique greeted Menéndez inscrutably, and then Menéndez brought out his gifts: first, for the cacique, a shirt, a pair of silk breeches, a doublet and hat, ornaments for his wives, biscuits and honey and quince jam for the Calusa archers. The cacique, handsome and in his twenties, was enchanted with his clothes when he retired to put them on. When he presented Menéndez in turn with a bar of silver, he said he hoped there would be even more presents. Menéndez assured him there would be, provided one concession were granted: the king of Spain wanted all his subjects, the Christians, returned to him. "I pray you to give them up; I will bestow many things upon you for this service, and will be your great friend and brother. If you do not, I will order you to be killed." Menéndez was nothing if not forthright. The cacique answered, through an interpreter, that he would send for the Christians of Calos. Within an hour of his command to one of his retinue, five women and three men were brought aboard. Hastily Menéndez put them into linen shifts while they wept with gratitude, and he ordered the ship's tailor to make proper clothes for them as soon as he could. The cacique promised Menéndez more Christians in the future— provided the flow of Spanish presents remained steady. When the cacique had finally departed, the rescued Christians warned Menéndez not to accept his invitation to Calos. The Calusa were murderous. Northward, the Christians said, there was an even greater harbor with more Christian captives, these in the power of the cacique of Tocabaga.

Menéndez sailed into Tampa Bay to find it empty of both Indians and Christians. The Timucua, sighting his ship, had fled with their white slaves to the interior. Discouraged, his hopes of his son dwindling, Menéndez turned back to the Bay of Calos, where he was joined by ships from St. Augustine full of enough soldiers to make it safe for him to go into Calos. If he were able to win as allies the Calusa, by all accounts the fiercest tribe in western Florida, he knew he would eventually conquer all the Gulf Coast, including the Bay of Tampa, Tocobaga, Ucita, Pohoy, the river of Mocoso, and the primeval swamp through which the de Soto expedition had slashed its way with machetes toward what became for most of the men a bloody doom. When Menéndez arrived in the village square at Calos the cacique embraced him, asked for his ration of presents, and stared at the new troops. He would like to regard Menéndez as an elder brother, he assured him. Menéndez and his retinue could hardly believe in the smoothness of the proceedings. Then Menéndez was stunned by a fresh promise: "I want to give you for wife my older sister, whom I love very much, in order that you may take her to visit the land of the Christians. If you send her back, I will become a Christian myself, for it appears better to me than to be an Indian." Christians had more presents available than Indians had, and the quince jam was tasty. The problem was not only that Catholic Menéndez already had a wife in Spain, but that her brother, Gonzalo Solís de Meras, was a member of his expedition and a spectator at his present dilemma. If he became a bigamist, he won souls for Christ and had a chance to locate his son; if he did not, he risked war with the Calusa and the loss not only of his son but of sovereignty on the Gulf. Back on his brigantine he spent a worried night. How could he extricate himself from the tangle?

On the next day, deciding he might be able to stall the cacique indefinitely, laden with gifts he took two hundred arquebusiers from his fleet and once more went to Calos to dine with its dignitaries. The leader of the Spanish troops carried aloft the Castilian flag. Behind him, and ahead of the arquebusiers, marched two fifers and drummers, three trumpeters, a harpist, a violinist, a psaltery player, and a dancing dwarf with a good singing voice who, Menéndez hoped, would keep the cacique amused. The cacique, when they reached his house, was entranced, and ordered the Indians around him to sing and dance likewise. Miles from St. Augustine, Spaniards and Indians enacted a gracefully preposterous pageant while each side secretly wondered how to prevail over the other. A chorus of Indian women piped in high, clear voices. The cacique led one of them to Menéndez. Here, he announced, was the wife he had promised him. She was in her thirties, ugly, clad only in moss, and completely silent as the cacique seated her beside his visitor.

Menéndez began distributing his bounty. This time he had brought two green gowns, one for the cacique's sister and one for his principal wife. He had also brought shiny glass beads, scissors, knives, bells, and mirrors. The Indians began gazing at themselves in the mirrors, laughing and crowding around them. Menéndez passed out biscuits and more quince jam, and as they ate them the Indians agreed this was far better fare than Calusa food. Continually the Spanish musicians blew their trumpets. The cacique listened as if bewitched. "Until you depart, let your men keep always singing and playing the instruments," he begged, and Menéndez assured him it would be so. "And now," said the cacique, "here is my sister. Go with her into the adjoining room and take her for your wife. If you do not, my Indians will be scandalized and will know that you are laughing at them and at her. In this village are more than four thousand Calusa."

With classic understatement Menéndez's brother-in-law Solís de Meras was later to write that the adelantado "showed a little perturbation." "Christian men," replied a worried Menéndez to the cacique, "cannot sleep with women who are not Christians."

"We are Christians already since we have taken you for our elder brother," said the cacique.

Oh, no! temporized Menéndez. It would be necessary for the cacique to study many doctrines, to hear wise counsels from Spanish priests. Desperately, under the eyes of Solís de Meras, he launched into a discussion of the Trinity, the Resurrection, Original Sin, and the Devil, "a very warlike and deceitful cacique" who presided over Hell. The youthful chief listened without moving a muscle. Finally he said Christian beliefs were evidently as impressive as Christian food and music. "Let there be rejoicing; baptize my sister and give her a Christian name. Then sleep with her, for it shall be a great beginning to our trusting one another." In spite of his dilemma, Menéndez realized he would eventually have to if he was to maintain any diplomatic relations with the Calusa at all. He hoped Solís de Meras would understand. The worldly Solís de Meras did, even to watching calmly as Menéndez's Calusa bride was stripped and anointed by her maidens, then dressed in the green gown Menendez had brought her. She looked, Solís de Meras thought, "much better than when she was naked." Menéndez, baptizing her, gave her the name of Antonia, hoping a tolerant St. Anthony would understand his problem. At last he retired with her to the bridal chamber the cacique had indicated, and the next morning Antonia "arose very joyful." When Menéndez finally left Calos he carried with him not only Antonia, whom he meant swiftly to deposit with priests in Havana for instruction in the faith, but several Calusa and some Christians who had been their captives. How the good fathers in Cuba explained to Antonia the Catholic position on marriage, adultery, and divorce is not recorded. When Menéndez had reconnoitered the southwest Florida coast and then put in at Havana to divest himself of his bride, he returned to St. Augustine. In future, with Calusa at his side, he would begin methodically the conquest of Tampa Bay and the river northwest of it which had defeated all his predecessors. Always, too, there persisted the tantalizing hope of his son.

Two months later Menéndez found it necessary to sail back to Havana in search of food and weapons for St. Augustine which had never arrived there. When he made port he was immediately greeted with accounts of how Antonia "was very discreet, and of such grave demeanor that she astonished those of the town." She had been studying her catechism so diligently that already she had been confirmed. She had felt "very sad, because of the absence of his lordship"; now she would be delighted that he had returned. Menéndez ordered one of his men to buy her some new clothes; then he attended to commissary business for two days. Finally he set forth to call on her. He found her depressed. Why? he asked her. Had he not brought her many gifts?

"I wish God might kill me!" she answered in tears. "When you landed you did not send for me and take me to your house to eat and sleep with you!"

Ah! Menéndez invented an ingenious reply on the spot. This was because knights of the Catholic order of Santiago, of whom he was one, might not sleep with their wives until eight days after they had gained safe harbor.

Antonia smiled through her tears. Was it so? If she could only believe he was telling the truth, she would understand, and be happy. She began to count on her fingers. "Two days have passed already. When the remaining six have passed I will come to your house!" Then she laughed like a child.

Come then by all means, Menéndez told her. When he left her he breathed a sigh of relief.

The relief was short-lived. That night Antonia devised a plan. She roused the Spanish woman with whom she was lodging with the explanation that Menéndez had ordered her to come to him. Together the two women hurried through dark Cuban streets. When they reached Menéndez's rooms the porter let them in without question, believing Antonia's breathless tale. From him she took a lighted candle and marched straight with it into Menéndez's bedroom, bringing the candle to the bed to see if Menéndez was, or was not, sleeping alone.

Dazed, he rubbed his eyes. "What is this, sister?" he exclaimed as he recognized her. The Spanish woman interpreted for him and explained that she had obeyed what she had thought was his command to bring Antonia to him. Menéndez couldn't help laughing, even as he repeated to Antonia that the eight days required by the Vow of Santiago hadn't yet passed.

"Let me lie in a corner of the bed, then," Antonia begged. She wouldn't come near him, she promised. When she returned to Calos, she could truthfully tell her brother she and Menéndez had slept together, that Menéndez hadn't mocked her by refusing. Did he want the friendship of the Calusa, or didn't he? Didn't he want them all to become Christians? Sighing, Menéndez opened a drawer of the chest in his room, gave her a new chemise, a mirror, and a glass necklace and let her stay. What happened after that to the Vow of Santiago is unknown, but Antonia was observed to be very cheerful in the succeeding days as Menéndez made preparations for the return with her to her brother. The adelantado also intended to take along Father Juan Rogel, a Jesuit missionary, and he had already sent ahead Captain Francisco de Reynoso, whom he had ordered to build a fort at Calos. San Antonio, he named it, possibly not without a chuckle.

Father Rogel was an ideal choice. He held a degree in medicine as well as arts. He was quick at learning Indian dialects and along with his zeal for the conversion of Florida's natives he felt becoming compassion for them. He was unruffled when he landed at Calos with Menéndez and his companions and began hearing the stories Captain Reynoso had to tell. Several times since Reynoso's arrival the Calusa had been caught plotting to kill the whole Spanish garrison. Great was their veneration for the cross, however, reported Reynoso—all except the cacique. He had been making a nuisance of himself by laughing at Christian prayers. The cacique, happy to see Antonia, received Menéndez politely enough.

Point-blank Menéndez asked him if he knew of a waterway that led from Florida's west coast northeast toward St. Augustine. The time for the question was propitious, Menéndez felt; hadn't he done his best by Antonia? To secure his hold on Florida he had to be thoroughly familiar with its interior passages.

There was indeed such a river, the cacique said warily. But it flowed inland from the vicinity of Tocobaga, on Tampa Bay. The cacique of Tocobaga, a Timucua, was his enemy. If Menéndez and Reynoso would march with him to make war on Tocobaga, he would show them where the river was.

To this proposal Menéndez returned a flat refusal. The king of Spain had sent him to make peace, not war, among Gulf Indians. If the chief of Calos had a quarrel with the chief of Tocobaga, he himself would mediate it. Then he would see that the people of Tocobaga also had a chance to become Christians, "in order that when they die on this earth they may go to God in Heaven, who is the Lord of all the earth." The cacique of Calos was disappointed, but asked if he could go along with Menéndez anyway. On Tampa Bay they could all discuss peace together. Menéndez consented. Three days after his landing at Calos, he made preparations to sail north to Tampa Bay. Father Rogel had begun learning Calusa, and the Indians were building him a palmetto-log chapel under the watchful eyes of Captain Reynoso. On a black, moonless night disturbed only by a south wind blowing softly, Menéndez's brigantines arrived at Tocobaga just an hour before daybreak. No sooner had their crews sighted shore than the Calusa chief began begging Menéndez to let him and his Indians go ashore, burn Tocobaga, and kill all its inhabitants. No! Menéndez roared. He would make a treaty between the Calusa and the Timucua, and he meant to rescue any Christian and Calusa captives they had. This mollified the chief again; one of the captives was his and Antonia's sister. Menéndez also still dreamed of finding his son, though his hope had grown steadily fainter. It was never to be fulfilled. Ashore he sent several Timucua Indians who had been prisoners in Calos with the message that the Spanish meant Tocobaga no harm. When the Tocobagans had seen the ships in the harbor, they had known all too well what they meant. They had begun to scatter, though the chief of Tocobaga listened to what Menéndez's messengers had to tell him. When the chief framed his reply, it was tactful. He sent it by a man he said was the only Christian captive he had. He, the ruler of Tocobaga, was grateful to the Spanish for not killing him or burning the village. His people had all left; only he remained, in the temple of his gods, and he "would sooner die than forsake them."

He was to stay, Menéndez sent back word through the Christian. The Indians of Tocobaga should return to their village, for the Spanish would do them no harm. By eight o'clock in the morning Menéndez had stepped on the sands of what he began to call the Bahia de San Gregorio, more fitting than the heathen name of Tampa. Slowly the chief of Tocobaga greeted him and led him into his temple and seated him in a chieftain's place.

"I had not thought the Christians were so good," Tocobaga's ruler said dryly. "I well realize they could slay me and my people, and burn my gods and my village. I have known for a long time that Christians go about in my country. They have sent to tell caciques of this land that they must give them corn or be killed. . . . Afterword there came other Christians who killed the first, and the caciques wish to know who they are." Menéndez assured him that he was the latter, not the former, type of Christian: a true one. He would kill any false Christians on sight. He only wanted to teach salvation to the people of Tocobaga, as he had begun to teach it to the people of Calos. When he invited the chief of Tocobaga to board his brigantine to meet his Calusa rival in peace, the chief consented. Once on board, quick harsh words flamed up between the two Indian leaders but Menéndez's skillful parrying prevailed. Let all the chiefs of the land be called to Tocobaga, he ordered. He would make a compact with them.

Three days later over fifteen hundred warriors gathered among the palmettos and mangroves of Tampa Bay. They carried bows and arrows; they were tall men, formidably striking in appearance to the short olive-skinned Spaniards who watched them uneasily. Menéndez shrewdly told the Tocobaga cacique that he had better keep present only the tribal heads and send away the rest of the armed warriors; he, Menéndez, feared his own soldiers would want to fight such a convention. The deception was successful, and Menéndez began to harangue the assembled Timucua and Calusa officials about peace, Heaven, the king of Spain and the High Pontiff called Papa. Where, he asked them finally, was the river which flowed northeast from the bay?

Undoubtedly, replied the Tocobagans, Menéndez must mean "the river of Macoya." The river of Macoya flowed through the territory of a hostile cacique. He would never let Menéndez and his soldiers pass without a fight; he had unfortunately seen the "false Christians" who had come his way under the earlier adelantado, de Soto. Menéndez listened with a sinking heart. He didn't have enough soldiers with him to engage in battle in unknown territory. A few leagues from the river of Macoya, he was stymied. The chiefs at his feet would tell him nothing more about it, and regretfully he knew he would have to return to Calos after he had made the Timucua and Calusa agree to a wary tolerance of one another. Behind him he left one of his captains, Martínez de Cos, to build a Spanish fort in Tocobaga. Martínez protested vigorously, but had to obey. On the way to Calos, the mercurial Calusa cacique began raging at Menéndez for making peace with a Tocobaga rival he had long hated. In these protests he was joined on his home ground by Antonia, of whom Menéndez confessed to his brother-in-law that he was beginning "to have no good opinion." She was furiously partisan toward her brother. The pleading bride who had begged Menéndez to let her sleep in a corner of his bed was now accusing him of treachery. Why hadn't he burned and killed the Tocobagans? "You have two hearts, Adelantado!" she shouted. "One for yourself, and one for Tocobaga. For me and my brother you have none!"

Menéndez, after futile attempts to silence her, decided he could only return to east Florida. Behind him he left Father Rogel and Captain Reynoso to face the music at Calos—literally, for the chief and Antonia persistently demanded that the Spanish play and sing to them. Captain Martínez de Cos was shakily installed at Tocobaga. The nearby "river of Macoya" had to be left unexplored. Wearily, Menéndez assessed his progress on Florida's west coast. Two tiny forts had been established; they were all that stood between the fury of the Indians and the regularly shipwrecked Spanish they captured off their shores. Whenever a hurricane roared up the Gulf in a swirl of iron rain and lashing wind it brought with it hapless Christians who could only look forward to lives of misery unless Reynoso or Martínez de Cos or Father Rogel remained to intervene with the Calusa and Timucua headmen on their behalf. On the east coast, Menéndez knew his position was surer. There he had done what his predecessors had failed to do: he had established a permanent and growing settlement.

Success in the west, however, had become a mirage, an ever-retreating illusion. It had yielded no gold or silver, but only the discovery of two plants, sassafras and nut grass, decoctions of which appeared to keep the Spanish soldiers in good health. As their wine ran out, they came to depend on sassafras tea. It "relieved the liver," drove away fevers, restored the appetite, "voided the stone," quieted toothache, cured gout, "preserved from pest" and was "most serviceable in all cold sicknesses." Nut grass less impressively relieved only stomachaches. The long tradition of health-seeking by visitors to the Suncoast had begun. But among the Indians even sassafras and nut grass proved powerless to stem the fatal effects of the Spanish sicknesses they began to acquire—measles, syphilis, gonorrhea, smallpox, whooping cough, and influenza. At both Calos and Tocobaga epidemics started, making devastating inroads among the men whom Father Rogel sought to bring prosperity and consolation in Christ, but who had no immunity to European infections.

While Rogel was struggling to perfect himself in Calusa and trying to compile a dictionary of it for his successors—for he knew well enough that his life expectancy was a gamble—he began teaching his charges the Lord's Prayer, the Creed, and the Ten Commandments. He concentrated especially on Calusa children but he soon found that "children who assembled to chant the doctrine recited only the call of hunger." When his Cuban cornmeal ran out, so did his audience. Disheartened, he made several expeditions to Tocobaga, hoping that the Timucua and their cacique would be better scholars. The cacique proved able to "discuss Christianity intelligently," but when Father Rogel asked him to destroy the images of his tribal deities he answered that if he did, his wife and children would leap into the flames and perish with them. The Timucua believed in a kind of reverse reincarnation:

> When a man dies [Father Rogel reported to his superiors] his principal soul enters an animal or fish, and when this dies enters a smaller one, and so descends till it reaches nothingness. Hence it is difficult to convince them . . . of the Resurrection.

But the principal objections of the Indians were not theological. One of them summed up matters eloquently:

> The friars take from us our women, leaving us only one and that in perpetuity, prohibiting us from changing her. They stop our banquets, dances, feasts, celebrations, fires, and wars, so that by failing to use them we lose the ancient valor and dexterity inherited from our ancestors. They persecute our old people, calling them witches. Even our labor

disturbs them, since they want to command us to avoid it on some days, and be prepared to execute all that they say, although they are not satisfied . . . What can we expect, except to be slaves?

One of the targets of missionary wrath was the Timucuas' ball game. "Striving together," wrote an apostle horrified at their nakedness, "some will fall on top of others, and on these, others will climb up, making steps of their bodies, and others again will climb over their faces and heads or bellies, all the time kicking face or body, pulling and striking and interlocking with reckless fury. When the pile is broken up four or five are stretched lifeless, others have their eyes gouged out and many arms and legs and ribs are broken. Buckets of water are poured on the survivors while substitutes replace the disabled, and the game starts all over in the hot sun, and so it goes on until sunset." The picture drawn by the offended evangelist is cruel; the alternative of Indian lassitude and blind obedience to the clerics among them was even crueler.

Soon Father Rogel found himself running short of supplies at Calos and at Tocobaga. The Indians at both outposts grew restless; where were their gifts? Plots to murder Captain Reynoso at Calos and Captain Martínez de Cos at Tocobaga were uncovered. In one skirmish at Calos, three Spaniards were killed and Reynoso was wounded. Reynoso found that the scheme had originated with the cacique himself. In spite of Antonia's pleadings he had him executed and made his brother, whom the Spanish called Don Pedro, the new cacique. For a while, all went well. Don Pedro permitted Father Rogel to hack to pieces the images of his gods, all the exquisitely wrought paraphernalia of the Calusa Death Cult on which long-gone Calusa artisans had lavished their skills. Then Don Pedro announced that he intended to marry his sister and the scandalized Father Rogel flatly refused. Promptly Don Pedro began plotting as his brother had plotted before him. When he was betrayed by some Calusa women who had attached themselves to the Spanish garrison, Reynoso had him beheaded along with fourteen of his friends.

The downfall of Calos's fortunes was gradual. A tiny bell still summoned halfhearted Calusa Christians across saw-grass prairies and dimly humid pinewoods to Mass. Calusa voices were raised in simple Spanish hymns the Jesuit had taught them; their confused intonations echoed strangely with the harsh chattering of boat-tailed grackles in the mangroves. Diseases continued their grim ravages, though slowly, and many of the Indians could no longer fish or hunt. At Tocobaga, morale was even lower than at Calos. The Indians there rarely saw Father Rogel. They, too, were growing constantly more lackadaisical. Tocobaga was possible only so long as Calos was possible, Father Rogel understood. In the hope of encouraging his charges he made a trip to Havana for more cornmeal and shinier presents. When he returned to Calos, he put ashore his supplies and then proceeded directly to Tampa Bay. There he found waiting for him the end of his Tocobaga projects. All the Indians had banded together against the garrison. When its soldiers had been out foraging for wild grapes and grasses and berries they had killed them, all but three, and the three were murdered as soon as Father Rogel's ship was sighted. Then the Indians burned Tocobaga to the ground. What awaited Father Rogel were unburied Spanish corpses rotting in the sun, the charred ruins of Martínez de Cos's blockhouse, smoking remnants of the village temple, abandoned potsherds, refuse piles of oyster shells, and forlorn fragments of Spanish majolica dishes which the Tocobagans had scattered behind them. The saga of Christianity on Tampa Bay was over, Father Rogel realized.

Heartbroken, he turned back to Calos. There the new cacique submitted to his instructions by day and defiantly took part in traditional Calusa ceremonies by night. One morning the Indians rose in rebellion against the garrison and overpowered it. Captain Reynoso and a few survivors fled for their lives to their ships in the harbor. The Calusa then burned their capital to embers, and vanished into the dark recesses of adjoining cypress swamps. Father Rogel retired to Havana. For a while a successor tried to create a new mission from the wreckage, but he soon realized the futility of his efforts. The swamps of Calusa country were impenetrable. From them the Indians would harass the Spanish until they had driven them out to a man. Without a Spanish stronghold at Calos, the Gulf Coast was closed country. So was the mysterious river which fed it from a fabled swamp in an interior now real only in the memoirs of de Soto campaign chronicles, pages gathering dust on monastery shelves in Cuba and Spain. Menéndez had founded a city in St. Augustine, but south of it, on east coast and west, now stretched only a vast mosquito-ridden wilderness of forests, swamps, scrub, gallberry flats, beaches, and watery prairies over which vultures circled monotonously on quivering currents. On a visit to Spain, Menéndez died. Franciscan fathers established by his efforts at north Florida missions made a few attempts to colonize southward, and for a while they had hopes of

Tocobaga and the nearby Timucua village of Pohoy. But the bay Indians proved ultimately intractable. Conquistadores? One of the Franciscan priests smiled wryly: "We are the ones who are bearing the burden and the heat. We are the ones who are conquering and subduing the land."

In north Florida this was true enough—for a time. Horses, cattle, hogs, sheep, goats, rabbits, cats, dogs, wheat, sugarcane, oranges, lemons, olives, bananas, pears, plums, limes, roses: all came to north Florida with Spanish soldiers and missionaries and all would eventually spread southward. But now Tampa Bay and the river of Mocoso sank slowly into twilight, the Indian shouts along their shores growing fewer and fainter as the tragedy of the dwindling Timucua and Calusa progressed. Once again the calling of rain crows dominated the Green Swamp, and the shrill challenges of gulls screamed and waned over sea beaches where water danced platinum bright during the day and at night fragile bay creatures shone in pale mimicry to beguile the savage eyes left to see them. Conquistadores and crusaders were no more. Gradually their quarry too were following them into the shadows.

On both the river and the bay, it began to be clear that man had failed.

7

El Río
San Julian de Arriaga

There were so many ghosts. Cadences of Spanish names must have
drifted elusively through the fading memories of drowsily aging caciques
to be echoed in the night winds combing riverbanks and beaches . . .
Narváez; Bahía de la Cruz; de Soto; El Bahía del Espíritu Santo; Menéndez; Bahía de San Gregorio . . . Fray Luis Cancer and his "Hail Mary's";
the stern commands of Father Rogel. . . . Echoes too of Mocoso and the
river whose name he had borne, soft Timucuan syllables blending with
the sharper consonants brought by Castilian warriors of sword and
cross who had dreamed and ravaged and succored and been defeated.

"Earth has no need of man," poets have written. It is perhaps the
hardest truth man has had to accept during his brief tenancy of the planet.
History began long before his birth; when he abandons land in which
he has dwelt for a time its history does not stop. On the Hillsborough
and Tampa Bay, life burgeoned richly even as Spaniards retreated and
Indians were being struck down by Spanish illnesses. The great food
chains of salt and fresh water still cycled endlessly, from the most minute
algae and protozoa up through insects and fish and land animals. In the
tide pools of the bay sea cucumbers slowly thrust themselves forward
through its currents. If larger animals ate them, they would survive by
escaping from their predators' stomachs and regenerating new internal
organs. Ghost crabs continued digging their burrows on the beach, and
long tides mixed the male and female cells of seaweeds to perpetuate

them. In the river's freshwater eddies, fairy shrimps swam back and forth on their backs. Tadpoles tried clumsy appendages each spring, the peepers developing into frogs in short weeks, the larger bullfrogs only after a year or more. Insects restlessly flitted in the yellow cups of pond lilies. Duckweeds spread carpets of green through the slower water, and with them the tiniest seed-bearing plant in the world, *wolffia*. Half-sunlit eelgrass writhed beneath beetle ripples. Kingfishers plunged sharply down for fingerling bass. All were vital parts of an Eden basking in rich, new peace.

Especially there were the mayflies, unforgettable even today along the river in their translucent clouds. When William Bartram, the great Philadelphia naturalist, made a voyage into Florida late in the eighteenth century, he described them on another river. But his prose poem fits perfectly the pageant they have made for centuries on waters where Chief Mocoso and Juan Ortiz once lived:

> I observed this day . . . incredible numbers of flying insects . . . emerging from the shallow water near shore, some of them immediately taking their flight to the land, whilst myriads crept up the grass and herbiage, there remaining for a short time; as they acquired sufficient strength, they took their flight also, following their kindred to the main land. This resurrection from the deep . . . commences early in the morning, and ceases after the sun is up. At evening they are seen in clouds of innumerable millions, swarming and wantoning in the still air, gradually drawing near the river. They descend upon its surface, and there quickly end their day after committing their eggs to the deep; which being for a little while tossed about, enveloped in a viscid scum, are hatched, and the little larva descend into their secure and dark habitation in the oozy bed beneath, where they remain gradually increasing in size, until the returning spring; they then change into a nymph, when the genial heat brings them . . . into existence, and they again arise into the world. This fly seems to be delicious food for birds, frogs, and fish. In the morning, when they arise, and the evening, when they return, the tumult is great indeed, and the surface of the water along shore broken into bubbles, or spirited into the air, by the contending aquatic tribes; and such is the avidity of the fish and frogs, that they spring into the air after this delicious prey.

Bartram made one error; in Florida mayflies do not hatch in spring but all year round, except during transient freezes. Joe and I had seen their discarded nymph cases in high summer on our trip down Mocoso's river, and I have seen them shimmer there in February, frailly perfect architecture which has served its use and been discarded. Florida mayflies have been little studied; science has not regarded them as glamorous enough, perhaps. But there is nothing lovelier than the lacy filigrees they make in dawning sun along the river. The lives of its inhabitants reveal secrets of the river itself.

Always, too, during these years of peace in the 1600s, plants crowded each other on the riverbanks: needle palms, cretan-brake ferns lush along the shore though twenty miles farther north they could not survive winters; wax myrtles and buttonbushes and cornels, small relatives of the flowering dogwood. Water thrushes sang, and prothonotary warblers perched in slender itea willows thickly white, in spring, with long starry blooms. In the strength of the light, the river's ripples were mirrored on the undersides of branches where brown-banded water snakes stretched out in perpetual warmth. Hernando de Soto had marched this way. Calusa and Timucua warriors had crept elusively through; de Soto survivors had told their tales, and other writers had begun to make myths of them. Yet while the great bay, Tampa, was known in the Old World now, the river was not. It had been discovered by the white man, never possessed. Its warriors had guarded it well. And it was to remain inviolate for two centuries after Father Rogel had abandoned it.

From Spain's foothold at St. Augustine it continued to govern Florida, even though it left the Suncoast empty. Sometimes the missionaries of St. Augustine would worry about remaining heathen at Tocobaga or Pohoy on the bay and send Christian Indians as delegates to them. When the messengers returned the priests would listen to a familiar tale of disease, hostility, and hopelessness. Sometimes, too, governors worried about possible foreign settlements on the Gulf. In 1603 Captain Fernando Valdés was sent by Governor Pedro de Ybarra in a Spanish frigate to explore the west coast from the Bay of Calos up to Apalache, the golden destination of Pánfilo de Narváez. Captain Valdes found not a trace of colonization, and though he probably suspected Spanish refugees from shipwrecks must still be living in scattered Timucua and Calusa villages he was powerless to do anything about them. A few years later some Timucua from Tocobaga and Pohoy, in an unexpected burst of vitality, began raiding Spanish settlements to the east. Governor Juan Fernandez de Olivera, who had succeeded Ybarra, wrote a report to the king of Spain after he had reconnoitered the west coast with the launch and canoes which were in the river for the punishment of the caciques of Pooy and Tocapaca, after having warned them. I sent word to the heirs of these caciques that henchforth they were not to harm the towns of the Christians, as because of their predecessors having done so, this punishment was made. . . . The lieutenant and pilot assure me that all this coast from near the river to where the launch is . . . a short distance from Pooy and Carlos is the best and most free from dangers that can be desired, and so soundable that one can get close to land on all of it with big ships, and that there are rivers and a bar so that one can go within, particularly the bay of Pooy which is where the Indians say the Adelantado Hernando de Soto landed . . . There was no opportunity to sound and explore it this time, but it will be done and I shall send a chart of the whole coast.

Would His Majesty be interested in a settlement on the bay of Pohoy which had been Tampa, Espíritu Santo, and Bahía de la Cruz? The river which emptied into it? His Majesty would, but a weakening Spain was losing its battle with Britain for dominion of the seas and Spanish commanders were reluctant to risk new forts they could not maintain. The record of loss on Tampa Bay had been too consistent.

From time to time bands of British traders wandered along the Suncoast, and enterprising pirates in search of treasures to raid. Neither traders nor pirates found much to interest them. The Catholic Bishop of Cuba, in 1674, reported to the king of Spain on the state of southwest Florida only by hearsay: "Four leagues beyond [Calos] is the Bay of Tampa; at six . . . from Beach of Pusale to Pojoy river; at twelve leagues is Tocopacas." A remnant of pagans lived there, he had heard, existing on fish and roots. Successive Spanish monarchs were no doubt as baffled at the bewildering variety of geographical names on the Suncoast as later historians were to be.

Late in the seventeenth century the Calusa had a renaissance of sorts. They had abandoned hopes of their own conquest of Tampa Bay and had retreated to a rebuilt Calos. As decades passed without further conquistadores and slave traders, they began to trade with Cuba. On twenty-four-hour trips their canoes navigated the Florida straits loaded with bark, amber, fruit, animal hides, and caged cardinals, much fancied by Cubans as pets. The colonists paid ten dollars for them and hung them in bamboo cages above their sheltered stone patios; the captive cardinals never sang, though. The Calusa traders in turn brought back a few

Spanish dishes. Later they received silver from Mexican expeditions, seed beads from the east coast, and a few hunting knives. Never guns; although Calusa were no longer a military menace Spanish memories were long. In 1697 a band of Franciscan fathers from Havana decided to try Christianizing the Calusa once more. They landed on an island in the Bay of Calos where they promptly staged a procession with robes, crosses, and candles. Calusa memories were as long as Spanish ones. In a body they drove out the friars who took refuge in the Florida Keys where a few Catholic Calusa had fled before them. By 1712 a war party of mainland Calusa had crossed from the Everglades to the Keys to murder what was left of their brethren there. So many bleached Calusa bones lay strewn on one of the keys afterwards that it became known as Cayo Hueso, "bone island," which sounded to later English sailors like Key West.

Not until after 1700 did Cuba begin to take advantage of the real treasure on Florida's west coast, huge schools of tarpon, snook, red snapper, grouper, pompano, speckled trout, and bonefish. Each year, from late summer until the following spring, Cuban fishermen built camps or "fishing ranchos" on Gulf Coast islands all the way from Tampa bay southward to the Keys. The fish were dried on the ranchos and then sent to Havana; a third of the profits went to the owner of the fishing schooner and two thirds to his crew. The fisherman bought their salt from the king of Spain's warehouse and had to pay "an outrageous price" for it, but even so the profits were tempting. A few of the men stayed out the summer on stray islands, sheltered by palmetto huts, living undisturbed by natives inland. Not only were the Indian populations still waning, but a new hazard had come: English slave traders were beginning to make their way south from Georgia and the Carolinas. One of their leaders may have explored as far south as Lake Okeechobee. With them the traders often brought Creek Indians from the colonies bordering Spanish Florida on the north. Unlike the Timucua and Calusa, the Creeks had proved hardy and soon became resistant to disease; possibly a more temperate climate, and English medicine, had something to do with their survival. Along with English fortune hunters the Creeks devastated Franciscan missions in north Florida. On each successive expedition they pushed the Apalachee, Timucua, and Calusa southward. A merchant from Charleston observed in 1755 that the Creeks had driven all the Florida tribes so far south that "the finest part of the country is uninhabited." When did the last Timucua vanish from Tampa Bay, Ucita, Pohoy, Tocobaga, and the river of Mocoso? Did any survive to join forces in the Everglades with the remaining Calusa? No one knows. By the time of the last Timucua on the bay, they were only staring in wonder at their disused temple mounds, hardly remembering what their ancestors had built them for. The proud glitter of gilded fowls de Soto had admired had been replaced by the tawdry glitter of glass around red throats. Spain, which never recovered from the increasing sea power of Britain, had become a floundering empire fighting for its very life.

Britain was getting very much interested in Florida's Gulf Coast. In 1745 a Captain Braddock had sailed down from Virginia, rounded the tip of the peninsula, and proceeded up to Tampa Bay—"or Spiritu Santo" —which he carefully surveyed. His map has not survived, but English explorers after him were to know it and hold it in high regard. At court in Madrid, rumors of the English expeditions caused alarm. If Spain could not hold Florida, what of her North American ventures west of the Mississippi? Nearly two hundred years after the death of Pedro Menéndez de Avilés, a Spanish naval officer arrived on Tampa Bay by orders of his government with weapons of compass and sounding line. Not only would he chart the bay thoroughly with the latest instruments, but he would ascend the river in his longboat. Carefully he would observe natural resources of wood for Spanish ships, pine resin for turpentine, and evidences of inhabitants. Don Francisco María Celi had sharp eyes and precise habits of investigation, and he kept a detailed journal of his adventures.

His ship, the *San Francisco de Asís,* was a small three-masted xebec, its mainmast square-rigged and its foremast raked forward. It had no oars, though its longboat did. It was commanded by Lieutenant José Jiménez, who was to leave his mark on the Suncoast while his commander in chief was probing inlets and bars and rivers.

Wednesday, April 13, 1757, dawned hazily sunny on the bay; a soft breeze was blowing from the east when María Celi's ship anchored. Immediately he began sketching the entrances and channels, "whereupon I gave it the name of San Fernando, in memory of the King my master. . . . In coming to this bay of Tampa, newly called San Fernando, one should attempt to proceed along the coast at a distance of about one league and a half from the land." On Thursday he took the longboat to what is now Egmont Key "and in the name of God and Most Holy

Mother began to measure said island." For more than a week he searched out other keys, passes to the Gulf, and beaches. To one point of land he gave the name Punta Pinal de Jiménez—the piney point of Jiménez—which was to become modern Pinellas County and the site of St. Petersburg. He found it "suitable only for fishing boats," though he ordered some of the longboat's crew to tap the pines "even though it is not the first of the moon" to test the quality of the resin. For days María Celi continued his sketching, sounding, and observations of the pines and mangroves and the clarity of the water. Not until Friday, April 22, when he had worked his way back into the bay toward the river, did he see any evidence of human inhabitants. That morning a canoe was sighted. When it pulled up alongside the xebec, four Indians boarded it with muskets in hand. Jiménez quickly presented them with honey, tobacco, corn, and chickens and sent his regards to their chief who, they said, was standing on shore. The next day another canoe arrived; this time Jiménez gave the Indians tobacco, honey, corn, bread, and rum and let them sit in his chair. They smiled and gesticulated. They were soon joined by some companions; that night eight rum-satiated Indians slept aboard the xebec. Jiménez and María Celi had no idea what tribe the savages belonged to, but they suspected their muskets had come from British traders to the north; the British, unlike the Spanish, saw no harm in selling guns to the natives with whom they traded. When the Indians—probably far-ranging, hungover and gratified Creeks—had departed, María Celi took his crew and longboat and entered the mouth of the river which had been Mocoso's. Ceremoniously he christened it the River of San Julián de Arriaga. Saint Julián's identity has been lost, but he may well have been a Spanish friar martyred long before by Indians at Arriaga, Mexico, a town on the Pacific coastal lowland in the same province of Chiapas over which Bartolomé de las Casás had so compassionately presided. With difficulty María Celi's men steered their longboat clear of oyster bars in the river's mouth and began slowly to make their way inland. Along the banks there were trees suitable for ship masts, they found, as there had been on the Piney Point of Jiménez; these, however, were only "middling in quality. Some are longer and thicker, and so the same with other kinds such as the laurels, walnut, and live oaks with their acorns, and the arbor of vines entwined on the trees along the banks of this river with its shoals." Navigation became increasingly difficult. The crew had to leave their grapnel, hawser, and two barrels of supplies ashore to give the longboat buoyancy. When they came to a barrier of sharp stones they had to stop. María Celi called it "The Waterfall," though he noted that the water did not flow from a much greater height. He had probably encountered the swift set of rapids which sing today over the river's stones in the Hillsborough River State Park. On the bank near the stones María Celi and his men ate lunch; then they began wading toward the western edge of the river bottom: "Upon walking in the river about one and a half leagues, there was found in this distance 31 trees from 21 to 28 inches in diameter, and 34 to 38 cubits in length, suitable for main topmast yards of two pieces, and many for make-shift main-masts." The river of San Julían de Arriaga had become important for the maintenance of the Spanish navy.

For three days María Celi and his men explored the river by longboat and on foot. On a serene dawn they finally raised the longboat's mast again and made their way downriver into the bay:

> I report that the tide enters this river of San Julián de Arriaga with a rise and fall inside of it for about a league and a half to two leagues, and in this distance the water remains brackish because it is mixed with that of the bay. Further upstream, however, the water is fresh and very delicate in taste. The crew reveled in it and all drank of it, for it was good as well as clear.

Perhaps María Celi and his men had wanted communion with the river in 1757 even as I had wanted it on my canoe trip with Joe in 1970. To drink of a river is to belong to it; perhaps they understood.

At the xebec María Celi learned that more Indians had been aboard. They had come for rum, but the crew had grown reluctant to give them any. They had plied them with food instead, but one of the Indians was so angry at being cheated of his liquor he took an axe from his canoe and hacked it into the xebec's side. Then, haughtily, he departed.

From the hand of Francisco María Celi came the first map of what is now the city of Tampa, its bay, and its river. Even today natural features are clearly recognizable, and Port of Tampa pilots have marveled at the precision of the navigational information. María Celi was no poet— except, perhaps, in his heart for a moment by a waterfall as he drank; his dry journal abounds in mathematics. Through it, even so, there runs an undercurrent of excitement, and a modern reader of it who knows the river can still recognize much of the landscape northeast of Tampa's urban sprawl. Tall trees on the river still bear their burden of vines; acorns still fall gently from the moss-hazed branches of live oaks; squirrels still scramble for chinquapin nuts in sandy tangles where woodpeckers rap. Some things that María Celi must have seen are gone: the vivid gleam of green gold on parrakeets' wings, the harsh "Kent! Kent!" of ivorybills calling, clouds of migrating passenger pigeons high above the dark tracery of forest treetops. But the river flows on, and the feathery flapping of wings mingles with the rush of its diamond rapids and the faint fragrance of crinum lilies nestling like patches of snow along its shore.

By 1760, on the North American continent, the French and Indian War had begun to blaze. Far from the river and from Florida a young English colonist named Washington was witnessing the struggles of British generals in American forests as the English fought back the encroachments of Canadian French and the ferocity of the Frenchmen's Indian allies. Spain panicked. If Great Britain succeeded in driving the French from North America altogether, what would happen to lingering Spanish hopes of empire? In 1761 Spain declared war on England and sided with France. It was one more mistake; France's energy in the wilderness and the Indians' persistence could not sustain themselves. In one of the war's naval battles Havana fell to Britain and with it Cuba. At the Treaty of Paris in 1763 Spain had to endure the humiliation of being able to ransom Cuba only by ceding Florida. The long legend of the conquistadores played itself out in the scratching of diplomats' quill pens. The Land of Flowers became a British colony and her forests and savannas lay ready to welcome explorers and settlers who meant to continue building a thriving trade with the Creek Indians of Georgia and Alabama. Florida was ready too for the Creeks. Wandering bands of them had already found the river and the bay; some had found the Green Swamp. These wildernesses were far from the neatly disciplined comforts of British trading posts. Florida's newest wave of red settlers had elected an alien frontier. "Siminoli," the Creeks back home called them: wild men, roamers. The English called them Seminoles.

Florida had little in common with her English neighbors to the north. The colonies of the Atlantic seaboard were already torn by the political passions of rebels who resented taxes imposed by Great Britain without colonial representation in parliament. Florida was still sparsely settled, though Menéndez's St. Augustine was older than any city north of it.

Florida spoke Spanish when it did not speak Indian dialects. London's King George III and his ministers were a long way off; what could they possibly have to do with life in a newly acquired subtropic outpost except to regulate its business in a very nominal way? Spain had never been a democratic country. Its erstwhile subjects in Florida found it impossible to understand, for instance, why the British in Massachusetts objected to a tax of pennies on imported tea. In the beginning, Britain paid Florida little attention, though military officials were sent to Pensacola in British West Florida to introduce discipline, order, medicine, and modern gardening methods to the phlegmatic Spanish inhabitants. British West Florida had a governor and British East Florida, all the peninsula east and south of the Apalachicola River, had one too. Both governors were responsible to the Colonial Secretary in London. The Colonial Secretary had worries enough with the fiery speeches of Virginia's Patrick Henry and Massachusetts' Samuel Adams and Pennsylvania's Doctor Benjamin Franklin without adding Florida projects to his burdens. The river and the bay were at first ignored, though British ships continually cruised the Gulf. Cuban fishing ranchos continued their commerce with Havana; Seminoles in the interior traded occasionally with them. The tradition of the area was deeply Latin when it was not Indian. The sovereignty of Britain seemed almost an irrelevancy.

In the spring of 1768 the Earl of Hillsborough, a seasoned Irish peer, became Britain's Colonial Secretary, and he wanted to secure Britain's Florida rights. Since it was Lord Hillsborough who controlled future pensions to the British surveyors and navigators he sent to the colonies, it was therefore politic on their parts to commemorate his Lordship in all the place names they could. Florida, with its cumbersome Spanish designations, presented a fertile field. Exactly who it was that turned the River of San Julián de Arriaga into the Hillsborough is unknown, but the name Hillsborough appears on a British map of 1769 by Thomas Jeffries. Probably, too, some explorer decided that a body of water bearing the name Holy Ghost Bay was improperly un-English. The Indian "Tampa" seemed simple enough for the bay as a whole; the west fork became Old Tampa Bay and the east fork—naturally—Hillsborough. A tiny inlet on Florida's lower east coast was also christened Hillsborough; the name persists. But there was never any controversy about what river was meant when reference was made, simply, to "the Hillsborough." It flowed into what the English navigators, like the Spanish before them, realized was a splendid potential harbor and a rich source of wood for the British navy. Early in office, Lord Hillsborough developed a special fondness for Florida. Not only would his name be perpetuated there (as it would be in other colonies) but its people never gave him any trouble. Floridians were loyal, he said repeatedly. It was his "favourite colony."

In 1769 he commissioned Bernard Romans, an experienced navigator and surveyor, to examine the coasts of the British provinces of East and West Florida. Romans, in his report, paid particular attention to "the Bay of Tampe, or Spirito Santo."

> Imagine . . . a country gradually rising into a ridge of highland, very barren, sandy and gravelly, a few places excepted, intersected with abundance of rivulets, and variegated with ponds and lakes, whose banks being in general lined with oak, Magnolia and other trees, exhibit the most romantic scene imaginable . . . the country is covered with roe deer and turkies.

On one of his trips overland from the Bay of Tampa to St. Augustine, Romans stared curiously at vestiges of Spanish settlement: maize hills, a rotting stockade here and there, orange trees, all of them weathered and wild but none older than the time of de Soto. The "Bay of Tampa" he considered "the most proper place in all America, south of Halifax, for the rendezvous of a large fleet of heavy ships, the country around being plentifully timbered and watered." He marked the mouth of the Hillsborough River, its marshes and its channel, and gave specific directions for entering the bay. He also catalogued the plants and sent specimens to the territorial governor, who sent them on to Lord Hillsborough. Romans was, the governor told him, "an ingenious man and both a Naturalist and a Botanist—I think him worthy of some encouragement." Lord Hillsborough agreed, and awarded Romans a pension of fifty pounds a year.

Many plants, Romans reported, would succeed in the region of the Bay of Tampe and the Hillsborough River. Especially he recommended coffee trees, their first fruit marketable by the third year of cultivation and easier to care for than sugarcane harvests. First, however, there had to be colonists. The country Bernard Romans saw was universally wild. The cypress knees in river swamps amazed him. "This vegetable monster I do not remember to have ever seen mentioned anywhere." He found formidable also the girth of what he called "the bottle-arsed tupelo," and the matted abundance of trumpet vines. It was a garden, but a garden that would require hardy men and hardier equipment. Salt winds quickly reduced metals to rust. The danger of sunstroke for pioneers would be everpresent. Romans was a realist; at the same time he was mesmerized by Florida's beauty.

So, at a distance, was Lord Hillsborough, though when he died years later as the first Marquess of Downshire he still had not seen the Elysium which in the twentieth century would bear the title of his Hillsborough earldom.

8

Life on the Lockcha-popka-chiska

At a negotiation table in 1783, a Britain which had lost its war with America and with her French and Spanish allies, was forced to return Florida to Spain. "Hillsborough" became a name on fading maps filed in dusty Admiralty archives in London. Once more royal Madrid turned its thoughts to El Río San Julián de Arriaga and Espíritu Santo Bay as timberlands for its navy. Bernardo de Gálvez, a Spanish commander who had defeated the British navy at Pensacola during the American Revolution, ordered an inspection of the Gulf Coast from Tampa, Florida, to Tampico, in Mexico. The man he picked to carry out the journey was José Antonio de Evia, a veteran of the Spanish main who had been Gálvez's courier during the war and a hero of several naval engagements in his own right. In September 1783, Evia left Havana in a two-masted lugger, the *Comendador de Marsella,* and began to chart the Florida Keys and the lower west coast. By October he had discovered that Florida weather was capricious; what in the morning were delightfully fresh breezes from the Gulf could turn by afternoon to fierce northers which whipped sails and turned the Gulf to spume. In spite of contrary winds he sailed up to Tampa Bay, which he found to have "a good bottom for any frigate, with several channels of two fathoms depth and good shelter for small vessels." The river and its banks, he noted, were heavy with forests of pine and oak. He did not tarry there long; instead he set out for Pensacola, but on the way north the weather turned so violent that he was afraid his ship would be swamped. By mid-November he was back in the bay waiting for a ferocious storm to blow itself out over grey-green billows. The skies darkened to gunmetal; his lugger pitched and rolled in the swelling seas; the crew was nervous.

When the weather cleared Evia was visited by a party of Indians who said they were Yuchees, Tallapoosas, and Choctaws. The first two were Creek tribes from Alabama, and the Choctaws had come from Mississippi to join them in a hunting party on the bay's shores. They were all mounted on British horses; they meant to take pelts, they said, and then sell them to English traders in return for guns and ammunition. They also told Evia they were friendly to the Spanish as well as the British who had stayed behind after the Revolution to barter with Indians, and to prove it they gave him some fresh meat they had killed and dressed. He remained to take soundings; then he left.

For ten years no white explorer ventured after him. Cubans were still scattered on their fishing ranchos; Creek bands hunted bay and river shores regularly, and a few Creek Seminoles, "wanderers," settled down to stay. Never did the Seminoles consider themselves members of one tribe. In fact, they disliked the name; they thought it made them disreputable vagabonds. Some of the wanderers spoke a Creek dialect called Muskogee, and others spoke one by the name of Hitchiti. Neither group, though their Creek ancestry was common, could understand the other. The Muskogee-speaking Indians began to refer to themselves as "people of the peninsula." The Hitchiti considered themselves, simply, "red men." Time and the encroachment of American settlers into Florida, not brotherhood and identity, were what would make the Seminoles a tribal unit capable of defending themselves. As the eighteenth century drew to a close they were still only far-flung groups of colonists who sought escape in Spanish territory from land-grabbing Americans, and who provided a refuge for escaped American Negro slaves. Slowly new sounds began to settle on evening mists along the river: high-pitched Seminole flutes, an occasional echo of Africa, and the solemn chants of Seminole medicine men over their dying old:

> Come back.
> Before you get to the king tree, come back.
> Before you get to the peach tree, come back . . .

The "king tree" had large white blooms and was the first to flower in the spring. Probably it was the dogwood, whose drifts along the river each March heralded the end of cool north winds and winter rains. The river's oaks were also important to the Seminoles. *Lockcha-popka-chiska,* the Hitchiti speakers began to call the erstwhile Hillsborough: river where one crosses to eat acorns. They fished for bass and bream in the waters of an inland lake they called *Thlonotosassa,* "field of flints"; there were large flint deposits near its shores. When they had planted a settlement of tobacco fields south of the river they named this *Hickapusassa*; by the 1890s it would become Plant City, in commemoration not of tobacco but of a more flamboyant plant—Henry, the railroad czar.

By 1793 the Spanish had realized that to hold Florida they must settle more of it. An empty Tampa Bay would prove too tempting to Americans in search of warmth and timber. Captain Vicente Folch y Juan of the Spanish navy was ordered to the bay; if he approved the site for a village, he was to gain the consent of "the lower Creeks" to the building of a Spanish trading post and fort there. The shade of Captain Martínez de Cos, who had commanded the sixteenth century Spanish blockhouse at Tocobaga among the Timucuans, must have smiled grimly. The conquistadores and missionaries hadn't needed to ask the Indians for any permissions! But Spain, then, had been a formidable world power. Now she was far from that, and though she had allied herself with America in the Revolution her fear of Americans was deep. They were reckless and expansion-obsessed. Unless Spain planted a settlement at Tampa Bay, it would be only a matter of time until Americans did. America had begun to make it clear that she wanted Florida for herself.

Folch y Juan sailed to the bay in the autumn of 1793 and found its banks "frequently subject to floods . . . heavily overgrown with mangroves, sea grapes, myrtles, and thorns, so that in some places it is impossible to penetrate them, and in others very difficult . . . There are, however, some stretches of beach here and there, where the swampy ground which precedes the solid ground extends for more than a mile." To Folch y Juan Lockcha-popka-chiska sounded like Acachy; its timber was as impressive to him as to his predecessors. He also decided the wide meadows which broke outlying forests here and there would be ideal for cattle grazing. Everywhere there were bubbling springs. At Indian villages he called Cascavela and Anattylaica he found that the chiefs would not only welcome a Spanish trading post at Tampa Bay but they would settle their people nearby. It would be far more convenient to sell furs at Tampa than to make the long journey north to St. Augustine or Pensacola. Folch y Juan envisioned a post at Tampa which would

rival those of the north, where the Indians "are given blankets . . . breechclouts, striped and white shirts, glass beads, vermilion, Limbourg shawls,
saddles, bridles, spurs, woolen strips of various colors, knives, combs,
mirrors, carbines, shotguns, powder, bullets, flints, chintz, flannel, nan-
keen, thread, needles, bracelets, pins, and various other gewgaws of this
kind." For a start the trading post would require a garrison of fifty men
plus their commanding officers. There would also have to be "gunners, a
chaplain, surgeon, medic, royal quartermaster, interpreter, armorer,
mason, carpenter, calker, baker, blacksmith, two shipmasters, twelve
sailors and a generous supply of convict labor." The Florida chain gang
had been proposed.

Back in Madrid, officialdom did not think as big as Folch y Juan did.
A tiny garrison was eventually sent to Tampa Bay. They lived in a cluster
of hastily built palmetto huts and ·longed for the refinements of home
and Cuba during days of endless heat and boredom. Finally they left,
and once more the bay and the river belonged to the Seminoles. A few
Seminole bands wandered as far south as what had been Calos. There
they found a straggling remnant of the once-powerful Calusa and some
Spanish from Cuba who had established fishing ranchos in the Bay of
Calos, which the British had retitled Charlotte Harbor after George III's
wife. The Seminoles, Calusa, and Spanish slowly began to mix and to
create a band of "Spanish Indians" whose lives were dependent on the
sea. The Seminoles of Tampa Bay and the Lockcha-popka-chiska to the
north were agricultural. They grew melons, Seville oranges, pumpkins,
corn, pineapples and sugarcane, and they were heavily dependent on
British and Spanish trade goods. When they discovered iron cookware
they abandoned the art of pottery making altogether. They began, too, to
piece scraps of cloth into intricate geometrical designs with which to
trim their clothes. The men made turbans out of Scottish clan plaids;
the colors of Buchanan and MacGregor were flamboyant in torrid cornfields where their wearers cultivated long green rows with British hoes.

Often the riverbanks rang with the shouts of young Seminoles at
their games. Seminole fishermen penetrated the Green Swamp in dugout
canoes they made of palmetto trunks. Seminole women murmured softly
to each other as they ground corn and pounded zamia roots into coontie
flour. When an infant came into their world they welcomed it formally.
As the laboring mother was being given sassafras tea to drink, the women
around her intoned:

You day-sun, circling around,
You daylight, circling around,
You night-sun, circling around,
You, poor body, circling around,
You, wrinkled age, circling around,
You, spotted with gray, circling around . . .

Birth and death, day and night, infancy and age were all part of the same eternity. Mothers crooned their babies lullabies about wild deer and the turkeys that called shrilly back and forth in the hammocks. Children ran naked in the camps, laughing in the light, tending tame otters they kept in pens as pets. At night little Seminoles slept in fiber hammocks or on deerskins or the yielding ground. In Georgia and Alabama their parents had been builders of log cabins. In Florida all a family needed was a palm-thatched shelter with a long floor raised above the earth to avoid flooding in wet weather. Beneath chikee roofs heavy cauldrons of cornmeal mush, *sofkee,* bubbled on slow cookfires and everyone ate during the day according to his hunger. Dark girls were taught to stir the long-handled wooden sofkee spoon. As early as the age of four a child was assigned household tasks of his own: pounding coontie, watching the fire, kneading dough for bread. Boys begged their fathers to take them along on the hunt, and they learned early how to freeze motionless in front of a deer so that it would think its stalker was only a tree trunk.

Adolescents toiled in the fields and fell in love. When a brave neared twenty he began to think of taking his first wife. There were rules he had to follow carefully. Seminoles belonged to the Wind, Tiger, Otter, Bird, Deer, Snake, Bear, Wolf, and Alligator clans. A Wind could not marry a Wind; a Tiger could not marry a Tiger. Always a mate must come from another clan. When the suitor had chosen his girl he sent her family a delegation of his friends, who proposed for him. If she and her kindred consented to the match, his female relatives brought them presents: blankets, cotton fabrics, sometimes a ruffled bed canopy. In turn they sent him the gift of a wedding costume: a new shirt. On the betrothal day, at sunset, he went simply to the bride's chikee to live. Seminole descent was reckoned in the female line, and to children of the marriage their mother's brother would be as important as their father. Divorce was simple; the husband departed.

The zenith of the Seminole year was the Green Corn Dance, a June ceremony that preceded the eating of the year's first corn crop. Men, women, and children tidied up large dance grounds along the Lock-cha-popka-chiska and the bay, clearing them of weeds and rebuilding the ceremonial chikees. Some of the men went hunting, their footfalls as soundless as ever in forests where they waited for wildcats and panthers and other game. They brought back enough for tribal feasts during which high flames sculptured shadows in branches at the edge of the clearing. When the Green Corn Dance began formally, a shaman took a ritual bath in the river and then gave his orders. Fresh wood must be brought for the dance fire; goalposts for a ball game between men and women must be raised. It was gentler than Timucua and Calusa ball games had been, but still the elders and children cheered the participants vigorously, their shouts bouncing through streamside thickets. At night the fragrance of pine smoke hung suspended, and chuck-will's-widows called insistently. The Seminoles danced then, their bodies writhing to the beat of pumpkinseed rattles and turtle-shell anklets. The next day, in a large chikee in the center of the dance ground, the men ate together. Women and children had to go back to their clan camps in the woods. One of the men left during the feast to go hunting, this time for a white ibis whose feathers would be used in a coming pageant. When his arrow struck home, the bird's anguished flutterings sounded briefly and then stilled. As the sun dropped swiftly the dancing began once more, faster and faster now, the cries shriller, the rattles stronger. At midnight the men began to fast. On the morning of the third day the shaman and his helpers bathed once more and then brought out medicine bundles containing bunches of dried herbs—wild savory and rosemary and red bay leaves and mint—and fragments of animal bones, a dried ear of corn on the end of a stick, seeds, a flint, and a piece of steel. No women were allowed to see the contents of the bundles when they were opened, though they saw the sticks of corn planted in the ground with a sudden thrust, the corn-cob pitched toward the east. While the shaman chanted, a group of men brewed the Black Drink, *Asi*. The Seminoles drank it as the Timucua and Calusa had drunk it, and a singer of Black Drink songs was called a crier, *Yaholo*. From long horizontal poles other men suspended ibis feathers which they carried in the Feather Dance. At noon the elders began to hold a court of justice.

At the Green Corn Dance, Seminole punishments were meted out swiftly and dramatically. If an offender had broken a moral law considered sacred he would be killed soon after the festival was over. By the time the judges had finished their sentencing, dusk fell once more and with the flint and steel from the medicine bundle the shaman lit a separate fire over which a fresh Black Drink was being brewed, this one a special and potent concoction of roots of the southern red willow, button snake-root, ginseng, red bay and sweet bay leaves, pennyroyal, wild blueberry, muscadine grapes, red cedar leaves and mistletoe, and the wild blooms of lizard's tail and rabbit tobacco. It was full of caffeine; white men who had tasted it had found it like unusually strong and bitter tea. Again the dancers gathered. At midnight the drink was passed out among them; then the shaman began droning slow, magical legends Seminoles and Creeks had woven around their history from time immemorial—around, too, the creatures and plants they knew. Surviving Calusa hunting songs had also become a part of the Green Corn Dance: visiting "Spanish Indians" from Calos had brought them. The river of Mocoso which had heard the Calusa long ago now heard their refrains on Seminole lips. For them its springs still poured forth the water which from the beginning had drawn red men to its banks.

After the Black Drink had been passed from hand to hand, boys in their early teens received new names which had been chosen for them by the shaman or by clan officials. They were adults now. The shaman scratched their bodies with sharp needles; this helped to ensure lifelong health. When the eastern sky glowed faintly coral the remains of the last Black Drink were poured on heated stones in a closed chikee the men used as a sweathouse. After they had steamed themselves over the sizzling rocks they plunged into the river and prepared to feast once more. This time they ate the first corn of the new crop. Another year had begun. Next June other fires would light the convolutions of the Alligator and Catfish and Eagle and Buffalo and Woodpecker dances, and new drums would beat along the Lockcha-popka-chiska.

Some time around the year 1804, a child was born in southern Georgia to a mixed-blood woman of the Muskogee-speaking Creeks, Polly Cop-inger. She was living with a white trader; Americans near the Creek settle-ment called her child Billy Powell. When Billy was a boy war flared bitterly between Americans and Creeks in Georgia and Alabama. Ameri-cans were stripping the Indians of their lands, and the Indians were re-taliating by stripping the invaders of their lives in ruthless massacres conceived by a race desperate at bay. After one particular holocaust Polly

Copinger fled with Billy Powell to Spanish Florida, where she and several other Creeks sought a haven among Seminoles. She settled in northern Florida at a village variously called Tallahassee and Fowl Town. Just when Billy Powell first journeyed south from Fowl Town to the Lock-cha-popka-chiska is unknown, but he was to know the river well. When he was an adolescent he was given his tribal name; one of the duties assigned him then was to chant over the Black Drink, for his voice was strong and clear. Asi-yaholo, his elders named him as Black Drink criers had been named before him. Asi-yaholo grew hardy and proud, and to the Seminoles who had welcomed him he was so attached that he denied the existence of his white blood. When white men heard of him in Florida they wrote his name down as Osceola. Because of him the river would once more turn ruddy with the mingled blood of conquerors and conquered, and the bay would witness his people's despair and, finally, their passing from its shores forever. In the Green Swamp, Suncoast romancers say, you can still hear the Seminoles mourning on windy, moonless autumn nights while silent birds rest high in the cypresses under the stars.

PART II

Pioneers

9

Mr. Hackley's
Real Estate

To a youthfully ambitious United States, Florida became more than a dream. By the first decade of the nineteenth century it was an obsession. Adventurers constantly harried Florida Seminoles as other adventurers were harrying Indian tribes to the west. During the administrations of Thomas Jefferson and James Madison, Louisiana was purchased and the Far West was explored. In Washington, over official dinner tables where the crystal and silver of the rich gleamed softly, there were casual references to the annexation of Canada. But it was Florida which tantalized most of all. "Storm the walls of St. Augustine!" cried slaveholding planters as well as rough-hewn farmers in Tennessee and Georgia and Alabama and Virginia. "Storm St. Augustine!" echoed shrewd Yankee merchants. In the judgment of one observer, "the persistent desire of the United States to possess the Floridas, between 1801 and 1819, amounted almost to a disease, corrupting the moral sense of each succeeding administration." Moral sense may have been deteriorating; certainly the young nation's insecurity was increasing. The British hadn't liked losing a war. They began to raid American sailing ships for crewmen with whom to staff their own navy. British traders wandering through Florida began inciting the Seminoles into freshly violent hatred of American squatters on Seminole lands. In June 1812, war broke out between Britain and America once more. At first, Spanish Tampa Bay felt no repercussions, but in Washington and London alike it was known and ardently desired. Whoever commanded the harbor it offered would have taken a long stride toward command of the Gulf.

Soon Great Britain had sent to Pensacola—with no objection from the Spanish authorities—Captain George Woodbine, whose duty would be to train Seminoles in systematic warfare. The Seminoles were delighted with the opportunity of exterminating Americans by means of raiding expeditions into the United States. In full feather and paint, in red turbans and multicolored jackets and silver gorgets and egret cloaks, bands of them turned up on Pensacola's village green to be put through military paces. "Such scenes," pronounced a witness, "of preposterous costuming, of tripping over swords, of hopeless drilling and mad marching and counter-marching as the common of Pensacola then witnessed can be imagined only by those who know precisely what sort of creatures Indians are. Captain Woodbine might as well have attempted to train the alligators of the Florida lagoons for the British artillery service." Captain Woodbine, in turn, had his own deficiencies; what he failed to understand was that the indigenous Seminole tactics of ambush and massacre were what worked in the wilderness, not neatly ordered columns of tidily uniformed troops.

Everywhere along the borders of Alabama and Georgia the traders were whipping up Indian anger. Other British agents carried messages of warning deep into East Florida. The Seminoles of the central peninsula heard of Indian leaders from distant tribes who had allied themselves with the British: the Shawnee Tecumseh, Francis the Prophet, a Creek, the Georgia Seminoles Big Warrior and Boleck, whom the white men called Bowlegs. In Alabama war broke out between Creeks and American homesteaders. Perhaps, as rumors reached him at his fishing rancho on Tampa Bay, Cuban settler Andrew González wondered uneasily if all the tumult would come south. Since 1808 he had been living in a palmetto hut at the bay's edge. His wife and children helped him tend fifteen acres of orange and lime trees and ten acres of corn. "The lands at Tampa Bay are of no value, and no one is interested in them," a Spanish official had told him. He knew better. So did Joaquín and José María Cáldez, who came to the bay in 1812 and began cultivating citrus of their own. Prieto, Artiaga, Gómez, Alvárez, Trasia . . . the fishermen-farmers who were the bay's first white residents were Latins willing to adopt a policy of live and let live with the Seminoles and the escaped black slaves who had sought Florida sanctuary. The Seminoles saw in the Latins' small number no threat like that of the restless hordes of Americans who did not buy land but seized it, more and ever more of it, and then claimed that such robbery was the will of their God. God was, above all else, an expansionist.

The Creek and English wars flamed garishly toward their conclusion. Andrew Jackson marched against Alabama's Creeks and dealt them a decisive blow at the battle of Horseshoe Bend. By the autumn of 1814 he had captured British-held New Orleans by charging redcoats in the murky depths of cypress swamps. Behind him had marched an army of buckskin-clad frontiersmen and stray pirates in search of loot. The War of 1812 ended, but in Pensacola lingered such Britons as Captain Woodbine and a colonel who, without either Spanish permission or orders from the British army, decided to "protect" the Seminoles of Florida. "I have ordered the Seminoles to stand on defense," he announced, "and have sent them a large supply of arms and ammunition, and told them to put to death without mercy anyone molesting them, but at all times to be careful and not put a foot over the American line." The colonel's concern was touching; less touching was the reality that British trade with the Seminoles was profitable and would continue to be profitable as long as there were Seminoles in Florida with whom to trade. Soon the colonel was taking Creek and Seminole chiefs to be wined and dined in London, where Francis the Prophet was presented with a golden tomahawk and a jeweled snuffbox.

Captain Woodbine also wanted to protect the Seminoles, but he was not content to stay quiet in Pensacola for long. By the summer of 1815 he had boarded a British warship and sailed south to Tampa Bay, where he gathered bay and river Indians near their village of Watermelon Town and told them to defy both Spain and America and found a kingdom of their own. In private he fancied himself as the king.

For adventurers like George Woodbine it was a time for visions. A whole continent was opening. Spanish Florida was one of its most glamorous wildernesses. *Filibusteros,* the Spanish called the empire builders: freebooters. It was before freebooters of debate in the United States Congress were to earn the title for themselves; Woodbine was a filibusterer in the earliest tradition. On the bay's long shores where the sandpipers ran ahead of a teasing surf he parlayed with Seminoles and with the runaway slaves. Runaways cleared his land and planted his crops and earned wages in solid British currency for their labors. Woodbine was not satisfied with charming Seminoles in the immediate area, however. His gifts were munificent to Seminoles who lived farther north. A band of them esteemed him so highly they presented him with further tracts of land and a casual promise that if Spaniards or Americans tried to drive him off, fifteen hundred warriors stood ready to attack on his behalf. Woodbine pondered, as he sat on his palmetto-thatched porch and watched the glitter of the bay and heard the mockery of its laughing gulls. To be King of East and West Florida would be a glorious destiny, but one which could not be accomplished alone. And then he heard about Gregor MacGregor.

Gregor MacGregor's filibustering ambitions included all of Mexico. In Baltimore he had recruited an army of his own "to wrest it from Spain." Although he claimed to be the brother-in-law of South America's liberator Simón Bolívar, he failed to kindle in Mexican hearts any desire to follow his leadership. Seeking another haven in Florida, he sailed to Fernandina north of St. Augustine and just south of the Georgia border. From Fernandina he and his ragtag and bobtail troops took control of the lower St. John's River and began a blockade of Fernandina harbor. Its dismayed Spanish commandant hurried to St. Augustine to get advice after he had received an ultimatum from "Gregor MacGregor, Brigadier General of the Armies of the United Provinces of New Granada and Venezuela, and General-in-Chief of that destined to emancipate the provinces of both Floridas, under the commission of the Supreme Government of Mexico and South America."

In Fernandina the fortunes of Gregor MacGregor rode high at first. He had style. Throwing Scottish thrift and caution to the winds, he gave huge banquets for the local citizenry. Every day he issued documents gaily sealed in multicolored waxes and tied with gaudy flying ribbons. Each man in his army was ordered to wear on the left arm "a shield of red cloth and a wreath of oak and laurel leaves embroidered in yellow silk." Gregor MacGregor also meant to "plant the green cross of Florida on the proud walls of St. Augustine"—the green cross, of course, being his own. His quill scratched out elegant commands far into nights echoing the roar of the Atlantic. His literary compositions helped him forget that his army was not nearly large enough for the task he had set it. Today Fernandina and tomorrow St. Augustine? In his heart of hearts he began to doubt it.

Captain Woodbine arrived in Fernandina enchanted with reports of Gregor MacGregor's desire to seize Florida. He knew where *he* could get an army, he told him. He would enlist the Seminoles who had promised him their fealty. MacGregor must sail for Nassau, on the Bahamian is-

land of New Providence. In Nassau hundreds of British soldiers from
disbanded regiments of the War of 1812 could be recruited; peace had
left them restless. In Nassau, MacGregor could also get ships for a sortie
to Tampa Bay. At the bay all the newly acquired British forces would
join Woodbine's Seminoles, and from it a mighty army would go
from strength to strength, Seminoles and Britons hand in hand.
They would march northeast along the banks of the Hillsborough toward
St. Augustine; then they would vault the capital's ancient stone and coquina gates to win the day.

Gregor MacGregor listened to Woodbine raptly. Then, obediently,
he set out for Nassau. Among the coconut palms and lime trees there he
recruited his lieutenants. One was Robert Christie Armbrister, a handsome veteran of the battle of Waterloo who had afterwards been selected
as one of Napoleon's guards on St. Helena. Transferred soon to the West
Indies, Armbrister had been disgraced in a duel and suspended from rank.
So dashing was he, however, that the daughter of a West Indian banker
fell in love with him and promised to marry him if he would get back into
military service. What better service than that of Gregor MacGregor and
George Woodbine? Armbrister was ordered to proceed to Tampa Bay,
gather the faithful Seminoles in Woodbine's name, and wait for reinforcements.

MacGregor, Woodbine, and Armbrister were soon joined in their
scheme by a fourth confederate in search of glory. Alexander Arbuthnot
was a canny Scottish trader of eighty who had just laid in an immense
supply of knives, guns, lead, powder, trinkets, tools and cookpans. Being
an octogenarian didn't stop him from going to Tampa Bay with Armbrister; when they arrived Arbuthnot quoted the Seminoles prices far
below those which traders had given them. The Seminoles rejoiced in
their bargains and they were cordial enough when Armbrister moved
into Woodbine's house. Arbuthnot went north to trade with Seminole
bands near Apalachicola, in West Florida. Armbrister remained on
Tampa Bay, but he found his eloquence failing him as the Indians listened
politely to his speeches and then quixotically refused to become an army
for him or anyone else. Their memories of Woodbine's more compelling
oratory were short.

The filibustering army never materialized. Gregor MacGregor lingered in Nassau with Woodbine, who had joined him there. Discouraged,
Armbrister finally went north. Near the Suwannee River he stopped to

become friends with a chief and flirt with his daughter. American troops, in MacGregor's absence, marched into Fernandina to "hold it in trust for the King of Spain" and put an end to MacGregor's ambitions. When Armbrister finally managed to tear himself away from his Indian maid he walked into the village of Old Town and straight into the midst of more American troops, these commanded by Andrew Jackson. Old Hickory headed an expedition whose ostensible purpose was to punish the Indians who were harassing American borders. The Seminole War was under way. At Old Town, Jackson took Armbrister prisoner, and soon he found Alexander Arbuthnot in the area. Both men protested their innocence when Jackson accused them of stirring up the Indians. Jackson was not convinced. A court-martial of fourteen American officers, under the leadership of American General Edmund Pendleton Gaines, gathered at St. Marks, a Spanish fort on Apalachee Bay in north Florida. In short order they found both Armbrister and Arbuthnot guilty; Arbuthnot, they said, should be hanged, and Armbrister, as a military man, shot. No sooner had the court pronounced sentence than it began to have doubts. How strong was the evidence? The case of Armbrister was reopened and this time the officers recommended that he be let off with fifty lashes and a year in prison. Andrew Jackson would have none of such clemency. However vague the charges against Armbrister and Arbuthnot, he wanted them both out of the way. Accordingly the Americans put them to death. In the moldering little Spanish fort of St. Mark's, Robert Christie Armbrister listened calmly to the approaching fifes and drums of the platoon that would fire at him. "I suppose that admonishes me to be ready." He smiled. "It is a sound I have heard in every quarter of the globe, and now for the last time."

Diplomatic Europe was horrified. Mighty outcries were sent to Washington, which was also horrified—officially. But Andrew Jackson was the swashbuckling hero of the day. Who could resist his ambitions and his daring? When he proclaimed himself the head of an American government in Florida the rest of the country cheered. As for Spain, it saw the harbingers of destiny. Luis de Onís, the Spanish minister in Washington, began conferring with American minister John Quincy Adams about selling a land Spain had already really lost.

General Gaines had a few parting words for the Seminoles of East Florida before he and Jackson moved on to mow down others farther west. "You are a very bad people," he told them. "You harbor a great many of my black people among you. And there is something out in the sea—a bird with a forked tongue; whip him back before he lands, for he will be the ruin of you. I mean the name of Englishman."

To this the Seminole chief King Hatchy replied, "You charge me with killing your people, stealing your cattle, and burning your houses. It is I who have just cause to complain of the Americans. When the Englishmen were at war with America, some Negroes took shelter with them. It is for you white people to settle these things among yourselves. . . . I shall use force to stop any armed Americans from passing my towns or lands."

King Ferdinand of Spain was no happier with the Americans than King Hatchy was. While de Onís and Adams haggled, Ferdinand decided to make three royal grants of crown land to favorite courtiers. America would have to honor these grants if he made them before a purchase treaty was signed. Don Pedro de Vargas, treasurer of Ferdinand's household, and Count de Punon Rostro, a chamberlain, were presented with sizable Florida tracts. To the duke of Alagon, Captain of the King's bodyguards, went El Río San Julián de Arriaga and the Bahía del Espíritu Santo. Adams was furious when he found out what the king had done. In October 1818, he told de Onís that all grants made after 1802 in Florida must be held null and void. De Onís in turn suggested January 24, 1818, as the cutoff date. That would still include the recent grants to Algon and the others, he knew, for they had been made on December 17, 1817. Adams flatly refused. Of all this the three courtiers were never told. They thought their claims were secure.

The duke of Alagon, an imposing enough grandee, needed money. Spain had recently been ravaged by Bonaparte wars. Certainly the duke had no thought of settling in a howling wilderness. In February 1818, oblivious of the horse trading being carried on by Adams and De Onís, he sent to Florida his agent and attorney, Nicolas Garrido. Garrido was to register the Alagon grant and take possession of Espíritu Santo Bay and the river of San Julián de Arriaga. On June 26 a deed was duly registered by Garrido with still-Spanish authorities in Florida, and when he heard of it the duke rejoiced that he now had some negotiable real estate.

Richard S. Hackley was the American consul in Madrid. He was an ambitious, middle-aged attorney from New York. When he heard of the duke's desire to sell nearly half of Florida he immediately approached him with an offer. True, the possession of Florida was under negotiation, but at the moment it was Spanish and that was all that was necessary for his business, Hackley thought. He was prudent enough to tell American embassy officials in Spain what he meant to do, and they gave their consent. In the spring of 1819 he returned to New York and announced to his family that he had acquired a staggering Florida acreage. He had a long document with which to prove it. How much he paid he never revealed, but he was sure he would make back the fortune many times over. The newspapers he read devoted much space to America's coming preemption of Florida, and in one of them there was special encouragement:

> From what we hear of Tampa Bay, though its shores are not now inhabited, it will probably contest with Pensacola the honor of being ultimately fixed upon as the site for the southern naval depot of the United States. The bay is said to be easier of access and to have more water than that of Pensacola; the neighboring country is fertile and abounds in oak valued in the construction of ships, and a short canal will unite the bay with the great River St. John's.

The Cross Florida Barge Canal had been born, in theory if not in fact. As for Tampa Bay's lack of people, who counted Cubans, Indians, or Spaniards? Not American newspapers.

Richard Hackley settled down to closing his law practice and planned soon to leave for Tampa Bay. But when the press of profitable business increased, he decided he would not be able to go himself. His son Robert was twenty-one; young, true, but Richard Hackley trusted Robert to begin building the Hackley empire in Florida in his stead. He bought Robert a schooner and loaded it with materials he would need to build a house and barns: lumber, wooden pegs, varnishes, hammers and axes, farm tools and linens and iron kitchenware. On the way down to Florida Robert stopped to buy two oxen, eight cows, and a flock of Dominecker chickens. He also hired sixteen men to help him clear his fields and begin the Hackley plantation.

The November morning his expedition landed not far from where Narváez and de Soto had landed three centuries before him was soft with the smoky haze of a Florida autumn. Long strands of moss swung from the limbs of live oaks at the mouth of the Hillsborough River. Palms rustled, and Robert noted that thick mats of shrubbery lined both the river's banks. Obviously the land was good. The oak grove would be an ideal site for his plantation house. Immediately he ordered his laborers to begin work on the Hillsborough's east bank. In a few days some Seminoles stopped by to visit him. He was building on land granted by the

King of Spain to the duke of Alagon, he said: his father had lawfully purchased it. Though he was an American, the Indians decided he could mean them no harm. He had no troops. He was soft-spoken, not raucous like the hip-shooting yokels Andrew Jackson had commanded. Robert gave the Indians presents: beads, mirrors, knives. The next day they returned with a deer and a brace of wild turkeys for him. They stood by as the Hackley schooner was unloaded. Robert wanted "a house of superior style and quality for a new locality." He planted long rows of oranges and grapefruits and lemons for his table. He and his men ate the game of the forests along the Hillsborough. They gathered oysters in Tampa Bay. By the end of December Robert Hackley knew he had made a good beginning. The house was nearly ready, and his foreman was trustworthy. Surely there could be no harm in taking a vacation. Robert, like any young man, longed to see Pensacola with its Spanish señoritas and its teeming harbor and exuberant night life; in Pensacola he could also do further shopping for luxuries like crystal and china he had had little room for on the schooner on his way down from New York. He was positive his father would understand. Smiling, refreshed by the prospect of a rest from his Tampa Bay labors, Robert authorized his foreman to carry on the work without him. If the foreman needed advice, there was neighbor Máximo Hernández, who had a farm on the bay's east shore and who "knew every passage, channel and shoal in it." With a half-breed Seminole servant, Máximo Hernández farmed and fished and spent time visiting fellow Latins in Spanish Town Creek, a settlement just west of the river's mouth. Máximo Hernández was wise in the ways of the subtropics. He would be glad to help.

As Robert Hackley's schooner sailed up Tampa Bay once more he cast a proud backward glance at Hackley's Plantation on the slowly flowing Hillsborough. The leaves of live oaks and palms were starry with tiny flashes of light; a winter sun shone high and serene in a cloudless sky. Gulls wheeled and swooped. Terns plunged down like swords after myriad fish, and pelicans flapped slow wings in comic phalanxes. It was bracing to look forward to the trip, but in that moment Robert Hackley knew it would be even better to return to the Eden he himself had created at this distant outpost. It was a proud thing to be the owner of the Hillsborough River and Tampa Bay, and the shores of both he would make bloom for himself, his father, and the descendants he would leave after he found a bride to bring to what he already thought of as his home.

10

"The Oysters Grow on Trees!"

When Spain ratified the Adams-Onís treaty and Florida became a United States territory, the American public were in a fever to learn everything they could about the balmy paradise now open to mass settlement. They pored over the books of Bernard Romans and the naturalist William Bartram. New York publishers were looking for a manuscript more up-to-date, however, and when *Sketches, Historical and Topographical, of the Floridas* appeared in the offices of C. S. Van Winkle and Company of Greenwich Street the editors knew it would have a brisk market. The author, James Grant Forbes, was actually a native of Florida. He was the son of a Church of England clergyman who had served in St. Augustine before moving to London. James Forbes had been educated in England and then had gone into business for himself on the West Indian island of Santo Domingo. He hadn't prospered there. When he returned in 1821 to St. Augustine it was to accept an appointment as United States Marshal for East and West Florida. His Spanish was fluent; Andrew Jackson liked him when he paid a visit to Pensacola; the people of St. Augustine made him their mayor. Who was better qualified to report on America's latest acquisition?

Forbes knew nothing of Robert Hackley and he probably had little firsthand knowledge of the river or the bay, but he was enthusiastic about both:

Espíritu Santo Tampa, or Hillsborough Bay, is the most spacious
bay on the west coast of the peninsula. . . . It must, in the event of possession and improvement by the United States, afford protection to her own
trade and be of vital importance to her naval grandeur. These con-
sequences are derived from the necessity under which the fleets of
merchantmen in time of war are, of coming through the Gulf of Mexico,
and making the Tortugas, thus rendering this depot the Gibraltar of the
West, and of incalculable advantage in the hands of an enterprising
belligerent. . . . The land about the coast of this invaluable bay is very
barren, sandy, and low, and cannot be seen from a ship's deck when in
seven fathoms water. There are several low sandy islands and marshes
covered with mangrove bushes, lying before the main land, which serve
as a resort for the greatest number of sea fowl and fish which it is
possible to conceive. You may, at a particular season, load a ship with
either, or with eggs, in a short time. . . . The head of the bay is well
adapted for advantageous settlement; for although the land is chiefly
pine, yet the resources of a fine river, which falls into the east branch of
it, are well calculated to promote emigration in that quarter. . . . If, as
is stated, there is on this coast a large quantity of building stone, how
propitious this circumstance for erecting fortifications, as necessary at
all times for the protection of our western coast and trade, as it is politic,
in the event of war.

On the necessity of fortifications the United States Army thoroughly
agreed with Forbes, and it sent scouts to Tampa Bay.

Robert Hackley, amusing himself in Pensacola, was unaware of the
scouts' coming. So, apparently, was S. S. Seymour, a friend of his father's
who was traveling in the south and stopped by Tampa Bay. "There are
two entrances of easy access," Seymour reported to Richard's father. "Egmont Key is situated between these entrances and forms a complete de-
fence against all winds blowing from the Gulf of Mexico." Hillsborough
Bay's bottom was "an excellent holding ground for ships." The quantity
of fish in the Hillsborough River was enormous; the sheepsheads, bass,
mullet, and turtle were unsurpassed; the fat of the manatee was as valuable as the purest lard; oysters were "exhaustless." Of the river Seymour
noted:

> There is not a more beautiful one in this world. I ascended this river
> ten miles. The water is fresh down to its mouth and abounds with fish
> innumerable. It is navigable for vessels thirty miles. . . . At the rapids
> are invaluable sites of water power; the bottom of the river and its sides

are composed of limestone. . . . The river will furnish stone and lumber
for the settlement. . . . A most important point I would impress upon
the minds of all who wish to purchase lands in this country is that after
you have tilled a field until it will produce no longer profitably, throw it
out, and the climate will resuscitate it in three years without any other
aid than the saline breeze of the ocean. . . . The never-failing sea-breeze,
familiarly called The Doctor, surely blows about 9 in the morning, and
brings with it health and comfort.

The era of Florida fables had begun.

It never occurred to anybody that the Indians had any claims to this
paradise. "What is the right of the huntsman," rhetorically asked John
Quincy Adams, "to the forest over which he has accidentally ranged in
quest of prey? Shall the liberal bounties of providence be claimed by a
few hundreds? Shall the lordly savage not only disdain the virtues and
enjoyments of civilization himself, but shall he control the civilization of
the world? What is the Indian title? It is mere occupancy for the purpose
of hunting. It is not like our tenures; they have no idea of a title to the
soil itself. It is overrun by them, rather than inhabited." From the beginning, Americans turned blind eyes to Seminole cornfields and cattle herds.

In September 1823, the United States presented Florida chiefs with
a treaty. All the Seminoles must move. Each Indian forced to vacate his
land in north Florida would receive the princely sum of two dollars, which
he was to use toward the purchase of fresh livestock. An extra dollar and
a half per year was provided him to help maintain a tribal school and a
forge. In case the Seminoles objected, a military fort would be established
near their reservation. Its garrison would see to it that none of them
strayed northward. In Washington, Major General Brown E. Kirby
decided on what seemed to him an ideal location; the army's scouts had
brought back glowing reports of the Gulf near the "Espíritu Santo Bay
of Tampa." Kirby sent an order to Brevet Colonel George Mercer Brooke,
stationed near Pensacola. "Brevet Colonel Brooke with four companies of
the 4th Infantry will proceed with as little delay as practicable to Tampa
Bay, East Florida, where he will establish a military post. He will select
a position with a view to health and in reference to the location of the
Florida Indians about to be removed to that vicinity agreeably to the
late treaty. . . . The quartermaster's and subsistence departments will
furnish the necessary transportation and supplies and will make such
further arrangements as may be required for the accommodation of the

troops at their new station." What was healthier than a house? George Brooke arrived at the bay in January 1824; soon afterward Robert Hackley returned from Pensacola to find the army cosily settled on his plantation, which, Colonel Brooke immediately proclaimed, now belonged to the government. The United States had the right to seize the place in the interest of security against the Seminoles. The astonished Hackley left for New York, where his father began rounding up brother attorneys to fight the case. For decades the Hackleys and the United States wrangled in courtrooms. The Hackleys petitioned presidents; it was their "duty to the Civil Liberty of the land," they said. By the time the validity of the Alagon grant was ultimately denied by the Supreme Court, Richard Hackley was long dead, his last years embittered. His heirs, who protested until 1905 that they owned nearly half of Florida, never received an indemnity.

"We are situated on the northeast bank of the Hillsborough River," Colonel Brooke advised his superiors, "immediately on its entrance into the Bay of the same name." Brother officers wanted to call the camp Fort Brooke; modestly, Brooke called it Camp Hillsborough "till the pleasure of the war department shall be ascertained." The pleasure of the war department was accommodatingly in favor of Fort Brooke. Brooke neglected to mention that he had evicted Robert Hackley. He was simply influenced, he said, "by the quantity of cleared land which was at once adapted to gardens for the officers and men."

For George McCall, one of Brooke's lieutenants, the river and the bay were enchanted country. "The oysters grow on trees!" he wrote home to his brother and his father of mangrove shallows where the trees' lower branches were covered with shells. At night the exiled Yankee soldiers could hear raccoons cracking the shells; coon oysters, some of them began calling them. The fishing was "unbelievable." Once McCall had gone out into the bay with seven friends and they had hauled a seine net. When they had dragged it into shoal water they had found it so full of redfish they couldn't take it back to Fort Brooke. The fish weighed thirty pounds and would bite on anything, but salt pork was best. Twice a week a fishing detail rowed out from the fort into the bay; a separate boat in tow had to be reserved for the catch. When the detail returned to the wharf, the bugler blew a "fish call." Sergeants appeared with wheelbarrows and loaded them for their companies. Officers had first preference. If any Seminoles happened to be in camp, they were offered fish of their own. What was left was buried to make compost for Colonel Brooke's garden.

The hunting, George McCall told his family, was as good as the fishing. Deer could be taken any time anybody wanted venison. The fort was rising: commissary buildings, a sutler's store, barns, wharves, buildings for the quartermaster and blacksmith, barracks and storage depots for tents and supplies. There was plenty of pine, and the fort headquarters stood in the grove of live oaks Robert Hackley had admired. Their branches were festooned with yellow jasmine that had been blooming ever since the soldiers had arrived. On Egmont Key the men hunted for turtle eggs and learned to be careful of the rattlesnakes who had burrowed into holes made by gopher tortoises. The sea breezes always broke the heat of noon. Nights were "perfectly glorious." The Indians who lived in the area were taciturn, though one of them became friendly enough with George McCall to teach him how to predict rain. If a black cloud rose with the sun, "a sensible man will seek a place to camp and peel a pine tree to make him a tent," the Indian said. When it was dark, the Indians told time by the positions of the stars.

Among the soldiers, discipline was strict. Careful attention was paid to hygiene. "No more than fourteen men," pronounced the post medical officer, "are to use the same toothbrush." Several times a week Colonel Brooke ordered expeditions into the bay "to look for pirates." What George McCall found on one such expedition were five tall sandhill cranes feeding at the water's edge on mollusks and saltwater insects. As he approached them quietly with his rifle in hand, the cranes paused and then took wing. Several of the men began talking of "the spirits of a ship's crew reported to have been murdered by pirates off the mouth of the bay not very long before." The spectacle of the soaring cranes was too unearthly in its grace to be real to them.

When the soldiers had finished building they began work on a military road which would lead to newly established Fort King, near modern Ocala. The Fort Brooke–Fort King Road crossed the Hillsborough, and George McCall found it hard work hacking through riverbank jungles. The men made jokes to keep up their spirits; when the company's doctor lost his glasses in the river it became "a fair subject for a good hearty laugh." The glasses eventually turned up in a Seminole village.

Colonel Brooke, who had been less than frank with his superiors about Robert Hackley, was more candid when he reported conditions among the Seminoles living near his fort. "The major part of the nation are, and have been, suffering for some time in extreme want. Some have

Major General George M. Brooke

died from starvation, and many have lived on the roots of the sweetbriar as a substitute for bread." While their corn was tasseling it had been parched by drought; several of the Indians who arrived near Fort Brooke to live within the reservation established by the treaty came too late to plant, and others had to clear new land which would produce no crop the first year. "It is impossible to me or to any other officer who possesses the smallest feelings of humanity to resist affording some relief to men, women and children who are actually dying for want of something to eat." Brooke asked Washington for extra rations. Near Fort King a party of Indians drove an American family from their farm and then made off with their provisions. Seminole chiefs bitterly complained of poor land within the reservation; they wanted to go north across the Suwannee again. Yet Secretary of War John C. Calhoun was saying confidently, "Immediate measures need not be taken with regard to the Indians of Florida. They have ceded the whole northern portion . . . and have had allotted to them the southern part of the peninsula, and it is probable that no inconvenience will be felt for many years either by the inhabitants of Florida or the Indians under the present arrangement." The inconvenience of dying, however, was considerable to the Seminole to whom it happened.

Seminoles were not primarily fishermen. William DuVal, the recent successor to Andrew Jackson as governor of Florida, came south from the territorial capital of Tallahassee to see for himself what those near Fort Brooke were enduring. On the Hillsborough the Indians were restricted by treaty to the river's upper portion near the Green Swamp. "The lands of Hillsboro' river within the Indian boundary are of so little value that there is not one Indian settlement on any of them," DuVal found. The villages were clustered southwest near Thlonotosassa, the "field of flints" which Americans could pronounce only as Thonotosassa. DuVal found the landscape depressing. "I . . . suffered much from drinking water alive with insects, from mosquitoes, intolerable hot weather, and my horses were reduced by the journey. . . . I have never seen a more wretched tract. . . . I entered a low wet piney country spotted with numerous ponds; I had much difficulty to pass through them, although the season has been uncommonly dry; had much rain fallen, I never could have reached Tampa Bay. . . . After riding all day and until eleven o'clock at night in the hope that I would find a dry spot to sleep upon, I was compelled to take up my lodging on a low wet place for the night. No settlement ever can be made in this region, and there is no land in it worth cultivation." Governor DuVal's pessimism was a contrast to the enthusiasm of men like Robert Hackley, who had seen the river and the bay as plantation country, and George McCall, who loved the hunting and fishing they provided and didn't mind the heat. "Croakers," McCall dubbed men who found no good in the place. But Governor DuVal had come upon the smoldering remains of a forest fire beyond the Hillsborough. "The whole of the timber for this distance as far as the eye can survey has been killed by fire; the burnt and blackened pines, without a leaf, added to the dreary poverty of the land, presents the most miserable and gloomy prospect I ever beheld."

Other men besides George McCall disagreed with DuVal. One was a doughty New Englander named Levi Collar whose wife Nancy, on the way to Fort Brooke, presented him with a daughter born in a deserted trapper's hut. The Collars had toughness and spirit. Another was a boyhood playmate (he said) of Napoleon Bonaparte who arrived on the bay possessed of the idea that growing oranges there might be made to pay.

11

Gifts and
Givers

With more truth than poetry the United States christened the territory surrounding Fort Brooke Mosquito County. Poetry was supplied instead by elegant Odet Phillippe, whose tales about himself captured the imaginations of the more prosaic Collar family and Fort Brooke's soldiers. Phillippe had been born in Lyons, France, in 1769; he was of royal birth, he declared, though he was vague about his exact relationship to the Bourbon dynasty. How he had met the child Napoleon was another mystery he never elucidated. As a youth he had studied medicine and several languages. When Napoleon came to power he appointed Phillippe a surgeon in the French fleet, and in 1804 gave him a commemorative medal. By this time Napoleon and English Admiral Horatio Nelson were skirmishing their way across European seas. At the Battle of Trafalgar, Phillippe was captured by Nelson himself. Nelson ordered him sent to the Bahamas, where he spent two years as a prisoner until he was finally released. Then he went to Charleston, South Carolina, where he began practicing medicine and married a Charleston belle. She presented him with four daughters and then died. Phillippe married again, but his second wife's beauty was palliated by her bad temper. His calamities were compounded when he cosigned a Charleston promissory note which he immediately was forced to make good. He had to sell his Carolina property; with the last of his money he bought a schooner which he christened the *Ney* in honor of one of Napoleon's marshals. In the *Ney* he made his way south to Florida's lower east coast, where he was enchanted with the Indian River. He decided to go to the Bahamas to purchase supplies for an Indian River settlement.

On her trip to Nassau the *Ney* encountered a pirate ship flying the Jolly Roger. The pirates stormed aboard the *Ney* and Phillippe was powerless to resist as the skull and crossbones fluttered ominously overhead. He had nothing to give, he said; he was on his way to buy implements for his plantation; he was a doctor. At this the pirates brightened. Several of their men were sick in the hold of their ship. If Phillippe could cure them, he would be permitted to go his way. In three days, Phillippe later claimed, all the ailing pirates were on the road to recovery, and their leader, John Gómez, was so grateful that he presented him with a chest filled with golden treasure. Safe in Nassau, Phillippe bought orange trees, ploughs, axes, tobacco seeds, and tropical shrubs. Then he returned to the Indian River.

He loved the Indians there, he always maintained. Such was their devotion to him that on one occasion when they were planning a raid they warned him to leave. He and his wife and his family of daughters boarded the *Ney,* and on their way out to the ocean they could see the smoke of burning homesteads. Nor had their adventures ended; what should turn up but another shipful of sick pirates under the command of John Gómez? By now Phillippe considered himself "unofficial surgeon" to these privateers of the bounding main. Again he nursed the invalid outlaws to health; afterwards Gómez was moved enough to take him aside and show him a map.

"Here," said the pirate (according to Phillippe), "is Espíritu Santo Bay. If there is a God, surely this is his resting place. There is but one bay to compare with it—Naples. I have seen waters all over the world and you can find no place like it. A sunrise from the west shore is beautiful; a sunset is grand. All the hues of the rainbow blended together reflect from the sky to the water. A moonlight night is exquisite. On its shore you will find flowing springs where wild beasts come to drink, and where almost any time you will see an Indian quenching his thirst or filling his deerskin with water. Often they are seen carrying a whole deer hide full of honey."

Moved by the pirate captain's fulsome fluency, Odet Phillippe immediately set his course for Tampa Bay. From it he made his way along the shore of the Pinellas peninsula which had been the Piney Point of

Jiménez until he came to a high Indian mound at what had been Tocobaga, where de Soto had stared at the Timucuan temple and its fowl with gilded eyes. Phillippe built a house near what is now Safety Harbor; his orange groves stretched in neat rows on the site which commemorates him as Phillippe Park. Soon he had begun a profitable business with Fort Brooke. His groves became a local landmark, and visitors from north Florida where oranges could not endure the cold often stopped by to stock up on Phillippe fruit. To his friends he gave it by the bushel. He named his plantation St. Helena in memory of Napoleon's final exile. There he established a herd of cattle and with slave labor he planted cotton. When a roaring hurricane swept in from the Gulf to raze St. Helena and kill all the citrus trees, he began another grove undaunted and rebuilt his plantation house more splendidly than before. When his shrewish wife died he did not marry again, but lived out his days in Panama hats and natty linen suits as the cigar-smoking squire of St. Helena, adored by his daughters. He reached a hundred before he died; as he told and retold his story neighbors would gather to listen; it got better every time. Always he kept a jug of Hillsborough River water beside him. "This is God's own country," he proclaimed, "and this water is his medicine, stirred by His hand and deposited on our shores to heal man's suffering."

So went the legend Odet Phillippe created about himself. Possibly some of it was true. In sober fact, he was recorded later in life as owning two pool halls in the newly founded city of Tampa, a pair of bowling alleys, and an oyster house. On his land at St. Helena lived two slaves, "five horses and a colt, four mules, five cows and six calves, a certain number of hogs and my hunting dogs, and a wagon and barouche with several sets of harness." That he grew citrus profitably was emphasized by his prosperity; his pool halls and bowling alleys may well have been built on a liquid foundation of orange juice. It did no harm to his business that he was reputed to be a sprig of the royal house of France.

He was not the only pioneer who claimed imposing ancestry. In Spanish Town Creek lived Juan Montes de Oca, "a Spanish gentleman of high family." He taught himself both English and Seminole; soon, along with Máximo Hernández who fished the bay, he was drawing a salary as an interpreter for Fort Brooke. One day he mounted his horse and went riding up the Hillsborough to Thlonotosassa. Here he fell in love at first sight with a Seminole girl he found "lovely of soul as well as of person." They were married, and when their daughter was born they named her Victoria. Victoria's mother fell victim to a fever and died; the child was reared by Levi Collar's family and grew up to marry a Virginian who settled in Tampa and founded its first newspaper.

In the early days of Fort Brooke, though, there was no Tampa. At first nobody wanted to buy land that both the U. S. Army and the Hackley family claimed. Technically, the area upriver was a part of the Seminole reservation and no American was permitted to settle on it. Matters were complicated by the appearance of one Henry Eckford, an American who said he had bought from Don Pedro Miranda of St. Augustine a tract of land twenty-four miles square which included Fort Brooke. He swore his claim antedated Richard Hackley's. To the tortuous technicalities of the Alagon grant were now added those of the Miranda grant, and American courts were taking their time about hearing both cases. Fort Brooke officers decided to declare surrounding forests a permanent timber reserve; this land, too, would be closed to settlement. Levi Collar had tried to establish a farm near Fort Brooke only to be told to move. Defiantly, in sight of the fort, he began building his cabin on the Hillsborough River's west bank; this time no one stopped him. The Seminoles didn't interfere; Colonel Brooke had confiscated most of their weapons.

To amuse themselves the soldiers began to stage horse races. News of a three-day derby at Fort Brooke, the first in Florida, traveled all the way to Pensacola, whose newspaper reported its results:

> *First day*: Mr. Page's horse Bacchus, Mr. McCall's horse Packingham, and Captain Dade's horse Richard the Third, were entered for the three mile heats—won by Bacchus in two heats, which were well contested.
> *Second day*: Captain Yancy's horse Uncle Sam, Mr. Collins's horse Beppo, and Mr. Morris's horse Bob Logic were entered for the two mile heats. First heat beaten by Beppo. The superior bottom of Uncle Sam gained him the second and third.

Captain Francis Langhorne Dade loved horses and history; during these days of calm at Fort Brooke he had no idea that he himself would one day become history. With his brother officers he visited the establishment of William Saunders, a trader from Mobile, Alabama, who had set up a general store at the fort's gate. It was the first on the lower Gulf coast, and army wives admired its bright calicos and household gadgets. Saunders was unworried about legal titles. People wanted his business, and he could, if necessary, take it somewhere else in the neighborhood. His relations with the officers at Fort Brooke were smooth; he promised them not to sell whiskey to the Seminoles. Word of Saunders's store reached the Cuban and Spanish proprietors of fishing ranchos; they, too, began to buy from him. Trappers traded him their pelts, and whenever an American family arrived to stay it built a log cabin as near the store as possible. Possession was nine tenths of the law, newcomers reasoned. Word of Saunders's prosperity spread. Soon a shoemaker joined him, and a boat-builder set up shop. One of the laundresses at Fort Brooke began taking lodgers in her cabin. Professional gamblers arrived, flashy and glib, splendid in spats and flowered waistcoats; they milked the soldiers of their pay in rigged card games. When prostitutes joined them they, too, built cabins on the river. Fort Brooke was suddenly an embryo town, and the government gave it a regular mail service. The Tampa Bay Post Office became Fort Brooke's first link with the world beyond.

Augustus Steele was a north Florida editor whose newspaper, *The Magnolia Advertiser,* had failed. Unruffled, he proceeded to get an appointment from Andrew Jackson, now president, as Deputy Collector of Customs at Fort Brooke. At once Steele began promoting the idea of a city called Tampa, the seat of a county all its own. In Tallahassee he lobbied for his project and spoke persuasively with Governor DuVal. He was rewarded with the designation of the County of Hillsborough (no more unsalable Mosquito!), and the name of the Tampa Bay Post Office was changed, simply, to Tampa. The young town acquired a brick-mason who began to build houses for settlers increasingly less worried by the Alagon and Miranda claims. The brickmason's wife went into the business of raising fighting cocks which she sold for extravagant prices to the men of Fort Brooke. Betting stakes were high, liquor flowed freely, and the daughters of joy on the waterfront were enjoying a booming trade. Not even the arrival of a Baptist missionary affected Tampa's lusty vigor; discreetly, he settled fifteen miles east of town in a hammock where he began preaching to the Seminoles. Once again, red men on the river and the bay were made acquainted with angels and the devil; this time, however, the High Pontiff called Papa was also a villain.

The missionary was horrified by the conditions he found in the Seminole villages. So was Indian agent Colonel Gad Humphreys:

> There is not at this moment . . . a bushel of corn in the whole nation, or any adequate substitute for it. The coutee and briar-root, which have hitherto been to them a tolerable dernier dependence, are almost entirely consumed. For nearly a year they have been compelled to rely mainly on

these and the cabbage tree. . . . What they are to do another year I cannot imagine. They have not corn for this year's need nor can I procure it for them. . . . The situation of some of these people is wretched, almost beyond description, those particularly who . . . were robbed of their guns have been absolutely famishing. . . . Toward a people like the Indians, whose chief dependence for subsistence is upon the chase, a greater cruelty could not be practiced than to deprive them of the implements so important and indispensable to their mode of life.

As more and more Seminoles died of hunger, their survivors were filled with a desire for vengeance. They began raiding outlying farms, burning buildings and scalping families; they stole corn and cattle because their own had been wrested from them; in the fastnesses of the Green Swamp they could not be captured. An idea began to grow in American settlers' minds: every Indian ought to be deported from Florida. Then conflict would come to an end, and white men could enjoy their lands in peace. Tampa would never develop as a city until it was safe to live there. The soldiers of Fort Brooke, gathering around their fires in the evening to bet on their fighting roosters, laughed with an uneasy gaiety. Were the Seminoles massing in the interior for a second Seminole War? Rumors cropped up everywhere. The Indians had a new leader. He was young and strong, he hated whites, and he drew the Seminoles to himself like a magnet. When Osceola spoke, other chiefs listened, and those whom the Americans had cowed into submission lapsed into silence. The Seminoles had had enough of submission. "I will make the white man red with blood," Osceola vowed. "I will blacken him in the sun and the rain, where the wolf shall smell of his bones and the buzzard live upon his flesh." Deportation? Osceola laughed outright. At one conference with Indian agents he hurled his knife deep into the pine table which separated the Americans from Seminoles. "The only treaty I will ever make is this!" he shouted; then he stalked away in grim and voiceless dignity. As his threat echoed, all present knew that inevitably red and white blood would mingle in the clear waters some called Lockcha-popka-chiska, and others the Hillsborough.

Tampa was on edge. Twenty-six citizens signed a petition asking the secretary of war for more troops at Fort Brooke. Soldiers began to station lookouts when they went turtle-hunting in the Gulf. Yet as word of the restless and starving Seminoles traveled to the industrial North from the river and the bay, so did word of the riches of the waters in both. In Baltimore a sea captain named William Bunce pondered all the reports he heard and then decided to set up a fishing rancho on Tampa Bay's south shore. His live catch could be sold at a profit in Havana, and he would dry and salt fish for Cuban as well as American consumption. When he arrived full of plans an officer at Fort Brooke found him "one of the most intelligent men on the coast" and "highly respectable." He began hiring help for his rancho, and in addition to the Latin seamen who had known and plied the bay for decades he found another source of labor: the Seminoles. When Fort Brooke's officers found this out they thought him far less respectable, but their doubts didn't prevent him from being made a Tampa Justice of the Peace; most of the local settlers were impressed by his dignity and seamanship even as they feared his Seminole workers. He made money immediately. With an outlay of "numerous fishing boats, conoes, seins, fishing tackle, buildings and everything necessary," including a fishing smack and a small sloop, he created jobs for a hundred and fifty workers and took in an annual profit of six thousand dollars, a fortune in a frontier settlement where barter was still the rule.

And then something strange began to happen to Captain Bunce; he took to liking and admiring the Seminoles he knew. With them he was sharing the sea wind, the adventures afloat which became campfire fables at night, the Gulf's alternating squalls and deadly white-hot calms. The Indians told him of the long succession of treaties they had had to make, the Americans' efforts to get them out of Florida. Conservative chiefs like Tsali Emathla (to Irish recruits at Fort Brooke he was Charley O'Mathla) might have given a weary consent to inspect the western lands where the government wanted the Seminoles to go, but militants like Osceola and Alligator and Jumper were determined to stay. The head chief of the tribe was Micanopy, fat, phlegmatic, pockmarked, and alcoholic, but no fool for all that. When Micanopy looked at his braves from beneath his hooded eyelids, they always knew he was taking their measure. All these things the Seminoles confided to Captain Bunce; he was their friend because he paid them fairly, and he listened with increasing sympathy though at first he kept his counsel.

But one evening, warmed perhaps by rum, he could keep it no longer. "You Indians are all fools!" he exploded. "The whites want to get you all in Tampa Bay and then they will send you off to a very bad country where your old people and children will die. You don't know anything about reading and writing, but I look into the papers and I see it all. If you wait a little while you will have plenty of people to come here and assist you. The reason the white people want to get you off from here as quick as they can is because they know that if you remain you will have people come and help you." What helpers he didn't specify; perhaps he had conjured up in his mind protesters against Indian exploitation as vocal as slavery abolitionists were becoming in the north. The effect of Bunce's outburst on the audience was electric. Antonio, a Seminole Negro, told the nephew of Chief Cloud about it; Chief Cloud's nephew told his friend Athlugee, who in turn sent a message to the village of Chief Tustenuggee. It was inevitable the tale and its effect of inciting Indians to rebellion eventually reached Fort Brooke; officers had only to listen to food-seeking Indians from Tustenuggee's village as they recounted how Bunce had asked the Seminoles and Seminole Negroes not to reveal his name. The treason of Bunce would be hard to prove, the officers knew; the story had come through too many people. But from this time on Bunce was watched, and eventually an American detachment found it necessary to burn all the warehouses of his fishery to the ground, where they became a smoking ruin beside seas dancing oblivious in the summer sun.

At Fort King the new Indian agent, General Wiley Thompson, talked with the party of chiefs, Tsali Emathla among them, who had traveled to the Indian Territory of Oklahoma at government expense. The chiefs had been willing enough to go, but now one of them confessed it was just for the trip. "Your talk," Jumper told Thompson, "seems always good, but we do not want to go west."

"I never gave my consent," Boleck added. "The whites may say so, but I never gave my consent."

"I am sick," another said simply. "I am sick and I cannot say all I want to say."

In April 1835, when Wiley Thompson gathered another group of Seminoles at Fort King, Jumper told him bluntly that the Seminoles would fight to remain in Florida. For the first time Thompson, who had been transferred from another post, heard the name of Osceola. He stared curiously at the young chief. When Osceola tossed him an unrecorded insult Thompson lost his temper and ordered Osceola to be bound in irons and put in the fort's jail. At first Osceola bellowed in anguish for his freedom; then he appeared to calm down; the older chiefs interceded with Thompson on his behalf. When Thompson freed him, Osceola assured him his heart had changed. In turn, Thompson apologized for his temper. "I now have no doubt of his sincerity," Thompson wrote that evening in the dim light of his tiny oil lamp in the Fort King cabin which served as his office. "The greatest difficulty is surmounted." When Thompson was placed by his superiors in Washington in charge of Seminole emigration, his schemes grew elaborate.

The Indians would all be brought to Tampa Bay. From there they would sail to New Orleans; then, by riverboat, they would proceed inland toward their territory far from American settlements. At Tampa, Thompson would build "issuing houses" and cattle pens; the Seminoles' Negroes would be rounded up and, if they refused to go to Oklahoma, they would be chained and sent anyhow. Thompson wanted vessels "seaworthy and every way prepared and arranged for the convenience, comfort, and safety of the emigrants." They were to eat corn, "generally considered as most wholesome for Indians, and the most economical." As a change, and for the sick, there would be wheat flour. Fresh beef and salt pork would alternate as main meals. For every five hundred Seminoles there would be a doctor, an interpreter, and a man-of-all-work. To be excluded on the ships and riverboats, naturally, were "all intoxicants except for medical purposes strictly." And then, of course, a military force would be required to herd the Indians into the convenient, comfortable, and safe ships. Twelve days ought to round up all the "disaffected and stragling." Wiley Thompson was a poor speller, if a zealous military executive.

July was humid and oppressive. All morning a metallic sun burned over steamy pine forests; in the afternoon skies blackened and torrents of rain fell to the ground while winds lashed high palms. Thompson, as he wrote out his reports in solitude, listened to the rain sliding off the agency's thatched roof. He smelled the rankness of the acid earth, and he slapped exasperated at the buzzing mosquitoes which were constantly settling on his face and neck. What series of events had led him here? He had been born in Virginia and had early migrated down into Georgia. He had served with distinction in the War of 1812; he had ended it a major. Then for six terms he had represented his Georgia district in Congress. Now he was fifty-two, gaunt and grey and sickly, but he wanted to continue serving his government at the same time that he gave the Seminoles treatment that was "as fair and Christian as possible" under the circumstances. But what was the Christian Way of Eviction? Wiley

Thompson began to understand he did not know. He wished he did. He only knew that something about young Osceola moved him deeply; he wanted his friendship. Osceola was imposing in his buckskin robes; egret feathers waved splendidly in his jet black hair when he raised his head to speak. His eyes were always darkly keen. On his chest hung three shining silver gorgets which flashed in fugitive sunbeams under the pines. His long nose was Roman; the whole cast of his features spoke of the mixed ancestry he so vigorously denied. He was fitted for kingship. And so, perhaps partly because Thompson was lonely in his Fort King exile and needed a friendship, he acted on impulse. He sent a special order to a firm of gunsmiths in Savannah. They were to make a handsomely ornamented rifle; the cost was no object. When it came, he sent for Osceola and gave it to him.

Osceola's eyes went wide. Then he examined the gun carefully, his face impassive. But Thompson could see how pleased he was; truly now they were reconciled. With dignity Osceola thanked him for the gift; he promised him to use it well. From time to time after that Osceola paid formal calls at Fort King. Thompson believed that not only had he served Osceola by the gesture, but the American government too. Now there would not be the Seminole war everyone had begun to fear.

Thompson's mail from Fort Brooke came late one week in August. Private Kinsley Dalton had ridden out some mornings before intending to reach the banks of the Hillsborough the first night. There he would make his camp. When Private Dalton saw the group of six Indians waiting for him in a stand of cypresses along the way he did not spur his horse to flee. It would have been useless. As he approached them slowly, they said nothing. Just as he reached the cypress pond one of them seized his mule's bridle and another shot him from his saddle. The others began ripping off his uniform and opening his belly to drag out his intestines while he screamed and choked on his cries. He died soon, but not before his head had begun to spout dark jets of red from a scalp being lifted away from his skullbone. Afterward the Indians threw him in the pond where he was found by an investigating party days later. By then his corpse was bloated. Fighting back the gorge in their throats, Fort Brooke friends buried him on the pond's banks and then covered his grave with brush to protect it from wolves.

Wiley Thompson, hearing of the death of Private Dalton, was sure—almost—that the gun which had unhorsed him had not had a stock of Georgia timber finely carved and polished in Savannah, the cost no object.

12

Massacre

Tsali Emathla, passing from the autumn of his austere life into its winter, was tired. As he stood one November afternoon in 1835 with his three young daughters on the banks of the Lockcha-popka-chiska, the old man gazed meditatively at their slim grace and at the equally slender grace of pine trunks pale in the sun. Then he raised his eyes to the pearled half-clouds which would never, he knew, gather enough density this crisp day to rain. The heat of summer had waned. Orchids no longer bloomed. Klo-hi-lee, the squirrel, scrambled briskly along a hickory branch. Maple and willow leaves were floating slowly, soundlessly, out to the bay. The smell of blooming wild flowers was mingled with far-off sea and with sulfur from river springs. Tsali Emathla had learned to love this land.

It has not been his country originally; he had not wanted to come here when the whites had overrun Seminole villages in the hilly north. But he had come, because there had been nothing else to do. Nothing could hold the white men back. That had been true in the north, and now it was proving true on the Lockcha-popka-chiska and on the bay where other red men had lived and then vanished. Nothing was left of the Old Ones except a few songs that had become a part of Seminole ceremonies. Tsali Emathla was a philosopher. Let the hotheads, Osceola and Jumper and Alligator, protest their defiance of the Americans. They would lose out in the end. Rum-soaked old Micanopy was no match for the Americans either. If war came, it would mean that far more Seminoles would perish under fire than had already perished of hunger. And Tsali Emathla wanted his people to live.

It was why he had just brought five hundred of them to the clearing not far from Fort Brooke's gates to wait for removal. He would miss Florida as his people would. But attachment to the land would not ensure their lives any more than his; it would hasten the doom of all. Better to obey the Americans now and prepare his people to make the long voyage to the Indian territory in the west that he had already seen. Some day the Americans would want that too, he thought. But not yet; and he believed in fighting for time.

In October he and his braves had answered a summons from Micanopy and the militants to a gathering in the Green Swamp. Tsali Emathla had sat impassive in his palmetto canoe as the young men had paddled him deeper and deeper into the cypress shadows. He was planning carefully the words of moderation he meant to speak. But when the tribal council assembled, he swiftly understood it was not to listen to him. His counsels were interrupted before he could finish them. Most of the young warriors jeered. Sadly, he listened to the bellowings of Jumper and Alligator, the ringing defiances of Osceola who had managed to bring most of the Seminoles under his banner though he was not a chief of high rank. Osceola offered hope. He had collected a hundred and fifty kegs of good powder and he was boasting he would not leave Florida until it was used up. Then Tsali Emathla heard the men of his tribe officially adopt Osceola's attitude as their own. They would make a stand here in the Green Swamp and along the We-wath-lock-o and Lockcha-popka-chiska rivers. They would never go to Oklahoma. They would kill, burn, and raze everything they could, and the white men would not be able to find them in the vine-matted swamp's remoteness. At this announcement of resistance the swamp echoed with cheers.

Even so, the calm of Tsali Emathla had later prevailed with the faithful five hundred he had offered to lead here to Fort Brooke to await shipment to Oklahoma. Now they were hungry, and Tsali Emathla had just come from begging the officers for food. He had even delivered up his herd of cattle, willing to let an American colonel appraise their value and determine a fair price. Then he had shaken the hands of his oppressors. As he stood beside the river this afternoon with his daughters, he knew it was one of the last times he would ever see it. He hoped the girls knew why he was doing what he was doing. It was for them, and for other women and children who had no part in the wars of men. All these things he pondered wordlessly; then he motioned to his daughters in their bright patchwork gowns to follow him as he began the trek back to his village to collect the rest of his possessions. Small things like his headdresses and medicine bundles he would be allowed to take with him, the Americans had said. The girls would want to keep the familiar trappings of their daily lives: linsey-woolsey shawls, sofkee spoons, the mortars in which they ground their coontie flour. Did coontie grow in Oklahoma? Tsali Emathla did not think so. He had not seen any on those distant prairies where strange grasses sang in the wind. Out there the Seminoles would cling to the old ways as long as they could, and he would tell and retell to his daughters all the timeworn tribal legends. Again the Seminoles would be wanderers, exiles. For him he hoped the wandering would not be long.

Slowly he and the three young women moved northeast along the dappled trail which led from Fort Brooke, and the sunlit waters reflected ripples on fallen palm trunks. Leopard frogs barked persistently. When Tsali Emathla heard a slight rustle in the underbrush he looked up to see Osceola standing before him sudden and splendid in war paint and feathers. In Osceola's hands was the long gun General Wiley Thompson had given him. At once Tsali Emathla knew what he had to do. To protect his daughters, he lunged straight at Osceola. He heard the sharp crack of the young chief's rifle, and as he fell to the ground clutching his side he heard the tattoo of other rifles behind the trees and shrubs. It took nine bullets to finish him off. When the execution was over, his killers faded quietly into the pines and once again the only sounds were the lapping of river waters and the calling of frogs. The terrified girls stood woodenly alone with their father's body. Then they managed to bury him and fled back to their village where they told Holata Emathla, their uncle, what had happened. Dismayed, Holata Emathla and five other Seminole leaders who had favored emigration along with Tsali Emathla hurried to Fort Brooke, leaving behind them their stores of food and herds of cattle. Fort Brooke officers listened bleakly to Holata Emathla's recital.

He was asking for protection, but could you ever trust an Indian? The officers sent word of the murder to Wiley Thompson. This time Thompson was forced into the realization that it was Osceola who had done it. "The consiquences resulting from this murder," he wrote Washington grimly with his bad spelling, "leave no doubt that actual force must be resorted to for the purpose of effecting removal, as it has produced a general defection." He began to realize, too, that he and his small detachment of soldiers at Fort King were in mortal danger. Again Osceola would come calling, and this time it would not be for polite conversation. "I will use it well," the warrior had said of his rifle. Wiley Thompson remembered, and the remembrance brought a shiver. Hastily he scratched out a message to the commandant of Fort Brooke requesting immediate reinforcements.

Francis Langhorne Dade, now a major, knew the Fort Brooke–Fort King road well. Ten years ago he had led a group of soldiers to reinforce Fort King during a series of Indian attacks on squatters' cabins. He had marched from Tampa Bay at the head of a hundred men and a six-pound cannon. He never doubted he could make the march again. High on his horse Richard III whom he had once raced in a nearby field, the major was a handsome and arresting figure: fair skin, dark blue uniform coat, brass buttons glistening in the sun, the scabbard of a long sword shining at his side. He had been born to command; was he not a member of one of Virginia's First Families? His men all admired his poise. He would lead them safely to the rescue of Wiley Thompson. It would not be difficult as far as the first creek, the Little Hillsborough, which drained a slough called Harney Flat. There would be four crossings in all: the Little Hillsborough, the wide, dark Hillsborough itself, and the north and south branches of the Withlacoochee. The expedition would have to skirt the Green Swamp. They would be in the greatest danger when they crossed the rivers. If the Indians had left the military road's bridges intact, well and good; if they had burned them, officers and men would have to struggle cold and wet from bank to bank in disordered columns and they would have to find a way to float their cannon over on a raft. But Dade was stimulated by the challenge. He was almost jaunty as he rode Richard III back and forth in the Fort Brooke compound on the morning of Wednesday, December 23, 1835.

Most of the men were thinking of Christmas. Some were Irish and Catholic; this year they would miss Mass. Irish private Hugh Peery reflected that life was strange; he had grown up near Hillsborough in County Down, Ireland, where the powerful marquesses of Downshire lived in their stone mansion and from it ruled the subdued, foggy countryside whose grey-greens were so different from the harsh colors of Florida. Here he was at Fort Brooke, and once again a Hillsborough had entered his existence; this was a swift river where parrakeets chattered and painted heathens might lurk. Peery compressed his lips. Why had he ever left Downshire? . . . It had been army pay, of course. Some of Major Dade's men had been musicians in civilian life. But music hadn't been as profitable as military service either; they had come down to Fort Brooke cheerfully enough to mingle with former hatters and hairdressers and tanners and carpenters and shoemakers and the professional soldiers —officers like Dade, Lieutenant Basinger who was from Savannah, and Captain George Gardiner of Washington, D.C., who looked preoccupied because his wife was dangerously ill inside the fort's walls and the surgeon would have to leave her to go to Fort King. It would not be much of a Christmas for Captain Gardiner. The expedition's guide was a slave, Luis Pacheco. At river crossings and on rises in the ground, his would be the first life hazarded as he stepped ahead on lookout duty. Pacheco himself accepted this as inevitable. He knew some Seminole. His master's widow had hired him out to the army for twenty-five dollars a month which she would collect regularly for herself at Fort Brooke. He would be, in addition to guide, an interpreter if they met any Indians. Pacheco walked apart in the courtyard as he would walk on the trail, his shoulders rigid, his eyes distant. The wheels of the cannon carriage rumbled as a group of artillerymen shoved it into place. Above the fort the stars and stripes fluttered smartly in a vivid sky. The weather was cool. Major Dade announced that they should easily make the banks of the Little Hillsborough by nightfall.

Lanky Private Ransome Clarke of New York, a drummer, moved with the army's easy rhythm as Dade led them all away from Fort Brooke through a palmetto jungle and into a piney ridge which Luis Pacheco scouted for Indian sign and found safe. The sun rose high over the unbroken pine forest; perhaps later some of the hundred miles would be hot going. But there was water in Ransome Clarke's canteen, and at the rivers he could replenish it. He was confident as he watched broadbacked Major Dade in the lead of his troops. Major Dade never slouched. Behind, Clarke could hear the snorting of the oxen that pulled the cannon carriage. It was sweaty work for animals as well as men. By noon the army had gained four miles; the temperature had risen to sixty degrees and the men paused for lunch: pork, hardtack, bitter coffee.

After lunch they crossed a marsh, its tough yellow-green grasses motionless as the wind died down. When they were at last approaching the Little Hillsborough and Harney Flat, Clarke watched Luis Pacheco push ahead of the troops to scout the bridge. Had it been left standing? Holata Emathla had said the bridge had been there as he had fled from his village. Pacheco confirmed it, and the announcement was passed down the line. Pacheco also said he had seen Indian tracks. Major Dade nodded, apparently undisturbed. The men would make their camp at the Little Hillsborough's edge, surrounded on three sides by open field. It would be impossible for Seminoles to attack them unseen. That night the soldiers spoke in low voices around their fires under a grove of liveoaks. They made jokes as they readied their muskets. As darkness fell Ransome Clarke was grateful for the warmth of his army blanket. A cold wind had come up. Somewhere a barred owl was hooting; a chorus of peepers answered him. They were all lonely sounds; Clarke listened until he sank into sleep, and when reveille roused him he was stiff from the coldness of the earth. For breakfast there were pork and hardtack and bitter coffee again.

Today Dade's troops would approach the Big Hillsborough by way of Lake Thonotosassa. As they crossed the small bridge of the Little Hillsborough, Clarke found the steady tramp of their feet reassuring. Behind still lumbered the cannon carriage. As morning wore on the air warmed. Large grey rain clouds began massing overhead, and before noon there was a torrential shower. Clarke got soaked. But it had happened to him before. Several times he had carried the mail along the Fort King Road. Experience told him the heat would dry him out by the time he caught his first glimpse of Lake Thonotosassa. Droplets were quivering on the leaves of turkey oaks and hog plums and on high pine needles overhead. Beyond the lake the stretches of pinewoods would continue until they gave way to the Big Hillsborough's hammocks. There the army would spend Christmas Eve. Ransome Clarke wondered if General Thompson was celebrating at Fort King. Probably; so far the Indians were leaving the army unmolested, doubtless for reasons of their own. They were deep; it was hard to understand how their minds worked.

As a scarlet sun dropped behind jet leaves the men found the carcass of a cow. Clearly, Seminoles had been here. Dade ordered his column to move on, but by the time they reached the river it was almost too dark to see the carboned logs of its burned bridge. The river would have to be forded in the morning. The Seminoles had been here too. The army fanned out in the woods to fell trees for a protective stockade. They were more than twenty miles from Fort Brooke now. In the distance rapids gushed. As usual, owls called; or were they owls? In one way it was a desolate Christmas for Ransome Clarke, but in another it was not; there was the fellowship of the men, the bond of danger they shared. In the firelight tonight their faces were streaked with dirt, their eyes tired. But they still made jokes about sore feet and itching redbug bites and army coffee. Apart from the rest hunched Luis Pacheco. The black man knew enough to keep his distance, Clarke noted.

Christmas dawned rainy and raw. The river water was stabbingly cold as the men ponderously began to wade through it. Some of them lashed pine trunks for a raft on which to float their cannon. They managed to get the gun onto the raft safely enough, but the river's current was unexpectedly swift. It could be a treacherous river. It looked innocent, but its force could sweep a man off his feet even where its momentum seemed slow. Even so, the raft floated across without incident until a detachment prepared to roll the cannon onto dry land. The raft gave an unexpected lurch, and Ransome Clarke heard the splash of the cannon as it fell into the Hillsborough and quickly sank to the bottom. Fortunately ropes had secured it, and a group of cursing privates managed to pull up the cannon once more and drag it up the river's steep sides. One man wrenched his back and fell to the ground with a moan. Quickly the doctor hurried to examine him and shook his head. An injured soldier would be useless. Somehow he must be sent back to make his way to Fort Brooke alone. Ransome Clarke felt sorry for him as he watched him hobble away from the river swearing with the pain of motion.

After the army had made their ford they marched on. Rain was falling steadily now, and Clarke's bones ached with the cold. Pacheco and the detachment's flankers reported no Indian sign; that was something. The tramp of heavily booted feet mingled with the squish of wet leather. Major Dade led the column through a grove of wild orange trees and as the men tasted the fruit they grimaced. It was so bitter it puckered their mouths. Soon they were in unbroken pinewoods once more; here there were few shrubs, only a dense mat of saw palmettoes. In summer palmettoes were notorious for rattlesnakes. Hopefully, though, the snakes had already gone into hibernation. Where were the Indians?

Could they actually mean to let the army pass without a fight? And if so, why? The column passed an abandoned squatter's cabin. Someone had been attacked here by Seminole warriors and had fled. Then the column came on a Seminole encampment and found it deserted, its chikees empty and its fires dead from the sheets of rain that were falling so relentlessly. Pines gave way to the outskirts of the Green Swamp; the Fort King road edged it but never quite got into it. The Green Swamp was the heart of the Seminole kingdom these days. From it the tribesmen might rush out in a painted, whooping body. They didn't, though. The rain streaked on, and rain crows were calling funereally in the cypresses. Christmas night was as wet as Christmas day; the men made a stockade again, and their fires spluttered ominously. Ransome Clarke could not keep warm. The long night was broken only by the arrival of a courier from Fort Brooke. The commandant was sending more reinforcements. Everybody cheered, though they realized the reinforcements would have to proceed at a run if they were ever to reach them.

During the night the rain stopped. December 26 dawned mercifully sunny and warm. Mockingbirds began caroling in the trees, and in the deep forest warblers buzzed in tiny pipes. Still no Seminoles in sight! Pacheco confirmed it after a careful search of the approach to the Withlacoochee River. By noon the men had taken off their coats and were marching in shirt-sleeves. They had left the Green Swamp unharmed and now they were passing through level woods. Even Pacheco's report that the Withlacoochee bridge had been burned was not too discouraging. It wasn't too bad to ford a river in hot weather. But they didn't have to ford it after all, for Major Dade found the frame of the bridge still solid. It needed repairing but not rebuilding. Quickly the men began chopping trees and laying them across the bridge's still intact trestles. They were able to drag the cannon across the logs; the wheels of the carriage groaned. By now Ransome Clarke thought of that cannon with affection. It was security. Indians never had cannons. One more river after this, the Little Withlacoochee, and they would all be well on the way to the relief of General Thompson. At Fort King there would be whiskey and bread that wasn't hardtack and perhaps enough sugar to mitigate the coffee. There might even be a few girls, daughters of homesteading families who had sought temporary refuge from Osceola's anger behind Fort King's walls. But along the way to that haven, Clarke reminded himself, the army still had to trudge through country thick with an understory of twigs behind which crouching Seminoles could hide with ease. Pacheco and the flankers would have their work cut out for them.

December 27 was a Sunday. It began in a sea of freshwater grass; beyond lay Wahoo Swamp. Glassy ponds heralded its beginnings. Still the sounds were men's voices and heavy feet and the rumbling of the cannon carriage and the calls of the forest birds and, occasionally, the terse command of an officer. They were marching north and east now; soon they would turn west, and unless Wahoo Swamp had dried out after the Christmas rains the men would be sinking in slime up to their knees. Would the Seminoles descend then in a cloud of muskets? At the Little Withlacoochee, Pacheco reported that the bridge was out and could not be repaired. Fighting the sharp branches that hugged the river's banks, the men began making their way through them to chop pine logs. Steadily they swung their axes and then heaved the logs into place. Soon they were marching noisily across their bridge and still no Indian attack came. They were going to make it, Ransome Clarke felt almost sure. They still had Wahoo Swamp to get through, but a hundred times the Seminoles could have attacked Major Dade's vulnerable army and had not. Night drew on with an ominous lack of wind. The air turned sharp. There would be a freeze; Clarke dreamed of a cot and a dry blanket at Fort King, and wondered what Osceola's game was in permitting them all to live. Had General Thompson captured him? Where were Micanopy and Alligator and Jumper? Men shifted in their blankets and made sure their muzzle-loaders were close by. A single night heron flew slowly from a treetop to begin his evening search for food.

Reveille woke them all to a freezing drizzle. Mounted on Richard III, white gloves soaked through, Dade inspected his troops. "I can't tell you to place your guns on the cart," he told them, "but since it's raining you may hold them under your coats." They had already passed through the most hazardous country. The need for flankers was past. Luis Pacheco would merely warn them if he sighted Indians from his position in the advance guard. By eight o'clock the rain had stopped and the sun was shattering spent clouds. The men breathed in relief. Ransome Clarke watched Pacheco far ahead as he moved through high grass. Once Pacheco came on a browsing horse, old and bony and obviously Indian. He reported the animal to Dade, but Dade shrugged. A stray horse meant nothing. "Have a good heart!" Captain Gardiner encouraged his detachment. "Our difficulties and dangers are over now, and as soon as we arrive at Fort King you'll have three days' rest and keep Christmas gaily." Clarke saw Major Dade smile at the prospect as he looked back. When the hard report of a rifle exploded the men froze in their places. Then, unbelieving, they marched ahead a few steps until they saw Major Dade's body hunch forward in his saddle and slide in a heap to the moist ground. He was dead; the rifle shot had hit him in the heart.

At once the grass was alive with Seminoles. They vaulted shrilly from their hiding places, their war paint vivid, their rifles ruthlessly aimed. In bursts of gunfire from both sides Indians and Americans began dropping to earth. The acrid smell of powder hung down; the wounded were screaming. Clarke could see Luis Pacheco stretched out in a clump of weeds—dead, hurt, shamming? He heard Captain Gardiner shout at the men to unbind the cannon. In a breathless pause, both sides reloaded their weapons. The Americans began dashing behind pines and grabbing at their cartridges. A dazed artillery team wheeled the cannon into place and began firing it. The first volley boomed thunderously, and some of the wounded began trying to get up and fire their own weapons. "God *damn*!" Captain Gardiner was yelling. "God *damn*!" But no protest could rouse the lifeless body of Francis Langhorne Dade; nothing could change the fact that the army, half of them dead or dying, was outnumbered six to one. Indian shots came from everywhere: grass clumps, palmetto thickets, pines and oaks. Clarke caught a brief glimpse of an Indian he recognized as Jumper. Tensely he wadded his muzzle-loader and fired, but Jumper ducked down unhurt. The shooting sputtered until both sides ran out of ready ammunition. When the Indians began creeping away at last, Clarke stared around him. Everywhere bleeding men writhed on the ground. Were he himself and Captain Gardiner the only ones left standing? Half stumbling, he began taking the weapons of the dead and gathering them into a pile. A few men rose, lurching giddily. Aimlessly they began to fire; the Seminoles had gone, but surely they would return. Some of the less seriously wounded began axing pines and laying the logs in an improvised breastwork. Then Clarke saw a bright flash in the grass ahead—a Seminole turban. The Indians were gathering again. Swiftly he made a decision; he would not go behind the breastwork. The men were building themselves a cage of doom. When they had piled the logs several feet they went inside and once again Seminole war cries shattered the air. The Indians fired at the breastwork, their yells rising.

Clarke felt a knife of pain tearing at his right arm; with his left hand he could feel sticky blood gushing from it. He ran to a tree; a bullet grazed him on the temple, but still he kept firing. The cannon volleys thundered. Then the warriors began aiming at the cannon crew, while the doctor knelt over the dying on every side. The air was heavy with screams and the stench of torn flesh. When the doctor raised his rifle to fire, a shot cut him down.

In spite of the blood that had begun to pour over his eyes, Ransome Clarke saw him fall. Half-conscious behind his tree, he felt the fire of another bullet, this one in the shoulder. Then blood spurted from his mouth; the bullet had hit his lung. He slumped forward, not seeing the advance of a party of Seminole Negroes who were shooting not only at the living but at the bodies of the dead. Those who had no rifles tore into the whites with knives; one felled Lieutenant Basinger with an axe. "What have you got to sell?" the black men hooted derisively as they rifled corpses. Clarke was brought back to a red mist of pain when two Negroes turned him on his side and began arguing with each other. One wanted to stab him with his bayonet, but the other wanted him to die slowly so that he would suffer more. Finally the second Negro poured a rain of lead into Clarke's shoulder, and once more he fainted. When he woke at last, it was dark. Ragged clouds blew across the moon. There were no sounds now but wind and faraway frogs. Dimly Clarke knew that Dade's men were all dead and the Indians had gone away for good, the massacre finished. He tried to move; his right arm and clavicle were broken. His mouth was still bleeding, but he wanted water and with his unwounded arm he reached for his canteen. The liquid was cool and it gave him strength. When he had emptied the canteen he struggled to his feet; blindly, from time to time, he bent down and took the canteens of the dead, drinking greedily the water of the Little Withlacoochee they had crossed the day before. Fort Brooke . . . In a half delirium he began limping from tree to tree until he could feel the military road smooth beneath his feet. Still hemorrhaging, he began walking southwest toward Tampa Bay. Often he fell. Once someone helped him, and he stared up at the bloodied face of a private who had also survived. With morning came the hard pounding of Indian horses' hooves. Clarke ducked in the grass; he heard a shot, a single scream that ended in a gag, and the rip of the scalp from the private's head. Again he was alone. When the Indian assailant had gone he staggered up to try going back to the Hillsborough.

December 28 had also dawned rainy at Fort King. Nervously Wiley Thompson awaited the detachment being sent from Fort Brooke to strengthen his defenses. To distract himself he plowed into paper work; the rain stopped, and the sun began shining on the curved leaves of live oaks beyond his office window. All day long he busily wrote reports and letters. When evening came, he and a lieutenant were hungry and they ate early. They decided to go for a walk; Cuban cigars lit, they started down the path toward the sutler's store. In front of the building they paused in conversation. By the time they both saw Osceola behind the pine it was too late for them to move. Quick charges felled them both. Slowly Osceola started toward the man who had given him the gun he was using. When he came to Thompson's body he stared down at it for a moment. Then he drew a knife from his belt and plunged it into Thompson's heart. Afterward he grabbed Thompson's grey hair and neatly severed his head at the neck. In Wahoo Swamp he would meet Jumper, whose assignment had been Major Dade.

Night came to the swamp with a cold, thick mist. Veils of it blurred the twilit outlines of cypresses and gums. The braves who were building a ceremonial fire had to rub their hands together to keep them warm, but their mood was exultant. Not only had Osceola killed the Indian agent, but Jumper's attack had also scored. He had even captured Dade's supply of medicinal whiskey. Tonight the Seminoles would have a celebration, dancing and feasting and drinking. Bright in their patchwork they gathered around the high fire when it was lit and roaring and began passing whiskey canteens from hand to hand. Grandly Osceola strode into the clearing, in his hands a pine pole with Thompson's head on top. Around the pole a column of Indians began a heavy shuffle in the orange light. Then one of them paused to launch into a mocking speech, imitating Thompson's slow Georgia drawl: "The Indians who do not go peaceably, the Great Father will remove by force!" All the Seminoles swayed with laughter. Then they drank and danced some more, while high on its pole bobbed the grey head of Wiley Thompson, its unshut eyes staring down at the spectacle beneath. At last Osceola smiled too.

13

The Trail
of Tears

The Second Seminole War ended more than a hundred and thirty years ago. Yet today, along the Hillsborough River, its traces remain. There is something eerie about coming to the long double ribbons at the edge of the Green Swamp which were the Fort Brooke–Fort King Road. A group of historians was able to hike its entire length less than five years ago. Its well-worn sand tracks run parallel and nearly clear. It is true that between the tracks yuccas have begun to claim the road for the surrounding forest, and bordering palmetto and gallberry thickets advance by inches every year. But how has the road escaped being devoured by the rank growth of the subtropics for so long a time, I asked a naturalist of the Florida Park Board?

"It was used," he told me. "U.S. Highway 301 down from Ocala didn't exist until the 1930s; the Fort Brooke–Fort King Road carried traffic. Today a few local people still use it." They are farmers and cattle ranchers reluctant, perhaps, to abandon the familiar security of a path they know for the rushing traffic of a federal highway. The Fort Brooke–Fort King Road is not the only reminder on the river of the war. On my canoe trip with Joe I had seen the protruding log foundations of what I later learned was Fort Alabama, a military outpost built in the spring of 1836 after the Dade Massacre and the murder of Wiley Thompson had shocked America into the realization that the Seminoles were one Indian tribe who weren't going to give up their fight to stay in their homeland. Both massacre and murder were blazoned across the nation's front pages. Generals massed at Fort Brooke: iron-jawed Gaines, Jesup and Clinch and burly Winfield Scott, who took charge as the fort's commandant. Fort Alabama, up river, had a life of exactly thirty-five days, but they were tempestuous.

On March 12, eight companies of volunteers, many of them from Alabama, and two of regular troops marched out from Fort Brooke to build the new outpost. Vividly the men thought of Francis Dade; they had listened to the horrors recited by Ransome Clarke after he had stumbled half dead into Fort Brooke a mass of mud and blood and maggots. Ransome Clarke had survived, as had the private who had wrenched his back and had to leave Dade's army before the battle. So had Pacheco, as a Seminole slave, but no one knew it yet. Clarke had already become a celebrity, and New York lecture agents had approached him about a nationwide tour. But perhaps because he had had such a close brush with death many of the men at Fort Brooke avoided him, afraid that their own luck might break if they acknowledged the possibility of his ordeal. When the Alabama volunteers and regulars reached the Big Hillsborough they began chopping pines for a stockade on its south bank. By March 20, Fort Alabama had been completed, and most of the troops returned to Fort Brooke. Those who remained had to fight off Jumper and four hundred Seminoles when they attacked a week later. The Americans lost only two men; they had built sturdily. But when the news reached General Scott at Fort Brooke he ordered Fort Alabama's immediate evacuation. The Indians were hiding in the Green Swamp and would stay there. Any usefulness Fort Alabama had had was outweighed by its vulnerability.

Fort Brooke cannons

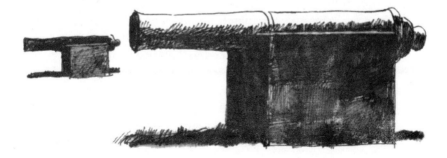

"We had built a magazine of foot-square hewn timber matched close," one of the volunteers wrote home. "One of our company, John Shackelford, got leave to place two kegs of powder and an old musket pointing to it with a string attached to the trigger and to the door, so when the door was opened the gun fired. We left and after about two miles we halted for dinner. When the explosion took place it shook the ground where we were." Jumper lost four of his scouts to the device.

The retreating troops encamped a few miles south of the fort, and again thoughts of Major Dade filled their minds as they stirred uneasily in the firelight, their blankets clammy with spring dew. Marsh rabbits thumped noisily in pools red with cypress tannin. The next day the men got as far as a dense hammock near Lake Thonotosassa and tiny Flint Creek. They were surprised there by a volley of rapid firing; four infantrymen were killed and nineteen wounded. For fourteen hours the firing went on; then what was left of the troops stormed the hammock's depths in a charge of desperation, and the Indians faded into invisibility. There had been a thousand of them; now there were none to be seen, and once more lonely bird calls broke the silence over a smoking battlefield where survivors began to bury their comrades.

In December the army tried once more to build a fort near the Hillsborough bridge. This time General Scott sent Colonel William Foster of the Fourth Infantry, U.S. Regulars; the purpose of the fort would be not only to guard the bridge but to be a supply depot for detachments fighting Seminoles in the Green Swamp itself where Jumper, Alligator, Micanopy, and Osceola were keeping their warriors ready. Vulnerable or not, a fort at the river had become a necessity again, decided Fort Brooke officials. A soft December wind was blowing as Colonel Foster approached the river; here and there a yellow jasmine bloomed. So far there had been no frost; what that would mean to the men of Fort Foster did not at first occur to the colonel. The fort was built on the site of Fort Alabama. Almost immediately its immates began to come down with malaria. The winter continued mild; by June the men were so sick that Fort Foster had to be abandoned as Fort Alabama had been. This time General Scott decided never to try another stronghold at the Hillsborough bridge. Expeditionary troops, however, continued to cross it regularly on their way to the Green Swamp.

To Myer Cohen, a sensitive young officer from Charleston, South Carolina, the Hillsborough River's associations of horror were outweighed by its fascination. In the Green Swamp one twilight he marveled at the reflection of the sky's burnished clouds in the clear water below. That night he stared up at a sky thick with diamonds and thought of a line from Shakespeare: "The stars do wink, as 'twere with overwatching." The next day Cohen and his men came upon a deserted Seminole camp. Here they found a tall orange tree. The sweetness of its blossoms assailed their senses "achingly." The soldiers also discovered "a remarkable pea . . . " Was it native to Florida or had the Spanish introduced it? Myer Cohen did not know, nor do modern naturalists, but conch peas are still sold at vegetable stands near the river and they taste delicious cooked with smoked bacon. The Hillsborough, to Cohen, was "beautifully bordered by varied foliage." He hardly minded the parched corn he and his men had to live on far from the sutlers of Fort Brooke. His language was florid, in the spirit of his age, but he had a sharp eye.

> The rich hammock land, the Magnolia grandiflora, king of the forest; the dark green of the pine, russet-trunked; the pale verdure of the silver shafted water oak; the babbling stream; the proud glories of the lilium superbum; the far reaching prairies of brown and yellow-brown straw which skirt the forest; the sunlit lakes in the center of these prairies—all harmoniously blend in one delightful coup d'oeil. Then the occasional dwelling abandoned; the few rude implements left there; the old chair unoccupied (the back bent, as is common with age), all remind one of similar scenes in traveling through some of the Southern states, where the small farmers have "broken up," as they phrase it, and with stock and store emigrated to the far west.

On the river the scene is repeated today; but the empty houses are those of blacks gone north.

Some of the Seminoles had by now turned as hopeless as Tsali Emathla had been. In straggling little groups Indian families began walking along the Hillsborough down to Fort Brooke. They were the old, the women, the undernourished, the children. At Fort Brooke the army camped them at the edge of a mangrove shallow; for the refugees the Trail of Tears had already begun. Always it was to begin on Tampa Bay; on Egmont Key the army built a stockade where Seminoles were penned like cattle as they awaited shipment out. A large group of Indians was rounded up at Fort King by Lieutenant Joseph Harris, who later reported to his superiors the events of his trip to Oklahoma. On the way from Fort King to Fort Brooke, fifty-five out of five hundred and twelve Indians died of malaria and malnutrition. At Fort Brooke one of the children died. More than half of the remaining Indians were felled by fever on the way from Tampa to New Orleans. From New Orleans to Little Rock, Lieutenant Harris wasn't able to remember much; he himself had been too sick with malaria, and not long after he wrote his account he died.

Lieutenant John Van Horne, in charge of the removal of Holata Emathla's band, kept a diary. In May he led them all into Arkansas where they refused to obey an American doctor and insisted on washing their sick in cold river water. Local farmers objected to the use of farm timber for campfires. Why did Indians need to be warm?

> *May 14*—Issued 4 days' rations of corn and started west 4 miles. Had to go back after four wagon loads of corn and meat, of which there was a surplus because of sick Indians—and dead Indians.
>
> *May 17*—Indians wanted to camp until sick got well. Tried to get more teams but without success. A principal man very low, they begged me to let them stay till he died. He died and was buried.
>
> *May 19*—Hotulge Yohola, Indian doctor, dying. Indians insisted on staying until he died and was buried. Roads deep in mire. Wagons had to be hauled for miles through deep mire, ten yoke of oxen to each.
>
> *May 22*—Started at nine o'clock. Made 10 miles to Poteau river. Road boggy. Poteau not fordable. An axletree gave way. After dark a Choctaw introduced a gallon of whiskey into camp, which I took from him.
>
> *May 23*—A constant scene of vexation and toil. About half the party have been and are still sick. Many continue very low and must die. Three died yesterday, three this morning. It has rained powerfully every day flooding the streams and making the roads deep.... The wife and daughter of Black Dirt, 2nd chief and a principal warrior, have just died. . . .

On and on went Lieutenant Van Horne's recital. "From one, two and three deaths per diem we now have four. The effluvia and pestilential atmosphere of the wagons, where some twenty sick or dying lay in their own filth, and even the tainted air of their camps, is unsupportable." By June 3, Holata Emathla himself had succumbed to dysentery. His body and his medicine bundle were encased in a horizontal wooden pile five feet above the surface of the earth. The neighboring ground was carefully cleared of grass and leaves, and a fire was left burning nearby. Had

Holata Emathla known his destiny even as he ran down the Fort Brooke road, across the river and south to the bay to gasp to the officers his news of Tsali Emathla's killing?

"I have no gun to kill squirrels and birds for my children," one of the chiefs complained in Oklahoma. "No axe to cut my firewood. No plows or hoes with which to till the soil for my bread." Back in Florida generals were now speaking confidently of a "war of extermination" of the Indians for whom the Trail of Tears had no attraction. "I was in hopes I should be killed in battle," Coacoochee, the Wildcat, lamented bitterly, "but a bullet never touched me." And then the Seminoles and Americans alike were electrified by news from the headquarters of General Jesup. During a conference about a possible peace treaty, Osceola himself was captured under flag of truce. In a war of flaming defiance such as he had led, niceties of honor couldn't be afforded. Osceola was thrown into chains at St. Augustine and then shipped to the high security prison of Fort Moultrie, on Sullivan's Island off South Carolina's Charleston Harbor. He was accompanied by Dr. Frederick Weedon, a St. Augustine surgeon, for treatment of the swamp malaria he had contracted. The army considered itself benevolent when a party of officers took him to a Charleston theater to see *The Honeymoon,* a comedy of white domesticity. Charlestonians stared as Osceola entered his box, egret plumes waving from his dark head, his silver gorgets shining brightly in the candlelight. He sat stony faced and did not speak, but something began happening because of the very pride of his silence: an American audience was moved to admiration. Had he not, after all, been defending his own?

The nation's conscience began to grow uneasy. Newspaper editors printed the laments of Seminole chiefs as they were herded togather at Tampa Bay: "If suddenly we tear our hearts from the homes around which they are twined, our heart strings will snap. The river and the bay were our home when the game was plenty and the corn high. If the deer have departed and the corn tassels not, they are still our home." The courageous words of Osceola were recalled: "When I make up my mind, I act. If I speak, what I say I will do. If the hail rattles, let the flowers be crushed. The oak of the forest will lift up its head to the sky and the storm, towering and unscathed." The oak still stood against the storm, but how long it would endure Dr. Weedon, in Charleston Harbor, began to wonder. Constant bouts with malaria were daily weakening the imprisoned chief. The bones of his face were growing more prominent. When artist George Catlin arrived at Fort Moultrie to paint him, Catlin noticed that the daily sittings left Osceola exhausted. He developed a sore throat and had to take to his bed. "Probably," Dr. Weedon confided to Catlin, "he will not live through the winter." The doctor pressed his remedies; but from one of the men at Fort Moultrie, Osceola learned disturbing information. Dr. Weedon was the husband of Wiley Thompson's sister Mary. Was Weedon trying to kill him? Osceola refused to take any more medicines Weedon prescribed for him. Instead a shaman was brought in, and the shaman's chants droned through late autumn nights sharp with chill in the island fortress. Both of Osceola's wives and two of his children were brought to Fort Moultrie from Florida. As he grew even weaker with the "violent quinsy" sore throat, his family kept vigil at his bedside; so did friends he had made among the soldiers who admired his dignity as the Charleston theatergoers had. George Catlin waited in a corner, watching Osceola's struggle for breath and life. On the night of January 27, 1838, he thought Osceola was dying. The shaman intoned his spells; vainly Dr. Weedon and a colleague begged Osceola to take their remedies; his women wept unashamed. But when dawn broke he was still alive. Two days later Catlin left Fort Moultrie believing Osceola would recover. On January 30 the chief made a request. He wanted his war costume.

When his wives brought it, he eased his frail body slowly out of the bed. Then, in a pageant of slow and bitter pathos, he began to dress—his calico shirt, his deerhide leggings and moccasins, his fringed war belt, his bullet pouch and bone powder horn and the high turban with its egret feathers. Beside the bed, on the floor, he laid his knife. Then he called for red ocher. While one of his wives held a mirror before him he began to streak one half of his face, his neck and throat, his wrists and the backs of his hands, and the handle of his knife. Then he placed his knife in its sheath on his belt and sank back to rest. But once more he rose. This time he extended his hand to Dr. Weedon and the soldiers. Wordlessly he shook hands with them all; a gentle smile was on his lips. He shook hands with his wives and with his children. Again he signaled the soldiers to help him into his bed. As he lay silent there, he drew his scalping knife from his war belt. Grasping the knife in his right hand, he laid it on his breast across the left. A moment later he took a deep breath, and died without a struggle. The only sounds from his prison room then were the rising lamentations of his wives. Asi-Yaholo would cry the Black Drink in the Green Swamp no more.

He was buried on Sullivan's Island, but not before Dr. Weedon had taken a bizarre memento. When Osceola had lain motionless in death after his family and friends had left the room, Dr. Weedon approached the body and deftly decapitated it. When he transferred the corpse to its coffin he left the head inside and tied a scarf around Osceola's throat. The people who came to pay their last respects never knew. Just before the funeral, Weedon removed the head and closed the coffin's lid. When he returned to St. Augustine he took the head with him, and made sure of its preservation by an embalming method he had developed himself. Wiley Thompson, after a manner, had been avenged. At home he took to hanging the head on a bedpost in his small sons' room whenever he felt they had misbehaved. Years later, grown Weedons remembered the ordeal with repulsion. Five years after Osceola's death Weedon presented the head to his daughter's new husband, also a doctor, as a token of esteem. The young physician did not keep it long. In the fall of 1843 he gave it in turn to Dr. Valentine Mott, of New York University's medical school. "I am aware," he wrote Dr. Mott, "that the classic lands of Greece and Rome, the isles of the sea, and many a well fought field of Europe, have alike given up their evidences of life, and in your cabinet of heads we travel into the distant past and hold communion with those times that were."

Dr. Mott was punctilious. Osceola's head, he assured its donor, would be "deposited in the collection and preserved in my library at home, for I fear almost to place it in my museum at the University—temptation will be so strong for someone to take it. Your letter will be attached to the head." Fifteen years later the catalogue of Valentine Mott, M. D., Ll. D., Emeritus Professor of Surgery in the University of the City of New York, listed item number 1132: "Head of Osceola, the great Seminole chief (undoubted)." Just after the Civil War Dr. Mott's museum caught fire, and the head of Osceola went up in smoke. Possibly the Weedon family, who were to give their name to Weedon Island when they settled on Tampa Bay, breathed sighs of relief.

For four years after Osceola's death the skirmishes of the Seminole War persisted on the Hillsborough. Chief Billy Bowlegs had inherited Osceola's mantle. "Me whip Governor of Florida and his long knives *damn* quick," Billy vowed as he led bands of Seminoles to refuge deep in the Everglades and the Big Cypress swamp. The army knew Billy Bowlegs' Indians were escaping the threat of deportation, but what civilized man could penetrate the Everglades after them? Once the watery prairies had belonged to the warlike Calusa; now the Seminoles had inherited their fastnesses. The Green Swamp was too close to civilization. Slowly, in dugout palmetto canoes, processions of Indians began floating from the Green Swamp down into the dark hammock and sawgrass thickets where poisonous manchineel trees stood guard. For the refugees English became a forgotten tongue. Even today, many a Seminole woman making patchwork skirts and blouses for fashion-conscious American women speaks only Seminole. Joe Dan Osceola, Osceola's great-grandson, has a college degree and during his recent chieftaincy of the tribe he managed its business affairs with acumen; nevertheless he has not left the Everglades. Retreat had been possible from the Green Swamp, but south of the Everglades lay—and lie—only the ocean and oblivion. This the Florida Seminoles have long understood; in their camps it is a matter of grim amusement that in the last century their status has changed from that of feared peril to tourist attraction.

The drama of Seminole removal continued into the eighteen forties. The stockade on Egmont Key was seldom empty, and from it the weeping-reddened eyes of captives watched for the last time the terns riding the green shallows of Tampa Bay. How many of their Seminole brothers were finding refuge in the Everglades they had no idea. The Indians in the stockade had escaped the spellbinding defiance of insurgent Billy Bowlegs. Now they only hoped the army would keep its promises to them of axes, ploughs, hoes, and stock to be delivered in Oklahoma. Ironically, one of the staunchest pleaders for fair compensation to the Indians was now General Jesup himself, the capturer of Osceola. He had seen too much in the intervening years not to be stirred to pity. He won the friendship of Coacoochee, the Wildcat, whose band gathered on Tampa Bay in the autumn of 1841. Eventually Coacoochee was to begin dreaming of an independent nation for Seminoles and Negroes in Mexico, far from American rule, but when promised agricultural implements for Oklahoma were slow in coming he still had faith in the Indian Territory and he asked General Jesup to intercede for him. When Coacoochee reached his exile the hard winter froze his bones, and through his interpreter he sent Jesup a message: "We are *very hungry* and do not expect to make much corn. . . . All the promises made to us have not been fulfilled." Jesup soon saw that they were; he wrested kettles and shovels and rakes from Washington and from his own pocket he bought Coacoochee a rifle. When Coacoochee returned to visit Florida, he was entertained by Mrs. Jesup and the Jesup children. Back in Oklahoma he recalled the scene with satisfaction: "I send my respects to Your Wife. She gave me a *good dinner!* I remember your children—they can sing! If the Great Spirit will allow me, I shall visit your wife and children again and shall sing to them. This *Coacoochee* says."

On the Hillsborough and the shores of Egmont Key and at Thonotosassa where Billy Bowlegs was still trying to maintain his old home with a handful of followers, occasional Seminole songs could still be heard. Faint fires glowed in chikees here and there. The nutlike smell of boiling sofkee hung over scattered camps. But slowly the songs became fewer, the fires rarer, the tang of cooking sofkee infrequent. The procession of docile Indians to Oklahoma continued until the country of the Green Swamp and the river were almost, though not quite, empty. In the opposite direction, into the heart of the Everglades, went the processions being led to safety by Billy Bowlegs. The Indians were passing. Victorious soldiers at Fort Brooke wondered at their own dawning emotion: they felt deprived. The great days of the fort, the color and tumult of huge Seminole gatherings, the stirring din of battle: these things were over, weren't they? The post which had been the headquarters of the Army of the South began to sink into drowsiness even as the town of Tampa brimmed with the excitement of new settlers and the schemes of fresh real estate promoters. Farmers' wagons rumbled along narrow, unpaved streets laden with produce to be bartered for mullet, which city dwellers found easier to come by than corn. Fort Brooke wives began to occupy themselves increasingly with dressmaking; they made a fresh variety of social occasions for themselves. Their husbands built them a wooden Chinese pavilion on the edge of the bay, and in it they fluttered in their gowns and ruffles at ice cream parties. The men laughed and joked and tapped their pipes on the pavilion's wooden railings where they retreated to smoke together in the evenings. Each knew what was in the minds of the others. Fort Myers, south near the Everglades, was now the important army post in Florida. At Fort Brooke you could listen to the sharp routine of the bugle calls in the morning and evening, you could drill and do paper work and go to all the parties and spend hours fishing in the bay where trading vessel masters wryly complained their passage was impeded by the numbers of fish. The climate remained idyllic, island and bay sands glittered fitfully, inland the forests stirred in tossing winds. But the river and the bay were no longer centers of action, and soon the soldiers began to be bored.

14

"Credit Is Dead and Bad Debts Killed Him"

In August 1842, the Second Seminole War safely over, Congress passed an Armed Occupation Act which brought pioneers to the Hillsborough and Tampa Bay in droves. A hundred and sixty acres in central Florida were announced to be due any head of family or bachelor over eighteen who could bear arms; all he had to do was build a "fit habitation" for himself and cultivate five of the acres for five years. To the ranks of Tampa veterans like Levi Collar and Odet Phillippe, to numbers of discharged soldiers who had decided to stay on, to fishing ranchers and waterfront madams were now added go-getting dreamers of the American dream who began arriving by sea in schooners and sloops and, by land, on horseback or oxcart or—if they were penniless—on foot. The Fort Brooke–Fort King Road saw regular cavalcades; other hardy souls hacked paths far from the highway through the river's forests with machetes, trampling ferns and young cornels as they went. Mule teams pulled wagons laden with household possessions: spool-carved bedsteads from the North, cast iron cookware, a few pieces of blue willow china, spinning wheels and carding combs. Herds of cattle lowed in Tampa streets as their owners drove them along to chosen sites. The few Seminoles still living on Lake Thonotosassa gruffly made friends with the white newcomers. Billy Bowlegs intended to keep his base.

The sandy soil, even where it was enriched by leafmold and pine needles, was stubborn. The settlers discovered that farming methods

145

which had worked in the North would not work on the Hillsborough. As soon as you watered the ground, for instance, it drained itself as the water seeped through the porous limestone beneath the surface to be caught in underground caverns. In summer there was so much rain that vegetables turned black with molds their growers had never seen before. Fungi flourished on corncobs; nematodes burrowed into the roots of fruit trees and killed them. Beets and potatoes could not be grown in the heat and rain; they rotted away before they could be harvested. Lettuce and collards, too, had to be grown in the cooler months, and then the problem was not rain but drought. The homesteaders' wives filled out lean rations with starchy dumplings and rice dishes. They cooked squirrels and raccoons their husbands brought them and made salad of the palm hearts they called swamp cabbage. At harvest time they pickled and salted furiously; half the time the pickles rotted no matter how salty the vinegar brine in which they were packed. The women discovered tropical foods like mangoes. They made cornbread more substantial by adding pork cracklings to it. But there was one luxury most families hadn't often enjoyed in the North: oranges. Many farmers abandoned vegetables for citrus, and successful planter Odet Phillippe was courteously helpful when he was asked about his grove methods. Spanish fishermen taught the Americans to cook chicken *pilau,* with celery and rice. People who couldn't pronounce it called it chicken purlow, and central Floridians still prepare the dish. Merchant ships from Jamaica brought ginger roots; the women baked them into cakes and topped them with guava syrup.

Along the river American log cabins began to rise in fresh clearings. But here the roofs were of palm thatch, not the cedar shakes of the North; window shutters were kept closed in winter and thrown open in summer, when they banged at the timbers during cloudbursts too torrid in which to bolt them. Flies and mosquitoes swarmed; fevers and malaria were commonplace, though no one knew their cause. "Muschetto netting" was a popular item at Tampa's newest emporium, the Blue Store; mosquitoes were not considered carriers of disease but their stings made humid nights sleepless in the rainy season. Sometimes, when rest was impossible, the women stayed up to spin and card wool for winter. Nobody wore shoes except during freezes. Cooking was done outdoors; the heat of the fire was unbearable in the house. Every fall mules turned sugarcane mills which ground out the syrup used on coarse grits and pancakes.

The forest was frightening to lonely wives and daughters at its edge.

Wildcats and panthers screamed to terrify them at night. Wolves howled; bands of them still roamed the woods unchecked. When the tattoos of marsh rabbits disturbed the darkness the women at first did not know what it was. On the shore of the bay another noise reminded Tampans of the roar of surf: mullets, frantic in their attempts to escape pursuing sharks and porpoises, jumped high over the waves croaking in fear. For humans, too, the bay had its hazards. In a tropical storm which swept inland from its shores, planter Hector Braden was returning to his fields one evening; when he tried to ford a creek, his horse stepped into quicksand. Both he and the horse were drowned; a few days later a party found Braden's body still upright on the horse; "his eyes were wide open," one imaginative witness reported, "and in his hands were clenched the bridle reins and his riding whip." The surviving Bradens had grand ideas; when they replaced their pioneer cabin with a brick plantation house they christened it Braden's Castle. Nearby, south of the Hillsborough on the shores of the Manatee River not far from its entrance into Tampa Bay, Robert Gamble, a grandee who had once owned a now-defunct Tallahassee bank, built a mansion in Greek Revival style with tall pillars and high, spacious rooms. Gamble slaves burned bay oyster shells into lime and mixed it with sand, water, and scallop shells to make bricks like Braden Castle's which were as hard as stone when they dried. Inside the Gamble mansion candles fluttered in their sconces; slaves sang African work chants as they toiled in Gamble fields. The Bradens and Gambles, however, were exceptions to a homely rule. Most of the settlers had few slaves, and Tampa had no rigid plantation society to amuse itself with tournaments borrowed from the pages of Sir Walter Scott. The southern legend never fully flowered on the Hillsborough. This was not cotton but cattle country, and the settlers who had driven in stock from other states or taken confiscated Seminole animals avidly increased their herds. Slowly their town became a livestock trading center. "A head here is worth four in your home state," hawkers vowed to the latest arrivals. On the Hillsborough a healthy cow brought the fine sum of ten dollars; if a river rancher shipped his cattle to Cuba, however, he could sell the scrawniest of range cows for at least thirty. Florida cattle farms were never fenced; open range became a state tradition. The river land was choice pasture when it was cleared; even today the cattle ranches remain, though their owners nervously eye the spreading boundaries of the metropolis to the southwest.

Three of the men who were to become Tampa patriarchs came during the eighteen forties. Each of them helped to make it the boom town it became. Archibald McNeill was a Scotsman who had sailed around the world. Tampa Bay appealed to him more than any other port had done; in time, if only the government would release the land still held by sleepy Fort Brooke, he envisioned a Utopia, and he began to acquire all the deeds he could. Frederick Tresca was a Frenchman from Dunkerque who had no intention of letting Odet Phillippe keep Napoleon all to himself. "I was a cabin boy on the ship which conveyed Napoleon to Torbay on his way to St. Helena," Tresca announced. In his sea life he had learned five languages; now his sloop the *Margaret Ann* plied the Gulf Coast from Cedar Key down to Key West. He technically turned homesteader and took out American citizenship, but he followed the career of master mariner to build a thriving coastal trade.

From Thurso, in Scotland's County Caithness, came James McKay, who had become a master seaman before he was twenty-five. In Edinburgh McKay had fallen in love with sixteen-year-old Matilda Cail. Her mother disapproved, and took Matilda to America where she settled in St. Louis. Immediately McKay followed the Cails; "Madame" finally relented, and she accompanied the young couple when they moved to Mobile. There McKay opened a general store, but he soon decided that better opportunities existed at Tampa, which Alabama veterans of the Second Seminole War were constantly telling him about. McKay chartered a schooner and moved south; north of Tampa, the same storm which killed Hector Braden on his horse raged at the schooner until its weakened timbers gave way. McKay and Matilda swam to shore, and so did the formidable Madame Cail. She was still with them when they arrived at the mouth of the Hillsborough; with her son-in-law she began investing in what downtown Tampa real estate was left. McKay bought a schooner which, with fine impartiality, he christened the *Sarah Matilda* after both women; in it he began making trading runs to New Orleans. Soon he was buying two steamers, and at a federal auction in Key West he purchased a condemned slave ship appropriately named the *Huntress.* Another steamer, the *Magnolia,* became his cattle ship; when bulls, cows, and heifers were sent to Havana they usually made the journey on vessels of the McKay line.

McNeill, Tresca, and McKay were empire builders. When the aristocratic Gambles were engulfed by debt, Archibald McNeill bought their mansion. Tampa bustled with the excitement of the captains' ships coming and going. It was still only a village, but some day the government would surely succumb to pressure brought by the trio to open up Fort Brooke. Inside the fort's gates, on radiant nights, the soldiers built fire platforms of pine logs and sand; flames flickered along a parade ground festive with the camp's perpetual parties. On gala occasions the soldiers threw wads of paper and resin into the sky; the humidity always put the fireballs out before they fell back to earth. Nearby a party of Tampans built a long swimming and fishing pier. The night in 1845 when Tampa celebrated Florida's entry into the Union as a state was particularly gay. The fort band played, fireworks soared overhead, and the waterfront Chinese pavilion was decked with lanterns. McKay and Tresca and McNeill ships rocked gentle at their wharves while fifes and drums amused troops and townsmen alike.

"Tampa is a neat little village," pronounced a visiting Englishman. At the fort he was charmed by the appearance of the garrison with its white-washed buildings and its grassy parade ground; around the cottages in which the officers and their families lived grew rows of orange and lime trees thickly covered with golden fruit. In front of the barracks the "noble group of liveoaks" still offered shade from the sun's scorching. There was a quiet and "sylvan beauty" to the scene curious in a military establishment, the vistor thought. The quiet wasn't disrupted by the occasional visits of stray Seminoles who came to the fort to trade. At nights they might stage an "Indian ball" in the courtyard there and drink and dance under military supervision. The evening usually ended with a war dance; it was all very tame. The war was over. Nobody worried. Fort Brooke soldiers helped a party of Tampans build a bridge upriver at what had been Fort Foster; downtown a ferry at the foot of Lafayette Street began carrying passengers and goods from bank to bank. A few rugged individualists decided Tampa was not to their taste and joined old Máximo Hernández on the Pinellas peninsula. One couple built a hut on Terra Ceia island, and later a cabin of cedar logs and clay bound with Spanish moss. The house's mistress, Mrs. Joseph Atzeroth, was content with a chimney made of sticks and mud, but she imported glass windows from New Orleans. Then, with new respect, people called her Madam Joe. She and her husband raised truck crops they shipped to Fort Brooke thirty miles across the water. In 1847 Fort Brooke's numbers briefly swelled. It became a point of departure for troops going to fight in the Mexican War, and the outpost was lively again with blue-clad officers whose gold braid glittered as they marched in stiff columns. This war was too distant for Tampans to take seriously; instead they kept badgering the government to release its grip on federal land. They wanted their Eden to expand. When calamity came it was neither military nor governmental. Nature proved even to the most sanguine Tampa boosters that it still governed river and bay destiny.

On Saturday, September 23, 1848, the skies were leaden. Low tide on the bay was unusually low; sand dollars and spiny sea urchins lay exposed on the flats, and marine worms tunneled in deeper beside them. By Sunday the rain began; a high east wind started lashing Fort Brooke. Shutters banged drunkenly on the hospital and commissary buildings, on warehouses and stables. Objects the soldiers had thought securely tied down—wagons, saddles, blacksmiths' tools—began sailing through the air and lodging in the tops of bending oaks. In the midst of the tumult a lookout sighted a schooner rocking in the bay. It was bringing the soldiers' payroll, he knew. A cry went up in the fort; a crew boarded a tipsy sloop on the river and managed to get out to the schooner, to which they threw ropes. After breathless hours both schooner and sloop put in at the fort dock. On Monday the wind of the hurricane shifted to the south. Torrents of rain swept earth and buildings and ships and horses ahead of it in wet sheets. The wind was blowing Gulf water into the bay and from the bay it blew the spume farther north. Gargantuan waves roared at piers. Whole islands were inundated. Men could not stand erect in the blast; whenever they had to go outside, they crawled, clutching at grass and weeds and shrubs. The commissary building was finally swept loose from its foundations and crashed into the sutler's store; both buildings were forced by the wind and the rain up the Hillsborough. Refugees began crawling to the solid house of Captain McKay, who had built to withstand tropical storms as others had not. The schooner carrying the army payroll lurched back and forth; finally wind blew the hull of an abandoned sailing ship into her side and broke her cables. The schooner, with its own crew and the payroll still on board, careened into flooded pinewoods. Liveoaks swayed and then crashed down. The terrified group huddled in McKay's sanctuary began to pray. Ceaselessly the wind screamed on as it drove the rain horizontally. It did not begin to subside until late Monday; the eye of the hurricane was passing. Then both wind and rain redoubled their fury until the final lull began to fall and dazed Tampans gaped as they stared around them and smelled the bodies of rotting fish. A few enterprising citizens found some barrels of whiskey from the sutler's store floating in what had been streets. They tapped them and in their despair they got gloriously drunk.

"What a scene of destruction Tampa is," the fort chaplain's daughter wrote to her sister.

> There are but five habitable houses left and these more or less injured. The water rose twelve feet higher than it ever has been known to rise before; at one time it rose five feet in fifteen minutes. The row on which we lived, the Chapel, the Commissary building, the Sutler's store, Mr. Allen's house—all gone! Not a vestige of them remaining, and in their place for two or three miles up the river are piles of rubbish, leading one to ask, "Where did it all come from?" Mr. Clark's schooner lying at the wharf was carried way above the Lime Spring and nicely lodged some distance from the shore. Mr. Allen remained in his house till the lower story gave way, sliding the upper one down to a level with water in which he was obliged to wade up to his armpits some distance in order to reach dry land. He saved nothing, not even a change of clothes—money, papers, everything gone . . . There are a great many families without even a roof to cover them, stripped of everything. Everywhere may be seen the same destruction, and could you see it you might well say, "Tampa is no more."

The only comfort Tampa had was that no lives had been lost. Soon the beleaguered citizens began building makeshift thatched huts; as they worked they had to shoot hordes of rattlesnakes which had been driven from their burrows. The bodies of dead chickens, pigs, and cows stank under what had been foundations. A message from the payroll schooner in the pinewoods was heartening, however; the food on board was intact, and so were the money and the crew. Military and nonmilitary divided it up as fairly as they could, and began taking inventories of possessions which had been saved by being blown into wind-tangled treetops.

Out of the tragedy came a second boom. Almost immediately, as news of the disaster spread to surrounding states, carpenters and brickmasons and painters began turning up asking for work. Tampa had to be resurrected. Many of the most recent wave of newcomers decided to stay. Every Saturday was market day for backwoods families hoping to sell the latest arrivals their produce. In a few weeks, Tampa's mucky little streets were teeming once more. Snuff-dipping Crackers milled with cigar-smoking slaveholders in front of construction sites. The department store of Robert F. Núñez rose proudly to carry "all human needs from the cradle to the grave," including General Concha cigars and Green Head Whiskey and French Brandy. For boys' knee pants Núñez charged thirty-nine cents a pair; Tampa mothers fumed at the inflated price. Patrons who didn't want to buy their liquor legally from Núñez could buy it illegally from José Vigil, the moonshine broker, who sported a vest as long as his coat, a huge watch and chain, and pockets full of jingling silver. His fierce eyes and bushy moustache were intimidating, but Christmas proved that his heart was golden. In front of his establishment be erected a nativity scene, and to the building fund of the Catholic church he gave fifty dollars. Virgin mother and virgin brew, to José Vigil, were never incompatible.

And then Tampa heard that a handful of Seminoles downstate had killed an Indian River planter. No matter that there were less than four hundred Seminoles in all of Florida. At Tallahassee, the legislature began clamoring once more for Seminole removal. The local chief concerned in the slayings, Assunwha, made quick reparation; he put one of the murderers to death and brought the others in to federal authorities. But the state legislature was adamant. The Seminoles must leave Florida.

"We did not expect this talk," Assunwha replied. "When you began this new removal matter I felt as if you had shot me. . . . When a few bad men broke the law—a thing that can't be prevented among any people—did we not hasten to make atonement? . . . I will not go, nor will our people. I want no time to think or talk about it, for my mind is made up."

Someone in Washington had a bright idea. Hadn't Coacoochee, the Wildcat, and General Jesup become friends? Why not send Coacoochee from Oklahoma to talk to Chief Billy Bowlegs and tell him about the wonders of the prairie? When Billy heard about this proposal, he held his breath for a long moment. Then, with slow deliberation, he gave a cryptic answer. "Wildcat is my great friend! Tell him not to come into our country until I send for him."

What was needed, Washington authorities decided, was to show Billy Bowlegs the superior might of the white man's civilization. Accordingly they invited him on a tour of eastern seaboard cities, among them Washington and New York. Billy accepted; he enjoyed traveling, especially when he was entertained sumptuously and treated as the dignitary that he was. At hotels he was duly registered as Mr. William B. Legs, and graciously he acknowledged the greetings of the Yankee curious. It was a great disappointment to his escorts at the end of the trip when he told them he had enjoyed the adventure but he didn't think much of American civilization after all and preferred being a Seminole in Florida. "The settlers want the Indians removed," editorialized a north Florida newspaper, "but we cannot afford to evict the Indians or start a war. If it cost the United States government thirty million dollars to whip and ship one half of the Seminoles west, what would it cost the state?"

In the late summer of 1850 a boy named Daniel Hubbard was found murdered up the Hillsborough. Immediately the Seminoles at Lake Thonotosassa were blamed. Vigilantes caught three young Thonotosassa braves and hauled them into Fort Brooke. Before their trial their bodies were discovered one morning hanging limply from high trees over the parade ground. The army said it was suicide, but Billy Bowlegs did not. He said it was lynching, and he took the cue to round up all of Thonotosassa's Indians and lead them south into the Big Cypress.

With Billy's band gone, Tampa's boom accelerated. The Orange Grove Hotel rose to accommodate touring promoters. Speculators and confidence men moved in until one exasperated merchant put up a sign: "Cash or country produce only, as credit is dead and bad debts killed him." Since Tampa was still rising like a Phoenix from the hurricane, its artisans had a lot of cash; it was the newly established banks which were extending loans to citizens who needed them. The *Tampa Herald* began publication near the pillared courthouse rising on Lafayette Street; soon it changed its name to the *Florida Peninsular*. At Pass-a-Grille beach, on the Pinellas peninsula, a newcomer discovered a freshwater well. He was John Gómez, in the past the pirate patron of Odet Phillippe. Gómez forsook his pillaging to build picnic tables and benches at Pass-a-Grille, and soon he was advertising that he was the proprietor of an ocean resort. Phillippe endorsed him with enthusiasm.

To everyone but Phillippe, John Gómez was a mystery. Tales began to fly. He had murdered someone in Cuba and had had to run for his life. There was a price on his head for smuggling. He had been a desperately wicked privateer. He never denied his piratical past; he was proud of it. He had even sailed, he told wide-eyed listeners who came for entertainment as much as picnics, with the terrible José Gaspar, the scourge of the Spanish Main. José's villainy was common knowledge; he had named Sanibel Island near Fort Myers for Saint Isabella, for he was religious, but Captiva Island he had christened because it was where he

kept all the women he had kidnapped. José Gaspar's legend soon became
a staple of Tampa folklore. Gasparilla, people dubbed him familiarly
with the Spanish diminutive. When anyone gave his neighbor a dark
scrutiny it was duly noted as a "Gasparilla look." John Gómez was
patronized at Pass-a-Grille as the romantic "last of the pirates," and when
his patrons asked for further anecdotes of Gasparilla he obliged with
gusto. Every year, under his care, Gasparilla got a little fiercer and his
imprisoned harem a little more beautiful. The reign of John Gómez as
the peninsula's first huckster came to an end only when he shot and killed
a man in a Tampa bar in a dispute over a woman. Then he vanished south
into the Big Cypress and was not heard of until almost two decades later.
But when he emerged from his exile, he was still full of Gasparilla stories
and at last he became, like Gasparilla, a local institution.

Tampa attracted its share of clergy and they began building churches.
A military visitor to Fort Brooke named Thomas Jonathan Jackson, not
yet "Stonewall," gave a donation to the Methodists. But Tampa's reputation was far from pious. It was a "sporting town," addicted to rotgut
liquor and gambling dens. "Disorderly and uproarious conduct" was a
common charge. On one occasion a grand jury brought in an indictment of
fifty-five Tampans who turned out to be leading citizens and a substantial
part of the town's population. Hastily the court pronounced "not a true
bill." After that such unlikely names as Miranda and Leonardi were
found on the roll of donors to the Baptists. But nothing quenched the
gambling. "On our return from the garrison," wrote an officer who had
been inspecting Fort Brooke, "we missed our way and went into a place
that had a light in it and there saw a long table with a miscellaneous
crowd—soldiers, Negroes, etc.—seated around it playing Keno."

> A man at the table turned around a calabash filled with numbered
> blocks, and at each revolution drew out one of these blocks and called
> out the number. The players were furnished with cards bearing different
> combinations of numbers and as any block was called that was on their
> card they would mark with a grain of corn, and the one who had his
> card filled first would call out "Keno!" and take the money staked, each
> player having put up ten cents each. The banker paid himself by a
> percentage of the amount staked on each game.

There were various ways of raising gambling funds. "No mail delivery today," the *Florida Peninsular* might casually report. "The post
office of Tampa was broken open last night and robbed of all the letters

on hand. The object of the thieves must have been to secure money." In another column readers might see a "Found Dead" item: "The body of a man was found hanging in the suburbs of our city. Various rumors are afloat that he may have committed suicide professionally, as the tree was near the racetrack. However, the jury of inquest has declared that he was hung by persons unknown." The stand of the *Florida Peninsular* was strongly anticrime:

> Our city is now infested with light-fingered individuals who are making nightly demonstrations of their skill. Just last night Captain Cooley's store was entered and robbed of all accessible money, and last Thursday night a man was found concealed in Mr. McCarty's store. We understand a vigilant police force is to be kept out during the nights in the future.

But there had been trouble in paradise from the beginning; Tampa citizens were having to be only as wary as the conquistadores had been centuries before them.

Schoolmasters began to arrive along with the pickpockets and they began waging a war of their own. "Tampa people are people for novelty," said a bemused parent. "When any new school starts they are for sending their children to it if for nothing else but change. There was a female school established here not long since and Mr. Glover's patrons have been so high-headed and foolish as to forsake him. He says that he will stick it out for this year and no longer. He will not teach the Tampa people after this year for they have treated him shamefully." But social amenities were encouraged. "Do you still have female prayer meeting?" a Tampa housewife's erstwhile guest inquired. "Has Mrs. Fatty Jones paid her promised visit yet?"

Billy Bowlegs and his tiny band of Seminoles in the Big Cypress seemed remote. When the Tallahassee legislature began to talk of draining the Everglades for truck farms new agitation for Indian removal stirred. A persuasive agent managed to spend forty-eight thousand dollars bribing thirty-six Big Cypress Indians to move west. State surveyors entered the outskirts of the swamp; Billy Bowlegs protested to the War Department and it scolded Florida for stirring up the natives but did little else.

One day a party of engineers discovered an extensive stand of bananas on Everglades boundaries, and a chikee of such size and ceremonial decoration that it obviously belonged to a chief—probably Billy Bowlegs himself. "Let's tear the hell out of his garden and see what he does!"

one of the engineers shouted in a frolicsome mood. The others bellowed their assent and began stooping to uproot potatoes and tear pumpkins loose from their vines. The entire planting of bananas they slashed to pieces. They were still at their work when Billy appeared. He demanded that they leave, but not before he had been paid for his losses. The engineers howled at the joke. One of them tripped Billy and he fell to the ground. When he climbed to his feet, his face was smeared with Glades muck. For a long pause he stared; then, silently, he disappeared into the brush. That night Indians charged the engineers' camp, wounding several and killing two. Over a banana patch, the War of Billy Bowlegs had begun. Once more shrill Seminole cries resounded in Florida wilds, and pioneers nervously looked toward the walls of local forts wondering when they would have to take refuge inside.

The *Florida Peninsular* expressed the general feeling of outrage:

> The Indians have violated every treaty and now occupy no middle ground. They are in an open state of hostility, and hurl defiance into our very teeth. It is high time the United States Government, which is the boast of every American, a government which has the fear and respect of all civilized nations, should assert her supremacy in her own territory and teach these marauding outlaws that they have rendered forbearance no longer a virtue, and administer rebuke so richly merited that will rid Florida of this non-amalgamating and dangerous population and enable her to stand out renewed, invigorated, and regenerated to compete with her sister states.

The Seminoles' response to this was to "lose all reason." They began burning and pillaging once more; state volunteers built a network of new outposts. A band of Indians wandered north from the Big Cypress and attacked Braden's Castle. This so terrified Tampans that they forted up their wives and children at hurricane-dilapidated Fort Brooke for months in the spring of 1856. In June the Seminoles killed a squatter near the Peace River to the south. Tampa merchants were vocal. Not only was there now the Indian menace, but a renewed one of "predatory interruptions by small piratical privateers from Cuba and Mexico under pirate flag at whose mercy the village now finds itself." Tampa preferred its pirates legendary. If the sound of danger was not a Seminole whoop, it became in the imagination of many a Tampan nurtured on Gasparilla tales the sinister flapping of the skull and crossbones.

Ten companies of state militia gathered at Fort Brooke. The trouble, their commander found, was that Billy Bowlegs' War was mainly one of raid and chase; when there were no Seminoles in the vicinity of Tampa itself militiamen didn't take the war seriously. They kept returning to their farms to cultivate crops. Many thought their women at home needed more protection than Fort Brooke did. But there were heroes—Andrew Canova, an Italian from the east coast, had settled in Tampa and now began patrolling Florida from the Kissimmee River far down into the Big Cypress. Ceaselessly he chased Billy Bowlegs and portaged a canoe on lonely, unnamed Glades rivers while Seminoles hiding in the reeds watched. Wiry Tampan Jacob Mickler commanded "a sorry looking set of ragamuffins" that became far more efficient at Indian hunting than had their more elegant counterparts in the official state troops. Mickler, splendid in a denim shirt and sky-blue overalls and a broad-brimmed white felt hat and high snakeskin boots, rode in front of men who were shaking with malaria and ague as they marched; others had faces yellow from jaundice. Their horses were "wretched looking beasts . . . both men and animals appeared as if they were in the last stages of consumption. Coming into the village from the east they resembled a ragged funeral procession." But that procession knew how to fight Seminoles on their own ground, which is more than most raw Florida recruits did. Had the Seminoles not been a ragged remnant themselves, Billy Bowlegs' War might have been more disastrous. As it was, it was never a war of pitched battles; but that it was a real war nobody doubted. A tiny girl immigrating with her family to Tampa from the east remembered for the rest of her life their journey by stagecoach, riverboat, and covered wagon. When they reached Tampa they found "only a handful of people" living there, besides the small detachment of soldiers at Fort Brooke. But belligerent Jacob Mickler kept bringing in renegades; on one occasion he and his motheaten lieutenants delivered up forty Seminole warriors. "I will have every Indian captured and shipped out of the Everglades in two months!" Mickler boasted. Yet in two years the Seminoles remained in the Everglades as elusive as ever, and the United States War Department confessed they had "baffled all efforts" to remove them. This time the army offered money to Seminoles in Oklahoma who would journey back to Florida and persuade Billy Bowlegs' band to follow them. There were several takers; the Seminoles of Oklahoma, authorities in Washington pledged, would be a quarter of a million dollars richer if their oratory succeeded in uprooting Billy and his

Billy Bowlegs

guerrillas. In February 1858, the Oklahoma mission entered the Big Cypress; the military force accompanying them waited behind at Fort Myers. Then a soldier saw a flag of truce fluttering in the twilight; soon afterwards one of Billy's Negroes came into the fort. After a month of negotiations and bribes a tired Billy agreed to move. In May, he came with thirty-eight warriors and eighty-five women and children to the Egmont Key stockade, where the steamer *Grey Cloud* waited. By the time his band had boarded it the vessel was badly overcrowded. As it began its journey to New Orleans, an ancient history of fever and pain and death was repeated. When the ship was forced to put in at St. Mark's for fuel, several warriors asked permission to go ashore to gather herbs for the sick. On land, they scattered into the marshes and began a long trek back to the Big Cypress. Billy, wise and beaten and fatalistic, remained on the *Grey Cloud* because he had given his word of honor to his Oklahoma brethren who needed money. In Washington, President James Buchanan sat up late in his White House office reading report after report on Seminole removal. It was a sordid business, he concluded. It had been bloody, expensive, and heartbreaking, the worst Indian trouble the United States had ever had. Since Billy had surrendered the War of Billy Bowlegs was over; a gesture would be politic. Buchanan made up his mind to ignore any Seminoles who might be left in the Big Cypress. There were too few to be aggressors any longer, and now they had no chief.

At Tampa the Seminole menace was succeeded by another. During the summer after Billy Bowlegs' departure, a ship docked in the bay carrying yellow fever. Soon Tampa was melancholy with the rhythm of jolting iron-spoked wheels on death carts, and makeshift infirmaries were echoing the strident cries of delirium. Not until frost did the fever abate. Soon another disaster came.

During the boom Tampa citizens had circulated enthusiastic rumors of a projected railroad. Had not Florida Senator David Levy Yulee, an industrialist and sugar planter as well as a politician, promised the west coast its own line? The state of Florida gave him a charter providing for a right of way from Fernandina, where Gregor MacGregor had once yielded to fantasies of empire, down to Tampa Bay. The state guaranteed the interest payment on the bonds of Yulee's railroad; the Senator promised tantalizing land compensations to cooperative property owners yielding up tracts he needed for railroad connections to the north. Tampans began envisioning a mammoth national trade in cattle and citrus and tropical fruits; imported northern tools would come to them in turn. The latest agricultural machinery could be acquired for such stubborn sands as those on Terra Ceia Island and the Pinellas peninsula; a few families still struggled there to establish themselves securely. Gandy dancers finished the laying of mile after mile of track, and the musical chinking of spikes resounded through the pinewoods north of Gainesville, itself north of what had been Fort King. From Gainesville the railroad was to come straight to the mouth of the Hillsborough. And then the *Florida Peninsular* broke a story: Senator Yulee had decided against Tampa after all. He would extend his line to Cedar Key, a hundred and thirty odd miles to the north, because he had real estate holdings there.

Tampa was outraged. A gang of men made an effigy of Yulee out of rags and cornstalks and when they finished it they carried it by torchlight to the grounds of the courthouse. There an audience gathered to watch the effigy hung from a spreading oak branch; the flames of the bonfire below crackled upward until they devoured it, and the burlesque form of the Honorable David Levy Yulee was nothing but a tiny pile of ashes fluttering down to a carpet of rotting leaves. In the exhilaration of the moment the revelers repaired to taverns, but when sobriety descended the following morning they knew the extent of the calamity their bravado had done nothing to change. How could Tampa be a national port, and the bay a mecca of the world's merchant ships, if there were no railroad to transport goods back and forth? Was Tampa ultimately doomed? How could its people depend only on the Hillsborough and the barges it might carry back and forth? And if commerce failed, what else would bring fortunes into the pinewoods and mangrove labyrinths that now began to seem an eternally hopeless symbol of wilderness on every side? The industrial North never willingly helped southern cities. Tampa had its share of zealous "Southrons" who blamed Yankees for everything not chargeable to Senator Yulee.

Music master James Austin Butterfield, an English lodger in the home of Fort Brooke's current commandant, was not concerned with economics except as they affected the number of pupils he got at the musical academy he had established in the city. Young Mr. Butterfield was in love with a Tampa belle. He had great plans: he would recruit a Tampa municipal band; local wives would sew it uniforms of scarlet wool and gold lace and they would decorate the musicians' hats with egret plumes like

Osceola's. Butterfield intended to deliver plenty of pageantry for the lesson money he got. Patiently he began recruiting artists for his ensemble. "The weird noises which are wafting in on the cool evening air may some day turn out to be excellent band music," noted the *Peninsular,* "but that is hard to believe." Mr. Butterfield's artists proved to be not very artistic. Still he worked at the composition of a ballad he hoped would please his sweetheart when the band played it to her; he gave her the dedication. The lyrics were by George Johnson, an obscure Canadian poet; Butterfield's gentle melody brought them to life, and even today they are inseparable from it:

> I wandered today to the hill, Maggie,
> To watch the scene below:
> The creek and the creaking old mill, Maggie,
> As we used to long ago.
> The green grove is gone from the hill, Maggie,
> Where first the daisies sprung;
> The creaking old mill is still, Maggie,
> Since you and I were young.
>
> . . . .
>
> They say we are aged and gray, Maggie,
> As sprays by the white breakers flung;
> But to me you're as fair as you were, Maggie,
> When you and I were young.

In picnic pavilions along the river, and on the bay at Ballast Point where parties of young people went on calm afternoons to gather agatized coral, Butterfield's strains moved tenuously across the pale waters. White-trousered dandies strummed them on their banjoes, while blushing girls in crinolines sang the phrases Mr. Butterfield had taught them how to enunciate. The nostalgia of the song soon touched the country at large, and James Butterfield was surprised to find himself the composer of an American hit. The chords begun on the banks of the Hillsborough became an enduring national romance.

Romantic, too, in July 1860 on the courthouse lawn, was the Glorious Fourth. Past the city council on their reviewing stand paraded Butter-field's redcoats; half the local militia followed, then the soberly clad city clergy and the rest of the militia, "ladies and their escorts, several societies, assorted citizens, and mayor." There was so much speechmaking that afternoon that the *Peninsular* said it had no space to report it all. In the evening Tampa danced, and a party went cruising in a paddle-wheeler on the bay. The average Tampan that night knew his country was troubled over the slavery issue, and he hoped the Yankees weren't going to elect gawky, dangerous Abraham Lincoln of Illinois to the presidency in the fall, but now citizens felt secure in the very remoteness they had paradoxically wanted Senator Yulee to invade with a railroad. Who needed a railroad anyhow? Wasn't Tampa shipping more than four hundred head of cattle to Cuba each month on McKay ships? In the innocence of its Independence Day revelries, Tampa looked south, not north, for its fortune. Old Glory rippled over Fort Brooke until sunset. Then an honor guard lowered and carefully folded it away. Afterwards, over the river, fireworks soared, and the half-misted moon quietly unfurled itself like a pallid flower nobody noticed, to shine feebly back from a corner of the Hillsborough's rocket-spangled surface of waves.

15

"The Devils
Are Coming!"

On January 13, 1861, the Gainesville stagecoach pulled into the courtyard of the Orange Grove Hotel in a cloud of dust. Quickly the driver
leapt down from his box and rushed to the courthouse with his news:
Florida had seceded from the Union. No longer did it owe its allegiance
to Lincoln, the ruffian Republican in the White House; now Tampa
belonged to the Confederate States of America. When the tidings had
started to spread people began gathering on the courthouse lawn, as
they had done that Independence Day six months before. Mr. Butterfield's band once again began marching down the streets, and super-
annuated cannons at Fort Brooke roared in triumph. That night local
ministers delivered prayers for guidance. The celebrations lasted for
days of rhetoric and rocketry. A company of Florida militia marched
into the fort to hold it for the Confederacy. Sturdy adolescents began
building earthworks at the Hillsborough's mouth. Carts rumbled by with
their cargo of ammunition. Five giant guns dating from Osceola's days
were soon guarding the waterfront as well. When the federal navy
sailed into Tampa Bay to take charge of Egmont Key, nobody worried at
first. Egmont wasn't Tampa. Captains McKay, Tresca, and McNeill
would find ways of running the blockade. The first time the Yankees
on Egmont bombarded the city a shell fell near the blacksmith shop of
Addison Mansell. When Mansell thought the shell had cooled off he
picked it up and poured out the powder from it; then, experimentally,

he poked a hot wire into it. Flames roared up to singe his eyebrows, burn off the front of his hair, and temporarily blind him. He was merely indignant; how dared the Yankees invade his privacy?

It was not that there were more slaves than before in Tampa. The great cotton empires of north Florida were still remote. Tampa even had its racial iconoclast, William Ashley, for whom one of the city's main streets was named. When Ashley died, his mistress, a black house servant, died not long afterwards. Both were buried in the same grave in Oak Lawn cemetery, and the Ashley estate's executor followed instructions in Ashley's will "to commemorate the fidelity which each bore to the other."

> Here lie William Ashley and Nancy Ashley. Master and Servant; faithful to each other in that relation in life, in death they are not separated. Strangers, consider and be wise—in the grave all human distinctions of race or color mingle together in one common dust.

It was not the sexual relationship itself, but the open acknowledgment of it, that was unusual. The tombstone remains, a point of twentieth century pilgrimage. Tampa also had its share of Free Persons of Color. Tampans wanted to fight less for slavery than for independence from a North which was now, to them, irrelevant. Bad enough that they had to acknowledge the control of Tallahassee. Soon all males between the ages of eighteen and forty-five were being drafted; volunteers as young as fourteen and as old as fifty were also welcomed. The Tallahassee legislature passed a law which entitled Confederate troops in Florida to seize beef, corn, and pork and pay for them in Confederate money.

On Egmont, where once the departing Seminoles had wept, incoming Union troops began building a fort. Farther east, on the shore of Old Tampa Bay, rose Captain McKay's new saltworks, which Tampans knew must be protected at any cost. Without salt they could not preserve the meat they needed to survive. Merchants, unable to get stock, closed up shop; Tampa began to look like a ghost town. The proprietor of the Blue Store took to blockade-running along with Captain McKay, and the most prosperous local families were either those whose incomes were swelled by contraband trade with Cuba or those who lived close enough to the wilderness to feed unconcerned on its bounty. On the Pinellas peninsula settled Abel Miranda, a fishing rancher, who found Pinellas "one vast wilderness full of game and varmints." He killed eleven bears and a panther his first year; geese and ducks and turkeys were constantly being felled by his muzzle-loader. He boasted that he never had to go farther than half a mile from home.

Abel Miranda's independence irritated the Union navy. Some of its sailors stole a fishing smack at the Hillsborough waterfront under cover of night and then put out toward their base on Egmont where they took on a cannon. Then they cruised up to Pinellas, and when they were opposite Miranda's rancho they fired. The startled Miranda and his family fled to Boca Ciega inlet for safety; when Miranda returned home he found only smoking ruins. His orange grove had been hacked to the ground. His livestock had all been stolen. The chickens and pigs the sailors had left they had maimed; Miranda had to shoot them to end their sufferings. The Federal raid began Miranda's bushwhacking career as "Miranda the Cat," whose fire repeatedly felled foraging Yankees on shore raids. Once he and a party of rebel cohorts dressed themselves up as slave women and began making enticing signs to the blockading Yankees to come ashore. When several swallowed the bait, Miranda killed them; then he retreated to Tampa to brag about his feat. A Union sympathizer threw him into the Hillsborough, but he was rescued by a black servant and continued a "red-hot rebel." Ultimately he refreshed his immortality by introducing the avocado, or "alligator pear," to Hillsborough County gourmets.

The Sunny South Guards paraded regularly at night by torchlight through Tampa's main streets. Their morale continued high, though the closing of local grain mills had deprived them of breakfast grits. Captain McKay was their hero, and when the war touched him it touched all of Tampa too. In the autumn of 1861 he was commanding his ship *Salvor,* which flew a British flag. In an inlet in southwest Florida the *Salvor,* on its way from Havana with contraband, encountered a Federal steamer. The raiding Yankees found on McKay's vessel two thousand sacks of coffee, four hundred thousand cigars, four hundred revolvers and rifles, half a million percussion caps, and piles of clothing. McKay protested indignantly. The *Salvor,* he claimed, had been sold to British interests while in Havana, and now he was taking it for delivery in Nassau. And what, asked the Union navy, was he doing in southwest Florida if he were on his way to Nassau? McKay replied that he had slaves on board he wanted to unload in Florida; if he took them to Nassau, they would gain their freedom. The Union navy was not convinced; the *Salvor* was sent to New York, condemned by an admiralty court there, and sold. McKay and his son Donald, who had also been on the *Salvor,* were sent to prison. After five months busy McKay attorneys won a hearing with President Lincoln, and the McKays were freed seventy thousand dollars poorer.

While McKay was in prison, Frederick Tresca regularly made the Nassau-Cuba run. The Royal Victoria Hotel in Nassau, stately with wicker, chandeliers, dense palms, and the elusive fragrances of a tropical garden, was a Confederate rendezvous. Rum and fruit juice flowed from its flagons. Nassau reveled in the southern cotton and turpentine the blockade runners brought in. Archibald McNeill, at first, merely delivered the mail from Tampa to Manatee River settlements southward on his sloop the *Mary Nevis.* When the Union navy intervened, he jumped overboard and swam ashore; afterwards he graduated to the Cuba-Nassau run and carried more than mail from his Hillsborough river wharf. He, too, became a habitué of the Royal Victoria Hotel in Nassau. It was a good place to meet fellow Tampans in peace.

To the Federals waiting out their blockade at sea, the winter of 1861/62 was tedious. They wanted action and there was little. Restlessly they began urging Lieutenant Colonel William B. Eaton, their commander, to capture Fort Brooke and Tampa. Privately Eaton thought neither worth the bother; what use was the fort, with its trappings that dated from God knew what bygone Indian wars? But to hearten his men he made for an island in the bay nearer the mouth of the Hillsborough, and from there he sent a message to Fort Brooke's commander:

> Sir: I demand in the name of the United States the unconditional surrender of the town of Tampa, Florida, together with all the munitions of war and ordnance stores contained therein. If these terms are not complied with I will give you twenty-four hours to remove all the women and children to a proper distance and then bombard the town. I have the honor to be your obedient servant.

When the commander declined to surrender, Eaton began his attack. One of his cannon balls ripped a hole in the courthouse wall; another went through the front window of a residence, careened into a hall mirror, and finally dropped on the kitchen floor. A few stray minié balls landed in the courtyard at Fort Brooke. Its chief then sent a bitter message out to Eaton; did the Colonel know he was endangering women and children? "Sir," replied Eaton,

> I regret that my design of commencing an attack on Tampa did not meet with your approval, but I would say that in justification of my course the

threat to bombard the town was an inadvertance and should have read "fort" . . . I have been here with my vessel nearly six months and after a short period of inaction I was naturally anxious to give my officers and men an opportunity to show their mettle and afford them the chance which they so desired of doing something, if ever so little, toward crippling the enemy.

Probably the humor of this put-down escaped the men of Fort Brooke.

The Civil War, in Tampa, lacked dash. Its most stirring hours had been lived by the blockade runners. Optimistic Captain McKay put his ship the *Scottish Chief* back to sea after his release from prison. On black, moonless nights he went out beyond Egmont Key to the Gulf; his crew were forbidden to light pipes or cigars to give the blockaders a clue to their whereabouts. Water lapping at the bow could be a disaster. So could the creaking of cables. Six times McKay glided noiselessly out to Havana and Nassau. When he returned it was always with guns and ammunition and wine and cigars. He was worried, however, about the barnacles which were coating the *Scottish Chief*'s hull. One day he took her up the Hillsborough to be scraped before she took on another load of cotton for Nassau.

Somehow Egmont's Yankees found out about it. They relayed a quick message to Federal troops at Key West, from which a lieutenant commander started north on board the U.S. gunboat *Tahoma*. At Egmont the *Tahoma* was joined by another ship and cautiously the two proceeded into the bay. On October 17 they began shelling Tampa; the militia fled Fort Brooke and civilians scurried into the backwoods. After dark a party of eighty-five Yankees went ashore near Gadsden Point, from which they marched to the Hillsborough. Six miles above Tampa they found not only McKay's *Scottish Chief* but his sloop the *Kate Dale*. Both were loaded with contraband cotton. Quickly the Yankees set them aflame, and the Confederate crew surrendered while hot timbers fell in cascades of flame to the decks. McKay, watching, knew that this time his career as a blockade-runner had been ended. He could not afford to refit. Instead, he began scouring the countryside for supplies for the Confederate Army.

The Yankees were so exhausted by their exertions on the Hillsborough that by the time they reached Ballast Point on the way back to their ships some were having to be carried. Within a mile of the Point groups of rebel soldiers began to appear; unknown to the Yankees, some of the troops commanded by Confederate General Braxton Bragg were searching the Hillsborough's environs for the cattle for which Tampa was famous. Bragg's men were delighted to join the Florida militia and a group of them charged the Yankees on Ballast Point's beach. In the ensuing melee three Union men were killed, twelve were wounded, and three were taken into Tampa as prisoners. The Confederates lost six men; seven were captured, and an undetermined number were wounded. The Battle of Ballast Point, Tampans called it. It was the only real battle the bay and the river were to know during the entire conflict.

When heroes weren't blockade runners they were adventurous spirits like Miranda the Cat and "Old Man" Joe Robles, a foreman at McKay's saltworks. One morning when a party of Union soldiers landed near the saltworks the Confederate troops normally stationed to guard it were away on a foraging expedition. Joe Robles knew he was alone. He fled to a rusty boiler, and from within it he opened fire with his muzzle-loader and began barking out imaginary orders to nonexistent colleagues. Many of his shots found a mark; the Yankees were convinced that they had been ambushed by "a strong force." After several fell, others returned to their gunboat; those who weren't quick enough to get away surrendered. Joe Robles, emerging from his boiler with his gun still in hand, was proud. He was exactly five feet tall and he weighed a hundred and thirty-five pounds. Jubilantly he marched behind his column of six-foot prisoners, their weapons confiscated, until he had arrived at the Orange Grove Hotel. "Viva el Sur!" he shouted in his native Spanish.

Tampa secessionists grew so accustomed to luck like that of Joe Robles that by the spring of 1864 they listened incredulous to the cry of a wild-eyed boy rushing through town to the courthouse. "The devils are coming!" he was shouting. Once again Yankees had landed on the bay shore; two companies of them were marching toward town; the boy had seen them as he squatted hidden in a clump of sea myrtle. He knew what he had to do then. "The devils are coming!" he cried once more. Not a single Confederate soldier in Tampa heard him when he got there; the home guard were rounding up cattle in the pinewoods, and Tampa's recently formed guerrilla band, the Beauregard Rangers, were raiding farms downstate. So it was that when Fort Brooke fell, it fell without protest, mourned first only by old men, boys, and the women who had been using it to house bazaars for "The Cause." At Fort Brooke their Cause came to an abrupt end.

Three gunboats full of white and black marines had landed on an island opposite the Pinellas peninsula. Swiftly they waded through the bay into half-deserted Tampa and took possession of Fort Brooke without a struggle. Then they sent out parties to confiscate cattle, food, the stock of the Blue Store, furniture from the Orange Grove Hotel, and anything else they could get their hands on. One Tampa citizen was unlucky enough to be carrying on his person eighty thousand dollars' worth of Federal bond certificates; he was left only with the suit he wore. At the fort the invaders made short work of their destruction. They hauled out several fifteen-foot brass cannons and scattered them to rust untended on the shores of the Hillsborough. Stockades were pulled down and machine shops destroyed. A group of marines raided the Masonic Hall and stole not only the ritual paraphernalia of the Masons but of the Independent Order of Odd Fellows as well. Tampans smarted under the shame of it and one of them, a carpenter, immediately began turning out ceremonial compasses and trowels. Another of the Federal insults was the lusty singing of Union ballads. "We are coming, Father Abraham!" chorused the raiders, and some of the black marines gave virtuoso performances by whistling war songs in thirds. Then all the Yankees mysteriously disappeared. When the fort commandant returned he could only wring his hands. It was useless; the old cannons that had stood against the Seminoles for so long had been hopelessly scattered. Morale among the soldiers was at a low ebb. After they abandoned Fort Brooke in disgust the Yankees returned. This time they stayed a month; then they concluded as before that Tampa had no real military importance. When they left for good its defenses were a shambles.

On the Manatee River near its entrance to Tampa Bay another drama took place late that summer. The captain of the blockading squadron in the bay was told that Confederate President Jefferson Davis himself owned a large sugar plantation nearby. Gleefully the captain went up the Manatee and ordered his men to put ammunition in the boilers and engines of the Gamble mansion's refinery. Then they set their torches to it; a series of explosions burst forth and the flaming refinery walls swiftly fell into a vivid skeleton. The mansion itself was left untouched; Captain McNeill and his new partner, Robert M. Davis, who was no relation to Jefferson, could only be thankful the damage hadn't been worse. After the raid the Federals proceeded to a nearby gristmill and razed it for good measure.

Captain Tresca's nine-year-old son Willie and several of his friends were catching turtles one afternoon in a pond not far from the bay. One of the boys shouted suddenly, "Look at the Yan-kees!" A patrol was marching north from Sarasota. The boys fled, including Willie, who had been turtle-catching with his pants off. He didn't stop to put them on. "Aim!" he heard the command of one of the bluecoats, and did not know it for the joke it was. As quick as a monkey he dodged behind a liveoak; then he began running once more, trying to remain behind the line of the barrier oak. Through a tangle of scrub and thorns he raced, his bare feet bleeding from the spiny sandspurs thick on the ground beneath. When he saw a herd of wild cattle roaming aimlessly he scrambled to the top of a palmetto; the Yankees marched by, and he was finally able to climb down and make for home. When he got there he found several children of the neighborhood gathered obliviously playing games. But Willie Tresca kept his decorum. Knowing he couldn't appear to warn his family and friends without his pants, he crept through a gap in the rail fence close to the kitchen and whispered hoarsely, "Oh, Mama, Mama! Bring me a pair of pants, *please!*" The Union troops did not stop at the house after all, and an exhausted Willie fell into bed after supper with a resolution never to let the Yankees surprise him without his trousers again. The Civil War had its comedies for the Trescas. Not until after Appomattox did it turn for them to high drama. The Confederate Secretary of State came to them fleeing for his life. A forty-thousand-dollar price was on his head. He knew it. "They will never take me alive," Judah Benjamin vowed, and the Trescas were ready to agree.

16

Mr. Howard

Judah Benjamin's career had been spectacular. "The Brains of the Confederacy," Northerners called him. They were not wrong. While Jefferson Davis's mind could shut like a steel trap against facts he did not want to know, Benjamin's worked resourcefully. He was at once shrewd and accommodating. He had been born in the Virgin Islands and on both sides he was descended from prominent Jewish families. When he was a boy his parents had moved to Charleston, South Carolina, an American center of Jewish culture and tradition. He was precocious; by the age of fourteen he was a freshman at Yale, though he left it two years later under a cloud. He had stolen money, went later Yankee rumors; no one knew the truth but Benjamin, who never elaborated on the circumstances that had caused him to quit the university a junior. His crime at sixteen, if there was a crime, could hardly have been desperate. From Yale he went down to New Orleans, got a job teaching English, and studied French and law. At the age of twenty-three he had published a landmark paper on Louisiana appeals cases, and it made his reputation. After he had served in both branches of the Louisiana legislature he was elected to the United States Senate. He was rich enough to buy a Louisiana sugar plantation by then, the dreaming Grecian Bellechasse under its canopy of wisterias. At Bellechasse he entertained on a grand scale. His wine cellar was famous, and so was the beauty of his Creole wife Natalie St. Martin, with whom he was ardently in love. Through Natalie came the

great personal tragedy of his life. When they both went to Washington ·
people noticed that she was "very, very gay" and "very, very unhappy."
She resented being married to a Jew, she said, although she appeared
to like his money well enough. Statesmen's wives reluctantly called, in
spite of whispered extramarital delinquencies on Natalie's part. "It is
better to call," one of them said tersely, "as a mark of esteem to a statesman of her husband's prominence." Perversely, Natalie Benjamin saved
her dinner invitations for the French legation. Finally, reported Mrs.
Clement Clay, one of the most respectable and "brightest ornaments
of Washington society,"

> . . . Arab-like, the lady rose in the night, silently folded her tent and
> stole away to meet a handsome German officer . . . leaving our calls
> unanswered, save by the sending of her card; and her silver and china
> and crystal, her paintings, and hangings, and furniture, to be auctioned
> off to the highest bidder.

Ironically, the highest bidder was Mrs. David Levy Yulee, wife of the
Florida senator who had denied Tampa its railroad. Natalie Benjamin
fled to Paris with her only daughter, and there she remained; Benjamin
immediately granted her a handsome allowance and whenever he was
in Europe he visited her without rancor. But he was heartbroken. At
first he thought of leaving Washington; David Levy Yulee urged him to
remain, and it was his lot to present what was considered "the ablest
defense of Southern policy" to the Senate in December 1860. But it was
too late for Judah Benjamin's congressional diplomacy by then. When the
Confederate government was formed, Jefferson Davis first made him
Attorney General, then Secretary of War, and finally Secretary of State.
The last promotion he received because Davis felt he had been unjustly
accused by fellow Southerners of being responsible for the South's
military defeats.

As Secretary of State, portly Benjamin worked feverishly for European
recognition; always it was denied. "He is the Poo-Bah of the Confederate
Government," scornfully noted a not very tall caller he had unwisely
addressed as "Sonny" because of his stature. "Mr. B. is certainly a man
of intellect, education, and extensive reading," said another. "Upon his
lips there seems to bask an eternal smile; but if it be studied, it is not a
smile—yet it bears no unpleasing aspect." His presence was "soft and
purring . . . He moves into and through the most elegant or the simplest

assemblage on natural rubber tires and well-oiled bearings." Jewish by blood, was a friend's verdict, English in tenacity, and "French in taste to his fingertips." Too late, complex Judah Benjamin offered emancipation to any Negroes willing to serve the Confederacy. After Lincoln's Emancipation Proclamation, even Southerners regarded this as a bad joke.

On Sunday, April 2, 1865, the Confederate cabinet's "flight into oblivion" from Richmond began. General Lee had sent them word he could hold out no longer; Federal troops were advancing on the Virginia capital. Benjamin was tired and his eyes were smarting as he boarded the train with the rest of the cabinet and a troop of militia at the Richmond depot; he had spent the previous night sorting secret papers, keeping the most valuable and burning the rest. The railroad itself was in bad shape from repeated battles; the train could only crawl along its tracks over broken crossties at ten miles an hour. The Secretary of the Navy, Stephen Mallory, thought he saw Benjamin's deep olive complexion grow shades whiter as the train so haltingly proceeded. But to keep up the company's spirits Benjamin began regaling them with tales of causes snatched from defeats more ominous than theirs. When the train groaned into the southern Virginia mill town of Danville, he found a room in the house of a local banker. There he made a point of attending Christian morning prayers, and with a fellow refugee in idle moments he genially argued the merits of the poetry of Tennyson over that of Dryden. Not until April 10 did news of Lee's surrender reach Danville. Benjamin pondered; then he decided to go on to Greensboro, North Carolina, with the cabinet; there, however, he would leave it.

"How is it possible for you to escape capture?" he was asked. He only smiled, and his questioner noted this time that the smile was pitiless. At Greensboro the townspeople had no welcome for the Confederate cabinet. They put them in a leaky railroad boxcar which a wag dubbed "the Cabinet Car." There Davis and his cohorts lived on a diet of bread and rancid bacon and in spring rains went begging to local farms for eggs. In the dripping boxcar Davis held a final meeting; he and Benjamin alone refused the possibility of surrender. But the only real alternative was continued flight, and both men knew it. Part of the Confederate treasury in gold bullion was sent ahead to Charlotte, North Carolina; some was distributed to the militia which had accompanied them, and the rest was reserved for Davis and the cabinet. Beyond Greensboro the railroad was too ragged for travel. The cabinet had to mount a series of sorry nags which stumbled from mudhole to mudhole. When it was dark Benjamin kept his cigar lighted to herd the party together while he recited Tennyson's "Ode on the Death of the Duke of Wellington" to them:

> A people's voice! We are a people yet
> Tho' all men else their nobler dreams forget . . .
> We have a voice with which to pay the debt
> Of boundless love and reverence and regret
> To those great men who fought and kept it ours,
> And keep it ours, O God! . . .

On and on fell the spring rains. Dogwoods were blooming in the Carolina glens, and wild azaleas turned orange in the hollows. Rain lilies were flowering along the roadside. The smell of fresh-plowed earth reminded the party that life was continuing, that men once more were working their fields. Not until they reached Charlotte did they learn that Abraham Lincoln had been assassinated, that any hopes the South had had for clemency must now be abandoned. Still on horseback, they pressed on through the mud to Abbeville. Davis was still talking of founding a Confederacy west of the Mississippi. Benjamin fell silent. At Abbeville, where he had friends, he left his trunk and with a smaller trunk and the clothes on his back he rode down to Washington, Georgia. "I am going to the farthest place from the United States if it takes me to the middle of China!" he told his comrades wryly. Then he put on goggles, pulled his hat over his face, and decided that if he met anyone he would pretend to be French, unable to speak a word of English. Did he dream momentarily of a refuge with beautiful and faithless Natalie in Paris? Natalie and his daughter would suffer now; for a while he could not support them in the elegance he had always given them. No, he could not go to Natalie. He had his pride, even as a hunted outlaw. Instead, he would try to get to England by way of Florida. His muscles were aching and his legs were saddlesore as he jogged into the pinewoods of its north. One day he stopped at a farm and pretended to be a South Carolinian looking for farm land to settle. The farmer's wife didn't know of any, but promised to make him a homespun suit like her husband's when he asked her; she soon guessed the importance of her guest. Southern newspapers had often carried his picture. She also gave him a mule. On his lop-eared mount, Benjamin pushed on toward the Green Swamp. Whenever he came to a wide road he turned southwest. Rough paths through pine forests and oak hammocks where Seminoles had hidden were the safest. Time after time the mule mired in sloughs. Benjamin took to riding by night and sleeping by day concealed in cane-brakes. When a late afternoon sun broke golden through a fluff of clouds, he turned west to follow it. The Atlantic coast would be alive with Yan-kees, and he must go to the Gulf.

On a dew-fresh morning alive with the rappings of yellowhammers he dismounted at a crossroads. Which way now? He knew he was too tired to decide, so he unsaddled the mule and sank his heavy bulk down to the grass, where he slept fitfully with his hat over his face. In his dream he heard the jaunty rebel cheer he had heard so many times before: "Hi for Jeff! Hi for Jeff!" His lips formed into their character-istic smile. Then his eyelids fluttered. "Hi for Jeff!" he heard again; now the sound was raucously close. Benjamin laboriously got to his feet and scanned the treetops. When he heard the cry once more, he could make out a parrot high overhead on a limb in the midst of a flock of jays. It had surely escaped from a farmhouse; obviously it was a pet belonging to southern sympathizers. Perhaps it could lead him to its owner. Hope-fully, he began pelting it with tiny stones in the hope that it would fly to the place it had come from. It did, and soon he was safe in the house of a Florida homesteader who was aghast when he learned his bedraggled caller was the Secretary of State. There was only one thing to do, said the homesteader. He would go for his friend Confederate Major John Lesley, of Tampa, who could lead Benjamin safely to the coast and a sea captain willing to carry him away in the teeth of Federal patrols.

Late one evening Major Lesley arrived from the Hillsborough at the Gamble mansion with a stout companion he introduced as Mr. Howard. Probably no one was fooled, but Major Lesley was cautious by nature. Captain McNeill, at least—still the mansion's proprietor—guessed Benjamin's identity; he knew there was a price on his own head as well, and already a constant watch was being kept from the mansion's second story for Yankee patrols. Mrs. McNeill conducted Mr. Howard to her best bedchamber, an airy front room on the second floor which led from a narrow vestibule. The shadows of heavy mahogany furniture were sharp against the white walls as sunlight streamed in cheerfully. In the room's southeast corner stood a massive four-poster bed, its scarlet canopy faded from years of use. A rocking chair had been placed beside a table with a frosted-globe oil lamp; Benjamin would be able to read his Tennyson on warm spring evenings. Pleased, he fingered the books on the table: Shakespeare, Byron, Irish Tom Moore. Then he turned to Mrs. McNeill and asked a favor; would she destroy his old caped overcoat? Someone might wonder at its quality in contrast to the homespun clothes the farmer's wife in north Florida had given him.

Little Fanny McNeill was enchanted with Mr. Howard, but her pride was stung when she went up to his room. "Boo," he only muttered at her and closed the door. Afterwards she and her small playmates on the front lawn stared up at Mr. Howard's round figure as he leaned against one of the porch's broad pillars and kept his spyglass trained on the Manatee River. Still the Yankees were cruising the shores of Tampa Bay in their gunboats, Fanny knew. She began to understand too that Mr. Howard was somebody very important, and that he was keeping away from the children because he didn't want them to talk about him. She already knew she mustn't say a word about her own father. One afternoon a party of Union officers appeared abruptly at the mansion's front door. McNeill and Benjamin barely had time to escape to the woods behind the house, while a woman guest began talking animatedly with the officers, showing them her children, and leading them slowly to the shade in the front yard. Unnoticed, Mrs. McNeill slipped away from the group to the backyard and began destroying the footprints the two men had left. Then she froze; the excited yelping of her husband's dog was clearly audible from the thickets.

Dismayed, McNeill picked up the dog and cradled it in his arms. Quickly he and Benjamin plunged deeper and deeper into the tangle; briers scraped their faces and tore at their clothes; their feet sank into the squashy soil. Once they heard northern voices; the Yankees were searching the woods. Breathless, the two waited, the dog still in McNeill's arms. One of the soldiers passed by so close that Benjamin could have reached out and touched him. Was he now to be betrayed by a whine, a growl, or a yelp? But miraculously the dog remained silent, and the party of soldiers moved on. Not until late that night did Mrs. McNeill dare to signal with her candle from the mansion's windows that all was well.

Benjamin now knew he could not linger. Ellen McNeill and her house guest had saved the day this time, laughing and joking with the Union officers when both felt "sick with uneasiness," but they might not keep their luck. Ruefully Ellen told Mr. Howard how she had bantered with the officers: "Your predecessors have taken all the booty we had." They had believed her finally, but everyone knew they might return. Whenever the McNeills heard the Manatee's waves lapping they started nervously; was it another boat?

Benjamin determined to get to Nassau. From there he would manage to book a passage to England. The weather was too hot now for his homespun clothes; Ellen McNeill and her friend began sewing him a suit of blue denim instead. They made uppers for his shoes out of the old overcoat she had saved and sewed them to a pair of leather soles she had been hoarding for just such an emergency. When the women had taken their last stitches and Mr. Howard was trying on the clothes, he relaxed his vigilance with the children and began performing a series of antics to amuse them. They laughed in delight. In his strange outfit, he was their friend after all. Fanny McNeill remembered especially his genial smile.

Archibald McNeill realized he couldn't take his guest to Nassau himself. He knew the well-traveled routes to the Bahamas, but not the inside channels that would have to be followed if Yankee patrols were successfully to be avoided. Therefore Benjamin proceeded southward to the house of Captain John Curry, who said he knew of a boat. Then he pressed on to the home of Frederick Tresca, the erstwhile blockade runner Archibald McNeill had said was most capable of saving the rebel statesman from detection and capture. Tresca knew the Gulf Coast as far down as Knight's Key; from there he could take a little-used passage to New Providence Island, where Benjamin would be safe.

"Mr. Howard"—though the fiction was wearing thin—was duly assigned a guest room in the Tresca household. This time he feared the children less, and Willie Tresca soon adored him. Mrs. Tresca began sewing pleats into Benjamin's denim suit; into them she stuffed the American gold he carried. It would have to sustain him in England until he found work. She made pockets for gold in his waistband; his stoutness would complete the deception. When the Trescas got word from Captain Curry that the boat was ready on Whitaker's Bayou at Sarasota Bay, Tresca and Benjamin and their crew of one, a sailor named McLeod, began jogging toward the bayou in a rickety old spring wagon. The June evening was heavy with the dampness of a recent shower; mosquitoes were buzzing. By the time the three men arrived at Whitaker's Bayou they were exhausted. The smell of blooming night cestrums there was somehow sinister. At every rattle in the brush Benjamin started. Under cover of darkness still, the three boarded their boat.

It was a yawl which had lain sunk in a creek for more than two years. Curry had managed to salvage it. Would it take them to Nassau? They did not know, but they had to try. Tresca knew the mangrove wilderness of southwest Florida as no other seaman did. McLeod, too, was acquainted with these waters; for him the incentive was Benjamin's money. By the morning of June 23 they were on their way; they carried no food. Instead, they stopped frequently on shore to fish and gather turtle eggs; instead of water they drank coconut milk. Near Gasparilla Island they sighted a Federal gunboat. Quickly Tresca and McLeod tacked into Gasparilla Pass, where they tied up in a jungle of mangroves. The Yankees began pursuit, but in the mangrove labyrinth they had to stop their boat; they were so near the fugitives could hear them talking. For two nights Benjamin and his companions huddled in their old open boat near Gasparilla Island; then they set forth once more and the yawl rocked in the high waves which heralded a rainy-season squall.

The second Federal gunboat sighted them while they were fishing and it proved too fast for them. Tresca formed a desperate plan. "Get to the galley, put grease on your face, and be *busy!*" he ordered Benjamin, who grabbed a chef's apron hanging nearby. When the officers of the gunboat drew up alongside the yawl they let down a small boat and boarded it. On the yawl's deck they found fishnets, tackle, and a string of fresh fish.

"Where are you from?" the officers barked at Tresca. "Where are you bound?"

"I am a fisherman supplying your troops stationed farther up the coast." Tresca's accent was faintly French, but not southern; probably it saved him. The officers, satisfied, departed, but not before one of them had stared at the fat cook bending over in the tiny galley. "By damn!" he exclaimed. "That's the first time I ever saw a Jew cook on a fishing boat!"

By the time the yawl reached the Ten Thousand Islands, Benjamin was noticing the alligators and crocodiles swimming beside them. From time to time a lone Seminole in his dugout palmetto canoe stared from the mangroves. The Seminoles did not seem friendly, but who could blame them? In a tiny Ten Thousand Islands village Tresca heard of a sponge boat with a leg-o'-mutton sail, the *Blonde*. With Benjamin's gold he bought it from its crew of spongers, and on it he began the next leg of his voyage to the Bahamas. The heat of the day had grown intense;

Benjamin began to sweat profusely. Early one evening the horizon
blackened with clouds. Tresca and McNeill took in the sail while the
wind began lashing at them and the *Blonde* began to lurch. Spray washed
across its deck. Tresca threw out the anchor; there was nothing to do
now but ride the squalls out. In a single minute two towering waterspouts
formed near the horizon. They were still a couple of miles distant, but
they began sweeping ahead of them a gale which bore down directly on
the *Blonde*. The furious whirl of the water echoed eerily close. When
the main squall broke, McLeod began bailing with a tin can, Benjamin
with his hat. Lightning coursed jaggedly down from the leaden mass of
the sky. Salt water surged and churned, stinging the men's eyes; they
could only turn their backs to its assaults and hope the wind would not
capsize them. Ahead of him in the east, to his horror, Benjamin saw
another waterspout. As the wind tore in at him from the west, he saw
the eastern spout begin to move in with frightening swiftness. There
were warring currents at different heights in the air, he understood; it
would be a miracle if anyone on the *Blonde* survived. In a sudden wrench
the first waterspouts passed not a hundred yards from the *Blonde* on
either side; they tore up the surface of the sea as they passed as if it had
been a pond; then they careened like dervishes into the clouds ahead,
where they met the third waterspout head on. Benjamin watched incredulous and fascinated as they continued their "awful race" into the
horizon. Fifteen minutes later an absolute calm descended. The stars
came out, faintly red-gold. Lazily, easily, the *Blonde* began heaving her
way once more toward the Bahamas and freedom as if nothing had
happened.

"McLeod," Benjamin confided, "this is not like being Secretary of
State." McLeod and Tresca burst out laughing.

"You're a nervy man, Mr. Benjamin," McLeod spoke up. "Yes sir,
a very nervy man!"

By the middle of July they put in at Bimini, which once Ponce de
León had sought for his own salvation. Tresca and McLeod lingered;
they planned to go on to Nassau to buy supplies for home and then return
to Tampa Bay. But Benjamin was restless. He set out immediately on a
sloop for New Providence Island with a crew of three Negroes. Thirty-
five miles from land the sloop foundered so quickly that Benjamin and
his crew barely had time to leap into the small skiff it was towing before
the sloop sank to the bottom. The skiff leaked; the Negroes took turns

with its single oar. They had managed to save a pot of rice and a keg of water. The skiff was barely five inches above the ocean; a storm now would mean certain disaster. Benjamin admired the courage of his companions as they started back toward Bimini. By noon they had sighted a ship. It was the British brig *Georgina,* which was inspecting coastal lighthouses. On board. Benjamin identified himself to the captain, who greeted him warmly and turned around toward Bimini. In port Benjamin chartered another sloop and started for Nassau the same afternoon. This time Tresca and McLeod insisted on going with him as crew. A stagnant calm alternated with torrential rains and violent headwinds. It took the sloop six days to go a hundred miles. When at last Benjamin and his companions climbed up the docks at the foot of Rawson Square they were almost staggering. Without resting he went to arrange his passage to England. And then? "Soon I may be penniless," he reflected moodily. Still, a London newspaper might give him a job. But no; it was not like being Secretary of State.

After an emotional farewell to Tresca and McLeod, Benjamin set out once more. Near the Virgin Islands, where he had been born, a fire broke out in the ship's hold. Furiously he and the sailors manned steam pumps to keep the flames back from the deck as far as they could. They barely managed to make St. Thomas; by this time there were seven feet of water in the hold from the pumps' overflow, and the fire had already burned away the deck in spots to within an eighth of an inch of its thickness. Now Benjamin was fatalistic; once more he had survived. Soon he grew characteristically cheerful. His voyage to England on a merchant ship proved to be without incident. His journey toward a second fame as an English barrister and Queen's Counsel was blessedly tranquil.

He would be the friend of prime ministers and princes. Soon, on long evenings of fog that, as a Southerner, he wondered if he would ever get used to, he would be entertaining London guests with tales of Tampa Bay, of the Gamble mansion and Frederick Tresca. Sometimes he visited Natalie in Paris. Whenever she listened she was charmingly polite.

On the first of September 1865, not long after Judah Benjamin had gained his English sanctuary, an old man lay dying in a house on Acton Green. He was the botanist John Lindley, famous as the author of *The Genera and Species of Orchidaceous Plants* and several other works. Though John Lindley never saw the latitudes where his beloved orchids flourished, he studied all the specimens people sent him. "Nothing is impossible!" he would bellow at his assistants when they were balked in a plant's identification. They knew him as a man "hot in temper and impatient of opposition." But he could be generous, they conceded; he was warmhearted and impulsive as often as he was angry. John Lindley had supervised the plantings at London's Kew Gardens; his advice had been sought on Irish potato famines; Queen Victoria put horticultural exhibitions in his charge. A lifetime of overwork had felled him with a stroke at sixty-six, and late that day he died without regaining consciousness. His son Nathaniel became Lord Lindley, a judge who often served in the British courts with Judah Benjamin. Years before, a correspondent had sent John Lindley a butterfly orchid. Where did it grow, Lindley inquired? It had been collected, he learned, on the Hillsborough River in Florida. He decided to call it *Epidendrum Tampense*: Tampa's orchid. Thus the city on the bay was given its talisman flower by a man who never saw Florida.

Epidendrum Tampense still blooms every summer in lavender-brown spikes touched with gentle green. High in the trees, it sways over the Hillsborough. Southward, near the shore of Tampa Bay, still stands the Gamble mansion; today it is a shrine dedicated to Judah Benjamin's memory. Far from the river and the bay in the English capital two men thought long thoughts of them both during their lives: John Lindley, whose London career ended full of honor in the last year of an American war, and Judah Benjamin, whose London career was just beginning. Perhaps whenever he passed the display of *Epidendrum Tampense* in the Royal Horticultural Society's greenhouses—for he adored orchids himself—his perpetual smile became more enigmatic than ever.

Mr. Howard had come a long way.

PART III

Developers

17

"A Bawdy Backwater"

Sylvia Sunshine was not the first and by no means the last Florida prophet for the Northern Ignorant after the Civil War. "Forty miles from Manatee," she told her Yankee readers in *Petals Plucked from Sunny Climes,* "is to be seen the remains of Tampa. Your morning slumbers will not be interrupted here by the hammers of rude workmen." Tampa, a shell of its former self, now slept. Sylvia was Abbie M. Brooks, and more honest than other prophets who saw no flaws in Eden; she noted things to praise, but also things to blame. Near the mouth of the Manatee River she found Tampa Bay charming; a few boardinghouses there offered a haven for the tubercular; the soil was suitable for grape orchards, and "a reliable firm" (therefore not Floridian) ought to come down and encourage wine making. This would eliminate the "beastly drunkenness from strychnine whiskey" which prevailed in the city, especially at the Hillsborough waterfront. If the strychnine in her whiskey was fancy, the beastly drunkenness was real enough. At Fort Brooke's very gates a fresh wave of Madams began to set up their trade. Newly freed slaves roamed the streets unsteady from cheap brandy. Many leading citizens had fled oncoming conquerors before the war's close. Tampa was a down-at-heels ghost town; Sylvia Sunshine felt it her duty to warn the public of its deficiencies—schools in particular. In the courthouse, classes were being held by "a genuine specimen of the Illinois backwoods race. His visage looked as blank as the door before which he sat chewing the

Virginia weed, firing jets of juice, evidently making a bigger effort with his jaws than with his brains. His pupils were undergoing a heavy cramming process. Meaningless, incomprehensible words were being wedged into their heads so tightly they could never be got out, either for use or ornament." Her departure from Tampa was good for some final barbs: "We do not take leave of this place as of a dear friend." Its sandy sidewalks were filthy with refuse. Houses were decaying on every side. "The place looks discouraged from sheer weariness in trying to be a town." Exorbitant rates were being charged by "indifferent houses of entertainment." Tampa was to be avoided; even Senator Yulee's rail-road to Cedar Key north of it was nothing to brag about. Sylvia succinctly reported the encounter of one of its tourists and a black train hand.

"Say, sir! Are there no refreshments coming in soon?"
"What is dem, miss?"
"Why, something to eat."
"I reckon dar'll be some groun' peas gwine round 'fore very long, or some cane stalks."
"I wish you to comprehend I come from *Boston!*"

Boston didn't approve of ground peas and sweetnin'. If Southerners had romanticized white culture, Northerners had idealized black; when North and South met, the result was often chaotic, and also often funny.

On Terra Ceia Island, Sylvia Sunshine found the farm of Madam Joe Atzeroth and her husband still flourishing; their glass windows shimmered irregularly in the sunlight. Madam Joe regaled Sylvia with tales of "the war whoop of the Indian, the howl of the jaguar, the scream of the catamount." What the Atzeroths had built in the wilderness was "a fairy-land . . . you constantly feel as though you were having a beautiful dream, which may be dissipated by some external interruption, and the spell broken." Warm winds, hesitant waves, the whisper of the Lombardy poplars the Atzeroths had planted, the fragrance of the orange trees: Terra Ceia was enchanted. In February roses bloomed, and at night, by moonlight, Madam Joe strolled her garden paths humming nostalgic German folksongs. But she didn't want to return to her native Rhine, she said. The air on Terra Ceia was "soft as the memory of a buried love," and she was also making money on bountiful crops of lima beans, pine-apples, tomatoes, peppers, and citrus. A few new settlers were arriving: an Alabama couple living on game while they built their cabin, for instance. The husband had lost an arm in the war; his wife went on his hunts with him to carry home the game. A few cattlemen had come to the island too and had built palmetto shacks. Fishermen had brought canoes in which they plied the bay's inlets. Terra Ceia and the Pinellas peninsula were infinitely more tempting than Tampa, Sylvia Sunshine decided. "It is a bawdy backwater," added another visitor; Tampa had its riproaring moments. A pioneering Reconstruction restaurateur boasted of his mettle by saying that he had never bothered to hire a bouncer or call the police; he handled his customers' fights himself. Once his chef insulted one of his waitresses; the owner asked his patrons to leave and began a battle royal with the culprit. While spectators pressed their faces aghast against the windows outside, the two men smashed tableware and kitchen utensils into each other until the offending chef was felled with a skillet. Once more the battered restaurant was open for business, and the waitresses weren't maligned after that.

In July 1865, Yankee occupation troops arrived at dilapidated Fort Brooke. Their first act was to emancipate a warehouseful of cotton belonging to Captain McKay, who had hoped to sell it abroad. The blow nearly, though not quite, ruined him. In the wake of the soldiers came gambling entrepreneurs flashier and more sophisticated than those who had flourished during the Seminole wars. Diamond stickpins glittered in Florida's afternoon sunlight along Tampa's main streets, and prominent on the scene were mulatto prostitutes who decked themselves in feathers and high-button shoes and promenaded enticingly in front of the fort's gates. While virtuous Tampa wives complained that the city had lost its morals, their husbands privately agreed that at least the occupation troops were bringing some life back into the place. The Dew Drop Exchange began to sell West Indian rum, and army sutlers prospered. But it wasn't safe to walk the streets; ex-slaves, their pent-up resentment exploding, were pushing white pedestrians into the mud and sand; to get whiskey money they burglarized Tampa stores and homes. A family couldn't go to church without leaving someone behind to watch the house, complained the *Florida Peninsular* when it resumed publication. Tampa was attracting newcomers, but unfortunately they were apt to be Republicans. They began orange groves on the city's outskirts, and it took a decade for die-hard Southerners to admit that some of them were "intelligent men" and "bona-fide citizens."

To the crudeness of Tampa several of its oldest families reacted in a typically southern fashion; they shut their eyes, hoping all the bad things would go away. At Christmas the newly formed Knights of Hillsborough began staging ring tournaments. The horsemen tilted their lances at a series of rings hanging ten feet high from horizontal bars; the victor got to choose the Queen of Love and Beauty, and a ball was held in her honor. More than one impoverished debutante's ball gown was bravely patched. When the courtyard of Fort Brooke wasn't being used for tournaments or military parades it harbored old Granny Cowart's cows. Nobody minded. Troops came and went. Granny owned the town's dairy, and she was also the local expert in midwifery and the castration of bulls. The babies she had brought into the world she called "my children"; what she called the bulls she never said.

One of Tampa's Reconstruction trials was a scalawag Southerner-turned-Republican named James T. Magbee. He had lived in Tampa since the 1840s, and during the war he had served in the Confederate army. Afterwards, sensing the way the wind blew, he turned ardently liberal and had enough admirers in occupied Tallahassee to get him a judgeship. Tampans gasped when he advocated racially mixed juries. Perhaps, in his championship, he was sincere, but Tampa voters believed he was out to humiliate whites. Judge Magbee had another fault: he was an alcoholic. One night when he fell dead drunk into the gutter a group of Democrats lost no time in gathering to pour over him a mixture of molasses and corn. Roaming hogs afterwards had a field day in it. Magbee was finally able to extricate himself and went home. Then he charged a Democratic suspect with the outrage. The suspect came into court with a sawed-off shotgun, which he pointed at Magbee. One of Magbee's friends knocked the gun's barrel out of the offender's hand and a load of buckshot went into the ceiling instead of the judge. Magbee, however, was moved enough to dismiss the case. Another time, when he was carousing in downtown Tampa, the Democratic mayor charged him with disorderly conduct. In jail, Magbee summoned his wife, who brought "the necessary papers." Promptly he issued a writ of habeas corpus ordering the town marshal to deliver the body of prisoner James T. Magbee to Judge James T. Magbee of the circuit court. When Magbee got to the courthouse he released himself; afterwards, pleased, he wrote up the case for a law review. He also founded a Republican newspaper, the *Tampa Guardian*, notable for the paucity of advertisements placed by ex-Confederates. But Judge Magbee was a lively writer, and his wife, as assistant editor, contributed her own talents. The *Guardian* flourished until Magbee died in the mid-eighties after giving his name to the Hillsborough River picnic site of Magbee Springs.

"For the piscator," one transient northern sportsman noted, "Tampa does not present many inducements." That winter economy was not summer profusion occurred to none of the newcomers. The society was "excellent," true, and the town pleasant—if you looked the other way from the floozy-filled streets near Fort Brooke. In winter, sportsmen found it necessary to go up the Hillsborough for good angling. A mule team could manage a boat and outfit for the round trip to where the redfish and trout had swum upriver to warm springs. There was some good fishing on Terra Ceia Island and the Pinellas peninsula, though.

"I judge Point Pinellas to be one of the most salubrious and healthful locations on the west coast," pronounced Dr. James Henshall, who went there to escape his native North. The fish in the Gulf were "regular snolligosters!" And if the Hillsborough was "a small and uninteresting stream," the Bay and the Gulf offered bonanzas. Dr. Henshall remembered for the rest of his life a Gulf sunset at John's Pass, where once pirate John Gómez had ranged. The sea was like molten glass, the sun a burning scarlet disk in a soft haze; then the ocean turned gold and orange and bronze, and on shore the palms were completely still. Under them sat pelicans and gulls and egrets and herons resting from their day's foraging. Farther south the birds were warier. Florida hunters had begun to reap a deadly harvest of egret plumes for the millinery trade, and an outraged conservationist left a description of their ravages:

> There were only a few aigrets flying in and out. We drove on up to the rookery and there were dead aigrets everywhere. The young were left in the nest to starve, and when we would look in a nest the young aigrets would think it was the old aigrets coming to feed them, and they would open their mouths and beg for food. . . . The plumes are prettier during the nesting season and the birds are easier to kill as they come in to feed their young.

On Pinellas, where Máximo Hernández had fished, the most active of the plume hunters was a Canadian named Chevalier. He sold not only egret plumes but the feathers and skins of herons and spoonbills and anything else he could lay his hands on. Thousands of pelicans were shot for their throat bags, which were made into tobacco pouches. In one season Chevalier got eleven thousand skins and plumes and thirty thousand birds' eggs; it took eleven of his men with blowpipes to blow the contents out of half the eggs. The rest spoiled, and were spread out and pierced for ants to consume. The empty eggs were then marketed as curios. One of Chevalier's boatmen saw a kill of a thousand egrets in a single day. Ten days later, as he rowed past the rookery, he was nauseated by the sight and stench of dead birds. "The heads and neck of the young birds were hanging out of the nests by the hundreds. I am done with bird hunting forever," he said. But within a few months he was back at it; money was too tempting, and Chevalier and his henchmen had the willing alliance of scattered Pinellas settlers who longed for a share of the bounty. They, after all, were the ones who had told him where the nests were.

The Hillsborough's egrets were largely ignored; flocks were more plentiful on the Gulf. On the river the cacophony of guns in rookeries was blessedly rare; the northern sportsmen who had come to hunt deer and doves were arrested instead by the minor music of black boatmen:

> I pole dis raft way down the river,
> O-ho! O-hoo!
> De sharks and sawfish make me shiver,
> O-ho! O-hoo!
>
> You thought you heard a gator beller,
> O-ho! O-hoo!
> 'Twas only dis black buckra feller,
> O-ho! O-hoo!
>
> De fish hawk kotched a big fat mullet,
> O-ho! O-hoo!
> But it foun' its way down the eagle's gullet,
> O-ho! O-hoo!

In and out of the mossy oaks the sounds were suspended, between the stark trunks of cypresses and over agate twilight pools to die slowly in a thickening blue night. At such moments, perhaps, sportsmen discovering the Hillsborough and Tampa Bay realized one of their charms was an exotic difference from any civilization they had ever known. River and bay became a haven hymned in the presses of frigid and frenetic cities far away, until from haven to heaven there remained only the distance of a letter.

For its own, whether native or newly settled, Tampa was fast becoming a cow town. The rebirth of the cattle industry was spurred by a Cuban revolution which began in 1868. For eleven years Cuba could not raise enorgh cattle for its own use. Captain McKay swiftly stepped in to fill the gap, and soon cattlemen along the Hillsborough were acquiring herds of five to ten thousand head. Their profits swelled; that decade they received over two million dollars in return for the scrawniest of cows. For every few hundred cattle, ranchers hired cowboys who branded them and drove them to market and at roundup time slept under the stars. Chuck wagons followed them with grits, potatoes, and coffee. In the evening, over their fires, they plucked out banjo tunes on the riverbanks and mouthed wailing harmonicas; also they compared notes on the feeding times of forest deer they had observed. You had to find a deer at moonrise, moonset, or moonsouth, when the full moon hung low on the southern horizon; that was when they came into the clearings to nibble at the tender shoots of willows and sweet gums. Even the fish answered the call of the moon; along the shores of the bay the cowboys at rest from cattle tending angled for sheepshead and speckled trout. "Moon's got more to do with run of the land than sun do," they said. They deadened trees and killed poisonous weeds like the sumac in the moon's dark; they charmed warts and styes then and took patent medicine for whatever ailed them. Moon's light was the time for slaughtering and for picking freshly ripened blackberries off the vines which festooned the edges of burgeoning rangelands. The best time of all for sorcery was moonsouth under, when the far-off white circle dipped to the edge of the equator.

The cattle trails down the Hillsborough through the wilderness east of Tampa saw massive drives. Some of the beasts were led to slaughterhouses beginning to spring up in Tampa itself; others were moved onto Tampa wharves from which they were loaded onto McKay steamers and shipped to Cuba. A favorite way station of the drovers was Old Lady Bunch's Roadhouse and Cowpens at Six Mile Creek. There they penned their cattle on the last night before reaching Tampa. In the inn they drank and jostled and told stories and cursed and admired each other. Often they were joined by such illustrious citizens as Dr. John Wall, a Tampa physician, and Colonel Frank Harris, a landholder who lived not far from the site of old Fort King. One night Wall and Harris got into an argument so fierce that Colonel Harris challenged Dr. Wall to a duel.

"As the challenged party," countered Dr. Wall, "I have the right to name the place of meeting and the weapons. The place will be Mrs. Bunch's cowpens and the weapons her shovels." The nonplussed colonel learned he and the doctor "could pitch cow dung at each other until one cried 'Hold! Enough!' " He didn't much like that idea so he changed the subject and stopped arguing.

Often a group of citizens, farmers and cowboys went into the woods to poison wolves. For this they killed a beef animal, put the flesh in a wagon and tied a rope around the hide and dragged the carcass where the wolves were known to range. The hunters wore gloves; wolves shied away from human scent. As the wagon bumped along the trail the hunters put strychnine into pieces of fresh beef they threw out on the path behind. Afterwards, they left wolves' corpses to rot and be scavenged by the eternal black buzzards of Hillsborough River forests. Afterwards they celebrated at square dances, to which the cowboys brought their banjos and guitars and harmonicas and for which they spruced up by giving each other bowl haircuts. Tampa girls who had no chance of being high society Queens of Love and Beauty found the knights of the range dashing.

The cows, in their roamings, fertilized the fields of local farmers. Swampland was available now to such farmers at seventy cents an acre. Adventurous homesteaders went into timber and began selling pines and cedars to newly established sawmills. In Tampa a familiar complaint began to be heard: Why did the government tie up all the valuable riverfront land which was Fort Brooke? The city still chafed at its federal restrictions. Its growth was also not being helped by the difficulty people had getting in and out of it. If you took the Gainesville-Tampa stagecoach, for instance, you were dependent on the driver, Old Man Roper, who cracked a long blacksnake whip and managed his lines between some of the healthiest curses his women passengers had ever heard. Old Man Roper's coach had been made in Cincinnati especially for Florida's corduroy roads. It was pulled by four swaybacked horses. Whenever it crossed streams, water leaked in through the coach's side doors; passengers indecorously had to keep their feet up. One would have the job of keeping his eyes fixed on the rear window to see if any baggage fell out, which was often. Springs broke down; during layovers Old Man Roper entertained his charges by spitting tobacco juice through the coach's front wheel without touching a spoke. Back en route, he enjoyed gopher-grabbing. Without warning he would leap down from his box and grab a sleepy land tortoise, which he threw up on the baggage rack and then traded to Negroes at the end of his trip. Negroes were partial to gopher stew, he explained.

Another hazard for stagecoach travelers was Old Man Roper's rival, Edgar Watson, horsethief, robber, and occasional murderer. He had buried three Florida wives under mysterious circumstances and was practiced with pistol and pocketknife. Eventually he had to flee westward, where according to river and bay legend he was downed by Belle Starr, queen of the Oklahoma outlaws. He survived, though; when he returned to Florida, this time to the Big Cypress, he killed several people who were working to clear land there. A posse found and lynched him; southwest Florida was strong on law and order.

In the early seventies, two new industries came to Tampa hardly noticed in the fever of the cattle boom. A modest brewery began to sell its beer beside the Hillsborough, and a Cuban named Molina set up a small cigar factory or *chinchal* not far from the courthouse near the river's banks. His family had all worked in Havana cigar plants and were skilled packers and rollers. Molina's product found plenty of patrons. He had other products too, though. Obsessed by cockfighting, he left most of the cigar rolling and bunching to his wife and children and himself bred, trained, and fought game birds. The best of them he imported from Cuba. Soon Tampa boys were pestering their parents for fighting cocks; groups of them wandered along waterfront streets with roosters under their arms looking for other roosters to pit their champions against. Townspeople began complaining of the disappearance of backyard fowl.

Cockfighting is illegal in Florida these days; its magic lingers. In hidden pits, inside modern Tampa and out of it, aficionados still gather at "mains" to watch their birds and bet for high stakes. Most of the bettors have reared their own contenders. At the cockpits—Cubans call them *vallas*—"English-bred" are matched against Jerezanos—first imported, tradition insists, from the sherry plains of Jerez in southern Spain. Most of the gamblers today are blacks who have taken over the sport from the Cubans who brought it. On summer nights lanterns still gleam over the improvised *vallas* in empty warehouses and barns, where they are fenced with makeshift wooden barriers. The contestants are weighed; corn liquor and bourbon and gin are passed from human hand to hand. As two cages are lowered into the *valla* sawdust by suspended wires, the cocks gaze at each other furiously. Then the comb-pared birds, spurs taped to their legs, are liberated to explode in a fury of feathers and rasps against a giddy counterpoint of shouts, curses, laughter and the clinking of change. The sport is cruel, puritans insist, but it is colorful. Bravery, whether human or bird, is not without its grandeurs. Neither is the ingenuity of the cornered. The mains go on until dawn, when the sun spreads down from the Green Swamp over the river into the city. Quickly the cockfighters fade into disappearing shadows. By breakfast they are bus drivers again, warehouse employees and sanitation workers and clerks in retail stores, dwellers in the ghetto of Sulphur Springs where the Hillsborough that once ran clear in a picnic nook now foams with surplus detergent. The cockfights must wait until dark again, but from the drabness of day they are relief sweeter for being stolen.

When the Yankees left Fort Brooke four years after they had entered it, they were serene in the belief that Tampa was rapidly being reconstructed by respect for cash, northern or southern. They were correct. Their parade ground stood empty then, more available than ever for Queens of Love and Beauty to preside over their Ring Tournaments when Granny Cowart's cows could be herded out of the way. Fort Brooke was hardly prepossessing these days; it gave the whole town a derelict look which led a visitor in 1876 to describe it as "the most forlorn collection of one-storey houses imaginable." He was the southern poet Sidney Lanier, and he had just registered with his wife at the Orange Grove Hotel. He had been commissioned by a group of northern railroads and shipping lines to write "a guide book to Florida which should also be a poem." This would not be easy, for he was dying, and at times as he strolled along the Hillsborough seeking an elusive February sun he knew it.

Always he had wavered between literature and music, this gentle Georgian with a high forehead, kind eyes, and resigned, half-humorous mouth. In college most of his time had been devoted to a study of the flute, and when he had left to fight in the Confederate Army he had taken his flute under his arm for solace. He had not liked secession, but he had loved his native state. "Gradually a change came about—how, who can say? It was in the atmosphere; we breathed it in the air; it reverberated from heart to heart; it was like a spiritual contagion—good or bad, who could say?" He had not been in service long when he was captured and plunged into the horrors of a military prison where he contracted tuberculosis.

"Here in this hell hole," a fellow poet and prisoner later wrote:

I met Sidney Lanier. One day while I was lying in my cot ill with fever the distant notes of a flute reached my ears from the opposite side of the camp. I was entranced. I said to myself, "I must find that man." As soon as I got out of bed I commenced searching, with the result that I found the flautist in the poet . . .

Lanier had already begun to write pleasant lyrics. After the war his poetry deepened; in despair and illness, lost in a sea of swarming Georgia klansmen and carpetbaggers and scalawags, he clung to his sense of humor, his love of music and his classical learning. He studied law and was admitted to the Georgia bar, but he could not stand what to him was the law's dryness.

His poems began to appear in national magazines. When he found a paying job he liked, it was as flautist with the Baltimore Symphony; he was to end his brief career as poet-lecturer at Johns Hopkins University there, but not before he had visited Tampa on his commission from rail and shipping magnates. "My physician had become alarmed at the gravity and persistence of my illness," Lanier wrote a friend on his way to Florida. "He might as well talk to the stars whose light hasn't yet reached us as try to persuade me that any conceivable combination of circumstances could induce me to die before I've written and published my five additional volumes."

First, however, there was his hackwork. In Tampa he described the species of fish expected of him and the sport of turtle-catching. The latter was simple; when the turtles came up on the shore to deposit their eggs at night, the hunter turned them over to die on their backs. The next morning he could eye their corpses with "certain titillating sensations in the diaphragm (where you laugh) and the conscience (where you do not laugh)." Conditions along the Hillsborough Lanier found shabby, but the people were hospitable and solicitous over his racking cough. He even convinced himself that Tampa was just the place for consumptives. He had so little to spend in it that his wife was surreptitiously selling her wedding silver to make ends meet.

Lanier wrote several poems in Tampa. *A Florida Sunday* described the bay's pelicans and the flocks of parrakeets that still flew over the Hillsborough in sweeping flashes of green-gold. *Tampa Robins* was a cheerful evocation of birdsong in a blooming orange tree. The robin's hopes were Lanier's own:

> I'll south with the sun, and keep my clime;
> My wing is king of the summer-time;
> My breast to the sun his torch shall hold;
> And I'll call down through the green and gold,
>   Time, take thy scythe, reap bliss for me,
>   Bestir thee under the orange tree.

At other times Lanier was bitter. Then the bay flats were "inexorable, vapid, vague and chill" when winter rains came, and they were "always the same, always the same. . . . Oh might I through these tears but glimpse/ Some hill my Georgia high uprears." As his Tampa weeks passed he finally faced the certain consequence of his disease and "The Stirrup-Cup" reflects his resignation to it:

> Then, time, let not a drop be spilt;
> Hand me the cup whene'er thou wilt;
> 'Tis thy rich stirrup-cup to me;
> I'll drink it down right smilingly.

Four years of invalidism and poverty later, he was buried in Baltimore under a boulder into which had been set a metal slab carved with rays. His epitaph was his own: "I am lit with the sun." He had loved it on the river and the bay, "the green leaves, the gold oranges, the glitter of great and tranquil waters . . . the heavenly conversation of the robins and mockingbirds and larks which fill my days with delight." But in the end both light and delight were useless.

Just a year after Sidney Lanier's burial in Baltimore a death took place on the Hillsborough. Often, recently, Fort Brooke had stood empty, its buildings tumbling into ruin, its orange trees festooned with unruly moss, its tools slowly rusting in successive suns and rains. In May 1880, however, a virulent epidemic of yellow fever in Key West prompted the army to transfer two companies from there to Tampa. They came in blue coats and pith helmets, they marched and countermarched on the ragged parade grounds and yelled clipped commands. In off hours, curiously, they examined ancient cannons and muzzle-loading rifles. The Seminole wars had belonged to their grandfathers. The Civil War had been their fathers'. Restlessly they whiled away dull hours shooting dice. They visited the prostitutes of "the town of Fort Brooke" and they drank rotgut whiskey as lonely soldiers do. In December 1882, they were transferred still farther north to Alabama and Saint Augustine. For the last time the flag of the United States was raised and lowered in the live-oak grove along the Hillsborough. For the last time stiffly booted feet echoed in the packed courtyard sand. The buglers blew; soon the tramping and the wagons' rumbling grew fainter along the military road, until Fort Brooke belonged only to its wraiths. A handful of Tampans tried to make it into a park. They failed; so did the group who hurried to Tallahassee to file land claims. Most of Fort Brooke had already been given to a Dr. Carew, the friend of an influential U.S. senator. When Dr. Carew moved in he commandeered the officers' quarters as Colonel George Mercer Brooke had long ago commandeered them from Robert Hackley. Squatters gathered nearby in ragged tents and shacks to protest, but meagerly paid day laborers were soon chopping down the live oaks on the river to make room for Carew warehouses. The Hackleys were still fighting in federal courts, but such technicalities hardly mattered to an investor with a U.S. senator in his pocket. Fort Brooke quickly became a commercial quarter and a slum, and the river flowing along its shore turned murky with slaughterhouse wastes. Gradually the lemon-lime flocks of parrakeets retreated back into the Green Swamp and then to oblivion. The cow town of Tampa would not be a backwater much longer. Its savior was waiting in the wings.

18

Enter the Tycoons

The savior was, however, immediately and colossally preceded by Dr. Frederick T. Weightnovel, who was to put the Hillsborough River and Tampa Bay to a use to which they had never been put before. Dr. Weightnovel said he was a Russian and a Nihilist. How he got his unusual surname he never explained, but he dropped hints that he had been forced to flee his homeland by swimming away from Siberia (presumably in summer) after plotting the overthrow of the Czar. He believed in the brotherhood of man, political reform, and helping the underdog. As soon as he saw the plight of the luckless squatters at Fort Brooke he announced himself their champion. For a start he armed them all with clubs and promised the rest of Tampa that he and his flock meant to found, by force if necessary, the model community of Moscow in what was now the Town of Fort Brooke. Dr. Weightnovel himself had more enthusiasm than his followers did. A few skirmishes took place between squatters on Carew property and the police; most of the conflicts were hand-to-hand. After a few weeks increasingly lackadaisical squatters gave up the idea of turning their toehold in Fort Brooke into a second Moscow. When Dr. Weightnovel tried to fan the flames of their discontent—perhaps it was the climate—he had no success.

It was not his way to stay out of the news. His appearance alone saw to that. He had a lion's mane of heavy black hair which he wore at shoulder length, formidable black eyebrows, and an enormous stomach.

Soon he was peddling hair tonic by pushcart on riverfront streets, along with patent medicines to restore lost virility and cure female complaints, consumption, social diseases, bilious fever, and the Curse of Drink. He also dealt in muscle-builders; his gigantic biceps offered convincing testimony of the benefit they offered. Furthermore, he advertised.

Usually he chose the bay for this, though a few times he used the river near Fort Brooke. His custom was to float belly up in the water until he had attracted a large crowd of spectators. Then he amused them by eating dinner from a plate balanced on his middle and by reading newspapers and smoking cigarettes. Often he staged his demonstrations at Ballast Point when he knew a party of picnickers would be there. The high point of the show was always his climb, shaggy haired and dripping in knee-length bathing trunks, to the shore where his wagonload of hair tonic and nostrums waited for customers. He was a stylish orator, with just enough accent to inspire confidence that he was possessed of startling European medical secrets.

But medicine was not enough for him. He was also philosophical, and soon he announced the foundation of the Tampa Free Love Society. Several of the city's most eligible bachelors promptly joined up. Things went smoothly at first. The meetings were secret. There were rumors of unspeakable orgies, but no one could be sure except the participants and they weren't telling. After a while the Free Love Society decided to stage a parade, after which they would celebrate at a banquet. Their torchlight procession attracted enough attention in itself, but their banquet attracted more. The Society had been indiscreet enough to choose a Tampa hostelry with floor-length windows. A lavish meal was served by a bevy of mulatto girls as naked as jaybirds; afterwards they danced topless and bottomless on the tables. Somebody outside called the police; somebody else called the Hillsborough County Sheriff. Both police and sheriff's deputies broke down the banquet hall door and captured all free lovers not agile enough to escape. They also captured Dr. Weightnovel; subsequently he was so heavily fined that he thought it wise to disband his organization altogether.

Adversity didn't keep him down, though. After an interval of obscurity he opened up a hospital near the Carew warehouses on Whiting Street. His principal clientele were women, particularly the inmates of bawdy houses in the Town of Fort Brooke. All of Tampa presently understood that he was performing abortions at a rapid clip, but nobody did anything about it until one of the girls died. The police raided the hospital then, discovered enough evidence to bring Dr. Weightnovel before a Grand Jury, and rejoiced when he was indicted. This was too much even for Dr. Weightnovel; it broke his heart, and he poisoned himself rather than submit to the penitentiary. Free love in the environs of the Hills-borough and Tampa Bay had a hard time of it after that. Eventually, even so, Tampa's shock changed to nostalgia for the doctor's breezy flamboyance. He was remembered even fondly as a risqué diversion.

Hamilton Disston—still not the Suncoast's ultimate savior but one of its more important benefactors—was cut of different cloth. He was a dreamer, but he got things done. His fortune came from a saw factory in Philadelphia; when he decided to invest it in draining swampland in southwest Florida, Tampans hailed his Gulf Coast Canal and Okeecho-bee Land Company as a potential source of growth. Floridians have always had a weakness for canals. At first Disston's dredging went on furiously. But Florida's finances were peculiar. Whatever unsold land the federal government had given to the custody of the state was put in a trust called the Internal Improvement Fund. A series of Reconstruction governors managed the Fund's finances so badly that charges on its debts soared past its revenues, and creditors began demanding payment. The Internal Improvement Fund's activities came to a halt, and so did those of Disston's canal company. But even in his frustration he saw a fresh chance. He bought four million acres of Florida land from the Internal Improvement Fund for twenty-five cents an acre, and once more he was able to begin dredging.

In 1882 he landed triumphantly on a Cedar Key steamer at the tiny settlement of Anclote in the northern part of the Pinellas peninsula. The tarpon fishing, villagers told him, was superb. He directed his planners to lay out a town called Tarpon Springs, and a year later its first hotel, the Tropical, opened its doors. Its wood had been shipped from Atlantic City, New Jersey, where Disston had a mill. He began touting Florida's winter climate in the north. Yankee newspapers carried advertisements about the splendors of Tarpon Springs; a fortune was said to be had in the seafood business. Even in Europe Disston's publicity made a stir. The Duke of Sutherland bought thirty acres at Tarpon Springs and brought his wife to a comfortable new house he built on the small lake which is now Lake Tarpon. Eyes in Tampa boggled. An English duke, especially one who lived on his Florida real estate in person, was heady

Tarpon fishing

excitement. He had made, it was rumored, a romantic marriage. He was a cousin of Queen Victoria's. It was anticlimactic when the duke's neighbors found him a simple man whose manners were unpretentious and whose tastes ran heavily to fishing. After a few years he tired of Tarpon Springs and went back to his British castles, but for years local promoters were able to drop his name with significant success. Pickled tarpon became a Tarpon Springs delicacy; tarpon sandwiches and boiled octopus were also popular.

With Disston's founding of Tarpon Springs, travelers began to discover the balminess and nearly perpetual sunshine of the Pinellas peninsula. Miranda the Cat still lived there, though after the federal raid on his bayou homestead he had built his second house in the woods. Somebody asked him why. "Well, it's just this way. If I had built on the bayou and it came another war, the damned Yankees would come in there with their gunboats and shell and burn me out like they done before. Now I'm where they can't get their gunboats through the woods to do it." His sentiments were shared by a kinsman and fellow veteran known on the peninsula as Charley the Daredevil. Other families were coming, too, and among their number was a solitary household of blacks. It was not a propitious time for Negroes who had ideas about farming their own land instead of working for someone else, but John Donaldson must have been a marvel of tact. He was a skillful vegetable grower and his larder was always full. Larger homesteads were left to his care when their owners went away. In later years he managed to get a contract to deliver the mail. He was also an efficient alligator hunter.

Compared to Pinellas, Tampa was a metropolis. Still, however, it lacked the one essential ingredient for permanence: a railroad. Senator Yulee's line to Cedar Keys held the west coast monopoly. Then Tampa newspapers broke a story. A Connecticut Yankee named Henry Bradley Plant planned to build not only a railroad which would have its western terminus in Tampa, but the most lavish hotel in the western hemisphere. Salvation was at hand! Firecrackers soared above Tampa thoroughfares, saloons opened their doors for drinks on the house, and riverboat whistles tooted jubilantly. The hotel would stand on the banks of the Hillsborough just far enough upriver to be out of sight of the Town of Fort Brooke. It would rise on the west bank and would boast a swimming pool, a casino, and a continual round of festivities which would range all the way from vaudeville to poetry readings and concerts by a resident orchestra. Mr. Plant's own musical tastes ran to Haydn, Mozart, and the hurdy-gurdy, he said.

He was the stuff of which capitalist gods are made. His greatest teacher, he revealed, had not been a university but experience. He had begun his career as a deckhand on a steamboat running between New Haven and New York. Sometimes the steamboat carried packages, but they were stowed apart in whatever corner might be handy and no one looked after them. Henry Plant's industry had so impressed the captain that he decided to set aside a freight area with Plant in charge. Plant's bunk was moved from the "dingy forecastle" to the express room, and he began learning the business of dispatching packages that would finally flower as the Plant System of railroads and steamers that ranged all the way from Washington, D.C., to Cuba.

Unlike many tycoons, he had charm. During the Civil War he had managed to convince Jefferson Davis that although his sympathies were with the North he would stick to running his express system in the South and refrain from military intrigues. He kept his word. His shrewd eyes and genial smile invited confidence. People said he looked like Buffalo Bill. As a young man he had fallen in love with a beautiful woman who had borne him a son and then contracted tuberculosis. Her doctors had advised Florida. It took the Plants eight days to make the trip from New York City to Jacksonville, and when they arrived there were no porters. Plant found two small black boys to carry his luggage to a hotel so dismal that the couple stayed in it only one night. After that Plant persuaded a private citizen of Strawberry Hill, a Jacksonville suburb, to take them both in while Mrs. Plant regained her health. By the spring of 1853, a few months after their arrival, she felt so well he decided to take her on a pleasure trip to St. Augustine. Again he was horrified by the difficulties of traveling. The road from Jacksonville to St. Augustine, grandly named the King's Highway, was so overgrown with trees and bushes it was necessary for a man to ride ahead of the Plants hacking down underbrush. Plant blazed trees along the side of the road so that he would be able to find his way back after the spring growth had come up. Even so, he and his wife got lost on the return trip and were preparing to spend a night under the pines when their Strawberry Hill landlord appeared; he had had a hunch a New Yorker might not find Florida easy going.

For the rest of her brief life Mrs. Plant spent every winter in Florida. Plant, too, fell in love with it, and after she died he kept returning. His climb in the express business was proceeding at a dizzying rate. He married again, and at the end of the Civil War he knew the south was ripe for expansion. He charmed other southerners as he had charmed Jefferson Davis. His afterdinner speeches, they said, "had no spread-eagleism in them, no declamation, but calm, quiet, easy suggestion, as if talking to a few friends he loved and wanted to help, and, better still, wanted them to help themselves. There is no alarm, but friendly admonition, wise counsel, and valuable instruction most kindly administered." Mr. Plant was, in short, a gentleman even if he *had* been born in Connecticut.

When he announced his plans to bring the Plant System to Tampa, he may have been soft-spoken, but he was far from unimaginative. In Dixieland, he told the town's leading citizens, he would make the desert "bloom like the rose, change waste places into fertile fields, the swamps into a sanitarium, the sand heap into a Champs-Elysées, the Hillsborough into a Seine, and reproduce the palace of Versailles on Tampa Bay." Plant system ships would "plough the Gulf of Mexico" and new industry would bring health and happiness "to many homes over which bereavement and sorrow are hovering like the black angel of death." He also believed in "the power of the fine arts over the mind"; his stations, and his hotel, would be sights to behold.

Persistent in Florida folkore is the tale that a south Florida school-teacher sent Henry Plant a bough of orange blossoms after a freeze had devastated northern groves, that this was why he chose Tampa for his railroad. The incident may well have happened, but Plant was too clever not to do extensive investigating before sinking a fortune into a town of about seven hundred people and "one or two shops." He rapidly began buying up the charters of other Florida railroads—the South Florida and the Jacksonville, Tampa and Key West—which had been authorized by the state to begin laying track. The JT&KW had actually done some grading. The city of Tampa provided early in the summer of 1883 a charter to the Plant Investment Company. Plant began paying good prices for land for his freight yards and depots. A large wharf was built on the Hillsborough at the foot of Polk Street, and soon Plant schooners and Plant brigs were sailing in from the bay loaded with wood, steel, and spikes. A former Confederate general decided he wanted a railroad of his own and built a second wharf, this one at the foot of Whiting Street, but after some preliminary publicity he retreated and it was generally assumed that Plant had bought him out.

Long summer days were lively with the chink of gandy dancers. On the river the activity at Plant's wharves was continuous. By August Tampa had had its first railroad accident; little Lee Ferris had fallen off a handcar on which he had hitched a ride; his knees were skinned. On September 1 a schooner brought in the first two locomotives, and half the town stood at the river to watch them being unloaded part by part. It took nearly a week to assemble them; then their boilers were fired, and Tampa began celebrating. Repeatedly revelers blew the engine whistles; Tampa had a railroad! Church bells rang; the engines began to heave and puff; the "monsters of the rails" were under way. The spectators were waving handkerchiefs and congratulating themselves. Small boys in sailor suits hopped from one foot to the other and demure little girls hid behind their mothers' ample skirts. Babies cried because of all the noise. To the Tampa City Council the uproar was sheer music, and Plant was grandly entertained that winter when he arrived at the Orange Grove Hotel. Soon he would begin his own; but the Hillsborough had not yet become the Seine. He and his wife cruised the bay. In mid-December, just before a balmy Christmas when the orange trees hung thick with golden fruit, the first regular train service was begun to a point thirty-five miles away. Fittingly, it was named Plant City. By January the last spike had been driven; Tampa now had connections with central and north Florida. "How this railroad kills time and space!" marveled a central Florida newspaper. "Only a little while ago it took two days to go from Ocala to Tampa and four days to reach Jacksonville. Now we can speed over the route in a few hours in comfort." It was possible to go from Tampa to Jacksonville in the unheard of time of twelve hours and twenty-five minutes. "What would a country be without its railroads?" rhetorically asked Henry Plant; his was an age of innocence during which passengers had not yet discovered just what a country without them would be.

The ensuing boom staggered even the imagination of Plant and the town fathers. They learned the world was waiting for newly discovered Florida phosphates. People began flocking to the city with suitcases in hand; the depot was full of dreams as future Tampans arrived, went outside, looked around at the palms and oranges, and decided it had been wise to come. Contractors began paving the streets. The place took on the vitality of a gold rush metropolis, southern style. Hot. Very hot. A brick factory was built and the city began sprawling into what to Francis Dade had been distant outposts like Sulphur Springs. The *New York Daily Tribune* felt it necessary to inform its readers exactly where Tampa was. It was "full of wide-awake citizens" who in a single year had spent three hundred thousand dollars on the construction of new buildings, among them a city hall and a courthouse two and a half stories high. In prerailroad days the customs revenue at Tampa had amounted to seventy-five dollars a year. Five years later the figure was a hundred thousand. Congress passed a bill making Tampa a port of entry; a Plant steamer, the *Mascotte,* regularly made the run to Cuba ."The streets of Tampa are not what they will be," admitted the *New York Tribune,* "but the roads on the west side of the river are naturally hard and smooth, giving fine drives in various directions. The water supply is obtained from one of the largest springs in the state and is abundant for all purposes." Another newspaper pronounced of the *Mascotte*: "Its staterooms are as dainty as boudoirs while its saloon is as exquisitely fitted up as any drawing room." By 1885 Tampa had grown to over two thousand people, and the city was increasing by leaps and bounds every week. The air rang with the hammering of construction workers, the sawing of carpenters, the rumble of mixing machines. Real estate soared. In the Town of Fort Brooke, not yet annexed to its more virtuous neighbor, the ladies bought new finery and did a brisk business undreamed of by their predecessors. Three Tampa hotels were hastily built—none of them Plant's Versailles, but enough to house throngs unwilling to wait for his architectural chef d'oeuvre. The new opera house had little opera, but touring players used it and it welcomed town banquets. For less solemn moments there were a roller-skating rink and multiplying pool halls. The city was a frontier boom town on a scale that dazzled even the most ardent boosters. Major John Lesley had to remind himself that only a score of years before he had had to lead Judah Benjamin toward his exile under cover of darkness. Now he was rich from real estate. Dr. George Weedon, of the newly formed Tampa Board of Trade, knew he lived in a world light years away from the time of his ancestor and Osceola. The Hillsborough was thick with construction logs being floated down from a lumber mill at Cow House Slough. The sternwheeler *Gopher* made the run from downtown Tampa to Sulphur Springs daily. Most incredible of all, the Pinellas peninsula was even showing signs of life.

In 1875 a Detroiter and former Union general named John Constantine Williams had come to Tampa looking for a place in which to found a town. But he hadn't liked Tampa, and the rest of Hillsborough County had also failed to impress him. Tarpon Springs he found charmless. Finally he decided to catch a steamer at Cedar Key and return north.

"Did you go to Point Pinellas?" a merchant asked him at Cedar Key.

"Damn Point Pinellas! I was told by a gentleman in Tampa that it's only four feet above tidewater."

"Not a word of truth in it. It's at least forty. It's the healthiest and best section in the state of Florida. It is a perfect paradise, sir."

The general ended by promising to go back to look. When he did, he was enchanted. The smell of orange blossoms floated by on trade winds. Gently Tampa Bay lapped at a pristine shore. The sky was bright. What a place for tourism! What Point Pinellas needed, decided the general, was a railroad.

In the sleepy central Florida hamlet of Longwood there was a lumber company, Demens, McCain, and Cotter. Peter Demens was fascinated by the general's dreams when the general came to see him. He also wanted to make money. A company called the Orange Belt Railroad owed him plenty; why not take over the company as creditor and get financial backing in the North? New York, Chicago, and Philadelphia capitalists must be induced to make loans. "Thees are beeg feesh an' we must cotch them," Peter Demens said. Like Dr. Weightnovel, he was a Russian.

Piotr Alexeitch Dementieff had been born in the imperial city of St. Petersburg. His parents belonged to the minor nobility. He had been handsomely educated to be trilingual, and when he was of age the czar made him a captain in the Russian Imperial Guard. Unfortunately Piotr also began to develop liberal ideas. "The democrat of aristocracy," his friends called him. When the Winter Palace was bombed by terrorists, they warned him that the time was ripe to "escape the tyranny of the Romanoff regime." He had had no part in the bombing but he had expressed questionable opinions and official Russian memories were long. His friend Leo Tolstoy stayed on. Dementieff soon discovered that Americans didn't like bothering with Slavic names; prudently, he became Demens. He had had considerable experience managing family estates in the Russian province of Tver; specifically he knew forestry. When he landed in America he heard about the wonders of Florida's climate, the land where there was never any winter. Perhaps the thought of such a paradise was doubly appealing to him because he had had enough of winter in Russia. Florida also had a lot of pine trees.

Demens bought the charter of the Orange Belt Railroad in 1885; then he began casting about for money. The first donor was a Swedish American named Henschen who also had uncomfortable memories of bitter winters. A Canadian, Harry Sweetapple, contributed also, but the total sum Demens now had of $37,000 was ridiculously small. The railroad got as far on the money as a central Florida crossroads Demens wanted to name St. Petersburg, but one of his backers insisted on Oakland. In Oakland, the cash ran out, and Demens was still far from the Gulf.

"You're crazy," people told him. "No railroad will ever make money in that wilderness."

But the wilderness would not stay a wilderness with a railroad, Demens argued. To his New York brokers he wrote: "The terminus of the road is the most important feature of the whole business and is in such a shape that I do not dare write about it—will only state that we have a chance to have the only harbor which exists in Florida on the Gulf Coast and to build a city of international importance." In Henry Plant's

Tampa there would be stiff competition to the narrow-gauge Orange Belt line, but Demens was optimistic. At first he thought of building a gigantic bridge out to Mullet Key. In a soberer moment he knew that General Williams's property would be best: "There is eighteen feet of water right at the shore, and a splendid townsite there."

His troubles had only begun. "A comic-strip railroad!" skeptics began jeering. He borrowed sum after sum only to see the construction of his tracks eat up funds at a horrifying rate. Steel and iron cost a fortune, he found. The moneylenders insisted on a whopping eight percent interest, and some of them reneged. Demens had no money to buy rails; without rails, he could complete no more tracks; without more completed tracks to show for his efforts, he could get no bond money. It was a "vicious circle." Finally he managed to buy metal for the rails in England. But then the rainy season began; the workers could not grade. Rumors of yellow fever frightened the laborers so badly that Demens was forced to spend days with them on the road bucking them up. Creditors clamored. Demens knew his back was to the wall. "Everything and everybody is disorganized and disgusted," he wrote his broker bitterly:

> I can do nothing without cash—all my time at present is consumed in trying to reconcile our creditors. They must be paid in order to have the thing going. When I wrote you that I want $20,000 between the 20th and the 25th, I meant it, have to have it—every delay hurts us badly. I am going today to Orlando to try to get the bank not to protest our checks. . . . One half of the creditors have quit, threatening lawsuits—we broke the contracts by not paying on time and are helpless . . . I am alone. How can you expect me to go ahead in such circumstances? I will have to give it up. It kills me.

Rapidly the crisis came to a head. Demens was three weeks behind on wages. Angry workmen began riding flatcars into Oakland from all sections of the railroad. There they gathered for a furious bout of fist-shaking oratory. When Demens mounted a stump he was shouted down. Then he was given an ultimatum; pay up by eight o'clock the same night or be lynched. He sent a telegram to New York. It want unanswered. A dramatic eleventh-hour rescue came when a group of his Yankee friends who knew southern mobs arrived with money in hand. Once more disaster had been staved off. Tranquillity reigned for a few days. Then a steamer arrived with two hundred and forty-five tons of steel and the captain demanded instant payment. Again Demens sent telegrams, now increasingly hysterical. Four days later a creditor, sighing, sent him an advance.

By this time a second cargo of steel had arrived and a fresh round of begging telegrams had to go out. When Demens had finished borrowing from the Chicago meat-packing house of Armour and Company, and from such Philadelphia millionaires as the Stotesburys and Drexels, his indebtedness had reached gargantuan proportions. Hamilton Disston—against his better judgment—loaned Demens money of his own; perhaps he was impressed by the excitable Russian's fanatical determination.

When the Orange Belt Railroad was completed, Peter Demens grandly rode into its terminus in a private car. He intended, he said, to build a splendid resort hotel in the city he was founding here. Half its cost of $10,000 he would pay himself; where the other half would come from God only knew, but the Orange Belt Investment Company, an aggregate of his lenders, would raise the cash somehow. In honor of General Williams's home town, the hotel would be called the Detroit.

When tragedy finally closed in, it was because the railroad failed to get the passengers and freight Demens had anticipated. He had worked himself into a nervous breakdown building it, and now nobody wanted to ride it or trust it with express. The competition of the Plant System was too much. The day came when the dogged Demens ran out of his last cent. Heartsick, he had to sell out to a Philadelphia syndicate. He had put nearly a million dollars of other people's money into his road; he had envisioned a fortune. What he emerged with was fourteen thousand dollars. The saga of the Orange Belt Railroad was, moreover, not finished. Demens had economized by buying secondhand locomotives. They broke down on nearly every run. The tracks refused to lie flat. The cars were constantly being derailed. Harry Sweetapple, the railroad's Canadian benefactor, died of sheer despair. Investor Henschen complained the road had "made him an old man." Demens pronounced that it had undermined his own health. "But it is a glorious success!" he protested. Did it not run through the town of Tarpon Springs, through the Duke of Sutherland's settlement, the hamlets of Dunedin and Clearwater and Largo? All would grow. So, it was briefly thought, would a vision Hamilton Disston had of founding a Disston City. Demens had no intention of letting the glory be captured by Disston City, however. Both he and General Williams wanted to name the railroad's terminus, but they couldn't agree. It already had a postmistress who was getting impatient; the mail could not be sent from nowhere.

"Name the town after one of its original backers," General Williams sighed. He had his Detroit Hotel; the nerve-racking saga of the Orange

Belt Railroad had disillusioned him about any delights to be gained from a Williamsville at its end. The postmistress pondered. Then she went to Oakland, the railroad's headquarters. There she found Mr. Henschen, who persuaded her that Sweetapple didn't have the necessary dignity even if it did commemorate a martyr. Modestly, he added that Henschensville would be hard to spell. Demens had wanted to call Oakland St. Petersburg? Why not call the town on the Gulf by that name? St. Petersburg, officially, had made the map.

Demens left Florida for Asheville, North Carolina, where he bought a mill. Three years later, bored, he went west to Los Angeles with plans to become a pioneer of steam laundries. In an arena of wet wash and rough dry he finally found himself. Four years later he had made a quarter of a million dollars. But then he got bored once more and decided to grow California oranges. On a grove near the town of Alta Loma he lived quietly; occasionally, he wrote articles on foreign affairs for California newspapers, and once he visited Russia. But California had granted him the success Russia and Florida had not. He spent the rest of his life at Alta Loma. When the Russian Revolution erupted he was elated. Many of the cabinet members in the Kerensky government were his friends. His daughter Vera had married Count Andrei Tolstoy and the couple had joined him in California to run the Demens estate on Tolstoyan agricultural principles. After Kerensky, the Bolsheviks shattered the Demens family's hopes. Peter Demens died a cynic. In the year of his death, 1919, St. Petersburg, Florida, had not yet become heaven for anybody. Only recently had it managed to get cows and rooting hogs off its unpaved streets.

By the end of the eighteen eighties, though, shores of the Hillsborough and eastern Tampa Bay were rapidly being cleared and settled as St. Petersburg's were not. The magnetism of Henry Plant had fascinated America. Fresh spurts of Florida literature flooded bookshops, and some of it was even realistic. "Look before you leap!" the editor of *Our Home Circle* warned prospective settlers. "Yes, Florida has malaria. But can you name a country or a state that has it not?" Loyally—for she was a Floridian herself—she added:

> Children who are racked and nervous and stand at death's door from the attacks of measles, scarlatina, or whooping cough, almost invariably recover rapidly if they are brought to Florida, and that too with little if any medical treatment.

Domestic help, of course, would be a problem. She had once found her maid dancing a jig over broken dishes in the kitchen:

> "Once there was six, now there's two;
> Hoo, hoo, hoo! Hoo, hoo, hoo!"

There were moths to be fought with turpentine, cockroaches to be routed with a mixture of borax and sugar. Every three months the careful housewife would empty all her closets and throw scalding water over all the shelves. "Surepop" and "Rough on Rats" were good for rodents, and so was powder made from the South African pyrethrum daisy. Today nontoxic pyrethrum insecticide is a Florida staple which may not completely rout the roaches so tactfully called palmetto beetles but at least slows them down. Of course, said the lady from *Our Home Circle,* you got used to fleas: "Always carry your little powder gun. Lizards? There is no harm in them, not even a particle."

In tiny towns like Thonotosassa, life on the orange groves was primitive in more ways than one. Children ran barefoot. Some of them, freed from the restraints of winter, turned half wild. Baptist Sunday School teachers made valiant efforts to civilize them. One afternoon a Thonotosassa mother heard the squeals of children and the meows of a terrified cat. When she hurried outside she found her brood stuffing the protesting animal into a grave they had dug. Were they burying it alive?

"We're baptizin' it, Ma. In the name of the Father and of the Son, into the hole he goes."

Near the newly founded community of Dade City, on the edge of the Green Swamp, backwoods offspring were even wilder. They were at "the clabber end" of Mr. Plant's territory and teenaged girls there bore little resemblance to the Victorian maidens they were supposed to imitate. In particular they took to holding "Ether Parties." A Dade City elder left a frank testimony:

> I as a kid stood amazed at what they did. Some cried, and some laughed and sang love songs, and went so far as to kneel down before a young man and tell him what they thought of him. It bordered on vulgarity.

During the pyrotechnic growth of post-Reconstruction southwest Florida, not all the trips went down Mr. Plant's railroad or the white rapids of the Hillsborough out to Tampa Bay. Some continued to the very Doors of Perception.

19

Messages
to Gómez

The bay was changing rapidly now. Where the curve of sunlight-dappled mangroves along its shores had once been unbroken, there were interfering phosphate docks, and wharves piled high with the cargo Plant trains had brought to be shipped out on Plant steamers: palmetto logs, turpentine barrels, cedar. Waters which had been as clear as Crystal Springs in the deep woods up the Hillsborough were now clouded—only a little, true, but as Tampa exploded, the soot and waste of industry became denser every year until corners of the bay were too dirty to swim in.

The river, too, was changing. Impatient of ferries, Henry Plant gave it a bridge across Lafayette Street. Freight of lumber lay heavily on the water beneath. As Tampa built, soil which had been held by the trees of its wilderness was overturned by construction gangs and piles of it were left to erode into a river that began turning browner, as if now it were drawing its source from some unending and unseen cypress pool. Overhead the hard clarity of the sky was an abrupt contrast to the murkiness below. Mixed with the smell of sulphur were other smells these days: citric acid from the orange peels a city discarded, sewage running unchecked where Timucuan water gods had once danced in the diamond light of springs. Pale willows still swayed at the river's edge. People planted tulip and magnolia trees along its banks when they built their houses there. The robins Sidney Lanier had loved still poured songs into winters that were not winter. Unmistakably, though, the Hillsborough was the river of a city—a great city, the loyal affirmed. Hunters had to go farther and farther inland for deer and doves and squirrels. It was a drama which had already been enacted in most of the rest of America. But the Green Swamp still towered against encroaching civilization. Its birds and trees were innocent of Henry Plant's trains. Each year the contrast grew between swamp river, forest river, suburban river, and city river. Sprawled along the bay lay Port Tampa, with its own quarantine station and immigration offices. At the end of a mile-long pier stood The Inn, which sheltered the arriving and departing. Among them was the naturalist Frank M. Chapman, who stopped at The Inn on his way from Key West to north Florida. Chapman was amazed at the forest of masts and rigging and funnels which were the Port Tampa docks, but he was also fascinated by the fact that birds were flourishing even so.

> There were more water-birds in Tampa Bay than I have seen elsewhere; laughing gulls in adult plumage were common, one to two hundred being observed. . . . All the buoys and stakes were crowned with either brown pelicans or cormorants and some were on the wing. Some of the channel posts have cross pieces nailed to them making five or six steps and occasionally each step would have its cormorant. Halfway up the bay to Port Tampa we sailed through a scattered school of devil-fish. There were at least fifty in twos, threes or fours distributed over an area two hundred yards in width and six hundred in length. They were all near the surface, some with the back out of the water, and the tips of the wings were frequently thrown up showing the white undersurface.

Chapman found the customs officers courteous and The Inn delightful. "There are many covered walks and lounging places, in fact it has been made very attractive." Near the hotel, the bay was clear. Mullets were leaping in late light, and lesser scaup ducks swam boldly up to the piers. Chapman paused to take in the scene: the vermilion-gold of a setting sun, white sails dotting the ruddy water, pelicans and cormorants and ducks riding soft waves together. He hoped there were no plume hunters nearby.

In several suburban yards Tampans had planted guava trees. Many had been brought from Cuba to the village of Sarasota decades before by a farmer named Valentine Snell. One of the persisting myths of modern Tampa is that flocks of mockingbirds spread Snell's Cuban seeds north to the river and the bay. True, perhaps, but Tampans enjoyed guavas too much to leave the distribution to chance. Guava paste and yellow cheese on hard bread were a latin staple. In the early summer of 1885 Tampa received two visitors particularly interested in guavas: Bernardino Gargol, a Cuban guava planter, and his friend Gavino Gutiérrez, a New York importer of the fruit. The trees they found in Tampa were unimpressive but both men were enchanted by the flooding sunlight and thick vegetation everywhere. Tampa was obviously a city on the way up. Fortunes might be made in something besides guavas. In New York, Gargol and Gutiérrez began singing Tampa's praises to a Key West cigar manufacturer named Vicente Martínez Ybor. Ybor was disillusioned with Key West; perpetual labor troubles had been dogging him. Why not shift his operations to Tampa? The Board of Trade, when he contacted them, offered special tax advantages. When a fire destroyed his principal Key West factory his mind was made up. He would establish the cigar business in Tampa on a grand scale. With his partner Eduard Manrara he began laying out a town on land which was sold him by Major Lesley. Ybor City, it would be named. As the Ybor y Manrara plant rose, plots began to sell; in less than a week newly arrived cigar workers bought two hundred and fifty lots. New York cigar magnate Ignacio Haya decided to join Ybor. Others followed. Within a few years, three thousand Cubans had come to Tampa to work in cigar factories. Now the city was not only a cow town, but a cigar capital, and Ybor City began its own tumultuous, particolored life a few miles east of downtown Tampa and the river. On Sundays the beaches of the Pinellas peninsula resounded with the excited laughter of frolicking Cubans on picnicking expeditions. Peter Demens's railroad actually began to make a little money.

America was a cigar-smoking country. In a halcyon era before anyone had suspected a link between smoking and cancer men puffed contentedly away at a variety of cigars from cheap stogies to expensive cheroots. Cigar smokers had their own folklore. "A thoughtful girl," one writer reported, "says that when she dies she desires tobacco to be planted over her grave, that the weed nourished by her dust may be smoked by her bereaved lovers." A poet was moved to describe how the lovers,

> . . . gazing on the plant, their griefs restrain
> In whispering, "Lo! Dear Anna blooms again!"

The jingle of the time was *A Good Cigar*:

> Oh, 'tis well enough
> A whiff or a puff
> From the heart of a pipe to get,

> And a dreary maid
> Or a budding blade
> May toy with a cigarette.
> But a man, when the time
> Of a glorious prime
> Dawns forth like a morning star,
> Wants the dark brown bloom
> And the sweet perfume
> That go with a good cigar!

Ybor y Manrara, Sánchez y Haya, Cuesta, Emilio Pons: all were prestigious names, and all were soon headquartered in Ybor City. Independent operators hand-rolled cigars in storefront "buckeyes." Ybor City was fragrant with the delicate aroma of *Vuelta Abajo* tobacco, which came from a district in Cuba and, when pure, made up a "clear Havana." One of the most talked-about inventions of the hour was a cigar-rolling machine dreamed up by the New York editor of *The Tobacco Journal*; it made a dozen at a time. He had also perfected a wooden cigar mold to insure uniformity in the finished product. When he died, nearly a hundred patents were to his credit; he was also fond of opera, and when he wasn't devising cigar-making machinery he was managing artists. His name was Oscar Hammerstein.

Today the cigar industry of Tampa is totally mechanized. But though automation has come to stay, there are still personal touches. People are needed to run the machines. On my first tour of the Hav-a-Tampa Cigar Corporation I was amazed to see sinks full of turnips. "Some of our workers have vegetable gardens," the manager explained. "In the morning they bring in their fresh produce to sell." It was, for me, a human touch in the midst of all that mass production, and an echo of the atmosphere of Ybor City's beginnings.

Cigar making by hand was (and is, for the scattered few buckeyes still doing it) an art. Cigar smokers like Thomas Edison were loud in the praises of their favorite brands. To Edison the only menace was cigarettes:

> The injurious agent in cigarettes comes principally from the burning paper wrapper. The substance thereby formed is called acrolein. It has a violent action in the nerve centers, producing degeneration of the cells of the brain, which is quite rapid among boys. Unlike most narcotics, this degeneration is permanent and uncontrollable. I employ no person who smokes cigarettes.

Cigars were blessedly guiltless. They were covered not by paper but by shade tobacco from the Connecticut River valley or the broad plantation fields of Gadsden County in north Florida, where the growing of tobacco under cloth screens or shades had been pioneered in America.

A cigar consists of two parts: the body, called the bunch, and the outer covering. The tobacco comprising the bunch is called the filler. Sometimes the bunch is first covered with an inside layer known as a binder. Otherwise the bunch is covered directly with the wrapper leaf. There are two types of filler, long and short. In long-filler cigars the tobacco leaves and parts are as long as the cigar itself. They are rolled together to form the bunch; cigars of this type command high prices. Short-filler cigars are made of chopped and broken tobacco. Sometimes the broken leaves used as fillers are called, with honesty, scrap. Three different types of leaf are needed for wrapper, binder, and filler. Color, texture, aroma, uniformity, blending properties: all are factors considered in the evaluation of tobacco. These days clear Havana cigars don't acquire their contents directly from Havana. Nevertheless Tampa's grading and manufacturing standards have remained rigid.

In the time of Vicente Martínez Ybor the cycle began with the sowing of tobacco in Cuban fields each September. In finely harrowed soil a series of plantings took place. Anxious eyes watched the skies for signs of a hurricane, which could destroy a tobacco plot and often a fortune overnight. In October the tiny plants were transplanted. The wrapper leaves were grown under slats or cloths; the filler leaves were left exposed. In January the mature leaves were cut and dried. Toiling Cubans with aching backs gathered the leaves under warm skies and strung the leaves by passing a needle and thread through the head of the stems. Then the leaves were left to dry for from two to six weeks. Again, rain and humidity could be a disaster. But with luck the winter in Cuba was usually dry, and the harvest could be processed promptly.

When the tobacco was dry it was moved by wagons into new fields where trained selectors sorted and graded it. Each "hand" of tobacco consisted of about fifty leaves; the hands were packed in bales protected by palmetto bark. Four hands, a "carat," were packed at a time. Eighty carats made a bale and weighed about eighty pounds. In mid-June the agents of the Tampa maunfacturers came to Cuba. If the tobacco was to be stored in warehouses before use, it had to be matured correctly. Stripping of the filler tobacco began when the leaves were watered and allowed to stand moist overnight. Then the lower parts of the stems were removed by hand. After the stripping the tobacco was put into barrels to "sweat"—that is, to age anywhere from several months to several years. Plant steamers to Tampa were heavy with the weight of it, and the customs house at the port was redolent of the slightly tart fragrance of the best *Vuelta Abajo*. Everywhere the language spoken was Spanish. Dark Spanish eyes glowed with pride as the barrels were unloaded. Spanish hands gesticulated, and Spanish voices bargained. It was all very colorful, conceded Anglo-Saxon Tampans, and the money it brought was nice; but why did these people have to be so . . . well, exuberant? Lower class Anglo-Saxons in Tampa, the "rednecks," were less evasive. They simply called the cigar people Cuban Niggers.

Not that the Cubans were happy with everything in their new home. The Town of Fort Brooke, in particular, rankled. It was too close to Ybor City for comfort. "Pornográfico!" exclaimed cigar manufacturer Emilio del Río. The Cubans took to calling most of the prostitutes *lobas,* female wolves. But the most famous was La Culebra, "the serpent." La Culebra was a mulatto who flaunted her satins and dingy laces along Sixth Avenue, near the border between the Town of Fort Brooke and Ybor City. Sometimes she stood boldly soliciting business outside Athanasou's Greek Café and Imperial Theater. When the Cubans complained to Tampa's city fathers, they were made to understand that nobody meant to do anything about a red light district which was at least relatively contained. It was a "Zona de Tolerancia," del Río concluded bitterly, "extremely disgusting to the honorable latin families of Ybor City." Secure in the free-for-all permissiveness, La Culebra sauntered on, her head top-heavy with a hat trimmed by the graceful plumes of snowy egrets from hidden bay rookeries. The rest of the *lobas* plied their trade unhindered. When a patron's enjoyments caught up with his health, he hurried off to visit the Indian Doctor on the Pinellas peninsula; the Indian Doctor wore cowboy clothes dyed black. Dr. Weightnovel had his successor. Respectable Tampa and St. Petersburg shut their eyes. They still do; recent urban renewal has merely shifted the base of sporting house operations.

In the beginning all Ybor City factories were dedicated to the Spanish hand process of actual cigar making. Every step in the manufacturing process was performed by a single worker. The tools he needed were a specially cured hardwood board and a curved knife; if he were a strict

Tobacco factory, Ybor City

traditionalist, he used no binder, only filler and wrapper. In the high wooden factories with their slatted windows facing east and west for proper light the cigarmakers were seated at long tables heavy with their workboards. The filler was never weighed; that would have been an offense against latin honor. It was assumed that no worker took any. He was allowed to smoke as many finished cigars as he cared to. It was a privilege he guarded jealously. To measure the thickness of his cigar he had a gauge, and to measure its length he used a ruler. First he trimmed the wrapper leaf to the size he wanted, depending on the type of cigar— panatela, corona, perfecto, queen, sublime. Then he formed the bunch, taking the filler leaves in his hand and setting them parallel to each other. In this way he created a draft for the smoke. It took years of experience to "get the feel of the hand" for the operation, veterans maintained. The tip of the leaf had to be toward the burn of the cigar, the side veins running upward toward the left. Whenever the cigar worker had ordered the bunch the way he wanted it, he rolled the cigar by starting at the lighting end—the tuck—and finishing it at the mouth end, the head. Then he completed the head by moistening it with a drop or two of gum tragacanth, a sticky but tasteless and odorless substance imported from Asia.

When he had completed fifty cigars he tied them in a bundle and put a number on it. This was his only record of the wages due him. Every day the bundles were piled thick onto rolling hand trucks, put on elevators, and taken down to the inspection room where foremen waited to inspect them the next morning. If a foreman wanted to inspect the factory itself, tradition decreed that he do so at noon and only at noon. If he criticized too many cigars from one worker, angry voices were raised. Every man in the plant had his own dignity, his own rights and privileges. When these were invaded epic feuds resulted which extended all the way to families and relatives by marriage.

Both picking and packing were two-man operations. At his table near the factory's windows the picker sorted the cigars into as many as a hundred piles of slightly varying colors. A picker's eyes were sharp after years of experience. When he had gathered a single pile of fifty identical cigars the packer arranged them in a box with the correct label. What the distant customer was paying for was not only tobacco, but the time of craftsmen. When the box had been packed it went to another table where each of its cigars was banded. The cigars had to be replaced in

Wrapping cigars

identical order. Then the boxes were sealed and wheeled to a humidified storeroom to await shipment north in Plant System trains. It was not long before Ybor City was an American institution, and the names of its founders familiar household words.

The first steps toward mechanization in cigarmaking came with the introduction of hand molds before the turn of the century. In this process the workers gathered in groups of three; one man made the bunch, two men rolled it. Molds necessitated the use of binder leaves; the result might still be a clear Havana, but it was a slightly different product from the luxury hand-rolled cigars which were Vicente Martínez Ybor's pride. The molds were wooden; most contained about a dozen cigar-shaped depressions. When the rolled cigars were bound they were pressed into the molds for about twenty minutes; then they were wrapped, and the steps of manufacture were the same as in Spanish hand-rolling. Gradually other touches of mechanization crept in. Bunching machines came into use after 1910. A suction-wrapping machine was also tried. Such developments frightened the workers, who felt new methods endangered not only their jobs but their justification as artists. A cigar worker in New York named Samuel Gompers at first protested bitterly at the use of the simplest molds and called for a massive strike. In old age, after he had founded the American Federation of Labor, he confessed: "From that time there came some light to my mind, and I realized . . . it was absolutely futile for workmen to protest against or to go on strike against the introduction of a machine, a new device, or a new tool." Accept the machines, Gompers advised Tampa, but organize the workers. The International Cigarmakers' Union had been started in New York during the Civil War. It flourished in Tampa, where collective bargaining earned Cuban workers the wage of seven dollars per thousand cigars. After mechanization began, a detailed list of labor rates for more than a hundred sizes and shapes and grades of cigars was drawn up. This was the "Cartabon," which soon became ironclad law. The rates never varied. At first the Cartabon was good protection

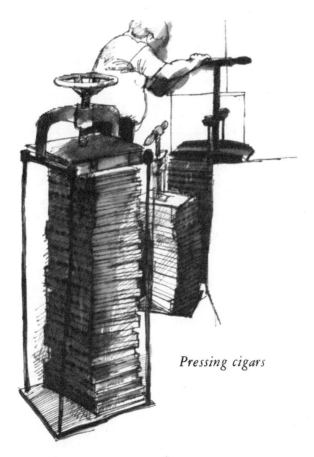

Pressing cigars

against rate cutting. Not until the Depression of the 1930s did it become the cigar industry's strangler. Periodically, through the years, Ybor City was rocked by strikes and violent protests. When machines came at last, unemployed cigar workers had to think of making new careers in other industries.

Perfectionists linger, though. On a small Ybor City side street near Las Novedades, one of the city's landmark Spanish restaurants, lives my friend Esteban Valdés. He and his wife work every evening in their small shop making with grace, care, and love the Tampanela cigars which are ordered by connoisseurs from all over the United States. Cuban tobacco has been replaced by Brazilian and Honduran, but the workroom of Esteban Valdés is still strongly reminiscent of Tampa's Havana past. Scales, boxes, rows of tobacco cutters and containers of gum tragacanth lie in precise order along his table. The odor there is subtle, faintly wheatlike. From time to time boys and girls with guitars drift in and play for Esteban as he works; his hospitality to the musical young is a byword. It was one night while I was standing in front of Esteban's that the spell of Ybor City and its traditions assailed me to an extent that was almost heartache. Many times since I have tried to sort out the elements which made up the scene, so vivid yet so elusive. In the east there was a hazy blue-purple twilight, and in it a single pallid star. Overhead a jacaranda tree shivered gently, a cascade of blue flowers and delicately traced green leaves. A train was rumbling through Ybor City on tracks Henry Plant had built; clattering, too, lurching yet muffled, its iron wheels singing low. In the west the sunset suddenly turned wild into a fire which faded slowly as the yellow globes of the old-fashioned streetlamps came on one by one. Fainter and fainter grew the rolling of the train which was carrying Ybor City cigars to the rest of America and to its ports. Behind his glass window still sat Esteban, his face impassive and beautiful. Las Novedades began to turn all light; I could hear laughter as couples began to go toward it for an evening meal of pompano or *arroz con pollo*. Whenever the restaurant's doors opened, fragmented strains of a flamenco guitar floated out only to wane as twilight waned and the night closed down. The rough bricks on the storefronts merged their outlines, the jacaranda fluttered, and because I had to leave, the dream was over. But I knew then that for me Ybor City had a beauty that the French Quarter of New Orleans would never have. The tourists come to Ybor City as they do to the French Quarter, but its vigor is still in cigar factories which are alive, not museums, not reconstructions. When you stare up at them it is easy to imagine the heyday of the handmade clear Havana, when workers were bent over their tables while a reader engaged by the company would intone everything from newspapers to propaganda literature for a free Cuba. The cigar factories were universities of liberation. The yoke of a decadent Spain, to Cuba, was becoming too heavy to bear. Apostles of Cuban freedom like José Martí were touring the United States trying to rally support for Máximo Gómez, the Cuban general who waited in the Antilles for the right time to march on Havana. From the beginning Ybor City had its part in the planning of the Cuban revolution. Ybor City Cubans were frank enough about it. They smuggled so much information about men and money to the general in boxes of perfectos and panatelas that they nicknamed their cigars "Messages to Gómez."

Always Ybor City was lively. There were the Christmas fiestas, when fat, bespectacled, benevolent Vicente Martínez Ybor sent wagons into the streets laden with gifts of suckling pigs and pastries for his Cuban families. There were, of course, cockfights, and Sundays so alive with the color of mantillas and lace-edged dresses and tight, elegant suits that onlookers from Tampa proper were horrified: it looked like a fair, and fairs were not decent on the Sabbath. The smell of thick Cuban coffee poured warmly from tiny restaurants. Always there were jokes: lovers were teased, a favorite reader would be hailed as he promenaded Broadway, the city's central thoroughfare. *El Lector* commanded respect, though hecklers would ask, "Señor, do you yet have warts on your lungs?" Ybor City bakeries provided thousands of loaves of Cuban bread each day. Kitchens were sweet with guava paste. Old people played dominoes at sidewalk tables under the areca palms each evening. The men of the community built themselves centers for them and their wives, where they danced and argued politics. The Centro Asturiano was for those of Spanish descent from the province of Asturias. El Liceo Cubano filled on Saturday nights with bright, gesturing crowds, electric lights, and potted palms. Slowly then the couples danced decorous Spanish dances while guitars urged. There were Ybor City parades, when blades disguised themselves as Don Quixote and Sancho Panza. The Order of Gentlemen of the Light, *Caballeros de la Luz,* serenaded primly shirtwaisted daughters tired from long hours over the cigar tables. Many families lived in "tenement houses" (the term was no disgrace) with pointed gables in the Spanish style, gingerbread porches, and tiny stone blackamoors which provided hitching posts at the curbs of streets that at first were sand and then, with affluence, brick. As far away as "el Río Hillsborough" young Cuban couples had their preferred steamer, *La Favorita,* which sailed them by moonlight (under strict chaperonage) out to Tampa Bay. But in all the romance there was always an element of pain. Ybor City has its poet, contemporary novelist José Yglesias, who has given grim testimony of Anglo-Saxon Tampa's failure to accept the cigar workers as Americans. Under such circumstances the Cubans felt doubly obliged to build institutions like El Centro Español, which was everything from a social club to a sanitarium. It boasted the latest X-ray machines, an operating theater, and hospital rooms; these were all upstairs. Below was the large ballroom with its waving palms, its blue ceiling and gleaming gold walls. A parquet floor glowed in muted evening light at the dances; around the dancing area the tables were covered in spotless white. Each sported a capacious ashtray for cigars. In the Centro's saloon the floor was of Spanish tile, and ice-cream-parlor chairs were ranged against an ornate wainscoting. The Centro also sponsored picnics. While the water of Tampa Bay sparkled beyond, everyone drank dry red Marques de Riscal wine. Tampa's clinic waiting rooms might be called the Salon of Hope, but they seldom were. To the fatalistic Cubans, a ride in an ambulance was usually considered one way. Life was to be savored while it could be.

And then the Italians came—from Sicily, mostly, and most went into the food business. Savarese, Nuccio and Lazzara became familiar Ybor City names. The founder of the wholesale grocery firm of Castellano and Pizzo came to Ybor City well equipped with dreams but not with cash. But Signor Pizzo soon got it as he catered for the large assemblies of the latin clubs. In a few years he was able to buy up most of his native Sicilian village of Santo Stefano, though he remained in Tampa. The Italians built a social club of their own. Ybor City real estate rapidly changed hands. Its latins were all lavishly hospitable and derided the stingy puritan decorum of the rest of Tampa. When a latin man said, "I'm workin' for the English," he meant for nothing.

In the shadow of The Clock, which fronted one of the cigar factories and early became an Ybor City symbol, the Cubans and the Italians mixed uneasily. Both races were proud; Spanish arrogance prompted

The Clock, Ybor City

Italian defiance of it. All were Catholic, but when a Cuban wanted to marry an Italian it was considered a mixed marriage, and families were torn asunder. Romantics shouted at nationalists. Many a youthful Italian suitor was told to leave Tampa by the first train out when he had dared to propose to a Cuban girl. When a Cuban met an Italian in a prizefight, the result was often a riot. Cubans sneered at Italians because, true to a rural heritage, they kept cows and goats and chickens and built brick bread ovens in their yards. The smell of oregano-rich spaghetti sauce mingled in Ybor City lanes with the fragrance of Spanish garbanzo beans. Over everything hung a perpetual aroma of black coffee and cigars. Any man rash enough to join the ranks of antitobacco crusaders invited a beating. Dieters were unheard of. Ybor City smoked and ate hard, and though its people had differences among themselves they united in a solid phalanx where Anglo-Saxons were concerned. Brave indeed was the pair of missionaries who established a Methodist Center in Ybor City. Astonishingly, they made some converts. Perhaps there were Cubans disillusioned with Spain's tyrannic foreign policies or with the dictates of the Catholic church. Periodically Ybor City was swept by fires; the jerry-built wooden houses of the cigar workers went up like tinder then.

Fires were not the only excitement; Ybor City had more than its share of pistol duels. Occasionally the social barriers between downtown Tampa and Ybor City were lowered. The son or daughter (usually a daughter) of a cigar factory owner might marry into what had become Tampa's Confederate Old Guard. But the Cubans and Italians were doubly suspect because many of them were well versed in the works of Charles Darwin and Karl Marx. Ybor City, said Tampa high society, was a hotbed of socialism and revolution. Partly this was correct. *Cuba* and *El Mosquito* were Ybor City newspapers which frankly advocated the freedom of Cuba from Spain by violence. From Ybor City began to issue speeches that eventually plunged America into war.

In 1868 a group of rebels in eastern Cuba's Oriente Province had proclaimed the country's independence. It was the beginning of the Ten Years' War which enriched Tampa cattlemen and sapped Cuba's vitality nearly to the point of death. At first the rebels were few—a hundred and forty-seven of them against the might of imperial Spain. But in a year rebel ranks had swelled to more than twenty-five thousand. Cuba was being ravaged by destruction and murder which made life and property perpetually uncertain. Plantations blazed up yellow into the hot black tropic nights. Rifles clattered in sugarcane fields. Women were violated and crying children starved. Horses' hooves beat a hectic tattoo on village roads as night riders on both sides marauded and laid waste. The land was full of blood and smoke, until the rebel leader Gómez was defeated in the province of Camagüey. Then the war degenerated into a series of petty conflicts between bandits. In 1877 Gómez was forced to sign a treaty with the Spanish Captain-General Martinez Campos. The Ten Years' War had cost Cuba two hundred thousand lives and seven hundred million dollars in property losses. But Cuba was aflame with its patriotism, and its prophet was the exiled José Martí, who travelled America winning sympathy for his cause.

As a boy Martí had been deported from Cuba to Spain because of his revolutionary ideals. When he came back to Cuba after the Ten Years' War he began making anti-Spanish speeches. Again he was arrested. After a spectacular escape he reached New York City, where he organized a Cuban Junta. Other cities followed suit. Key West soon boasted a total of sixty-one freedom clubs, and Tampa more conservatively had fifteen. "A tenth of all your earnings!" revolutionary leaders exhorted the cigarmakers. Martí vowed that his memory of Cuba was "a basket of flames." Every word he spoke was reported to Ybor City by Néstor Carbonell and his son Eligio, dedicated journalists who led Ybor City with the cry of "Cuba libre!" When the city suffered a particularly disastrous fire, Martí received the message that "even the Tampa fire would help make the desire for your visit there even hotter." The Ignacio Agramonte Club, named for a hero of the Ten Years' War, invited Martí to come himself to Ybor City and address them. He would find that on the shores of Tampa Bay Cuba libre was more than a slogan. Tampa's Cubans were homesick; in their hearts patriotism was all the more poignant because it was a link to the past.

Rain was pouring down in heavy sheets the night officials of the Ignacio Agramonte Club gathered at the little Ybor City railroad station to welcome Martí. This part of the city was known contemptuously as The Scrub. A group of young Cubans had to carry sticks to beat off rattlesnakes and alligators crawling in the streets because of the downpour. Lanterns swayed eerily in the storm, brief shafts of gold illuminating the heavy streaks of rain which fell ceaselessly on. For hours the delegation waited. Martí's train was late. The storm, perhaps, had made it impossible for him to come on time. Trees were down along the line.

But at midnight a train whistle rose mournfully at last above the rain's pattering. Slowly, the train puffed in. What a travel-weary Martí saw when he dismounted was a group of about fifty chilled and dripping men. The lanterns, and the sticks for the snakes and alligators, startled him. Slowly the brief procession of his honor guard sloshed its way through the mud toward Rubiera's Hotel, where a room had been reserved in Martí's name. At the door of the hotel he paused to smile. Turning, he told his audience: "I am happy to feel myself among warriors."

The following day the sun broke through. The bricks of cigar factories baked in the strong light of an October morning. Sun and shade made patterns on the slatted windows of Ybor y Manrara and Ignacio y Haya. (Ironically, the King of Spain smoked Cuesta cigars from Tampa.) Tiny Cuban flags rippled in the wind. Garlands of leaves had been wound around the posts of street lamps. Martí looked curiously at the workers' white frame houses on their stilts; here and there he saw gaps left by the latest fire. Vacant lots were crowded with rubble—roof shingles, clapboards, fence posts. With Ramón Rivera, the *lector* of Ybor y Manrara, he entered the door to breathe the tang of *Vuelta abajo*. The reader substituting for Rivera closed his book abruptly. There was a dramatic silence. Then, all of them as one, the cigarmakers rose to welcome their visitor with sharp taps of their leaf folders on the tables before them. José Martí smiled.

That night the dining hall of the Liceo Cubano was crowded. Its walls were hung with hastily executed paintings of famous Cubans, Gómez and the mulatto leader Macéo, Narciso López who had led an abortive revolution years before. Tricolor Cuban revolutionary flags hung from the molding. When Martí walked in an uproar of cheers echoed in the wooden building. Everyone began singing a revolutionary hymn. The Cuban stenographer imported from Key West to take down the proceedings was so agitated he broke three pencils. But when Martí gave the signal that he was about to speak, silence fell. The lighthearted Cubans who so often had parties in the banquet hall were sobered by Martí's pallid face and the tense way his hands gripped the back of his chair. He was a small man; his high forehead gave his face the shape of an egg, for he was balding. His nose was long and narrow, his moustache and goatee modestly clipped. In his mouth there was a firm line of purpose; in his eyes, pain. Martí had seen Cuba bleeding and broken; now he longed to mobilize the large latin community of Tampa to take action.

"If in things concerning my country I should be given the choice of one good over all others," he told them, "this would be the good I should choose: I should want the cornerstone of our Republic to be the devotion of Cubans to the full dignity of man. . . . Either the Republic has as its foundation the basic character of every one of her sons, his habit of working with his hands and thinking for himself and respecting, as if it were a matter of family honor, the unrestricted freedom of others—in short, the passion for man's essential worth—or else the Republic is not worth a single one of the tears of our women nor a solitary drop of a brave man's blood."

Inexorably, in tones hardening with urgency, Martí told his audience they must help him to banish "the colonial soul" in Cuba. They must accept "the generous Negro, the Negro brother" and cast aside fear of going barefoot "which is now a very common way of going in Cuba, since, between the thieves and those who help them, no one in Cuba has shoes except the thieves and their accomplices." Then he began building toward the climax he knew he must give his hearers if they were to act. "Now!" he told them. "Now! Form your ranks! Countries are not created by wishful thinking in the depths of the soul! . . . Let us rise so that liberty does not run any risk in its hour of triumph through disorder or indolence or impatience in its preparation. Let us rise for the real Republic . . . Let us place around the star in the new flag this formula of triumphant love: 'With all, for the good of all.' " Moments later Martí was watching the first row of his audience rise and begin advancing toward the stage. Soon he was lost in a sea of embraces. Women in the room were standing on their chairs and cheering, waving their gloves and lace handkerchiefs. Some were crying. "Viva!" everyone cheered, and José Martí knew he had begun his work in Ybor City well.

In the days that followed he went into the lace-curtained drawing rooms of the factory owners, and also into the cramped houses of the most menial workers. In the parlor of Cuban-black Cornelio Brito he founded the Tampa League for Instruction, a revolutionary study group. Hostesses offered him *garapiña,* fermented pineapple juice, to drink, and proffered glazed cakes. He saw posters in the clubs: "Viva José Martí!" Little Carmita Carbonell presented him with a pen and ink stand as a souvenir of the Cubans of Tampa, and he was moved to tears. At the Liceo Cubano he gave a second address. "Crime itself can be redeemed by love," he told his hearers. Cubans could not "live like jackals in a cage milling around in their own hate." Martyrs to the Cuban cause were "the heroic yeast which liberty needed for leavening." Then he paused, searching for a memory. It came, a brief vision of light near the Hillsborough River during the storm on the day he had been riding down to Tampa.

> Suddenly the sun broke through a clearing in the woods, and there in the dazzling of the unexpected light I saw above the yellowish grass proudly rising from among the black trunks of the fallen trees the flourishing branches of new pines. That is what we are: new pines!

The slogan ran like wildfire through Ybor City. By the afternoon of José Martí's departure a crowd of four thousand people had gathered in the street near the railroad station. Flags waved; a military band was tooting and piping and thumping. Martí climbed up to his car. Then his audience saw him step out onto the platform and wave a last farewell. He, too, was a new pine; small, vigorous and tough. The Tampa police who had been sent to keep order in the crowd had no idea of what all the excitement was about; latins were latins, they shrugged to one another, and it was like them to cry and rant at the sight of a short little man saluting from the rear of one of Henry Plant's trains.

He stands in Ybor City today in the tiny Park of the Friends of José Martí. His pale statue has been smoothed by successive rainy seasons. Feathery podocarpus bushes rise darkly around him. On his arm he wears a band of black cloth; Tampa Cubans are conservatives now and none of them has forgiven Fidel Castro, the twentieth century rebel of Oriente province. There are Tampans alive who remember Martí's comings and goings, the music of his voice, the clarity of his eyes and the depth of his compassion. They remember the alligators at the railroad station, the rain, and the slow voice of Rivera the *lector* as he brought Martí before the men and women of Ybor y Manrara, who then tapped their cigar sticks in greeting. Some, too, remember what a modern poet, Justo Sierra, has written of their idol:

> . . . In the peace of the funereal night,
> Like a lamp of glory, his solitary star burns on.

20

"Think You This Is Not the Alhambra?"

September 1887, was a torrid month. Near the end of it an importer of Cuban fruits died suddenly, and the news that he had died of yellow fever spread like the plague itself. A few days afterwards a housewife followed him to the grave. By the time the third victim had perished Tampa was in a panic. Two more deaths forced the city health officer to declare a state of epidemic. Tampans began piling their belongings on wagons and in carriages for flight up the Hillsborough into the country. Doors were left unlocked; in empty houses forgotten lights went on burning, grim sentinels piercing city nights sinister with heat and contagion. The editor of the *Tampa Tribune* left a young printer in charge. With two black helpers, he continued to grind out the paper, but each day brought a fresh list of deaths for them to put in type. Stores closed. On steaming afternoons tar barrels burned at street corners, sending up clouds of pungent black smoke which doctors hoped would kill the mysterious germs. They didn't. When the death toll had topped one hundred, a relief committee was organized; widows and children had often been left destitute. The city sent out emergency calls for more physicians and nurses, who responded. But the horror dragged on until a sharp freeze descended to kill yellow fever mosquitoes as well as young fruit trees. By January 1888, the epidemic was over. But now no northerners wanted to visit its site.

Once again, Henry Plant came to the city's rescue. The "father of

Tampa" announced plans to expand Port Tampa and to build the most fabulous hotel in the western world. Tampa would become a must in international society. He was shrewd enough to know that what mankind would not risk for the promise of fun it would gladly risk for fashion. Tourists would come because they had to come in order to qualify as seasoned travelers. St. Petersburg was all very well for the sort of individual who cared about careening down the toboggan slides the Orange Belt Railroad had recently built on Tampa Bay. Penny arcades might be good enough for people who came to live cheaply and enjoy the simple pleasures, but the Tampa Bay Hotel would attract captains of industry and royal families.

Already millionaire Henry Morrison Flagler, head of the Flagler System of east Florida railroads, had built his sprawling Ponce de León Hotel in St. Augustine. "The climate of the East Coast of Florida," pronounced his general passenger agent, "is nearer perfection than that of any other place on earth." Yellow fever wasn't mentioned in Jacksonville or St. Augustine, though both cities had had their share of it. Henry Plant was not a man to take a rival's publicity lying down. To better Flagler's Ponce de León, however, he knew he would have to come up with something freshly staggering to civilized man.

St. Augustine had long been laying claim to Ponce de León's Fountain of Youth. It was also the site of an early Catholic mission and was regarded by the devout as a shrine. Its stately Catholic cathedral dated from the late eighteenth century. Undeniably, with its old city gates and cobbled streets and jogging surreys, St. Augustine had charm. It contained the Oldest House, the Oldest Jail, and various other hypothetical Oldests within the continental limits of the United States. A mighty Spanish fort, the Castillo de San Marcos, still dominated the harbor. But the wonder of Americans was reserved for the Ponce de León Hotel itself. Nothing like it had ever been seen. Two pointed towers reminiscent of a Spanish cathedral—the lavish kind found in Spain—thrust upward into the St. Augustine sky. Fountains abounded in gardens that covered acres. There were Moorish cloisters, wrought-iron weather vanes intricately cast into curlicues and oranges, Gothic niches, and at the gate a portcullis which seemed to be waiting to let pass the armies of El Cid. At night, lowered, the portcullis kept out spooning couples. Soaring above date palms and bronzed magnolias and flaming red and white oleanders, the Flagler hostelry was a challenge which grew to obsess

Henry Plant as much as it delighted its patrons. Its lobby was splendidly furnished with a concert grand piano and velvet chairs with heavy fringes—"cardinals' chairs," though some of them approached the papal. And just as the Moorish cloisters began to grow monotonous, hymned a travel writer, the turning of another corner "brings the visitor upon a scene unparalleled in all his former travels at home or abroad." At the Ponce de León there were

> on one side, parklike grounds, sparkling fountains, tropical verdure and blooming plants . . . The round tower, the kneeling balconies, the wide parapets of a mediaeval castle give a mere intimation of the dimensions. . . . At the left is a gateway, lofty, arched, and grand in proportions, as rich in its finishing and as imposing in its entirety as any of the triumphal arches of foreign cities.

The Ponce de León's Grand Doorway was surmounted by a semicircle on which were carved the shields of noble Spanish families. Each shield bore a letter; together they spelled P-o-n-c-e-d-e-L-e-ó-n. On every side abounded "emblems and suggestions of sunny Spain." "It takes little imagination," gushed a northern society columnist, "to people the balconies above with dark-eyed señoritas, and the verandas below with spurred and booted cavaliers, fiery of eye and haughty of mien." For practical purposes what mostly inhabited the verandas were the rich, fat, and elderly in search of a respite from winter sniffles and rheumatism. "It is a daze of oriental magnificence!" they all told each other happily as their noses and bones warmed. They reveled in expanses of marble, onyx, and silver. The dining room, they marveled, held a thousand people. The hotel itself occupied a total of six acres framed by a fence of spiked iron balls. The style was "eclectic," boasted Mr. Flagler, who had sent his architects to Europe with simple instructions to think immense.

Henry Plant could think immenser still. The Tampa Bay Hotel would cost him at least three million dollars, he knew, but he would easily make that back when the throngs came. He and his architects settled on five hundred guest rooms. There would be gardens, electric launches, haute cuisine, antique furniture, and paintings raided from European noblemen in need of hard cash. Professional guides would be hired to take the guests hunting up the Hillsborough. He would build a casino, not for gambling but for entertainment. There would be a large swimming pool, and a concert room. When the Tampa Bay Hotel's shining minarets

The Tampa Bay Hotel

began to rise against the Tampa skyline, people gaped. Plant kept bonfires flaming so that they could watch the progress even at night. He even had an answer to Flagler's Fountain of Youth. The oak in the front yard of the Tampa Bay Hotel was, he declared, the same oak under which Hernando de Soto had treated with the Timucua Indians. The hotel, its bricks sprayed with disinfectant as a precaution against yellow fever, opened in February 1891. Flagler sent Plant a telegram: "Henry, where is Tampa?" Plant sent a succinct reply: "Follow the crowd, Henry." And the crowd came according to plan. Reporters abounded. So many of them tried to convey the wonder of the scene that finally Plant, standing one morning on a Plant steamer in the Hillsborough, told a party of personal guests: "Soon we shall be docked, and soon thereafter at that haven which has been so often described but to which no writer to my mind has done justice—the Tampa Bay Hotel." Perhaps Plant had detected the tongue-in-cheek attitude of the representative of the *New York Journal of Commerce:*

> It is not to be denied that this hotel is one of the modern wonders of the world. It is a product of the time. It illustrates the age, the demands of the people, what they enjoy, and what they are willing to pay for.

To the lasting credit of American journalism, none of the reporters was rendered speechless.

The *Saturday Evening Gazette* man from Boston, Henry G. Parker, certainly was not. Perhaps he was bored with the penny-pinching austerities of his native city of cod and beans. In the Tampa Bay Hotel, he told his readers, "nothing offends the eye or the taste at any point." Basically the architecture was Moorish; the horseshoe and crescent motif of Arabia kept appearing on the building's exterior. It was five stories high; Plant trains had brought in its red bricks from Atlanta. The floors were of brick, and the building was braced with steel beams. This made it fireproof. To walk the length of the hotel, including the solarium and dining room, the visitor was required to go twelve hundred feet. Plant had provided Chinese rickshaws for the fainthearted. Princes, dukes, marquesses, French and Italian counts and jaded English barons paid enthusiastically for the privilege of riding in them. The list of hotel guests read like a combination of the *Social Register* and the *Almanach de Gotha.*

In the drawing room stood a table which had belonged to Marie

Antoinette. (Plant's second wife Margaret had chosen much of the furniture.) Marie Antoinette had also contributed a sofa and two chairs. Louis Philippe had left four. Japan, land of the Shoguns and the Samurai, had been searched for inlaid cabinets. What royal palaces didn't yield up, Grand Rapids, Michigan, was commissioned to supply from its furniture factories. Thirty thousand yards of scarlet carpeting embossed with black lions covered the floors. Unfortunately, titled English resented the design and some refused to "tread upon the British lion." It was Plant's single lapse. In the music room a raised circular stage held an impressive orchestra. Six of the sixteen resident musicians had been lured from the Boston Symphony. The spectators were rhapsodic. Had de Soto himself gone up the Hillsborough, in a dream of the future "sporting in fantastic fandango with a dark-browed Señorita of fair Castile?"

> Was his dream a prophetic vision [asked Henry G. Parker] that there seemed to be an Alhambra just there under the lee of his ship, or did some grander palace with Moorish minarets and silvered domes, glistening with more silvery brightness under the rays of a tropic moon, topped with golden crescents that could only come from the Orient to ornament its towers high above the pines, seem to be here in this faroff land—a dream passing all realization? . . . I say, perhaps old de Soto dreamed all this when he landed here at Tampa, and if he did, behold 'twas prophecy, for the swaying pines have toppled and in their places have risen higher the crescent of the Orient, and the silvered domes and Moorish minarets that ornament a palace, and here at Tampa Bay, the Spaniard's dream has been realized . . . Think you this is not the Alhambra? Then you have not read of the Alhambra, nor seen the Tampa Bay Hotel.

More mundanely, he added: "The Ponce de León at St. Augustine may have cost more dollars to build, decorate, and furnish, and the name and fame of the Ponce de León have gone to the four quarters, and 'tis not intended to compare invidiously. But here at Tampa Bay, the surroundings take one back through the centuries even before de Soto came, and this may have been the very spot where he landed." The White House, he thought, suffered sadly by comparison. Every wicker chair on the Tampa Bay Hotel's porch had been woven large enough to conform to the measurements of the World's Fattest Man.

The hotel's art was varied. Louis XIV graced a drawing room wall, as did *Return from the Masquerade* and *Wine, Women and Song.* Two dwarfs modeled on Black Forest legends guarded the room's entrance. Close by were telegraph and ticket offices. The drawing room divan had flowers growing from its center, "and between the seat-arms, roses and calla lilies mingling their perfume where beauty holds sway." The upholstery was white and gold; the ground glass of the chandeliers overhead was slightly tinted to show it off to best advantage. Busts of Elizabeth I of England and Mary, Queen of Scots faced each other on opposite sides of a portrait of a dead duke of Savoy. The Sleeping Beauty slept in Carrara marble not far away. Trinkets of Queen Victoria had found a place on a whatnot shelf.

The guest rooms were hung with panels of pink watered silk. They also had telephones. Everywhere in the hotel were reproductions of Wedgwood pottery, "little plates designed by Moritz Fischer" on which guests ate their Italian ices, and life-sized bronze statues which held clusters of electric lights. Near the dining room entrance the "Grand Orchestrion's" interchangeable rollers played music ranging from popular airs to the classic productions of the great composers. The shining floor of the dance salon was suited to "terpsichorean uses, concerts, lectures, and tableaux." Here the electric lights had been blown into Arabian crescents. As magnificent as was the interior, however, nothing could equal "a stroll by moonlight down by the river under the palmettos." The Hillsborough reflected a sheet of broken silver. The silver moon shone on the bulbous minarets, and the electric crescent which was the hotel's standard blinked in a starlit sky. Everywhere echoed the whish of falling water from stone multicolored Japanese fountains. The perfume of orange blossoms lay heavily on the night. Beyond, phosphorescent Tampa Bay glowed in a heaving expanse. Steamers whistled mournfully. Oars softly cut the river water as lovers paddled their canoes and rowboats back and forth. In the distance, the night sky glowed with the lights of Ybor City. The first vision of heaven on the river and the bay belonged not to a conquistador but to a railroad czar as capable of wonder as a child.

The visiting teenage sister of a Tampa bride years later recalled the hotel's opening night.

In memory I see again the magnificent things, so accurately described by gaily dressed pages . . . Everywhere you looked there was a series of happy surprises. After greetings by the host and hostess, Mr. and Mrs.

H. B. Plant, you were directed to the spacious dining room so colorful with its flags of all nations. The Stars and Stripes stood out from all the rest. . . . In those richly equipped rooms you could "see yourself as others see you" in 110 beautiful mirrors. Imagine the many oh's and ah's as each lady adjusted a hairpin or two and powdered her nose. . . . I got such a thrill out of writing to my friends in Kansas City.

For the wildlife of the river and the bay the hotel spelled trouble. Professional guides on the staff took their clients up the Hillsborough at a fee of fifty dollars a day to hunt in its oak and hickory forests. The fee included food, rifles, bullets, hunting clothes, and transportation by wagon. During a single season guests of the Tampa Bay Hotel slaughtered five thousand and eighty-four quail and snipe, eleven deer, fourteen turkeys, and seven alligators. H. Lee Borden, the milk magnate, was himself responsible for the death of seventy-three quail and two doves on a single trip. From November until spring the forests Osceola had known echoed with bursts of gunfire as lethal as any the Seminoles had ever sent forth. Only the Green Swamp escaped. It remained a densely impenetrable tangle, its pine needles wiry in the winter sun, its waters wine-dark with the mysteries of alligators and snakes. Occasionally a panther cried—it was like the dying scream of a woman, thought one of the hunters from the hotel. He shivered. Sometimes even now there are screams and rumors of screams. The Green Swamp still mocks its would-be conquerors. But along the river, the animal life is only a fraction of what it was at the turn of the century.

The hotel has survived the vanished wild things, of course. It even survived the death of Henry Plant as the twentieth century began, though Plant heirs began stripping it of the treasures he had loved. It survived the thousands of troops milling on its broad lawns at the start of the Spanish-American War, the hectic operations of Clara Barton's Red Cross, and the competition it had to endure as other tycoons built other hotels, each one farther downstate. It survived the birth of Miami as a resort. What finally did it in was America's increasing sophistication. In 1927 it was forced to close its doors. Its thirteen minarets, each one representing a Moslem month, shone on in the sunlight on the Hillsborough's shore, but now the huge rooms were empty. Gradually the eighty carloads of furniture which had come in only a generation before on Plant trains decayed, disappeared, or were sold off. By 1927 the veranda as wide as a city street no longer had its rocking chairs but only memories: of John Drew and Winston Churchill, Theodore Roosevelt,

Anna Pavlova, actress Minnie Maddern Fiske and, much later, George Herman Ruth whom America loved as Babe. In 1933 Plant's Alhambra finally became the University of Tampa, as bizarre an academic setting as any in the world.

Walk through it between quarters, and its silence is deafening. Its granite columns still tower in the huge hall. Rays of sunlight fall on the darkly polished wood of the chairs that remain. A museum attached to the university contains a few souvenirs of the hotel's heyday. The wide staircases down which princesses made grand entrances are empty. Classrooms have reminiscent names—the Rough Rider Room, the Florentine Room once full of Italian marbles. From the veranda you see crowded gardens—thickly bending areca palms, mimosas which need pruning, heavy hedges of tropical bamboo. Mockingbirds trill obliviously in the de Soto oak, and from the river wafts a faintly fishy smell. Water hyacinths drift down it slowly out to Tampa Bay; they were not there in Henry Plant's time, because they had not yet become naturalized in Florida, but they are exotic enough to have delighted him. And after you have thought about these things, perhaps an ancient black caretaker with a gold-flecked smile will come up to you knowing what is in your mind. And he will say, softly, "They never did find the rickshaws, you know that? Every attic and warehouse in this town been searched, and nobody knows where they gone. The rickshaws, they just vanished." Then, quietly, he will move on.

When Henry Plant celebrated his seventy-sixth birthday at Plant System headquarters in Atlanta, southern newspapers extolled his civic munificence, the empire he had founded, the splendor of his achievements, and in particular the Tampa Bay Hotel. Only the *Atlanta Constitution*, however, ran a column headed "Mr. Plant and the Negroes":

> They are grateful for what he has done for them. There are over two thousand Negroes employed by Mr. Plant. A great number of them have accumulated homes, educated their children, and have nice bank accounts, and they all love him. He has contributed liberally to churches, schoolhouses, and other Negro enterprises. In fact, he has built institutions of learning for Negroes. A number of Negroes hold positions of trust, with good pay attached, as is not the case with any other system in the United States.

Today the tone of the column is uncomfortably patronizing. When it first appeared, however, it savored of radicalism. In a South moving toward segregation, Henry Plant had retained his Yankee convictions. He did not see why black men had to be porters when they could be accountants and agents.

His jubilee was a long one. All morning and afternoon the Plants and Plant's son by his first marriage, Morton Plant, stood in the receiving line at the Plant System building in Atlanta. The Tampa Municipal Band had been brought up to provide music. The family were mobbed. Finally Morton Plant got up to make a brief speech. "Ladies and gentlemen, members of our family the Plant System (cheering and applause), I desire to thank you in behalf of my mother, my wife, and my boy for the great compliment you have paid my father. (Great applause.) It is a great treat to me to be here and to thank you for your kindness, not only to my father, but to the name of the system which, by your careful, studious and painstaking application to its business, you have built up. Gentlemen, I thank you. (Great applause and cheers.)"

Henry Plant was sitting beneath the leaves of Tampa palms which had been imported for the occasion. They stood ranged in bronze tubs. One by one, the hundreds of his employees advanced, shook his hand, and returned his tireless smile. When it was over he stepped into his carriage outside. Then he turned and waved a final time. For the remaining years of his life he cherished that tribute. But those closest to him knew his heart was, above all, in his Alhambra on the Hillsborough River. Its decline would have broken his heart; and yet the daily echo of young voices and young laughter in the University of Tampa would perhaps have been a compensation.

The autumn of 1896 was mild on the river. Yellow sourwoods and beeches were a contrast to the crimson-touched dogwoods, green magnolias, and brown turkey oaks. Flocks of warblers came down from the north, though there were no longer any Carolina parrakeets. Not until December 29 did the first freeze come. It arrived without warning to damage—usually hopelessly—every citrus grove north of the bay and the Hillsborough until thousands of trees were ruined. The temperature plunged to eighteen degrees. Palms trembled in a coating of ice, their fronds flashing yellow and red and blue in a capricious sun. Then summer returned. Yellow jasmines bloomed in temperatures of eighty. But on February 7 the mercury had dropped to twenty-two by midnight. Then it began to snow. The white flakes fell on splitting citrus limbs, on bamboo vines and pepper trees and dying butterfly orchids and goldsfoot ferns. In the morning Tampa was hushed until the children woke. Then their cries of joy began echoing in the streets. Snow! Most had never seen a snowfall, and they began making balls of the white stuff and throwing them at one another. All day the temperature stayed below freezing. The river was covered with ice at its bends. Icicles hung from Tampa roofs. Water pipes burst. Frigid winds blew in from the bay. Hurriedly guests began leaving the Tampa Bay Hotel, hugging their light cloaks. Sarasota and Fort Myers would be warmer. When the calamity was over, citrus growers estimated their losses at eighty million dollars. Still, those who had suffered the most were from the northern part of Hillsborough County and counties north of that. The bay itself had fared better, the Pinellas peninsula better still. As America read about Florida's Big Freeze, people became increasingly familiar with the little town of St. Petersburg. For St. Petersburg had had no snow at all.

Its position was what had made it secure. There was the warm Gulf, then a row of barrier islands to the east, then Boca Ciega Bay and St. Petersburg and Tampa Bay. Usually the sun in St. Petersburg was uninterrupted. For the first time northerners began to be curious about Peter Demens's outpost, and the Detroit Hotel began having to refuse reservations since it was already full. The hamlet was positively on the march, and though few tourists dared swimming in the Gulf they began promenading along the St. Petersburg shore of Tampa Bay and dipping brave toes in it, while they exclaimed at the thickness of mangroves and pelican rookeries. Plume hunters had to retreat south into the Big Cypress to join renegade Seminoles. Nobody mourned. But more than in wildlife, tourists were interested in open-air trolleys with gaily fringed tops, in picnics in Chinese pavilions and bathing machines and grapefruit shortcake which they had never had before and in wicker chairs rolling sedately along municipal piers. Nobody paid much attention to Cuba. St. Petersburg began building. When Máximo Gómez landed on his native island to begin the revolution so passionately championed by José Martí, only Ybor City was aware that the signal to attack had been smuggled to the general—naturally—in a Tampa cigar.

21

The Charge of the Yellow Rice Brigade

America was spoiling for a war—a swashbuckling war, which would deliver a comfortably distant oppressed island people from the yoke of tyranny, a noble war which would unite domestic Yankees and southerners and make them forget lingering bitternesses. Was not Fitzhugh Lee, a former Confederate officer, now serving his country as the American consul in Havana? Vocal politician Theodore Roosevelt was frank about his own ambitions. He began to preach, "with all the fervor and zeal I possess, our duty to intervene in Cuba and to take this opportunity of driving the Spaniard from the Western World." When William McKinley was elected president Roosevelt became his Assistant Secretary of the Navy. Roosevelt's oratory grew hotter then, and his keen horse sense about personal publicity ensured that every incendiary word he shouted went the length and breadth of the United States. Did people look upon war with "sincere horror"? Convince them otherwise! Roosevelt counseled his aides. He became intimate with an army surgeon named Leonard Wood. On long summer afternoons in 1897 when the heat hung heavily over cement Washington sidewalks, he and Wood took brisk hikes together along the Potomac. As fall drew on they practiced "the strenuous life" more vigorously by kicking a football back and forth in an empty Washington lot. In winter they took to the outlying Maryland and Virginia hills to ski and ice skate. All the time they talked of how much they wanted a war with Spain. Somehow or other they would go to the fighting front; their solemn duty was to see that there was one.

José Martí had gone before them. After Gómez invaded Cuba, impassioned Ybor City journalists Néstor Carbonell and his son Eligio whipped up local patriotism to a frenzied pitch. Martí made trip after trip to Tampa, gazing each time from his Plant System train at the young pines of Hillsborough forests. He felt exhausted these days. "I am going to die," he said simply. He had to go to Cuba, he told Ybor City. "They will kill me with bullets or with some evil deed. But I still have the pleasure of knowing that men like you have loved me. I do not know how to say goodbye to you. Help me now as if you were never to see me again." His slow smile was slighter than ever. To his mother he confided:

> My life is like that of a glowing carbon filament that burns to light the darkness. I feel that my struggle will never cease. The private man is dead and beyond all resurrection. . . . But the vigilant and compassionate man still lives in me, like a skeleton come forth from the grave; and I know that he can expect nothing but combat and sorrows in the struggles between men.

Shrewdly, the Spanish sent spies to Ybor City in the hope that infiltrators could undermine Martí's eloquence. The spies began orations of their own on chuckhole-pocked streets shaded by palms and bananas and spreading kapok trees. "Martí is a thief!" they shouted. "He will take all your money." They insinuated themselves into the cigar factories and began sowing seeds of distrust. Did the workers know that Martí and Gómez had quarreled? That the Cuban Junta in New York was disillusioned with Martí? That he could get no more money in the Northeast? In every rumor there was a grain of truth. Martí and Gómez had had their differences, and he was finding money increasingly difficult to raise. Cigar workers who had not fallen under his spell began to have misgivings. One afternoon he walked into an Ybor City factory with Ramón Rivera, *el lector* of Ybor y Manrara. "Here comes the bandit," someone muttered, and this time no one rose in greeting.

For old Paulina Pedroso, at her cigar table, it was too much. She sprang up and ran to *el lector*'s rostrum. "Gentlemen!" she shouted in Spanish. "If any of you is afraid to give his money or go to Cuba to fight, let him give me his pants and I'll give him my petticoat!" The ice was broken. The cigar workers began laughing and applauding. Martí walked over to her and embraced her. When he had finished speaking to the workers their expressions of skepticism had vanished. Once again he had rallied them to the cry of "Cuba libre!" When he left, several men who had resisted his pleas were mysteriously beaten up, and nobody dared to ask any questions.

The trouble with Rubiera's Hotel, Martí decided that night, was that there was too much confusion there. He was constantly being interrupted. Gratefully he accepted an invitation to stay at a house nearby; two Cubans, one white and one black, moved in to serve him. They were loud in their praises of him as the Apostle of Freedom. One afternoon when they were out, Martí helped himself to a decanter of *coca de Mariani* wine they had left for him. As he touched the wineglass to his lips, he smelled a peculiar odor. The few drops he tried tasted strange. Quickly he spat them out. When Dr. Barbarrosa, the Ybor City physician who looked after him in Tampa, arrived on an afternoon call he found Martí sitting listlessly in an armchair staring ahead of him. Barbarrosa smelled the decanter when Martí haltingly told him what had happened. "Acid," said Barbarrosa. "Let me have it analyzed."

Martí gripped his shoulders. "About this—if it is true, my friend, not one single word."

But when Dr. Barbarrosa began insisting vocally in an Ybor City cafe that Martí be moved to another house, the news was out. The two "helpers," white and black, had fled; they had been Spanish agents, people said. Doughty Paulina Pedroso marched into Martí's room when he was out making speeches and she swept up all his possessions into his battered suitcase. How was it, she marveled, that he carried more books than clothes? Promptly she took the suitcase to her own diminutive house opposite the Ybor y Manrara factory. Martí soon capitulated to her insistence that he move in with her and her black husband.

The Pedrosos' house became very gay. Cigar workers climbed up the roof and affixed a pole and a revolutionary flag to one of the gables. Whenever Martí was at the Pedrosos' the flag was flown like a royal standard. In the evenings, while lapis dusk settled over Ybor City and the odor of Havana tobacco permeated the humidity and tiny frogs peeped from puddles in the streets and outlying marshes, people stood below Martí's window to watch him as he scribbled by the feeble light of his desk lamp. Always his light burned late. Sometimes, when his windows were open, spectators fancied they heard the very scratching of his pen in his endless appeals to the rest of America. Late one evening one of his

former "helpers" appeared. He was shaking. A self-appointed Martí
bodyguard rushed at his throat. Martí came downstairs, wondering at
the noise. When he saw the intruder and heard his pleas for forgiveness,
he motioned him to come into the parlor with him. Afterwards he
emerged with the culprit. "This man will be one of the first to fire shots
in Cuba." He was right; his forgiveness eventually spurred the would-be
poisoner to acts of bravery on the battlefield which won him a major's
rank. But Martí himself was not so lucky. When he returned to Cuba to
join Gómez he rode with the troops of the insurgents through a Caribbean
night in which quivering high coconut palms made grotesque shadows
on the moonlit ground. A quick volley of shots surprised the men. One
of them, little more than a boy, saw Martí clutch his breast and fall
with a thud to the ground. The youngster rushed up to his hero and
found Martí's jaw running streams of blood. Blood was gushing from
his heart. He was dead. "His eyes," whispered the boy under the white
moon. "I had not known that they were so blue."

The news plunged Ybor City into mourning. Houses were draped in
black bunting. Several cigar manufacturers donated two days' wages to a
revolutionary fund in Martí's memory. Soon a contingent of women
arrived from Cuba to seek jobs in the factories while their men fought
Spanish troops on Cuba soil. The list of visitors to Ybor City swelled: the
rebel general Calixto García, Quesada who was the secretary of the
revolutionary party, Palma who would become President of the Republic
of Cuba, and wily revolutionary general Castillo. All of them knew the
number of Ybor City cigar factories had swelled to ninety-seven, and that
the war for Cuban independence had to be fought as much in Ybor City
as it was being fought in the mountains of Oriente province and villages
like Daiquirí, on the south coast.

The Hillsborough River and Tampa Bay were soon alive with ships.
Cuban organizations from all over the country arrived with cargoes of
guns and ammunition for the insurgents. Guests on the porch of the
Tampa Bay Hotel, as they rocked back and forth in their deep wicker
chairs, often, these days, saw mysterious vessels sailing silently up the
Hillsborough without lights. Heavily cloaked figures would appear at
the docks where the vessels dropped their anchors; then the newcomers
would silently board them along with piles of wooden packing crates. A
few hours later the elusive ships would weigh anchor and glide noiselessly
down the river once more into the bay toward *Cuba* not yet *libre*. In

Havana, the Spanish Commandant Weyler (Ybor City called him The Butcher) grew red with apoplectic fury whenever Tampa was mentioned. He would show that upstart Florida city it had no business with his war! He announced an embargo on all shipment of Cuba tobacco to the United States. What money could cigar manufacturers raise for the revolutionaries with their sprawling plants shut down? Tampa's businessmen, Anglo-Saxon and German and Polish and Jewish as well as Cuban, were electrified. They needed Ybor City. In a body they approached Henry Plant, who agreed to send his steamers *Olivette* and *Mascotte* to Havana before the embargo's deadline to bring back enough tobacco to keep Ybor City alive. Weyler's hands were tied. He was not officially at war with the United States—yet. His deadline had to be honored. Impotent in his rage, he watched the ships of Henry Plant load tobacco even to the ceilings of their staterooms and then steam out of Havana's harbor bound for Tampa Bay and the Hillsborough River. From Plant System docks the cargoes of tobacco were loaded onto Plant System trains which rumbled ceaselessly into Ybor City, clanked to a ponderous halt on factory sidings, and blew shrill whistles to signal cigar workers to begin unloading. The factories were saved—for a while. Tampans of all nationalities now understood that it would be necessary to crush Spain completely if Tampa were to continue its marathon growth uninterrupted. Old Confederate families along the river's suburban shores who privately considered Ybor City "socially very, very much south of the railroad tracks" began clamoring for the freedom of their bronze brothers the Cubans. How admirable was the forthright militarism of Theodore Roosevelt and Leonard Wood, who were begging America to march!

On February 15, 1898, the U.S. Battleship *Maine* was blown up in Havana Harbor, rocketing to smithereens under tropical stars. "An outside agency" was the immediate verdict of American investigators. "Remember the *Maine!*" war hawks began crying. The fresh outrage of "the Spaniard" on American national honor must be avenged. A few feeble voices counseled patience; war was not a game. But nobody listened. American newspaper correspondents rushed down to Havana and chafed when they had to wait idly for news. Havana itself seemed tranquil. One of them, artist Frederic Remington, sent a disgusted telegram to New York: "Everything quiet. No trouble here. There will be no war. I wish to return." Remington was to become a great painter of the west, but his political intuition left much to be desired. From New York came a prompt answer:

REMINGTON

HAVANA

PLEASE REMAIN. YOU FURNISH THE PICTURES AND I WILL FURNISH THE
WAR.

WILLIAM RANDOLPH HEARST

Soon Remington was joined by fellow correspondent Richard Harding
Davis, who wrote a few articles on Butcher Weyler's cruelties in rural
villages and then left Cuba in disgust because the war was not coming
fast enough to suit him either.

Survivors of the *Maine* explosion were carried back to Tampa on
Plant's *Olivette*. At the harbor half of Tampa waited to cheer them as
they walked or were carried down the gangplank. That night the city
was ablaze with torches and Chinese lanterns to celebrate the homecom-
ing. Soon afterward the *Mascotte* brought in nearly a thousand Havana
refugees who had tales of rape and murder to tell eager Tampa audiences.
Consul Fitzhugh Lee landed on the river to find all of Tampa decked
with Cuban revolutionary flags. "Viva Lee!" shouted the crowds.

"What are you shouting for?" he yelled back. "Do you want to
fight?"

"Yes!" came the deafening answer.

"That's what I wanted to hear you say!" Fitzhugh Lee beamed at
them all. Later, he told reporters the episode was not for publication
because he was still a diplomat.

A goaded U.S. Congress declared war on Spain late in April. England
at once proclaimed her neutrality. Militant Admiral George Dewey began
steaming toward the Spanish navy in Manila Bay where it guarded
Spain's Philippine Islands. Outmoded Spanish ships of the line were no
match for the battleships of Dewey. He blew them as sky-high as the
Maine had been blown, and when the news reached Tampa by telegraph
the city once again went wild. Quickly bards sprang up to laud the
victory:

> Dewey! Dewey! Dewey!
> He has met the Don's array,
> And the *Maine* has been remembered
> In the good old-fashioned way—
> A way of fire and carnage,
> But carnage let it be
> When the forces of the tyrant
> Block the pathways of the free!

From the beginning, official Washington agreed that the forthcoming invasion of Cuba must be carried out from Tampa because it had a deep river to accommodate supply ships. It also had a Cuban climate and it had Henry Plant's port to harbor troop transports. It had a railroad too. Government agents began arriving by the trainload; U.S. ships appeared in Tampa Bay to take soundings of its channels and harbor and fortify Egmont Key. Tampa businessmen were soon jubilantly waving contracts with the army, the navy, and the marines. Night after night cannons boomed as citizens held patriotic rallies at the courthouse. Cuban banners hung everywhere. When the first military detachment arrived—five companies from Fort McPherson, Georgia—they were wearing Confederate grey. The eyes of Tampa mothers and wives and widows filled with tears. The greys encamped at de Soto Park on the bay's shore, where they were soon joined by the 69th Regiment from New York, clad in Yankee blue. But the cheering went on. Grey, blue, what did it matter? Bygones were bygones. The people of the river and the bay ached with the rest of their countrymen to proclaim to the world that America was now an international power capable of toppling kingdoms. And the toppling was to be engineered from Tampa, Florida! Nobody saw anything ominous in the prevailing nationalism. Today, popular emphasis on the glory of war frightens; by common consent the soldier of fortune has become a terrible ancestor, not a romantic hero. But seventy-five years ago America had no qualms about battle or suspicions that the vestiges of Spain's colonial empire were already doomed by their own bureaucratic decay. Nor did America have much of a sense of humor. The commanding general it planned to send to Cuba weighed one seventh of a ton—a long ton.

William Rufus Shafter, a native of Galesburg, Michigan, tipped the scales at three hundred and twenty pounds. He had managed to reach the age of sixty-three heedless of the adage that Fat Kills, and he was to survive well into his seventies. No steed could hold him for long. He rode into Tampa in a specially built buckboard wagon with heavy-duty springs; it was pulled by Percheron workhorses. No army cot could hold him either. His staff commandeered a door wherever they happened to be billeted, removed it from its hinges, and laid it flat to make him a bed. Sometimes, when he was exhausted with the effort of movement, he conducted newspaper interviews lying on the up-ended door. In spite of his bulk he was "a good army man," his soldiers thought, and he commanded over fifteen thousand of them. In honor of Cuba's national dish, Tampa wags dubbed them the Yellow Rice Brigade.

If General Shafter was not exactly dashing, Lieutenant Colonel Theodore Roosevelt was. He had survived a sickly childhood to preach calisthenics and he was so keen a hunter that nothing on the hoof in the wild was safe from his rifle. Paradoxically, he was interested in conservation; when he felled endangered species they were not yet endangered. His fondness for being photographed with his kill led to the introduction of the Teddy Bear. With Colonel Leonard Wood he headed a company of volunteers first called the Western Regiment because its ranks contained many cowboys. Then it was the Rustler Regiment and after that the Cowboy Regiment and Teddy's Terrors, but finally people took to calling it the Rough Riders, and the name stuck.

The Rough Riders came from what modern westerners call Standing-up Country. They were rawboned men used to scaling scarred buttes into the splendor of desert rainbows and rounding up dogies and descending into steeply solitary copper canyons. They hailed from the mesa country of clinging cliffrose and juniper, from baking cactus plains full of Gila monsters and oversized spiders and branched saguaros, from high mountains covered with Norway spruce and trembling aspens whose restless leaves shivered in oxygen-poor winds. Because most of the recruits had lived and worked alone, they were not easy to discipline. They couldn't understand why you didn't greet your officers with a friendly "Howdy!" or that army cooks weren't supposed to participate in the strategy speculations of officers at the dinner table. Some of the Rough Riders had been prospectors; others had been law enforcement officers; what several of the rest had been they weren't telling. Captain Llewellyn had been shot four times "in pitched fights with red marauders and white outlaws"; Lieutenant Ballard had "broken up the Blackjack Gang of ill-omened notoriety." They were used to the brash, pushing life of the frontier. They knew how to pitch tents and drive bulls, and they had names like Cherokee Bill, Happy Jack of Arizona, Smoky the Broncobuster and Rattlesnake Pete. Amazingly their numbers also included no less than four Methodist ministers who longed to subdue Cuba as a veritable Babylon of Roman Catholicism. Some of the others were Indians. Pollock, a full-blooded Pawnee, approached the regimental barber and asked in a rough voice, "Do you cut hair?" The barber nodded. "Then you'd better cut mine. Don't want to wear my hair like a wild Indian when I'm in civilized warfare."

To while away tedious hours in camp, first in San Antonio, Texas, and then at Tampa, the Rough Riders gave each other nicknames. One of the men who mentioned an aunt in New York was promptly christened Metropolitan Bill. A redheaded Irishman emerged unpredictably as Sheeny Solomon. A young Jew only laughed when he drew the sobriquet of Pork Chop. Hell-roarer was diffident, and Prayerful James had an arsenal of profanity that floored even army regulars. "My men are children of the dragon's blood," Theodore Roosevelt asserted. "If they had no outland foe to fight and no outlet for their vigorous and daring energy, there would always be the chance of their fighting one another." It was splendid to command such desperadoes; Roosevelt had two loves above all others—romance and press-agentry. Reporters at Tampa could not help being stirred by the sight of his Rough Riders in their slouch hats, blue flannel shirts, brown trousers, leggings, and boots, and red bandanas knotted carelessly around their necks. They were far better copy than the black regiments, whose members in Tampa knew they were in the South and acted with according deference. But even they were more interesting to write about than Roosevelt's officers, of whom he boasted: "I have never heard in the officers' mess a foul story or a foul word." Some people merely said that Lieutenant Colonel Roosevelt in that case must be deaf. He would have been delighted, as one of his biographers has noted, with Ernest Hemingway. Writer Stephen Crane he hated; he thought *The Red Badge of Courage,* Crane's deeply introspective Civil War novel, a lot of drivel: "I do not see among my fighting men the very complicated emotions assigned to their kind by some of the realistic modern novelists who have written about battles."

If Roosevelt worshipped the strong, silent men of the plains, he also admired the combination of blue blood and eastern football. Some of his Rough Riders had been personally recruited by him. They were William Tiffany, nephew of Mrs. August Belmont, a New York society matriarch; "Reggie" Ronalds, a drinking companion of the Prince of Wales and son of tobacco czar Pierre Lorillard Ronalds; Dudley Dean, who had captained the Harvard football team, and Horace Devereux, who had captained Princeton's. J. C. Clagett and L. M. Montgomery were gentlemen farmers from tidewater Maryland; Henry Bull had rowed with the Harvard crew; Guy Murchie was a Harvard football coach. Of Craig Wadsworth a wit said dryly: "He has led the Genesee Valley hunts for some years, and at other times he has led many a German in New York ballrooms." But Roosevelt was soon writing enthusiastically to President

McKinley: "We are in fine shape. Wood is a dandy colonel. . . . We earnestly hope we will be put into Cuba with the very first troops; the sooner the better."

In their camp at San Antonio the Rough Riders began training in heat and wind and dust in the very shadow of the Alamo. During off hours they gambled. On Sunday, May 29, Roosevelt marched them into the San Antonio railroad station for their journey to Tampa which, transportation officials said, was only forty-eight hours away. Roosevelt doubted it. The facilities for getting horses into the cars were inadequate, and nobody had thought of feeding or watering the animals. Roosevelt stormed until the negligences were put right. At every station along the way he commandeered oats and hay and stowed the horses in baggage cars. For four torrid days the train inched from Texas toward Florida. Whenever the men were given a breather at small country stations they managed to get hold of white lightnin' and get drunk until Roosevelt had to curtail their liberties. At each depot during hot sunlit hours the scene was always the same. Women handed flowers and fruits up to the train windows. The eyes of the older women were sad, and the eyes of young girls sparkled because they, unlike their mothers, had not seen the bloodletting of the Civil War. The girls waved miniature American flags and begged prettily for cartridges and buttons to keep as souvenirs. Then they fluttered their handkerchiefs as the train pulled away into more steaming May hours under the southern sun. When the troops reached Tampa, "in the pine-covered sand flats at the end of a one-track railroad," Roosevelt found no one to meet him or tell him where to camp. Henry Plant's railroad left him unimpressed and so did Henry Plant himself when Roosevelt exploded into his office asking for efficiency. Plant himself had come down to superintend Plant System operations.

"Unless this road runs more efficiently the War Department will seize it!" Roosevelt thundered.

"Seize it and be damned," said Plant, who knew the army didn't want to add to its burdens the supervision of a railroad.

For the Rough Riders' first twenty-four hours in Tampa, there was nobody to issue them any food. Other trains began to jam up along the track as fresh regiments arrived. Roosevelt and Wood bought their men food with their own money. The Tampa Bay Hotel, now the headquarters of General Shafter, was lively with officers and glamorous women and scores of reporters who sat in rocking chairs on its verandas as they waited for their stories. The Rough Riders' camp was austere by contrast; its long streets of tents were arranged in mathematical precision. Some of the Rough Riders from the West had never seen the ocean and gaped at the breadth of Tampa Bay. When a gust of wind blew off the hat of one of them, he shouted: "Oh-oh, Jim! Ma hat blew into the creek!"

The snarls of officialdom at Tampa grew tortuous. When army food was finally issued much of it was rotten. The hardtack brought in by boat had been "soaked first in sea-water, then by rain." In Tampa the season of daily deluges had begun, and Hillsborough County mud began oozing into the food crates. Pork and bacon wrapped only in cheesecloth were turning rancid. The canned beef, said the correspondent for the *London Times*, was "execrable—simply the offal of a beef factory." Some of the beans, soaked in pork fat, were "nauseating even to the Massachusetts troops." Clara Barton, founder of the American Red Cross and vigorous in her seventies, was horrified. When she arrived in Tampa she began writing letters to army officials. Miss Barton was an institution, but even generals could not make Henry Plant's trains run faster when there was only one track. He had not calculated on a war when he had laid his rails. To divert themselves the Rough Riders had their mascots: a young buff panther some of the boys had brought protesting all the way from Arizona, a bald eagle from New Mexico whose wings had been clipped. The third was "a rather disreputable but exceedingly knowing little dog named Cuba." Cuba was destined to see action. The regiment got its human mascot weeks later when a small boy, Dabney Royster, tried to smuggle himself onto a troop transport with a .22-caliber rifle and three boxes of cartridges. When Dabney was sent ashore he began crying bitterly, but the squadron staying behind adopted him and got him a little Rough Rider uniform. Then he was happy. He loved going swimming in the bay with his new-found comrades. The officers had a sandbar all to themselves.

Other regiments had other troubles. Private Charles Johnson Post was first stationed in the sleepy Florida town of Lakeland, thirty miles east of Tampa. The Tenth Cavalry, a black regiment, was designated as Lakeland's provost guard. The local sheriff stared curiously, and then turned to Private Post. "D'ya ever have nigra cops up no'th rounding you up an' throwin' you in the jug—like here?"

It was perfectly all right, Private Post explained. Army was army, black or white. "It is the uniform, not the wearer. It is just Provost Guard, wholly impersonal."

"Well." The sheriff scratched his head. "Just as you say—perhaps. You're in the army and maybe it don't make no difference in the army. But it shore gravels us folks around here. It ain't natural. Any you fellows ever punch the black bastards?"

"We are forbidden to punch bastards whether black or white," Private Post answered with poise; after that the sheriff gave up needling him.

To reach Tampa, Post and his company had to pass through Ybor City. They swung their Merriam packs over their shoulders and marched out of their suffocating railroad cars into an even more suffocating Ybor City afternoon. The station where José Martí had arrived to arouse his fellow Cubans was, to Post, "a siding and a tank." The sand was loose and ankle-deep. Troops had to wait under broiling light until all the staff horses had been unloaded and then saddled and put in front of the regiment. For the remaining three miles to downtown Tampa, foot soldiers were forced to keep pace with the officers' horses, restless after confinement in the train's close quarters. Infantry staggered toward their camp at Tampa Heights—a fifteen foot rise in the ground—with sweat pouring down streaked faces. Several of them collapsed from the heat before they left Ybor City, and ambulances had to be summoned. Awkwardly the horse-drawn vehicles rumbled down Ybor City's pathways. Residents began passing pitchers of cool well water to the exhausted soldiers. Some of the regiment were so tired they did not gain their camp until after taps, and Tampa Heights was so "barren of habitation," Private Post found, that when latrines had been dug the palmetto scrub made screen enough for their users. But when a group of privates took the trolley into Tampa the next day the city looked refreshingly urban. The minarets of the Tampa Bay Hotel were blinding; assembled war correspondents were fanning themselves languidly on the building's porch. They had ice water, steak, eggs, ice cream, and highballs. They even had Scotch whiskey, a drink newly fashionable in America. Richard Harding Davis was studying the *Social Register* to ferret out the elite among the Rough Riders; the man from the *New York Herald* "whose dispatches know more than it is humanly possible to know" sat close beside him; a Chicago correspondent was composing pages speculating wildly on the strength of the Spanish fleet. Only a writer named George Kennan seemed interested in Tampa doughboys and in what they thought of army bungling at the racy and riotous port.

Tampa had become a madhouse. Cavalry horses kicked up sand that stung eyes and throats. Empty fields rang with commands and fire as the men practiced bracing themselves for rifle recoil. The cars of wooden Plant trains backed up for still more miles, and in freight yards they clanked and groaned in protest as they were switched. Tampa's post office was piled high with mail for thousands of recruits. Merchants did a brisk business in pith helmets; daily, heat prostration took its toll. At Port Tampa the docks overflowed with Cuban refugees, all of them chattering excitedly in Spanish. Mules and horses walked unchecked along railroad crossties, the stench from their droppings doubly pungent in the heat. The bay was thickening with transports. Supplies were daily being piled high on the docks—tents, blankets, rifles, crates full of rations. From time to time reporters tore themselves away from the porch of the Tampa Bay Hotel to take pictures of the chaos on the bay. In their open-flap tents, regimental chaplains were baptizing nervous country boys, northern and southern, flocking for sacred insurance before they risked themselves on Cuban soil. At its headquarters the Quartermaster Corps began issuing accumulated tents and blankets to soldiers who were instructed in their use and then drilled and inspected. Medical officers were kept busy caring for dysentery and fever cases; dengue fever could hit a man so suddenly that one minute he felt fine and the next he collapsed into Tampa sand.

Private Post waited with the rest of his company to board one of the fifty-five transports in the bay. In the distance, toward the Gulf, dark thunderheads were rumbling. Jagged streaks of lightning plunged down here and there into the grey water. Post, after his own bout with dysentery, was too queasy to eat much. Down the main street of Port Tampa "old black mammies" were peddling fried chicken sizzling in hot grease on portable stoves and Buzzacot boilers. All Post wanted was milk. In search of some he began walking down the hectic avenue that consisted "solely of tent saloons, with one exception, a large two-storey house of lumber still in its first glare of raw, yellow boards." Maybe, somewhere, someone could give him milk. All he was finding were whiskey and beer, and his stomach rebelled at the thought. "Last Chance Street," the men all called the thoroughfare; the final drink before Cuba, and also the final woman. The Town of Fort Brooke had responded enthusiastically to the challenge of the military. It had sent them the best it had to give. On the building of raw lumber Private Post discovered a sign: Restaurant. He started up the steps when a soldier yelled at him,

"Hey, git in line!" Unworried, he continued to go indoors. To his amazement, the room was bare. The boards of its walls had never even been painted. "Hey, Doc, git in line!" came the shout again.

"I want the dining room," explained Post. Immediately the room reverberated with a chorus of guffaws. Then Post saw a door opening in the wall. A naked female arm thrust itself through it with a motion that unmistakably beckoned. The head man in the line went in, and everybody moved up one position. Post blushed; but the "sophisticates" in the lines gave him only the most casual of glances as he retreated. Outside the building, he found a group of soldiers who had just managed to get a ladder. It leaned giddily against the dirty window of an upstairs room. A pair of men were climbing the ladder and they began whistling when they could see into the room and note its activities. When they crawled in through the window, there was a scream, and then a volley of curses which would have done any military man proud, though the voice belting them out was feminine. Moments later the two ladder-climbers were kicked by an unidentified foot out the front door into the yielding sand of Last Chance Street. The line cheered them loudly; sheepishly, they took their places to wait as decorously as the others for their turns with Town of Fort Brooke belles.

By June 14, the transports in Tampa Bay were full of men, four batteries of field artillery, and four Gatling guns. General Shafter—slowly, because his legs were too fat to carry him any place in a hurry—paced the deck of his leading battleship. All had not gone smoothly. There had not been enough room for the horses of the Rough Riders, who would have to fight on foot in spite of their name. Only Lieutenant Colonel Roosevelt had his mount. What horses were on board would have to swim to the Cuban shore when they approached the target village of Daiquirí. Some of the nags, General Shafter reflected gloomily, would probably swim straight for the Florida Keys and get drowned in the process. His voyage to Cuba would take at least six days; with luck, the fleet would not encounter waterspouts or be buffeted in a sudden hurricane tumulting in from the West Indies or be challenged by Spanish Admiral Cervera and what was left of Spain's navy.

From the deck of the transport *Vigilancia*, Private Post watched the transports behind swing jerkily away from Port Tampa docks. Tugs were whistling and chugging. The *Vigilancia's* crew readied a steam winch for the lowering of the mooring chain. At a sharp command, crewmen began grinding the winch. The massive anchor was coming up. Gongs rang. Slowly, the *Vigilancia* turned into the line of cruisers, battleships, and transports ahead. Gradually Port Tampa's docks retreated, and the United States Army moved in its carriers out into Tampa Bay. On Egmont Key, the light was revolving and flashing, and on Mullet the hastily built fortifications had a raw and vineless look. Ahead lay Cuba and adventure. The fortunate, like Private Post, would return at summer's end to ticker-tape welcomes and a jingo-minded America jubilant with the knowledge that Spain had been thrown out of the hemisphere forever. Five hundred and six years after Columbus, the last chapter in the saga of Spanish conquest was about to be written; like most real-life endings, this one would be anticlimactic, no bang but a whimper. Where elegant Ponce de León had scanned the far horizon in search of gold, corpulent William Rufus Shafter was scanning it for the remnants of Spain's fleet undemolished by Admiral Dewey at Manila Bay. Where caravels and brigantines and pinnaces had tossed on turbulent waves carrying the glory-driven into immortality, the grey hulks of United States ships ploughed restlessly through the swells and ebbs of Gulf waves to shatter an ancient empire. Had Luis de Onís foreseen such a time when he had sold Florida to John Quincy Adams eighty years before? The laughter of the gulls swirling black winged in the hot sky echoed the riddle more mockingly than ever.

To Theodore Roosevelt, who was preposterously and gallantly to lead his Rough Riders up San Juan Hill outside the city of Santiago, Cuba would mean the White House. Perhaps even now, as he stood on the deck of the U.S.S. *Vixen* watching the gulls and terns, he knew it. Cuba would stir his soul in many ways: flame trees and royal palms would impress him with their high green lace, and the calls of bush cuckoos would ring in his mind long after men had died in the heat of Antillean afternoons. He would see his men live through—and perish from—yellow fever. He would see, too, more of the young English reporter who would be sending firsthand accounts of the conflict to his London paper; in Tampa Winston Churchill had been fretful at all the confusion and burlesque delay. Through the annals of the Spanish-American War were passing conquistadores' shades, men of the moment, and men of the future. Clara Barton would succor the war's wounded. One of the Rough Riders had talked to Roosevelt about the Cuban vultures which would be consuming the regiment's dead. Now Roosevelt thought he knew what he had meant. The man had not been afraid. There was a passage in the prophecies of Ezekiel he must have remembered: "Speak unto every feathered fowl . . . Ye shall eat the flesh of the mighty, and drink the blood of the princes of the earth."

PART **IV**

Pilgrims

22

Argonauts

The isles of Greece, the isles of Greece!
Where burning Sappho loved and sung,
Where grew the arts of war and peace—
Where Delos rose, the Phoebus sprung!
Eternal summer gilds them yet,
But all, except their sun, is set . . .

Not on the Hillsborough River, though. Pappas's Riverboat Restaurant
opens wide windows onto it from which you can watch autumn skies
turn at sunset from tangerine to smoky quartz. Last motorboats churn
their way upstream toward the Tampa Bay Hotel. Darkness falls to the
accompaniment of lights and a mélange of Mediterranean voices. You
smell Calamata olives cured in oil, Salonika peppers, feta cheese, and
egg-lemon soup. Eggplant moussaka steams up in coils from nearby
tables. Faces are swarthy; there are grey old men with hard muscles and
the profiles of heroes, wise dark-eyed women who have perhaps given
sons to the sea, young girls in black ringlets—Elenis and Sophias and
Aphrodites—whose necks are as arrogant as those of swans. Greece has
survived with little enough dilution here. Yet, somehow, Pappas's gives
you the feel of the river, from oil tankers to tugs to a paddle-wheeler for
tourists, as larger restaurants do not. Perhaps it is because the Greeks who
come in such numbers have always been men of the water. Pappas's is
only an outpost of the mother Greek community of Tarpon Springs

northward on the Pinellas peninsula. Even so, from it radiates a culture centuries have not been able to kill: the stately litanies of Greek orthodoxy, Byzantine icons and austere key designs and Homer and low whitewashed buildings that blind. Tampa has a sizable population of Greeks; St. Petersburg has fewer, as do Largo and Dunedin and Clearwater. On the Suncoast they have left indelible marks. Every January it celebrates Epiphany with Tarpon Springs, when burnished boys dive for a sacred cross in the chill of Spring Bayou while black-robed Greek archbishops from abroad bless what is left of Tarpon Springs's sponge fleet. The sponges are why, in the beginning, the Greeks came, and Tampa Bay has yielded up its share.

Spiro Agnew is a Suncoast hero not because he is a Republican but because he is Greek and managed to become vice-president. America—and especially the people of the Hillsborough and Tampa Bay—has not always been as well disposed toward the Greeks as a national group as it is today. The rise of Onassises, Niarchoses, and Livanoses into the firmament of glamour has been recent. The first Greeks on the Suncoast encountered backwoodsmen who stared and sometimes even shot. Crackers had gotten used to Cubans and Italians in Ybor City, but here was a fresh wave of outlanders who built polychromed shrines to saints in their front yards, had unpronounceable names, and buried their dead while their black-clad women pulled at long locks and screamed out a ritual lament. Names like Giallourakis and Papademetrios were a far cry from the Tampa familiarities of Sánchez and González. On the Suncoast, paradoxically, one of the oldest peoples in the world and the founders of modern western civilization was too new. Suncoasters were not always admirers of the classics. Deep in the pinewoods, there were people who had never heard of them.

Until just before the Civil War, America had imported most of its sponges from Mediterranean ports. A few West Indies spongers fished for yellow, grass, and glove sponges in the Bahamas, but not until the discovery of sponge beds off Key West did the United States have any part in the sponge trade. In an era before synthetics, sponges were household essentials. In 1873 a fleet of Key West turtlers found the sponging grounds accidentally. A local factory immediately realized their significance; it was not long before Key sponges began to appear on markets in New York and Philadelphia. The Florida finger sponge was prized as a tropical decoration for northern piazzas. During the Spanish-American

Sponge boats, Tarpon Springs

War the Keys spongers grew nervous. Where was the Spanish navy? There were sponges elsewhere in the Gulf, they had heard. Particularly there were rumors of rich beds near Tampa Bay. As early as 1890 a few sponge warehouses existed at Tarpon Springs; a friend of Hamilton Disston's, John Cheyney of Philadelphia, had visited Key West and had been fascinated by the gatherers themselves, most of Bahamian origin. They ate so much shellfish they were called Conchs. They took their sponges from the sea bottom with long hooks. They were wiry, tough, and agile, and in Key West they formed a group completely separate from Cuban cigar makers. Many of the cigar makers, of course, had gone north in the 1880s to El Río Hillsborough and Tampa Bay. John Cheyney hoped he could lure the Conchs north even before the Cuban revolution, but not until the ensuing war did the Conchs come: Tarpon Springs was safer than Key West. A small sponge market was set up on the banks of the Anclote River on the edge of town. Tampa would provide a necessary port. But business was slow; Key West was a national habit for sponge buyers from the northeast.

Tarpon Springs may have had a duke in its environs, but the town was rough enough the moment a tourist left the porch of the Tropical Hotel. Even the hotel had had its moments; there had been a shoot-out, after which town officials said, "Tarpon Springs is so healthy somebody's got to be killed to start a cemetery." From time to time arrived roving ambassadors of culture like the bandleader who called himself Professor Smeltz and had his musicians toot in the town bank. A former governor of Arizona came and built a wooden mansion. But with the coming of the Conchs, Tarpon Springs got rougher than ever. The city marshal, an ex-cowboy, was shot as he climbed down from his horse; the incident began a vendetta that ended in the murder of thirteen more people. Also, the Conchs drank. John Cheyney's sponge industry at Tarpon Springs was off to a poor start. Redemption came in the person of John Cocoris, a native of Kynourias, Greece, who had been working in New York City for a sponge company which had made him one of its buyers. The company's owners were Greeks from the Aegean island of Hydra, and they had heard of Cheyney's Florida warehouses.

John Cocoris didn't look much a latter-day Jason. He was short and good natured and wore pin-striped suits. Better than anything else in the world, he knew sponges, and he knew that from Tampa Bay to Apalachicola, in north Florida, the environment for sponges was ideal. In 1896

he settled near a Cheyney warehouse to supervise buying and processing
for his employers. A man named Morrison took care of the necessary
English correspondence. Florida's sponge business was growing as Amer-
ica's population was increasing. It was a nation of bathers—fanatical,
Europeans said—addicted to rubdowns. John Cocoris made a trip to Key
West to learn market conditions and prevailing prices there. When the
Spanish-American War arrived and with it, in Tarpon Springs, the Key
West sponge fleet, Cocoris, a family man, decided to send for a brother in
Greece. Later he sent for other brothers, and after returning to Greece for
a bride he came back to Tarpon Springs. There he found Cheyney's
fledgling industry having problems. The hooking operation practiced by
the Key Westers was too slow. But Cocoris was resourceful. He began to
have visions of discovering a better way of sponge gathering and of
building Cheyney's beginnings into a complex which would rival that of
his native Dodecanese islands. He left his job with the New York sponge
company and went to work for Cheyney as a bleacher. Buyers liked pale
colors for their bath loofahs. Cocoris persuaded Cheyney to hire his
brothers. His wife, Anna, settled herself happily in Tarpon Springs because the Gulf reminded her of her native Aegean. Not far away sprawled
the bustling city of Tampa, where other Greeks were beginning to come.
In Ybor City, the *barrio latino,* Athanasou's Greek Cafe had been joined
by competitors. All served delectable pastries and the Greek coffee Cubans
said was dark as death, thick as night, and hot as hell. Anna Cocoris
knew she would not be lonely.

For two years John and one of his brothers, Constantine, worked for
Cheyney. But unobtrusively, on Sundays and holidays, they took to rowing a small boat around the mangrove fringes of the islands off the
Anclote River and out in the Gulf. They scanned the ocean with glass-
bottom buckets, studying rocks and sandbars and sponge deposits. They
learned to know the blues and yellows and greens of the tropical fish that
swam offshore in summer, the purple sea fans of coral gardens and the
clawless Florida lobsters peering warily at them from submerged retreats.
There were, in the Gulf, bars and islands where no human foot had ever
left a trace. John and Constantine Cocoris mapped the sponge beds in
their minds until there was not a corner of them near the Pinellas shore
they did not know. John had been right; the sponges were there. The
brothers never spoke of their activities. The rest of the town merely
thought they were fond of boating.

Anna Cocoris became pregnant and her husband announced that he would take her to New York to have her baby. When he and Constantine left with her for the North, another brother, George, stayed behind with instructions to buy a large boat. Besides Anna, John and Constantine took with them to Manhattan eight thousand dollars' worth of Tarpon Springs sponges. From their sale they meant to realize the capital that would start them in a great experiment. Sponges, they knew, could be taken by divers. This was the custom in the Mediterranean. It would make more money in Tarpon Springs than hooking; it was faster. The Cocorises knew where they could find the men needed to dive. For turbulent, whiskey-soaked Conchs they had little respect. The dedicated and dynasty-minded men they wanted lived in islands flung whitely out in the turquoise Aegean south of the Greek mainland like a scattering of tears. Like Jason, Cocoris would lead his Argonauts to the Golden Fleece—the fortune to be garnered by mechanized sponge diving at Tarpon Springs. In Tampa was the railroad he needed for shipping. Mykonos and Delos and Kalymnos and Halki: their Greece would be reborn on the Pinellas peninsula. When Cocoris had sold his sponges in New York at a profit of four thousand dollars, he began sending messages to the old country. Then he began buying diving machinery.

In Manhattan he and his brother met a sponge merchant from the Dodecanese island of Aegena, Spyros Vouteres. Vouteres complained that New York merchants were offering him low prices for his own sponges because they knew he had had to lay out heavy sums of capital to start business in the city. Sympathetically, the Cocorises promised to sell their countryman's sponges for him. He was happily surprised when they presented him with unexpected profits. One evening John Cocoris confided to Vouteres the extent of Florida's rich sponge beds, an extent undreamed of by the Conchs. Vouteres was planning to go to Greece. Cocoris entrusted him with a large sum of money; Vouteres was to buy more diving equipment and hire a Greek crew to run a sponge-fishing engine and its accessories on a Tarpon Springs boat.

Vouteres found his crew in Aegena. He recruited a captain, two divers, and two deckhands who could double as lifeline tenders. They would be holding the diver's rope at one end while it bound his waist at the other. Whenever the diver tugged five times, the tenders would draw him up without delay; it was a signal his life might be in danger. Other pulling signals gave the diver more allowance of rope as he wandered in his two-hundred-pound undersea suit among coral gardens. Diving was dangerous as hooking was not, but it had made Mediterranean fortunes. When he returned to Tarpon Springs with men and machinery, Cocoris named his first boat the *Elpis*—hope. He was ready to begin his adventure.

On a blue afternoon in June 1905, while cumulus clouds massed slowly on the horizon, the *Elpis* set forth into the Gulf. John Cocoris was aboard. When the *Elpis* had reached the Anclote Keys, two islands at the mouth of the Anclote River, it anchored. On one of the islands the crew began building a communal house to live in, and on the other a sponge warehouse. Cocoris knew his rival Conchs; they would be hostile to his method of harvest as soon as they learned of its speed. He was right; the Conchs began circulating rumors that the heavy metal boots of divers would eventually destroy all the sponges in the Gulf. Cocoris knew he had to guard his sponges on the Anclote Keys day and night. In the hostility of the Conchs there was also a mystical element. No man before Cocoris had dared to walk the Gulf's floor. It struck the Conchs as blasphemous, much as man's conquest of the moon struck the timid as sacrilegious more than half a century later.

When the *Elpis* finally put out to sea from the Anclote Keys, the divers began their preparations in earnest. Burly Demosthenes Kavasilas, the first of them, was lowered into the ocean's cobalt depths where he found sponges lying by the thousands. Dexterously he began his work. Every ten minutes he sent up a basket loaded with wool sponges, the most durable there were. By evening the *Elpis* was loaded, and Cocoris knew he had his dream secure. In Tarpon Springs, John Cheyney welcomed him and became an enthusiastic buyer.

In a matter of weeks Cocoris had earned both the hatred of the Conchs and a substantial sum of Cheyney money. He bought a single-sail boat, the *Pelican,* on which he intended to transport sponges in from the diving boat and, on the return trip, food and drink for the divers. They could thus stay constantly on the sponging grounds. Cocoris's profits began to pyramid. One by one he added to his little navy: from Tampa came the *Leonidion,* which had begun as a bay fishing boat. The *Trayton* had been a yacht which had won a golden cup in England. *Amphitrite, Agia Trias*—the names were strange to staring Conchs. All the time were arriving Greek sponge divers who considered themselves spiritual offspring of the god Oceanus, men who had learned to mask fear and who could endure the loneliness of their work. Their hands had catlike grace which even the weight of diving suits could not still. They were fatalists about death; on shore they were retiring, "lions in body, meek as lambs, and bashful as young girls." They avoided local bootleggers and moonshiners, though the bootleggers were resentful at having to conduct midnight operations off the coast with sponge boats nearby. The divers also ignored the smugglers whose cargo was human—Chinese, Mexicans, and West Indians who wanted to enter the United States illegally and had to pay heavily for the privilege. If the smugglers sensed danger, they abandoned their cargoes on deserted Gulf islands or, more sinisterly, to schools of sharks which waited for the briefest scent of blood. A cut on one Chinese finger might mean the end of a boatload of human flotsam. Divers also felt themselves menaced by other smugglers who trafficked in drugs; the Anglo-Saxons of Tarpon Springs only thought all the foreigners and backwoodsmen were a wild crew. If Ybor City was "socially very, very much south of the railroad tracks," Tarpon Springs, they feared, was socially very, very much north of the Tampa Bay Hotel.

The spongers kept their bunkhouse yard fragrant with pignolia nuts and pickled grapevine leaves; over lightwood fires they drank *retsina* wine and talked of home. Their lives revolved around the two trips of six months each they made into the Gulf. The first journey began in January when often the north wind stung their faces as they stood on deck. The second trip began in July, when the trade winds blessedly mitigated the heat. The only contacts with Tarpon Springs were messenger boats which brought food and mail. Among themselves the spongers had friendly rivalries; those from Karpathos, the "country of the giants," gently mocked the Kalymnians as "letter-eaters." Kalymnians were notorious for building schools and supporting scholars in Greek Orthodox monasteries. Under the leadership of Cocoris they were soon able to send money back to the Dodecanese islands. Dark-eyed girls began arriving with gaunt mothers whose heads were modestly wrapped in black shawls. Also came the restaurateurs which had soon changed Suncoast cuisine forever to provide feta cheese in every pot and Greek salad with every fish. Tarpon Springs itself was being transformed into a Greek port where Greeks were gathering to serve their countrymen. The Conchs, in disgust, left. Streets echoed now with hawkers' cries and bouzouki music and the creaking of brightly painted ships at Anclote wharves. The air was fragrant with spiced lamb and olive oil. This was Greece as Ybor City was Cuba. Tarpon Springs shops began selling

delectable imports, Greek jewelry and textiles. It was not long before
Tampa and St. Petersburg adventurous began considering a trip to Tarpon
Springs a tourist essential. It was exotic as tidy, Presbyterian Scottish
Dunedin was not. As the number of tourists increased, they understood
Greek salad better than the culture of a people who built altars on their
sponge boats from which the serene figure of St. Nicholas, patron of
mariners, gazed out into the Gulf while divers and tenders knelt in
prayer before the descent into what they called "the wealthy sea." Divers,
to the tourists, were enigmas. Sometimes they still are.

To the emotionally volatile spongers, the sponges stood for many
things. They knew that Homer had written of sponges in the *Iliad,* in
which Penelope's maidens cleaned with sponges the dining table of her
suitors. Vulcan, god of fire, had used a sponge to wipe the sweat from
his forehead. Aristotle had chronicled Greek warriors who used sponges
to polish their shields. Pliny, writing of later Romans, mentioned the
beautiful women who bathed with *melathi,* very soft and delicate sponges
to be found in the Mediterranean's deepest waters. Ancient divers risked
their sharks for Roman Beautiful People who insisted on being kept in
melathi. Christ had been offered his sponge of vinegar and hyssop. Today, say some spongers, the sponge is still cursed because of it. Sponging
is "filled with labor, dangers, tears, blood, and sudden death."

The sponge is an aquatic animal. It clings to a hard object—rock,
coral—and through a system of chambers it ingests the plankton on
which it lives. From its openings issue larvae which swim to new rocks,
new corals; nascent sponges are constantly being created. Every two
months the growing sponge increases in diameter by half an inch. In
its natural habitat it is coated with a dark elastic skin whose openings
serve as nostrils through which the sponge breathes. Gurry, a grey,
gelatinous substance, is found between the external and internal skins of
the living sponge. The sponges long popular for domestic use were only
skeletons. Today—ending an era—they are synthetic, though Tarpon
Springs continues to market the real thing. Divers gently squeeze out the
gurry as they garner their sponges. Then they pound them down and
clean them. Sponges are covered with wet gunnysacks on the ship's deck;
the heat the sacks generate releases a gas that rots the sponges' skins.
They come in more than three thousand varieties, but only a few are
valuable. Florida waters yield the sheep's-wool, velvet, yellow, grass,
glove, reef, wire, and finger sponges. Tampa Bay is the southern limit of

what are called the Bay Grounds, and the Bay Grounds are especially rich in sheep's-wool and grass and yellow and wire and finger sponges.

Hooking and harpooning of sponges was practiced to a limited extent in the Bay Grounds until a decade ago. The hookers worked from small skiffs in depths of from ten to forty feet. With glass-bottom buckets they scanned the Bay floor, and whenever they sighted sponges they marked their location with a buoy. Hooks had five keenly honed tines. The skiffs were called *Gantzericas*—the Greek root of the word means hook. At sunset the decks of the *Gantzericas* teemed with activity; spongers drank thick black coffee and began stamping on their catch and scraping its skin. Sometimes, in the Bay Grounds, memories of ancient sea songs drifted on twilight winds. So did the tang of the spongers' meat, *kavourma,* and the less ethereal scent of decomposing sponges. In most of Florida's sponge grounds, the machine-diving method introduced by John Cocoris was the preferred one. Now it is used exclusively. The diver, in his unwieldy suit, carries a netted bag, the *apohe,* in which he deposits his catch. Today the divers of Tarpon Springs dive mostly for tourists. On a good day, descent after descent to the bottom, they may get ten dollars to show for their pains. But it is enough to buy *koukia* and *roka*—beans and salad cress—for their wives if the women aren't gardeners. Most are, and Tarpon Springs dooryards are fragrant with heat-paled roses nearly all year.

The embarkation of the sponge fleet, in John Cocoris's time, had its rituals. Sheep and steers were killed and their meat salted down. Cedar barrels were filled with dried stockfish. When the meat was seared it became the divers' *kavourma.* It was eaten with dry hardtack, *galetta.* Before the multicolored boats of the sponge fleet sailed, Dodecanese Boulevard swarmed with crews. *Bouzouki,* xylophones, and violins blended in sea chanties in the taverns, from whose open doors issued the smell of lemons and olive oil and honeyed *baklava* pastry. Inside, young girls danced and begged the spongers for money bills with which to deck their hair and clothes. Spongers were heroes. The partying continued until the hour for the fleet to put out. Then the dancing and the music and the laughter died on the very freshness of the sea breeze, and Tarpon Springs began to pray.

Aboard, the crew would have to turn the wheel of the diver's air pump as long as he was down, usually for hours at a time. In the stern the life-line tenders pulled two heavy oars weighted with lead; tenders

Tarpon Springs

usually ended their lives with misshapen, disjointed arms. Constantly they kept their eyes on the life-line, while the diver below walked in iron shoes toward his quarry. Sometimes he descended to depths so great that his struggle with the current exhausted him if he lingered longer than five minutes. In every sponger's heart lay dread of the bends, paralysis and turning blue-black all over. If a victim of the bends were dragged up on deck and his companions saw what had happened when they removed his helmet, they had to throw him back into the sea for his circulation to get started once more. Sometimes the cure failed, and the sponger was paralyzed for life. In a tiny back room of a Tarpon Springs cottage, he lay immobile on his cot, his face set stoically. His friends, kindly, prayed for his release.

The sponges were sold in the Sponge Exchange, a whitewashed building still fronting particolored Dodecanese Boulevard. There are occasional sales today. Twenty per cent of the sponges came from *Gantzerica* boats and the rest were from the deep-sea divers. Sponges were put into metal-barred cages in the Exchange's courtyard, vividly bright in contrast to the dungeon darkness of the cages which fronted it. Every Tuesday and Friday, except Good Friday, the sponges were sold whenever there were enough to tempt buyers. The boat captain was billed two and a half percent of his profit for the Exchange's services, and one half of one percent was taken for the support of St. Nicholas's Greek Orthodox church, a basilicalike structure on the town's main street. A penetrating whistle at nine thirty in the morning signaled the beginning of the sponge market; the sponges had been tied in bunches, *couloures,* which were spread out on the sidewalk. The time of sale, for the boat captain and his family, was one of heavy drama. In a few moments the rewards of six months' labor would be decided. The black eyes of the shawl-wrapped women and girls were anxious too; even children stared breathlessly at the sponge buyers who examined the sponges and then wrote bids secretly on tickets which they handed to the Exchange clerk. When the clerk called out the highest offer, the captain either answered with a ringing "Sold!" or else, if the price was low, "Refused!"

Afterwards, in the warehouses, the sponge shearers took over, carefully snipping at the larger sponges to make attractive shapes; smaller ones were left intact. When the shearing and drying were finished, the sponges were packed into bales and sent to wholesalers in New York, Chicago, Detroit, Cleveland, Pittsburgh, St. Louis, Cincinnati, and Los Angeles. These were the "sponge cities" and their caprices could mean prosperity or want to Tarpon Springs.

In spite of their uncertainties, however, its people were never without humor. Legendary is the tale of Calvin Coolidge, who came in the 1920s to board a sponge boat and embark upon the briny. If he had been mildly amusing in the campaign garb of a Blackfoot Indian, as a sponger he was preposterous. But he gamely insisted on his share of *kavourma* and *galetta* and feta cheese and drank the ebony coffee he was offered. The chairman of his reception committee was John Kananes, originally from Halki. Stout, conscientious John Kalafates was the captain. Coolidge didn't see Kananes when he walked up to Kalafates and whispered: "Knock the boat a bit and drag it on the sandy shallow bank of the river." Captain Kalafates did not think he had heard correctly. Grimly he kept his eyes on the hazards of the Anclote, but soon he heard: "Knock it a little, Kalafates!"

"What are you saying?" hissed Kalafates *sotto voce.* "Don't you see the President and his wife? Do you want us all to hang?"

"Knock it a little on the side. I tell you this," Kananes added benignly, "for your own good."

A few minutes later Coolidge was startled to feel the boat hitting a sandbar. "Do not worry! Do not worry!" Kananes rushed to reassure him. "It is all right!"

"What was that?" asked Coolidge.

"Mr. President, just a slight, slight wrong twist of the tiller on behalf of the captain. The canal is so very shallow and narrow, you see, that it is dangerous to navigate."

A week later, government drag-ships appeared at Tarpon Springs to begin the dredging of a deeper Anclote channel. John Kananes and Captain Kalafates smiled.

The ritual of Sanctification of the Waters was performed by the priest at the start of every voyage. The spongers were determined to preserve their Greek heritage intact. At home they were fiercely pious and authoritarian. Their wives and daughters, along with small children, were expected to keep silence when men were discussing affairs of the sea and the Sponge Exchange. Whenever a child misbehaved, its mother was also punished; did she not have the training of the child, and its instruction in the Orthodox faith which made obedience mandatory? Husband and wife never kissed in front of their children. "It lessens respect," the men said tersely. Girls did not date, and marriages were arranged These traditions have died hard; when Tarpon Springs daughters go off to college these days and meet Jewish or Lutheran men the resulting mixed marriages may be inevitable but they are violently fought by the girl's parents. If courtships in Tarpon Springs were austere, weddings were gay with the stamping of feet in Greek dances. Older women sang their blessings to the young bride, who had been elaborately dressed in Greek cotton and lace. Festivities ended only with the dawn. Afterwards, the couple was expected to continue obedient to their parents. What freedom there would be came only with age.

Spongers had their share of superstitions—Evil Eyes, black cats, ladders, owls, and dogs barking all had their hazards. To the women belonged the power of exorcism, a mystery of olive oil and candlelight and incantations. The most startling custom of Tarpon Springs was the death wail, the *xodi*. Over the corpse, perhaps of a drowned sponger, black-robed women screamed and tore at their hair and beat their bodies so hard with stones that arms and breasts often ran with blood. The chanters wailed of Hades and graves; raucously they mourned all the way to the cemetery. If a man's body could not be found after a drowning, his clothes were buried to the accompaniment of a *xodi* more terrible because its object was missing. The *xodi* originally came from Halki, but it spread through the whole of Tarpon Springs because death came so often and so starkly there from the Gulf. In their dirges the Greeks heard echoes of the *Iliad* which told of the women of Hector lamenting dead of their own.

The years, of course, have brought change. They have brought bitterly divided families and a generation of young which sneers at the tradition-bound society of their elders. America has always claimed the young. Graduates of universities where their fathers slaved to send them return to scoff at Tarpon Springs and its proscriptions. Still, however, they are a part of it too, and perhaps the emotional knowledge of that is what they fight. On Epiphany they still don white costumes and dance Aegean dances. In crises they are drawn back to St. Nicholas's Church. A way of life is passing, but it has not passed yet. Still the *Socrates* and *Agatha* and *Hector* rock gently beside the pier, bright in orange trim. They have been joined by shrimp boats. *Bouzouki* still pours from dim yellow bars after dark. The gaiety has weathered such tragedies as Red Tide, which began destroying the sponge grounds in 1947 and continued mercilessly until sponging was little more than a memory. On their decks the spongers stared at the ruddy fire and on land their families smelled dead fish. A night came swiftly down on Tarpon Springs; homes and stores were closed; bankruptcies abounded; the young faded away and did not return. The jobs and the laughter were in Gary, Indiana, for them, Illinois and Pennsylvania and Ohio. Older spongers and their wives—most spoke no English—were unemployable. 'The sickness ate us up like rust," a sponger told the visiting Greek ambassador. "Carcasses boiled over by the sea, our sponges. Dead are the old people, and those living are living dead. Our children went to the factories. We are left without heirs. The wounds of Pharaoh came upon us." American sponge merchants once again began buying on the Greek island of Kalymnos, and Tarpon Springs was all but forgotten.

Today, though, it is chic. The tourists and wholesale fisheries have come to stay. Society matrons rent motel rooms for guests they have invited to watch the Epiphany cross-diving. In gardens, bauhinias and Hong Kong orchid trees are laden with lavender and pink blossoms which rain softly in the wind. The sun illumines hibiscus bushes and bird-of-paradise plants. Artists and writers have descended and so have the very elegant, who live discreetly far from the sponge decks and belong to country clubs like Innisbrook, a secluded and lavishly landscaped retreat for golf and dining on the gourmet fare of Chef Charles, whose Crab Louis is matchless. Tourists find Greek jewelry and gold-bordered textiles along Dodecanese Boulevard. The Greeks are still a majority, but non-Greeks have invaded their stronghold for good. Still, Tarpon Springs is probably one of the few places in America where your friendly neighborhood drugstore sells Aristophanes and Plato. The color and bustle of a Levantine seaside village have been reborn because of the influx of outlanders. Pappas's Restaurant has become nationally known and sells Mama Pappas's recipes to its customers in enticing booklets. Because of tourists, Dodecanese Boulevard rings again with the rough voices of reminiscing sponge divers. The isles of Greece live on, changed but vivid still in a western home. For the tourists glitter the Greek cloth and Indian brasses, and for them are displayed the polished shell jewelry, batiks, straw baskets, and Italian filigree. There are plastic flamingoes, but there are also treasures. A Sponge-o-rama presents an impressive display about the sponge industry and its people. Southward, along the Hillsborough, Pappas's Riverboat is alive with the chatter of visitors and prospering Greeks alike. Tarpon Springs has become more than a town. It is an ambience now, one more fountain of Suncoast cosmopolitanism which so startles first-time visitors. And, loyally, the veteran sponge divers who eat at the Riverboat all smoke Ybor City cigars.

23

"Health City"

When phosphate czars joined cattle kings up the Hillsborough, they clamored for the dredging of Tampa Bay to accommodate the ocean liners they needed to transport their product. In 1905 Congress appropriated $350,000 for deepening the river channel and creating an island with fill. The island got the name of one of the engineers, Seddon. Phosphate elevators climbed into brilliant skies. Cattle lowed as they waited for passage to the West Indies; Florida breeders on the river had begun crossing their scrawny range cows with heat-resistant Brahma bulls, and the results were in demand. After it had become a world port, Tampa also became the destination of the first scheduled airline in the United States. Captain Tony Jannus flew a hundred and fifty feet high from St. Petersburg and the *Tampa Times* marveled, "He can go even higher if he chooses." By then World War I was in progress. Tampa was rocked by a cigar workers' strike that lasted nine weeks and resulted in three deaths, seventeen injured, and twelve thousand unemployed. The city survived the strike and a hurricane; its industries proliferated in spite of the fact that right-wing Ku Klux Klansmen had a way of kidnapping labor leaders and dosing them with castor oil. Shipping dynasties like the Lykes family replaced the gentle paternalism of small industry; Vicente Martínez Ybor was dead, and nobody distributed Christmas baskets in Ybor City anymore. It was all light years distant from little St. Petersburg across the bay, which finally demanded and got its own county. In their eagerness to shed the label West Hillsborough, St. Petersburgers forgot that the river was, literally, the very water of life to them. They had their minds on tourists.

B. W. Richardson of London, England, had been a doctor with a dream. He wanted to find the perfect climate; somewhere on earth, he reasoned, there had to be a sanctuary without snow, sleet, or tse-tse flies. Dr. W. C. Van Bibber of Baltimore agreed with him, and began scouting America for Health City. He busied himself with taking down wind, sun, rain and temperature data until he was able to report to the American Medical Association at a New Orleans convention:

> Where should Health City be built? Overlooking the deep Gulf of Mexico, with the broad waters of a beautiful bay surrounding it; with but little now upon its soil but the primal forests there is a large sub-peninsula, Point Pinellas, waiting the hand of improvement. It lies in latitude 27 degrees and 42 minutes, and contains, with its adjoining keys, about 160,000 acres of land.

The people of Pinellas were racketing around in a boundless Utopia of light and beach and sea. There were no marshes, doctors said. The average temperature in winter was 72 degrees; all the inhabitants of the peninsula had ruddy cheeks, which proved that the air was pure. "Here should be built such a city as Dr. Richardson outlined," Dr. Van Bibber declared. His colleagues began coming south to see St. Petersburg for themselves. To reach it, they had to use the Orange Belt Railroad.

The train, on occasion, could muster speed for twenty miles an hour. It was more than enough on the uneven rails. Half the time it broke down, and arriving physicians were treated to hours in steaming pine-palmetto woods where their only diversion was watching cows roam. "The train jumps the track about once a week," said a patron, "but I never heard of anyone being killed or seriously injured. The train doesn't go fast enough. When it rains, the wood fuel gets wet and then you can keep up with the train by walking." When the Orange Belt's successor, the St. Petersburg Land and Improvement Company, finally standardized the tracks and devised a timetable the doctors were happier. They liked what they found at the road's end. The sun shone nearly every day, even in the hot season of sudden tropical downpours. When the downpours were over, the zamias and palms and mangroves glistened like fire opals. "Even the lizards are healthy," noted a hiking medical man. When the doctors went back North, they wrote articles. Soon the arthritic and victims of the sniffles began visiting paradise. The railroad built them a pavilion on Tampa Bay where "you can get a fresh water bath after you take a dip in the briny blue. The proprietor is a clever, accommodating gentleman." Clever, too, was the town's only barber, a black man with impressive muscles who offered to "carve" you at fifteen cents a head. Then he rubbed turpentine into your cuts to stop the flow of blood. Paradise wasn't expensive, and you could buy venison and wild ducks and turkeys in the market. Straw-hatted farmers brought in oranges in squeaky, sun-bleached wagons and charged a nickel a hatful for their fruit. It was always fascinating to watch the alligators in St. Petersburg ponds, and people were hospitable. The city council passed an ordinance forbidding belled cows to wander in the streets; convalescents needed peace and quiet. The invalids and farmers and cattlemen and freshly arrived merchants all got along splendidly. Rheumatics discarded their canes and often stayed to open stores. A Philadelphia publisher of medical books built an electric plant; he also started a trolley line, but he found the tourists were walkers who used the trolley's bay bridge for fishing. Modest frame boardinghouses began to line streets shaded by cocos plumosa palms. One enterprising citizen built himself a tower a hundred and thirty-seven feet high and then claimed that Signor Marconi, the inventor of radio, was coming to St. Petersburg to conduct his experiments in it. Marconi never showed up and the tower was struck by lightning, but the city prospered. One merchant boasted that his artesian well was the original Fountain of Youth. Its patrons were frisky enough; when a local bank failed some of them forgot they had once been cripples and heart patients and marched downtown threatening to lynch the bank manager. They got only a fraction of their money back, but still they sang St. Petersburg's praises. Then the Philadelphia publisher began reprinting Dr. Van Bibber's speech to the American Medical Association and sending copies to newspapers all over the country. He also started a *Florida Magazine* which touted his electric station and streetcar along with the attractions of the Land of Flowers. Into every diagnostic discussion he brought St. Petersburg, and he wrote two pamphlets, *The Progress and Possibilities of St. Petersburg* and *St. Petersburg, the Queen City of Pinellas*. It was not long before half of the steadily growing population had originally been frail souls put out to pasture by their doctors. In St. Petersburg, pains vanished; nobody had ever heard of Dr. Sigmund Freud or psychosomatic medicine.

A train was chartered for aching residents of Ohio and Indiana, and the city sent a brass band to the station to welcome them. Real estate values began rising. As streets were paved and sidewalks were built, many of the curbstones were made to slope instead of ending abruptly; that way, users of wheelchairs would be able to get around more easily. It was no longer unusual, in hotel lobbies and rooming houses, to see elderly men with shaking palsy wearing bright sports clothes while fishing rods quivered in their uncertain fingers. Faces partially paralyzed by past strokes acquired sunburns, and onetime influenza patients swore they had been cured by orange juice. The Loyal Christian Temperance Union was so dismayed by the general atmosphere of celebration that it built a bronze water fountain in the yard of the Detroit Hotel to remind visitors that H_2O was better for them than liquor. In the autumn of 1908 an Arkansas lawyer arrived in St. Petersburg to publish a newspaper. Lew Brown also had an idea; he thought St. Petersburg needed a more cheerful label than Health City. Sunshine City had a more encouraging ring to it. Every day the sun failed to shine up to press time, Brown promised to deliver the paper to the city free. The national press was intrigued and gave the promise immense publicity. The Sunshine City! There seekers of lost vigor could bask eternally enough to ensure that the *St. Petersburg Evening Independent* only had to be given away five times a year. Brown also wrote poetry: St. Petersburg air was

> . . . like some rich old wine that thrills through every vein;
> Thy sunshine falls as gently down as some far music's strain;
> Thy soft perpetual breezes waft a life-balm rich and rare—
> Where all the time is summer, and every day is fair.

Another literary light had his own version of the creation of Pinellas County:

> The god of the sun said, "She is mine!" Over her fair breast of gentle hills and the breast of her waters he laid his veil of sunbeams. "She is mine!" swore the god of the great waters, "for out of the depths of my own heart have I cast her up on the rock of ages; day by day and night by night she bathes in the flood of my eternal fountains of the deep, and dries her velvet beauty in the flood of moonbeams." "No, but she is mine!" said the goddess of the trees and flowers.
> "Then will we all make Pinellas, fair daughter of fair Florida," sang the gods of mystic wonder.

It was all heady stuff for people coughing in Akron.

Noel Mitchell was a lyricist of another kind. "Mitchell the Sand Man," his real estate advertisements read. "The honest dealer. The man with a conscience. He never sleeps." Unaware of the irony of a sleepless man of good conscience, he did a vast volume of business in his office on Central Avenue. Many of his clients complained of tired feet; the town hadn't yet cured their bunions and fallen arches. Mitchell decided he could lure more lot buyers if he provided benches for them to sit on. From a local carpenter he ordered fifty and directed them to be painted a vivid orange. One weekend he planted them on the street in front of his office, hoping for results. He got them on Monday morning. The amazed Mitchell looked out the window to find the benches filled, and near them a waiting line. "Mitchell's Prayer Meeting," people began to call the footsore who flocked to Mitchell's for sitting room. Other merchants looked, pondered, and began asking Mitchell to lend them benches for their own establishments. He ordered a hundred more orange benches, and each one bore the legend of "Mitchell the Sand Man." Soon competitors were buying their own benches, which began to cover the sidewalk in a conglomeration of shapes and colors. The mayor was alarmed. Nothing matched. It would not be impressive to the tourists. He speeded through the city council a law which required all benches to be the same size. He didn't like orange; benches were to be green. They were a city trademark from that time on. The Sunshine City was now also the City of Green Benches, which began to be cherished not only by people with tired feet but also by lonely oldsters who were not above a bit of flirting with bench-sitters of the opposite sex. An impressive total of marriages resulted.

World War I slowed things up. Lots began to revert to plumes of dog fennel weed where promoters had envisioned retirement villas. America was preoccupied not with health but with anxiety over its sons fighting on distant European battlegrounds. People traveled less. St. Petersburg managed to stay alive, but there were bankruptcies. It was a pleasant little city, though. Steamships sailed blue-green Tampa Bay, pelicans flew over Boca Ciega Bay to the West where the Gulf beaches were, and red-tiled pseudo-Spanish roofs gleamed in the steady light. Hotels like the Detroit and the newer Huntington were still mostly full, though boardinghouses suffered. Naturalists, in particular, liked St. Petersburg. They could take the trolley out toward Maximo Point where black and yellow swallowtail butterflies flitted over Timucua mounds full of potsherds and flints under a cover of washed-up seaweed. Conch shells littered the white sand. The deep green leaves of cherry laurels rustled stiffly at night as the heavy perfume of their white blossoms mingled with the salt tang of the Gulf. Every spring and fall the sky darkened with flocks of migrating long-billed curlews. Tampa was less popular with the naturalists. "It is low, dirty, and behind Jacksonville in every respect," one of them pronounced, noting that it had such exotica as " a Cuban-inhabited suburb." Tampa trains which had belonged to liberal Henry Plant now dragged Jim Crow cars behind them as they chugged out of town. Naturalists from the North disapproved of segregation. They also disapproved of rising prices in St. Petersburg: "It's a place where the natives work less and have more to show for it than any place on earth. This is probably due to the fact that they charge northern suckers exorbitant prices for everything they buy. St. Pete is like neither heaven nor hell, for in both places you need no money and in St. Pete you need it every hour." On one of the green benches they were amazed by axioms: "Man is made of sand. Dust settles. Be a man and buy sand!"

The end of the War To End Wars filled the rooming houses once more. Hotel managers were jubilant at filled registers of guests. After a ferocious hurricane tourists arrived eager to see the damage, and many stayed after the torrential sweep to buy lots they reasoned were immune to damage because now that the Sunshine City had had the storm statistical chances for successors were low. On the eastern horizon, the smoke of Port Tampa sent up scattered spirals, but in St. Petersburg the air was pristine. Daily it dealt in miracles of testified recovery until the decrepit were being helped by a mystique of hope. They began writing home to younger relatives and friends that they had found a garden where old people were not only tolerated but courted, an American miracle. The eyes of sons and daughters widened as they read that Pa was playing shuffleboard while Ma was going to classes in ballroom dancing and neither had had a cold all season. What a place! Why spend another winter vacation up north coping with storm windows? The way to get to St. Pete was in the new flivver. The old folks might stick to trolley cars, but their children were adventurous. They were also, for Florida, the Big Boom.

24

Tin-Can
Tourists

By 1920, in both St. Petersburg and Tampa, the onslaught of winter visitors had grown to a deluge. They were even invading little Zephyrhills up the river. They were not, for the most part, the sick, nor were they the rarefied Stotesburys and Whitneys of Palm Beach, whose efforts to fill the time they spent in Florida were chronicled in society pages in New York and Philadelphia and Boston. The enthusiasts who came to the river and the bay from the north filled their trusty automobiles back home with supplies of canned food sufficient to last the season down south. Tin-Can Tourists: the label was at first derisive, then affectionate. When they came they were enthralled by St. Petersburg's city pier. What an experience to drive your Tin Lizzie out to its end over the bay where sharks still swam and were sometimes caught by startled anglers! On moonlit nights harmless youngsters spooned by the pier's railing, and occasionally, from a nearby parlor with open windows, echoes of piano ragtime drifted gaily out to mingle with the distant horns of steamers like the excursion boat *Favorita*. When a hurricane ripped part of the pier away, it wasn't difficult for the *Evening Independent*'s Lew Brown to spearhead a drive for its restoration. St. Petersburg was in love with it, and the new pier even boasted a casino. In 1925 the pier was rebuilt yet again, to the tune of nearly a million dollars. Soon the Million Dollar Pier was a St. Petersburg attraction pulling in middle America by the thousands. The city early set aside a campground for the Tin-Canners, and Tampa handsomely followed suit by giving them de Soto Park, on the shore of Hillsborough Bay. De Soto Park boasted plumbing and running water, and the Tin-Canners there who had children were required to pay Hillsborough County only fifty cents a week to enroll their off-spring in local schools.

A Tin-Canner's saga invariably began the same way. One morning he woke up in Ohio (Michigan, Wisconsin, New York State, Ontario, North Dakota) to find snow falling thickly and soundlessly to rigid ground outside his frost-frescoed windows. Groaning, he got out his snow shovel and galoshes; his wife began complaining about the probable coal bill. When he had finished shoveling the snow, there were "clinkers" of coal residue to be scraped out of the furnace. His water pipes were in danger of freezing. Snow had made his country into a picture postcard, but the picture postcards he started thinking about were those of palms waving on the shore of moonlit Tampa Bay. While he struggled at home knocking icicles from his eaves, he knew, people were pruning roses on the Suncoast. While blizzards swept whitely and fatefully across mid-America's prairies and piled high drifts at the edges of northeastern woods, the sun was shining on the Million Dollar Pier and the minarets of the Tampa Bay Hotel. The real-life fable of the Suncoast was in every newspaper—often. And if a man had a business—like storekeeping or farming—that could be left in reliable custody for the winter, he was crazy to linger in a prison of frost. Why, there were actually St. Petersburg and Tampa natives who had never even seen sleet! Storm windows? In Florida windows were flung open to health-giving breezes wafting a tender perfume of orange blossoms—every day! So why not chuck winter altogether?

Tin-Canners were on the tightest of budgets. None of them were rich, though Suncoasters liked to fool themselves into thinking the latest comers were doctors and bankers. A Tin-Canner was chary with his dollars, and some people said that before he spent a quarter he gave it such a fond farewell squeeze that the eagle on it squawked in pain. An efficient Tin-Canner had everything planned. He stocked his flivver with camp chairs and sheets and frying pans and mattresses and tents and tin cups and plates that nested to save space. His cans of food he stashed on the roof and beneath the seats, and he tied cartons of them onto the fenders. As you passed a Tin-Canner on the road, his car sounded "as though its owner were carrying a reserve supply of canned goods under the hood—loose." There was room for checkerboards and playing cards. Water sports had few attractions for the average Tin-Canner, who paid his homage to Florida instead by sitting in the sun clad in baggy pants, white shirt, and suspenders. He gambled at bridge for pennies. His wife enjoyed rubbernecking along St. Pete's Central Avenue where dress shops didn't cater to skinny flappers but to mothers with ample bosoms and spacious hips. In Tampa there were the attractions of Ballast Point and Sulphur Springs to tempt Tin-Canners on family expeditions. Such families naturally didn't bother with the dagoes of what they called Ee-bo City, these jabbering Cubans and Italians who waved their arms so wildly as they talked. In de Soto Park Tin-Can patriarchs had a kingdom composed of men and women like themselves, Anglo-Saxons and Dutch and Scandinavians and Germans, and it was here that they founded an organization, Tin-Can Tourists of the World. Everybody in it got to wear a tiny white celluloid button labeled T C T in navy blue. On his auto radiator a Tin-Canner was entitled to mount the symbol of a small soup can. He even had a password which he shouted to other Tin-Canners as he met them on the highway; it was such a carefully guarded secret that outsiders never did learn what it was. Conventions were held annually at de Soto Park, the Tin-Can Town of Tampa. By 1922 the society had more than thirty thousand members and before the Big Boom was over the figure had swelled to a hundred and forty-seven thousand. What a gold mine, collectively if not individually! A canny operator contacted a retired transportation engineer named Gandy and sold him on the idea of forming a company which would promise to build a bridge between Tampa and St. Petersburg. Gandy Bridge: Gandy liked the sound of that. The promoter began a campaign which included the presentation of Gandy to St. Petersburg as Dad, a folksy individual anybody could put his faith in. When half the shares had been sold, the promoter sauntered into Gandy's office. "Well, Dad, we've hit the million mark!"

"Yes." Gandy was beaming. "It won't be long now before we can start work on the bridge."

The promoter blinked. "Dad, did I hear you right? You're not really going to *build* it, are you?"

Luckily for his shareholders, Gandy was an honest man. Gandy Bridge is unimpressive these days compared to its more modern sisters which span Tampa Bay, but when it opened to traffic it was the longest bridge in the world, nineteen miles of it.

Tampa was as popular with the Tin-Canners as was what they always called St. Pete. A trolley connected de Soto Park with the downtown area, and in the de Soto camp itself Tampa erected a pavilion where Tin-Canners entertained each other on winter evenings just cool enough to require sweaters. The camp had lights and showers and its own hot water tank. The more the Tin-Canners camped in such grounds—other Florida cities established them too—the more the word got back north that there were free places to stay indefinitely. New hordes followed. They undercut local laborers by offering to work for a pittance, a habit which earned them the hostility of Suncoasters who began muttering that such folks ought to go back where they came from. Tin-Canners were supposed to spend, not earn. For some of the temporary workers the natives made things pretty hot, and they retreated. Was Florida becoming inhospitable, asked the northern press? The *Tampa Tribune* answered righteously, "The only Florida tourists beating it back to the north are the cut-rate, fly-by-night cheapskates who have been coming to the state and preying off the public . . . The state has enough of its own honest labor to take care of without opening its doors to the floater who is here to take the bread out of his brother's mouth for less than the honest price. The riff-raff, the confidence man, the fakir, the wage cutter and the public mendicant all get the cold shoulder in Florida." Thereafter fewer and fewer Tin-Canners had the temerity to seek winter employment. Instead they hooked their thumbs on their galluses, leaned back in their folding deck chairs, and contemplated the swelling bay. When they read Florida newspapers it was to relish headlines like *No Lives Lost in California Blizzard*. The worst, short of slaughter, had occurred in rival orange groves. It was a matter for celebration. Every fall California retaliated with gleeful accounts of hurricanes, a catch-all category which, out west, included the feeblest of southeastern tropical depressions. Florida's Tin-Canners weren't fooled. They knew that only in Florida could they get by for a winter on a hundred dollars, drinking orange juice all the way. Florida's roads might not be much—south of Tampa and St. Pete they certainly weren't—but they got a man where he wanted to go, in a vehicle to which his loyalty bordered on fanaticism. "This flivver makes forty miles an hour hardly tryin'," Tin-Canners told their hearers eagerly. "Nothing this old bus can't do, she sets her mind to it. Yessir! Mud? Don't bother her a bit." Sometimes the bus was merely a family automobile of uncertain years, and sometimes it was a converted delivery truck. There were Tin-Can wives who fitted up the windows in white dotted-swiss curtains, and who painted across the truck's sides their origin: Oconomowoc, Wisconsin. Spartans jeered such families as being "slaves to their belongings." Some Tin-Canners cooked breakfasts of bacon and eggs and coffee and had orange juice and maybe half a grapefruit thrown in. Others were content to chew Kellogg's Corn Flakes or other breakfast cereals that needed no preparation.

The average Tin-Canner drove a touring car, which had a fabric roof and open sides. His tent, set up, usually hooked on to the automobile's side. To his pride, his car was "a combination lavatory, sitting-room, chiffonier, clothes closet, pantry, and safe-deposit vault." He had thin, sturdy tires on his four spoked wheels, and he also found room for a tire jack, a set of wrenches, and extra water, if he was on the move, for times when the radiator boiled over. To Henry Ford, who maintained a winter home next door to Thomas A. Edison's in Fort Myers, it must have been a memorable experience to travel up to St. Pete and Tampa Tin-Can Towns to see what he had wrought. Nobody tied auto-camping mystically to ecology or meditation in those days. It was simply a lot of fun, and only a loony would want to stay up with the snowdrifts and birds that shivered over breadcrumbs instead of pouring out trills like mockingbirds did. Tin-Canners had their bard in author Kenneth L. Roberts, who immortalized them in his book *Sun-Hunting* with the same lack of suspicion everyone else had that by 1962 the convention of Tin-Can Tourists of the World would attract to Tampa's Municipal Trailer Park exactly sixty people. Flivvers, curtained and convex-roofed delivery wagons, and sagging canvas tents had yielded by then to the pretensions of the Mobile Home which contained its own Early American Stereophonic Sound System.

Early in the 1920s there were Tin-Canners who ceased to be Tin-Canners by staying in Florida for good. They wrote their friends up North, and often the friends came with confidence that they could earn a living one way or another, as most of them could. The cost of real estate began to progress geometrically.

HERE IS A TIP.
AN INVESTMENT IN A MUD HOLE LOCATED IN THE PATH OF A CITY'S
GROWTH WILL OFT-TIMES BRING HOME THE BACON.

Real-estate developments mushroomed. In the Sunshine City, hotels began rising in stuccoed and Spanish-tiled masses against the blue sky: the Don Ce-Sar, the elegantly pink Vinoy Park on the bay's shore and the Princess Martha downtown, named for the wife of Crown Prince Olav of Norway. Since many newcomers came to the Sunshine City from the Midwest, they were of Scandinavian stock. The St. Petersburg telephone directory began to fill with Thorkildsens, Sorensons, Haugens, and Olsens. A group of Czechoslovaks arrived to found Masaryktown north of the bay. Dunedin remained heavily Scots-Presbyterian. Tycoon Roger W. Babson—he who was to see prosperity just around the corner in the depths of the Great Depression—bought four hundred acres in Oldsmar, "The Wonder Town of Pinellas," and named them Babson Park. There was also a Babson Park inland. St. Petersburg began to fill with suckers and salesmen alike, and as they all started to build, the land values climbed to new heights. Snell Isle was for the rich, like doctors and dentists, and so were The Jungle and Shore Acres. On Gandy Boulevard rose Rio Vista, which vista-ed not the rio but the bay. The Florida Riviera and Five Thousand Acres of Sunshine erected impressive billboards and began to endow tracks in the sand with the designations of boulevards. Now, if the buyer could just visualize. . . . Bolder spirits began to sell land at the bottom of Tampa Bay, and when the victims found it out they weren't too disturbed. The bay could be dredged, couldn't it? Snell Isle was nothing but dredgings. *"DOUBLE YOUR MONEY WITHIN A YEAR!"* promised advertisements, and everybody believed them. Speculators bought on margin, and ethical developers competed valiantly with outright crooks. Integrity gave a man a hard time of it, for the gaudiest operations had the combined powers of Circe and the Lorelei to spellbind and immobilize the unwary. The labor of pitching was usually divided between two separate classes of entrepreneurs—knickerbocker boys and bird dogs.

The knickerbocker boys had dash. They wore plus fours and bow ties, and some of them sported visored caps like these of golf professionals. The plus fours were light in color, their fabric a forerunner of the Palm Beach suit. A knickerbocker boy was a crack salesman, and if he had previously been dealing in real or imaginary mines and wells the experience didn't hurt him any. He was cheerfully ready to plunder from widows and orphans, he was impossible to find after he had committed a fraud, and even if he were honest he made extravagant promises. The lot worth five hundred dollars today would go for a thousand next week, and before the year was over it would be worth a cool ten thousand. To the knickerbocker boy, dollars were "clams" and "simoleons." To keep the simoleons flowing in, he hired bird dogs—scouts who went out and mixed with the populace. Bird dogs favored green benches, churches, lodges, and political clubs for their prospects. A bird dog talked up his subdivision, and when his prospect was weakening visibly he called in the knickerbocker boy for the kill. For every deal, the bird dog raked off a commission of his own from his boss. The most successful bird dogs were handsome, silver-haired men in their sixties who knew how, in St. Pete, to pay gallant compliments to old maids and widows in their seventies. What looked like romance on a green bench was usually, now, a budding real estate transaction. Bessie would never forgive herself if she lost the golden opportunity to triple her savings; a lovely lady such as Bessie ought to have every luxury life could afford her. Would Bessie care to dine out that evening? She would? And how about taking in a flick afterwards? There was no sex discrimination in the employment of bird dogs. Some were women, and one of them, an attractive thirty-eight, short-skirted and cloche-hatted, was rumored to have made fifty thousand dollars in three years of being charming to elderly men whose blue-veined hands were still strong enough to reach for their wallets.

It was all very swanky, and the knickerbocker boys generally maintained carpeted offices in hotels like the Detroit, Huntington and Princess Martha in St. Petersburg and the Tampa Bay in Tampa. They also dispensed plenty of liquor if they were sure they weren't dealing with Methodists and Baptists. Prohibition was an unfortunate fact, but bootleggers along the Hillsborough and beside the bay were daring enough to dispense from the backs of their pickup trucks rum which had been smuggled in by night from Cuba. Moonshine went for five dollars a quart, about what it goes for today. Even the churches didn't protest too loudly; bootleggers kept them deep in donations, and the stipends of the clergy began vaulting. Church corporations bought and built. Three million dollars went into the development of downtown St. Petersburg in 1925. Fourth and Central was christened the Million Dollar Corner, a mate for the Million Dollar Pier. Everybody agreed it was ritzy. Newly rich businessmen built houses in Snell Isle, and there they entertained their clients with gin fizzes and Canadian Rye while victrolas ground out boop-a-doop music. One of the fanciest new subdivisions in Tampa was Temple Terrace, on the shores of the Big Hillsborough near the Little Hillsborough Francis Dade had crossed with his doomed contingent. Originally fifteen hundred acres of Temple Terrace had been owned by Mrs. Potter Palmer, a Chicago society matron. When she parted with it to a firm of nurserymen they planted it thickly with Temple orange trees. It 1924 their grove was taken over by a syndicate of developers, who built for their clients a country club among the citrus and promised them instant social conquest.

Not that everything was calm in the bay area. A long and bitter battle had begun between cigar laborers and factory owners which ended in a strike of sixty-four hundred workers in twenty-seven factories. Local unions had doubled their membership. The Mayor of Tampa, a descendant of Captain McKay, proposed "public assistance for the non-Unionists," and after visiting fifty homes in Ybor City reported that "suffering was acute." Tables were empty, but many of the workers (he said) had told him they were too proud to take help from the Salvation Army or the Red Cross, which the mayor had urged to set up operations in the shadow of The Clock. Cigar manufacturer A. L. Cuesta informed the press that the strike was "not in the least interfering with his business." The pride, upon investigation, turned out to be reluctance to take help from organizations brought in by the very coalition of Tampa officials and cigar manufacturers the workers felt were trying to destroy them. What was the Big Boom for them? Newspaper editorials intoned ominously:

> The people of Tampa are not going to tolerate the situation many days longer . . . The greatest menace today to the perpetuation of the rights and principles of the people and to the guarantee of free institutions of the United States is to be found in the destructive propaganda, aims, and practices of the American Federation of Labor which represents less than 3 per cent of the country's entire population.

Tampa wanted no economic chinks in its Big Boom armor. When the cigar strike ended, this time after ten acrimonious months, several manufacturers had gone bankrupt, unionists still had to bow to the principle of the open shop, and Tampa feared its image to the rest of the country had suffered. Oh, for another Henry Plant! Uneasily, there were Tampans who began wondering if the boom were eternal after all.

Dave Davis thought it was, though. His father had been a steamboat captain on the bay, and he still liked traveling on steamers. To show off he walked their side rails like a tightrope, even in the stormiest weather.

Dave's brains were as agile as his sea legs were steady. As a boy he had collected coon oysters on the mud flats at the Hillsborough's mouth. There, too, he had watched the scurrying of fiddler crabs, and he had listened to the plaints of herring gulls over his head. He loved those mud flats. While he went to high school in Tampa he sold newspapers and worked in a candy store as a soda jerk. At seventeen he took a job in a local business, but after three years, bored, he gave it up. Then he disappeared. Nobody in Tampa ever knew where he went. The Panama Canal Zone? Central America? By the beginning of World War I, he was in Jacksonville, where he got married and operated an army canteen. When the war was over, he and his wife took off for Miami, and there he found his destiny in real estate. Miami was a marketable swamp.

It was tantalizing for Dave Davis to watch the mud flats of Biscayne Bay being turned into islands full of shiningly expensive new houses sought after by millionaires. He remembered the islands in the Hillsborough and Tampa Bay he had tramped as a boy, all the while dreaming of Gasparilla's buried pirate treasure. Little Grassy, Depot, Big and Rabbit and Big Grassy . . . the islands had all been lush with spartina grass, and on their tangled mangroves coon oysters had been thick and fat. Why couldn't places like Little Grassy and Big Grassy be converted even as had been the islands in Biscayne Bay? Dave hurried up to Tampa and checked their ownership. They belonged to a rich merchant and to a cattle baron who had both expected Henry Plant's railroad to expand to the islands' borders. That hadn't happened, but they hadn't invested much at a dollar an acre. The city of Tampa now had ideas of making Little Grassy into a park, and it owned the tidelands between the islands. Dave began calling meetings of townspeople, attorneys, and prospective home builders. He soon learned he was going to have to pay more than a dollar an acre; before he could put his scheme into action he would need to raise a hundred and fifty thousand dollars, not counting the two hundred thousand the city wanted for Little Grassy. If he could complete his development in four years and build a bridge to the islands as well, and establish a city park, Tampa would return his purchase price. The project was enticing, and people began giving him their money. Dave Davis was a smooth talker, and he had a winning smile. He opened an office downtown whose walls were hung with grandiose drawings of the Davis Islands that were to be—dense tropical foliage, drifts of garden flowers, mansions, palms everywhere, and—naturally—an orange tree in every yard. He hired big-time knickerbocker boys who pounded it into public brains that Davis Islands would be the eighth wonder of the world. How could anybody afford *not* to buy a piece of them? Lines began forming outside Dave's headquarters, and his clerical staff were soon avalanched in a million dollars' worth of transactions. Celebrities began turning up. William Jennings Bryan came to the Tampa Bay Casino and told jokes when he wasn't preaching fundamentalism. (Downstate, an invalid Mrs. Bryan was confiding to newspaperwoman Marjory Stoneman Douglas, "If I had had my health, Papa would never have gone into this evolution business.")

In the bay itself things were jumping. Dredges pumped and rattled all day and all night until the mud flats of Big and Little Grassy had been stripped to sand as white as snow. Giant shovels hollowed out drainage ditches, and bulldozers graded roadbeds. Dave talked himself into borrowed money for a yacht harbor and an electric light system. One of the apartment buildings under construction he christened the Palace of Florence because it stood near the Venetian, and he felt every inch like a Doge as he watched his water-laced miracle taking shape. It only needed a Bridge of Sighs. Ground was broken for a hospital and whenever he wearied of watching cranes and shovels he went up to St. Augustine, where he was presently raising more money for a development to be called Davis Shores. As sunlit weeks passed he was so happy in picturesque St. Augustine, with its cobbled streets and old Spanish houses, that he stayed—and stayed—while the building of Tampa's Davis Islands went on without him.

Monday, December 7, 1925, dawned rainy in St. Petersburg across the bay. Long wet strands combed through palm fronds and sent tardily clinging dogwood leaves down the streets in gusts of wind. Waves dashed white against seawalls, and the foghorns of ocean liners echoed dolorously. It was obviously a day when Lew Brown would have to give away the *Evening Independent,* but it was more than that. It was the opening day of the convention of the Investment Bankers Association of America, and the bankers were incarcerated in their pseudo-Spanish hotels staring glumly out of the windows at what they had been lured into believing was the Sunshine City. The wind howled, and chilly drafts seeped through thin cracks. The disgruntled bankers played cards and backgammon and checkers and dreamed of golf courses. Some Sunshine City! Tuesday was even rainier, and Wednesday was worse. Thursday and Friday brought no respite from the chilling rain and wind. By then St. Petersburg was a soggy mess. The mercury plummeted every night. When the bankers departed, they went convinced that the weather in the Sunshine City, and the Sunshine State, was lousy. They freely told everybody back north exactly what had happened to them. They had been drenched, but not in Vitamin D.

They had many friends, had those bankers who were the agents of a major Florida disaster. During the previous autumn, land sales in St. Petersburg and Tampa had rolled up to staggering new totals. In December, after the bankers had floated back home, sales fell off dramatically. Northern newspapers began carrying stories about Florida's cold wave. The cold wave continued; when the rain gave way at last to sun the air turned sharper than ever, and at night outlying orange groves blazed yellow-black with smudge fires. Garden ferns browned and died; even hardy pansies withered in clammy blasts of air from the Gulf and the bay. Knickerbocker boys rubbed their hands together to keep them warm as they sat in empty offices. Bird dogs bundled themselves against the chill in outmoded northern overcoats. It was a standing joke that you could always tell a Floridian in the cold by his shabby clothes; Floridians never bought new overcoats because they so seldom needed to wear anything heavier than a sweater. That, at least, was what everybody had believed. Now the bird dogs found it increasingly hard to interest strolling Bessies in tripling their life's savings. Bessie wasn't buying anymore. Neither were northern millionaires, nor retired doctors and engineers and dentists from Ohio and Nebraska. Tin-Canners were streaming homeward. By spring, the real estate market had collapsed utterly in St. Petersburg. Half-finished buildings exposed naked beams to a sky which had turned blue and mellow too late. Knickerbocker boys faded into the shadows from which they had come. A lumber company tried frantically to sell its overstock of wood, and nobody could afford to buy it. Finally they made a high bonfire of it on Nineteenth Street South. The bright flames ate away at what had once been a part of Florida's future.

The banks tottered, and unemployment rose. Architects, engineers, carpenters, interior decorators, and plumbers all returned north where 1926 was still a golden era of prosperity, and pickle-faced Calvin Coolidge was prognosticating nothing but good for an unfettered capitalistic system. Rents dropped, and still the tourists did not come. Everybody knew what had happened to the Investment Bankers Association of America. By the fall of 1926 St. Petersburg had its new buildings, a new park on the shore of Tampa Bay, and a fraction of its former inhabitants and visitors to use them.

Dave Davis, up in St. Augustine, was having his troubles too. It had rained on the Davis Islands even as it had rained on St. Petersburg. All his money was now tied up in his St. Augustine development, and buyers of Davis Islands tracts were refusing to keep up their payments. Tennis tournaments and speedboat races failed to entice them back to the Davis fold. In panic, Davis hired a firm of auditors which issued a reassuring report. The financing of Davis Islands was "the soundest in the state." But to qualify for the honor, that didn't have to be very sound. Davis had to stop construction; there was no money with which to pay workers. Skeletons of houses stood raw, and the rainy season flooded half-finished parlors. Heartbroken, Davis knew he had to sell out. The buying syndicate formed the Island Investment Company in Tampa and he went back to St. Augustine determined at least to continue Davis Shores. From a New York bank he managed to borrow a quarter of a million dollars; this he put into the St. Augustine project. But his nerves were shot. What he needed was a sojourn on the French Riviera. His personal Monte Carlo had left him in need of a vacation. He wouldn't have been Dave Davis, however, if he hadn't begun bragging about sets of Davis Islands he was planning for France and Monaco.

He sailed from New York in October 1926. The northern seas were choppy and the liner *Majestic* rolled. He was never seasick; of that he was proud. He had grown up on a Tampa Bay steamer, and he boasted to fellow passengers bound for Europe that he could still walk a ship's rail in a storm. He would show them all by going from porthole to porthole outside the ship's saloon. The crowd of lighthearted spectators watched admiringly as D. P. Davis, Florida Real Estate tycoon, balanced himself on a rail slippery with fresh wax. Just then they were all pitched sideways by a tall wave. When it subsided, D. P. Davis had disappeared.

"Man overboard!" the cry rang. It began to rain harder. The waves waved white manes as they swelled, and even if Davis hadn't drowned in the rough sea below nobody could have heard his cries for help. The great liner rocked while its crew and passengers scanned fruitlessly the churning water. When the rain came down in solid sheets and the wind and waves rose, the *Majestic* started once more toward the sunlight of

the Riviera. Telegraph wires began humming with the news that Dave
Davis was gone. Murder? Suicide? Every Florida editor had a theory.
The truth was finally told to Davis's insurance company by one of his
friends, a fellow voyager: "Dave was just walking the rail again, and
this time he wasn't lucky."

Along with his body, into the angry Atlantic, had sunk the last of
the Big Boom. On the Hillsborough, where there had been hammering
and crane-swinging and drilling, there was now a silence as stark as the
silence in which Father Juan Rogel had stood in the realization of his
vanished missions three and a half centuries before. The river, and the
bay, had not been conquered yet. Conquest by man now depended not
on priestly prayer but on the most fickle force in Florida: the sun. In the
winter of 1927, for the thinning ranks of Tin-Can Tourists clustered
around their pavilion in de Soto Park, it came. Yet for every Florida
dream but the smallest, they told themselves, it came too late.

25

"The Craziest Drug Store in the World"

In St. Petersburg, the people were fatalistic. They were also agreed on the lunacy of James Earl Webb, a druggist with no common sense. What man in his right mind could be optimistic about the chances of success with a tiny store when the boom was over? Webb was headed for bankruptcy at a breathtakingly rapid clip. The store measured exactly seventeen by twenty-eight feet in a rented building on the corner of Ninth Street and Second Avenue South. Its Peruna-loaded shelves shook whenever trains rumbled past outside its windows; a block away another railroad contributed its share of the vibrations. Webb's Drug Store was, moreover, on the edge of a sleazy black neighborhood; what money could its denizens have to spend on patent medicines when some of them weren't eating regularly? Even Hayworth Johnson, Webb's partner in the venture they had started together in 1925 before the Investment Bankers had been rained on, shook his head. Webb had bought his own share of the business for five thousand dollars. It was all he had had in the world. When empires began collapsing on the Suncoast, Webb began lowering prices to a few cents above cost. Hayworth Johnson stood by helplessly until the store's unpaid bills totaled six thousand dollars and the cash register was full of scrip because money had vanished from the Suncoast along with the natty wheelers and dealers. "If you're mad enough to keep this up," Johnson warned Webb, "I'm leaving." Unperturbed, Webb cut prices still lower; a Johnson by now haggard from suspense sold out and left Webb alone to face what Johnson was sure was approaching funeral music as gloomy as anything in *Götterdämme-rung*. But Webb—"Doc,"· he called himself—only smiled and began making plans to lure customers in by providing them a show of trained ducks and chickens which could play ball, ride toy fire engines, and walk tightropes.

Doc had been born in Nashville, Tennessee, in 1899 to Scotch-Irish parents who embodied the usual puritan virtues. His father, a road contractor, and his mother, a gentle Baptist, could only watch nonplussed as their Jimmy began an energetic career at nine delivering the morning Nashville *Tennessean* and the afternoon *Banner*. Soon he was earning eight dollars a month and bossing a crew of fourteen newsboys. On his own route be began selling hot German bread. At home he started a garden and bought a cow. It was not long before he was peddling vegetables and milk along with the German bread and newspapers. When business got slow, he mowed lawns and sold lemonade and orangeade at a curbside stand he built. Every night he made his unsold fruit drinks into sherbet and proceeded to sell that. By the time he was twelve, he was so busy with commerce he decided to quit school.

"I hated that school," he reminisced recently. Doc's various press utterances have a certain sameness to them, but it is an engaging sameness. "Oh, how I hated that school. I would sit there in class not seeing the book in front of me. I didn't hear what the teacher was saying. I had a hell of a lot of things on my mind—things I wanted to do. I got lousy grades, played a lot of hookey and finally quit." He never quite made it through the fifth grade. The fact may account for his less than sympathetic attitude to efforts by the federal government to better the lot of the needy in St. Petersburg. *He* dropped out, didn't he? And became a millionaire? Millionaires are vulnerable to a particular weakness; what they have done, they think anyone can do. It is not that they are inhuman. They are merely geniuses, and geniuses have not historically been sensitive to the failings of their fellowmen.

When Jimmy Webb was twelve the family moved to Knoxville. He was heartbroken; he had built up his businesses and now he had to leave them. In Knoxville, though, he got a job setting up pins in a bowling alley, then started augmenting his income by jerking sodas and handling prescriptions at Knoxville's Economy Drug Company. At eighteen he was working sixteen hours a day seven days a week and he had a nervous

Webb's City, St. Petersburg

collapse. He had his own theories on what to do for it: for five years he lived (and thrived) on a regimen of milk and crackers. At twenty he was manager and part owner of Economy Drugs, and his customers, amused at his giddy rise, were beginning to call him Doc with as much relish as he had using the title himself.

He had a knack for knowing what people wanted. He made them Good Luck Bags containing Health Herbs; for moonshiners he stocked bottles and barrels. How could he know, he asked with a wry smile, what the receptacles were going to be used for after they had been carried out of the Economy Drug Company? He made up a liniment for stiff muscles which he christened Sorbo-Rub and sold for eighty-nine cents a bottle. Sorbo-Rub is popular in St. Petersburg today, though Doc says the formula has several times been improved. When he began his pharmaceutical career America was unburdened by testing regulations. When he brewed up a mixture of epsom salts, herbs, alcohol, and water and marketed it as Wahoo Indian Bitters, nobody stopped him. The laxative went for a dollar a bottle. He sold "tons of it." He wasn't as famous for his Wahoo Indian Bitters, however, as he was for his chef d'oeuvre, "Doc Webb's 608." It treated "unnatural discharges." In every public toilet in Knoxville Doc put up signs: "If this happens to you—get Doc Webb's 608." "This," of course, was gonorrhea. If Germany's Dr. Ehrlich could give humanity 606 for another barely mentionable ailment, Doc could go him two points higher. Since human beings were human beings, Doc Webb's 608 was required in Knoxville as frequently as was 606. Victims of V.D. in Tennessee were happy to pay five and a half dollars for a bottle of a miracle cure which contained gum acacia and sandalwood and cost Doc seventy cents to make. It was no antibiotic, in the austere age before penicillin, but it did its job no worse than competitive products. Since human beings were also human beings in Nashville and Louisville as well as Knoxville, Doc began getting orders by the barrel. His bank account hit figures that, to him, were astronomical. What would he do with all the money? Already he had discovered the fun of business wasn't actually making the loot but pitting his own resourcefulness and ingenuity against those of his rivals. Economy's owner was so impressed he offered to sell Doc a store of his own. But Doc had begun having yearnings to wander, to chart new seas. When a letter arrived from Hayworth Johnson, a former co-worker in Economy who had gone to reap fresh rewards in St. Petersburg, Doc began to see himself as the Ponce de León of Patent Medicine. Would St. Petersburg devour Doc Webb's 608 as Knoxville, Nashville and Louisville had done? He knew he had to find out.

When flying ace Eddie Rickenbacker rolled into Knoxville one afternoon to demonstrate the automobile he was manufacturing, Doc was a fascinated spectator. He fell in love with a blue beauty so smooth Rickenbacker could balance nickels on its running engine. Rapidly, in front of the astounded Rickenbacker, Doc counted out nearly seven thousand dollars in cash. "Mr. Webb," Rickenbacker managed to say at last, "the car is yours." Ponce de León had had his golden caravel; Doc now had his midnight-blue sedan, and in it he drove down to Florida, its trunk and back seat filled with his belongings and copious supplies of 608. He pushed the car so hard it began consuming quarts of oil at a time and emitting a sinister black smoke. On the edge of St. Petersburg the weary engine fell off the block. Doc's Rickenbacker was never the same after that, though he had the engine remounted. Finally he had to sell it for the ignominious price of two hundred and twenty-five dollars. But he had arrived in the Sunshine City and soon he was turning out more 608. The trouble, he found forthwith, was that St. Petersburg was far below the national average in venereal disease. It made less love. Timid romances which began platonically on shuffleboard courts and ended in pension-sharing companionate marriages were not apt to encounter the same hazards as back-street passion. The oldsters needed Wahoo Indian Bitters and Sorbo-Rub, but Doc Webb's 608 meant less than nothing in their lives.

When Hayworth Johnson hightailed it back to Knoxville and left Doc in sole charge of the St. Petersburg venture, Doc changed its name to Webb's Cut Rate Drug Company. He advertised, often flamboyantly, his opposition to price fixing, large profits, and fair trade laws. When he met a Tampa cigar magnate, Eli Witt, he found a kindred spirit. Cut rates, in the teeth of the Great Depression, made Webb and Witt so powerful by the mid nineteen thirties that the two of them were able to prevent a state sales tax for twenty years after that. Doc made no secret of the fact that he was on the side of the little man. He was a little man himself—literally, at five feet five. But what he lacked in height he made up for in a peppery vaudevillian flair that began captivating a Depression Suncoast in need of laughter. Chickens which could ride fire engines, play ball, and walk tightropes? By all means! The chickens began decorating Webb's Cut Rate Drug Company to the delight of pensioners, middle-aged invalids, and children alike, and by 1936 Doc had grossed his first million. Then he had a brilliant idea. Why not build a one-stop shopping center? It would be the nation's first. Why did a drug store have to stick to drugs? Doc decided to sell food and tobacco, and soon he was doing business in gasoline, tires, trees, typewriters, and beauty salon facials as well. "The World's Most Unusual Drug Store" was on its way into the American press. Even the sedate business periodical *Fortune* could only gape. *Cosmopolitan* reported that there were cooch shows in the cafeteria, sales of women's scanties at the cigar counter, and "a three ring circus in the parking lot with Doc himself playing the role of a clown cavorting in a high wire act with a galaxy of pretty and daring young ladies." Naturally, the original drug store had expanded. Eager buyers had literally knocked out its walls. Rival St. Petersburg merchants became so alarmed at Doc's Depression success that they called on him in a body and asked him to "co-operate"—that is, to stop cutting prices.

"You run your businesses and I'll run mine," he told them. They retaliated by forming a merchants' association that pointedly has never asked him to join. He has survived the exclusion nicely.

The merchants were not the only people distressed at the goings-on at Webb's Cut Rate Drugs which finally became, more simply, Webb's City. "It's the craziest drug store in the world," its patrons bragged proudly. One day Doc sold seven thousand fifty-cent tubes of Ipana toothpaste for thirteen cents apiece. Newspapers as far away as New York printed the intelligence in admiration. Not long afterward Doc had a visitor in St. Petersburg who stated that he was Mr. Bristol, of the Bristol-Myers Corporation which manufactured Ipana, and he was distinctly not amused. When Doc didn't promise to obey in the future, Bristol-Myers sued him. He went to court and won, cheered all the way by a St. Petersburg that had by now adopted him as a proud symbol of city recovery. To Tampans, Tampa Bay became a place which had a bridge across which you could drive to get to Webb's City. Even today Doc's birthday in St. Petersburg is half a holiday, and his admirers fill newspaper columns with their paeans: "We hail the birthday of Doc Webb, a genuine Floridian merchant prince to whom the business of business is democracy. An outstanding member of the business world—a race unique in history for its vigor, its paradoxes, and its dreams!" The stranger is tempted to answer, laconically, "Wow!" But big prose applies naturally to the commercial and spiritual—bigness of Doc Webb, who has remained the common man's champion in his pricing policies. Competitive in sports as well as retailing, he has managed to garner a series of tennis championships over the years and today, at seventy-two, he maintains six "hot lines" in his home that connect him directly and instantly to the downtown store. His wife, Aretta, herself a native of Knoxville, and a longtime maid who is now mostly a secretary help him to man the hot lines every morning, when split-second decisions have to be made about Romilar, Ben-Gay, My Sin, tire treads, freight cars full of Geritol, color television and dinette sets, and Swiss watches going at $6.88—SPECIAL! TODAY ONLY! Papaya juice, water lilies, and De-Moist Electric Closet Air Dryers get their share of the attention. Doc sells a thousand prescriptions a day in a store now covering ten city blocks. Within it, Doc's Original Drug Store has become a shrine. Seventy-two departments are located in Webb's City's seven buildings visited daily by sixty thousand people. They buy on an average of five thousand ice cream cones, and nobody has ever been brave enough to calculate how much Serutan they take home. Doc's customers worry less about being Beautiful People than they do about Being Regular.

His tactics, even in the thirties, bordered on the reckless. One day he advertised two thousand one-dollar bills for ninety-five cents each. The store was mobbed by people who proceeded to spend the ninety-five cent dollars on Webb's City merchandise. The following morning he sold twenty-five hundred dollar bills for eighty-nine cents apiece. They went in a torrent of enthusiasm, and came flowing back into Webb's City cash registers which clanged like instruments in an electronic band manned by drunks. On the last day of the promotion he offered to buy back any outstanding bills at a dollar and thirty-five cents. (They had, of course, to have the right serial numbers.) Almost none turned up. Doc already had them in his bank account.

It is his gaudiness as much as his price-cutting which has so endeared him to the Suncoast. He owns a hundred suits and fifty sports jackets. "Some," he says happily, "would shame the TV costumes of Liberace." His shoes number sixty-five pairs and every year he adds a hundred or so neckties. Then he takes fifty old ties downtown and distributes them to Webb's City employees. Nobody grudges him his extravagances. His fans agree that he has earned them. His price-slashing is no myth. In the autumn of 1971 he was advertising eggs for thirty-three cents a dozen, Pillsbury Buttermilk Biscuits at six cents a can, ten to the can, and sliced lean bacon at thirty-two cents a pound. U.S. Choice chuck roast went for fifty-nine cents a pound. Prices in the most budget-keyed St. Petersburg supermarkets were at least double on the items in question. "The *good* that man does!" retirees eking out existences on Social Security tell you. "Thanks to Doc Webb we eat regular and we can pay for our prescriptions." Doc lists drugs both by trade names and generic names, and if a customer can prove that Doc is being undersold anywhere in town Doc will lower his price below that of his competiter. One old woman in Webb's City told me earnestly: "If it wasn't for Doc Webb I wouldn't be alive. I got high blood pressure, see, and I got to take these pills. Doc charges less then half what another pharmacy wanted for 'em. If I couldn't get 'em cheap I'd have to give 'em up and just wait for a stroke to kill me." Diabetics flock to him for their Orinase and insulin, and young beachcombers from Gulf Sands make the pilgrimage from Treasure Island across Boca Ciega Bay in St. Petersburg because the $1.37 size of Coppertone Tanning Butter is ninety-nine cents at Webb's City. Chicken is twenty-five cents a pound, $6.95 will buy a 9 x 12 foot linoleum rug, and a three hundred and fifteen dollar name-brand color television set, with rolling base, retails at two hundred and sixty-nine. "Family day at Webb's City!" the banners beckon. "Mom, Dad, Come Bring The Kids and Spend The Day! See Doc's Live Animal Circus, Live Talking Mermaid Show, Replica of Doc's Original Drug, and Much More!" They come in droves. A trip through Webb's City can be as harrowing as a fifteen-minute sale at S. Klein's Department Store in Manhattan. Herds stampede, bargain-seeking hands snatch, and everywhere there is the smell of mixed Lysol and taffy apples, while babies squall and the bending old lean heavily on their yellow canes waiting for room to pass. Witch hazel, Dentu-Creme, and Tarot cards compete with city bus tokens and Gatorade for the consumer's attention while costumed Moon Maids welcome the customers upstairs. Doc, concluded *Fortune* years ago, "is an anachronism. He considers government protection of independent business both unnecessary and immoral, feels sorry for chain store managers enmeshed in red tape (and trading stamps) and is moved to wrath by the mere mention of minimum price-fixing, whether official or otherwise."

St. Petersburg skeptics learned just how powerful Doc Webb could be in 1965 when the state legislature gave the St. Petersburg City Council orders to redevelop shabby inner-city areas. Doc went up in smoke. "There are five thousand customers of Webb's City who live within two miles of the store and own their homes and all of them could be taken under this plan." He spent thousands in newspaper advertising attacking the proposal. When voting time came, every vote for was matched by three against. St. Petersburg had made its sentiments on urban renewal very clear and its regard for Doc obvious.

His customers are of all ages, but his special flock are the old, who regard him as their undisputed shepherd. They, after all, are what St. Petersburg became famous for. They built the Kum Inns, the Dens of Antiquity, and the Dun Rovin cafés. For them were erected the signs begging "Yankee Don't Go Home Pleeze!" St. Petersburg in modern times has been called, with some justice, "the haven of the dumped," the grandpas and grandmas (and pas and mas) that nobody wants back home. For them Doc has just built a two-million-dollar store at Sixty-sixth Street and Park Boulevard, so that oldsters who live in outlying areas need not travel all the way downtown. Doc's flock are the same people who join lodges and cherish extravagant titles. LIZARDS INSTALL GILA MONSTER, reads a headline ever a photograph of four elderly ladies in dunce hats:

> New officers of the Military Order of Lizards who were installed in ceremonies Thursday evening at the U.S. Veterans of Foreign Wars Hall are, from left, Mrs. Mary G. Aschenbrenner, Gila Monster; Mrs. Anna Kowalski, Gecko; Mrs. Verleen Johnson, Caletetophon, and Mrs. Mayalice Gainous, Past Grand Gila Monster.

When Elmer Schoebel, author of *The Bugle Call Rag,* settled in St. Petersburg years ago with gilded memories of the Hit Parade and Ina Ray Hutton's All Girl Band, he turned his talents to writing a battle hymn for his newest-found comrades:

The Senior Citizen

> You may have a lucky star,
> Makes no difference who you are,
> Who's the one ahead by far?
> The SENIOR CITIZEN.

> Love and life are never cold
> When the years have turned to gold,
> Who's the one who's never old?
> The SENIOR CITIZEN.

Days are bright and sunny
When you're not alone,
You can bet your money
It's a life to call your own.

If a problem should arise,
Ask a question just for size,
Get an answer from the wise,
The SENIOR CITIZEN!

Brave words. But the trouble in St. Petersburg as everywhere else is that no youths ask for wisdom; life and love can turn as cold on the Suncoast as in Ohio; and senior citizens are very old indeed and a prey to every tragedy from poverty to advanced arteriosclerosis, to say nothing of social segregation. The town they made, along with the doctors hunting for Health City, has recently announced its intention of adopting a new slogan, "Think Young!" When one group of residents sent green benches to the Florida State Fair for the St. Petersburg exhibit, another group hauled them out again. Fashion promotions in magazines like *Glamour* and *Mademoiselle* began featuring St. Petersburg Beach and Treasure Island-on-the-Gulf as places where Fun People congregate in discotheques and men are young, rich, handsome, and thoroughly eligible. For the ladies, bikinis and nothing over size fourteen. The pitch was obviously to vacationing northern secretaries with money to swell Suncoast coffers. "They're kicking us in the teeth," an elderly couple told me in a St. Petersburg Mobile Home Park. "Now the city wants everybody over sixty-five to drop dead, please, because our Social Security doesn't get into their pockets fast enough. It's a bitter thing, when they advertised to get us here in the first place." Stores such as fashionable John Baldwin's advertise their couture clothes in *The New Yorker* as well as in the St. Petersburg *Times*. But the half size and portly set continues to go to Webb's City. Doc may not be Yves St. Laurent, but he can sell you an ample housedress or outsize slacks that are color-fast, permanent press, and cheap. He carries, too, a full line of Dr. Scholl's Foot Comfort Aids, which are not prominently featured in *The New Yorker* editorially or otherwise. Doc's flock is also ministered to by a merchant who pushes "Ladies' English Walking Shoes." These are oxfords that lace up; they have posture-pedic heels and steel arch supports. Wedgies in St. Petersburg are no 1940s revival but the real thing. Doc's beauty salon specializes in blue rinses, permanent wave ringlets, and dry rouge.

The laureate of Doc's flock is Milton Paul Magly, author of *The Bell(e)s of St. Petersburg*, a novel issued by a vanity press in 1963. It is a very romance of retirement, and it is not without lyrics to rival Elmer Schoebel's:

> Oh give me a seat way down in St. Pete
> Where the aged and crippled may play,
> Where no one is told, "You're getting too old,"
> And the benches are crowded all day.
> Home, home in St. Pete! where the
> Northerners and Southerners meet,
> Away from the cold, in the sunshine of gold,
> And where nature is always a treat.

To question Magly's scansion would be quibbling. He is eloquent on the subject of radio station WSUN ("Why Stay Up North?") and he lovingly details the bank chimes that play four tunes according to the weather. Sunny? "Oh, What a Beautiful Morning!" Rainy? "Stormy Weather." Clearing? "It Ain't Gonna Rain No More." Colder? "Button Up Your Overcoat." Magly knows all his palm trees, as good retirees should. His hero's adventures are always couched decorously: "Going to the hotel, he was invited by a Mrs. Cora Wing, a widow, to play contract bridge, to which he consented." Afterwards he inquires, "How about Howard Johnson's for a thirst quencher?" In language which Doc's flock can understand, Magly is the spokesman of their myth that everything is for the best in the best of all possible cities. To read him is not to find out anything about the rest—actually the majority—of St. Petersburg's population, the coiffed matrons of Snell Isle and Maximo Moorings, the barefoot youngsters whose tape decks play acid rock on beaches where toddlers build sand castles and bronzed St. Petersburg Junior College students wrestle. There are many St. Petersburgs beside that of Doc's flock; but that is, in the end, the flock that haunts the observer. Whenever I read Milton Paul Magly I want to cry, and to beg the fates, "Please let it be perfect for them; let them keep their golden legend as long as they can."

Ed and Bertha Kramer live on tiny pensions in a trailer park which has a crumbling shuffleboard court and a rundown wooden recreation hall where the nearsighted and deaf and still-hale gather to play rummy on hot summer nights. As you watch, the anxieties in faces and the limits on lives led rub compassion raw. Ed and Bertha have air conditioning in their Mobile Home. Their three children are in the North. Ed is a retired railroad conductor from Alton, Illinois. Forty-seven years of his toil have managed to buy her a few luxuries—rubber plants, pictures of cypress swamps. She is proud of her possessions, especially the chenille bedspreads with the peacocks on them and the tables furniture stores call "the costume jewelry of the home." But she is also wistful.

"If we get sick," she tells you, "I mean if it's a stroke and months in the hospital, it's all over for us. It's welfare. We wouldn't want to take from the children. I tried selling shellcraft—I made earbobs and brooches —and Ed thought he might be able to get people to buy Christmas cards; there was this outfit in the magazine that promised you real good money if you took on their cards. But most folks we know live like us. Close to the bone, that's what it is. Nobody has money to buy anything frivolous." Neither he nor Bertha can afford to keep a car. If they could, their dimming eyesight would probably prevent them from getting licenses. Instead, they take the bus. "You ever tried to get from St. Pete to Clearwater by bus?" Ed asks. "Takes a whole goddam afternoon waiting for those things." But Ed and Bertha don't go to Clearwater much. It takes too long to make the bus trip to Tampa, and Tampa costs a pile when you get there. Cubans run the restaurants, and you can't get a decent digestible meal like you can at the Smorg-a-rama or Webb's when you want to celebrate something, say an anniversary. The kids write—two graduated college—but of course, how can they know how it is?

With television and air conditioning, Ed and Bertha are waiting to die. By the standards of developing countries they are rich. But in American society they are the people who pore over the bacon counter at Webb's City figuring whether they can splurge on real slices or settle for cheaper ends and pieces. They eat puréed canned corn. They have no steak and enjoy no wine. Ed likes beer, but he doesn't drink much. He takes Bertha to the movies about three times a year—they both liked *Song of Norway*—and naturally Mother's Day wouldn't be Mother's Day without dinner at Doc Webb's Cafeteria.

"Doc Webb!" Ed's face lights up. "Now, there's a real man. I'd do anything, vote any way he wants me to. I just wish that man could become President of the United States. You bet we'd have prosperity then, and no wars and no welfare chiseling either."

With Doc Webb to sustain you, waiting for death is just a little bit easier in St. Petersburg. As long as you have your health you can go down to Doc's to see the mermaids for nothing and forget your troubles. You don't think about that dark corner of your mind that whispers, *Anything but cancer! Please, God, let it be a heart attack....* And meanwhile, when your back aches, there is Sorbo-Rub, and when you're feeling pretty good and the kids send you a sawbuck for your birthday you can take Bertha down to the Senior Citizens Center when Rudy Vallee comes to town. That's where he performs these days. And won't it be just like old times!

26

Vigilantes

The river had changed. At its mouth, the water which flowed into Hillsborough Bay still sparkled but it was no longer fit for drinking. Tampa sewage now emptied into it a few miles upstream where once Timucuan flutes had sounded reedily in brief summer twilights. Now the sounds were those of far-off ocean liners in Tampa Bay, and of pleasure boats on the Hillsborough which in their wake vomited a film of iridescent oil. For scenery, river lots were considered choice, but the prudent didn't go swimming there anymore; too many gushing pipes spewed effluents into the channel down which floated water hyacinths in a tide of bacteria to the sea. Above Tampa, there were places where ornamental elephant ear plants had gone wild to form choking mats through which tourists' canoes had to be portaged. The hyacinths continued to spread, a lovely lavender obstruction, partly because there were no longer any manatees to eat them. River fishing fell off—slowly, at first, then more swiftly each year until anglers had to drive well out of Tampa and beyond Cow House Slough to the northeast in order to find largemouth bass, the channel catfish that tasted so delicious fried in cornmeal batter, pickerel and stumpknockers and shellcrackers and bream. Gars proliferated; so did chubsuckers and killifish. Fragile Florida swamp-darters retreated upstream. In Seventeen Runs an occasional ivorybill still called his loud and metallic single note of "Kent!" But there were more hawks than there had been, and to see less common warblers, bird watchers had to go up to Crystal Springs. Prothonotaries and smokestacks didn't mix.

Hillsborough State Park

Since the 1930s, eighty-one species of birds have vanished in what is now the Hillsborough River State Park. The darkly shining eastern glossy ibis has flown out of the cypress swamps never to return to them; Canada geese now stop each winter in north Florida, but no farther south. Wild ducks, the pintails and baldpates and teal, have become a Hillsborough rarity. The litany of the vanished is a tragic poem: swallow-tailed kites, Audubon's caracaras, duck hawks and purple gallinules and coots and Wilson's snipes, whip-poor-wills and nighthawks and red-cockaded woodpeckers that had probed clots of resin for insects high in the slash pines through which Francis Dade's army had marched on the Fort King Road. Brown creepers are gone, too, Bewick's wrens and Tennessee warblers and Florida prairie warblers. Bob-o-links no longer sing out their lilting rises and falls, and there are no fox sparrows to chatter in hickories. The Hillsborough is still a beautiful river, but for many species the water of its lower reaches meant death as early as 1900, and the increasing presence of man south of the Green Swamp was by then pushing back timid animals which had once abounded—panthers, black bears, bobcats with wary eyes and tufted ears laid back to distinguish footfalls. Tampa, conservationists began saying, was killing the very river which had made her; it should be called the Stenchboro. In Tampa Bay, St. Petersburg had power plants where mangroves had formerly been thick with spoonbills. Still, however, shrimp boats glided out from Tampa Bay wharves at dusk, their chains of lights twinkling softly over black nets and winches. Man's ties with the river and the bay were yet close in the late twenties. The Great Depression was seen not as a respite for nature —was nature really in much trouble?—but as a tragedy which brought St. Petersburg (Doc Webb excepted) and Tampa to a standstill.

On Wednesday morning, July 17, 1929, the Citizens' Bank and Trust Company of Tampa did not open. Neither did five smaller banks, including the Bank of Ybor City. Days before, the story had spread among cigar workers that the Bank of Ybor City was in difficulty. They began hurrying downtown to remove money from its affiliate, the Citizens. By Tuesday Tampans had withdrawn over a million dollars. When the money ran out, the affected banks clanged their metal doors shut with a finality that reverberated in every Tampa household. The city's people lost more than ten million dollars when the Citizens and its satellites failed because of a rumor that wasn't true—at first. Other banks managed to survive by bringing in reserve funds from Jacksonville; all night long worried bank officers and state bank examiners drank black coffee and smoked Tampa cigars as they pondered their unbalanced books. When the bank runs ended, Tampa was stunned. Three months later came the stock market crash in New York; soon grim jokes were being made about the bodies of investment bankers hurtling down to cement suicides past the office windows of their friends. Yankee tourists stayed home that winter, while starving crowds across the country stormed warehouses where the butter and eggs they needed were turning rancid and rotten because they could not pay for them. Wholesale firms went into receivership. Once-prosperous merchants appeared on street corners with apple carts; that, too, became a sour joke, but its sourness was based on reality. America stopped smoking so many cigars; it turned to cheaper pipe tobaccos and cigarettes. Tampa cigar factories were forced to lay off long lines of workers who had faithfully served them for decades in Ybor City. José Martí had seen Ybor City alive with political fervor and hope. In the 1930s Ybor City turned funereal. The factories slowly began to mechanize. Had not *el lector* in many a factory passed on the tale that had ended in the bank failures? For the factory readers, it was the beginning of the end. One by one they were dismissed. Cigar workers, passionate and resentful, gathered to protest. Who would educate them now that *el lector* was gone? Sporadic riots broke out and police several times came into Ybor City with guns and billy clubs. Between 1928 and 1934 twelve cigar factories closed their doors for good. Citrus growers on the river were hit at the same time by the Mediterranean fruit fly; without cigars and citrus, phosphate could not carry Tampa and its labor force alone. Half of its people were out of work by 1930. The city entered the most joyless decade in United States history with starving families and no large-scale public programs to help them. Other families tried to survive on five dollars a month. Private charities like the Seamen's Institute and El Centro Español did what they could, which was little. Slowly Tampa ground to a halt. The sun shone cheerfully on, while Tampa dinner tables stood empty. Not only was there no state program for the poor, but not even a rush to provide it. Factory owners murmured hallowed proverbs about self-reliance, while chemists sought to find a compound that would kill the Mediterranean fruit fly before it killed the Florida citrus industry.

None of the cigar workers were passive. They persuaded manufacturers to form relief committees in the shops, they collected bread from generous bakers, and they began a system of food tickets. Cigar manu-

El Centro Español

facturers who could afford it distributed staples to the hungry. The wages of the employed were cut by one fifth. Voluntary soup kitchens mushroomed in clouds of steam, and sad lines stretched down long Ybor City blocks while olive-skinned supplicants asked each other, "Why?" For the question, one group had an answer. Communist organizers came to Ybor City. Why indeed; they thundered, did a man have to demean himself by declaring himself a pauper before Hillsborough County would feed him—with five dollars a month for his entire family? To this, latin pride responded eagerly; pride and pauperism declarations had never mixed. In Tallahassee, an oblivious governor formed a committee to investigate Florida's troubles and then wrote Herbert Hoover a reassuring letter that everything in Florida was just fine; the state needed no federal assistance, thank you.

Cigar lord Cuesta became so alarmed at the bitterness in Ybor City that he formed an Unemployment Council. Among its aims were "to prevent riot and rebellion." The philosophy was that of fill-'em-up-and-keep-'em-calm. The Tampa Family Services Association found itself besieged by a crowd which demanded two dollars a day to feed their families. Madness! Gleefully assembled communists and anarchists and socialists, now arriving as a fresh wave of pilgrims on trains which had carried tourists, watched the bumbling and fumbling of official Florida and Tampa, and they grew increasingly confident that Florida's conservatism was making its own revolution. But by principle they helped it along; they held meetings, they made promises, and they sang stirring revolutionary songs. To many a harried cigar worker whose stomach was gripped by the pain of emptiness, communism began to look very promising indeed. Why should the Cuestas of this world give out charity only as they saw fit? Their wealth belonged by rights to all.

Anglo-Saxon Tampa watched Ybor City and was horrified. It began organizing itself into committees of self-appointed vigilantes who promised to protect Tampans from the saboteurs in their midst. West of Ybor City on the bay, the Great Depression was severe, but not severe enough to tempt Klansmen away from the fold. The Klansmen began abducting known leftists and forcing them to drink castor oil; it was like the good old days again, when men who were men covered themselves with sheets and rode by night to plant fiery crosses in the midst of the racially suspect and bewildered. A communist meeting at the Ybor City Labor Temple ended in a free-for-all as the Klan stormed in to scatter a rapt latin audience. Afterwards the homes of the radical leaders were raided; some of the Klansmen found Russian flags and held them triumphantly aloft to justify what they were doing. "Patience!" begged Mayor Chancey. But who wanted to listen when there was not enough bean soup or yellow rice in the larder? Workers began begging the state of Florida to take its convicts off road gangs and hire them for wages instead. "Unemployment," Governor Carlton said with satisfaction in Tallahassee, "is negligible." Tampa's joblessness may have looked negligible because Carlton saw it through a curtain of Tallahassee moss. In the North, newspaper readers construed his optimism to mean that there were actually jobs for the asking in Florida, and seekers began pouring in to claim their share of nonexistent booty. Private businesses contributed more funds, started food farms along the river for the poor, sent out crews to collect clothing that could be mended and salvaged for those in rags, and reiterated the doctrine of Roger Babson: "Prosperity is just around the corner." Stockbrokers were hanging themselves in basements up North and in barns down South, and suburban fathers were retreating to their garages to seal themselves in, start the car, and die of carbon monoxide poisoning. By the autumn of 1932 a full third of Tampa was desperate for food. It was no wonder that hungry Ybor City regarded That Man in the White House and Nosy Eleanor as saviors. The Roosevelts, in Washington, would do for them what Doyle Carlton, in Tallahassee, was not willing to do. When Carlton applied for loans from the newly formed Reconstruction Finance Corporation, the gesture came too late. Worse still, private businessmen stopped their charities. Why compete with government? Mayor Chancey wrung his hands and watched helplessly while his city tottered back into the dark ages. The salaries of his teachers had plunged to a bracket among the lowest in the nation. His schools had to be kept open by means of bank loans. Civil liberties in the 1930s were a joke as macabre and pertinent in Tampa as apple sellers had been in 1929 on Wall Street. The Klan promised to "protect government from the ravages of radicals." A "Secret Committee of Twenty-Five" specialized in "physical persuasion." Communist organizers were found, in alleys, half-dead from floggings. In 1934, a young liberal attorney was kidnapped, tied up in a bag, ridden out to a desolate Gulf shore and then castrated. The perpetrators of this particular deed, some said, were off-duty Tampa police. The vigilantes also administered beatings to leftists with canvas straps which left burning welts in the victims' backs as wretched as any welts Captain Bligh had ever ordered on the *Bounty*. Into the wounds of slashed dissidents the Klan poured hot tar; they also exposed their victims on freezing nights. When vigilante cases came to trial, defense lawyers airily explained, "The deceased was a communist." Gangsterism thrived, and rival gang leaders took each other up to oblivious Dunedin on "rides" which for some of the passengers were one way. The city of Tampa also began registering all men who had ever been convicted of any crime, regardless of whether they had served their sentences or not. The Mafia moved in; to this day, it has not left. Sedate middle-class Celts and Teutons turn the other way: if it's nasty, it wasn't, isn't, and won't be. Had the WPA not come into existence to bring hope to Tampa in 1935, communism would have had impressive success with a substantial portion of blue-collar workers who lived on or near the Hillsborough River and watched the phosphate barges moving slowly by as tokens of one of the few things that, in 1935, remained right with the state of Florida.

Late in November 1935, union organizer Joseph Shoemaker was kidnapped on Tampa's Florida Avenue. He was soon joined by two other prisoners, Eugene Poulnot and Sam Rogers, both socialists. The men were driven to a city dock. Iron-armed captors grabbed Rogers, began beating him with a hose, and then covered him with tar. They flogged Poulnot with a chain and a rawhide, then tarred him and feathered him for good measure. Shoemaker was covered with tar and then abandoned to a freeze. When he was finally discovered and brought to El Centro Español a doctor said: "He is horribly mutilated. I wouldn't beat a pig the way that man was whipped. He was beaten until he is paralyzed on one side, probably from blows on the head. He cannot say anything to you; he does not know what has happened. He can't use one arm, and I doubt if three square feet would cover the total area of bloodshot bruises on his body, not counting the parts injured only by tar." It was necessary to amputate Shoemaker's feet. Nine days later, he died.

Leaflets began appearing on Tampa streets. "The Ku Klux Klan rides again. YOUR COUNTRY IS CALLING YOU. The Klan rides to save America! Stop! Look! Listen! Think! Pray! Communism must go! America, wake up!" A coupon was provided for earnest readers: "Yes! I want to help save our country and am ready to ride with you. Name ————— Occupation————— Residence————— Address—————." Kidnapping, observed the New York–based Committee for the Defense of Civil Rights in Tampa, Norman Thomas, Chairman, "is a favorite Florida sport." City police were implicated in the Shoemaker case, and links between police and Klan, according to the Committee, were apparent. The American Civil Liberties Union and the Tampa Board of Aldermen posted rewards for the arrest and convic-

The University of Tampa

tion of the men who had done the torturing. Tampans were cynical. A lumberyard sported a billboard: "Tar Today—Whitewash Tomorrow." Norman Thomas began clamoring for mass protests to the mayor and to Florida's new governor, Dave Sholtz, who found the answer to Florida's difficulties in the promotion of racetracks. Racetrack Dave, in the fastnesses of Tallahassee, thought prudence lay in nonintervention in Tampa. Slowly, people forget.

The WPA, when it came, built an airport on the Davis Islands. It initiated a badly needed mosquito and malarial control project and began constructing a strong seawall on Bayshore Boulevard which bordered the bay from the east bank of the river toward Ballast Point. The job proved expensive; a seawall sponsored earlier by city and county had been badly built and had to be torn out. The Hillsborough got another bridge at Platt Street. In the Tampa Bay Hotel, the WPA had a field day. It started with a budget of $138,000. It also began adding to the landscape of Plant Park on the riverfront and built bleachers at Plant Field near the Florida State Fairgrounds, in which WPA improvements were also made. The WPA built Tampa an armory: white-collar businessmen made all the standard depression jokes about WPA workers leaning on their shovels and no doubt, in Tampa, the workers did. Summer sun could fell a man quickly if he didn't rest. But the labor went forward, and so did the conversion of the Tampa Bay Hotel into the University of Tampa. The Arabian Nights palace hadn't been so busy since Richard Harding Davis had sat on its verandah waiting for a word from General Shafter, and young Winston Churchill had paced impatiently back and forth. This time there were no telegraphs to tattoo out military directives, nor were there any crystal goblets to clink the champagne toasts of the hotel's heyday. The new university had its own sounds: the tramp of students' feet up and down broad staircases, and the coded directions of a football coach outside as he struggled to build a team for an already fanatical following. Florida would not have been Florida if the University of Tampa hadn't started football before it had granted its first degree.

Things had begun looking up. The WPA was clearing slums and even installing sewers in black neighborhoods. Streets were being paved. Again the Hillsborough was dredged, this time to thirty feet. Saloons began to get more business. Until the repeal of Prohibition, Tampa's gangsters had been heavily involved in bootlegging. Mysterious trucks rumbled at night over cobbled streets, and speakeasies flourished, their blue dimness thick with the smoke of Cuesta Rey and Hav-a-Tampa cigars. Trenchcoat collars, in winter, were worn high. The Cubans of Ybor City said the Italians were the criminals; the Italians pointed fingers at the Cubans. After Prohibition, Tampa's racketeers channeled their energies into bolita, a game in which players were sold individual tickets at "bolita houses" known to the faithful but hopefully not to the law. In bolita the balls are displayed on a tray for the spectators to see. Then they are put into a bag which is passed from hand to hand and shaken several times. Eventually the bolita operator throws it, and the player grabs it by one of the balls inside. The operator then opens the sack and releases the player's ball, which carries the winning number. Wily bolita operators who weren't quite wily enough were found black eyed and savaged in Ybor City alleys on Sunday mornings. Reforms have come and gone. Bolita is still a Tampa staple, and when a haul is made by police on the rampage the Italians say it shows the Cubans are back in business and the Cubans shake their heads over the lawlessness of their Italian neighbors. *Aunt Sally's Dreambook* is a steady seller on Tampa newsstands. Bolita players know that their dreams may be translated by Aunt Sally's interpretations into numbers that will win when the bolita bag is caught. For symbolism Aunt Sally puts Freud to shame. Only skeptics admit that her theories vary from edition to edition, and that a tall dark stranger may mean twenty-seven one year and thirty-nine the next.

A young man studying theology at the Florida Bible College in Temple Terrace, in 1937 and 1938, was interested not in the gospel of Aunt Sally but that of fundamentalism. William Franklin Graham— Billy Frank, to his devout parents in North Carolina—had briefly attended Bob Jones College in Tennessee, but he hadn't much liked it. NO GRIPING TOLERATED, signs in the dormitories had read; college monitors had been known as The Gestapo. Bob Jones College was Baptist with a vengeance, and its president, "Dr. Bob," frequently stated that he had never been wrong about anything. Billy Frank believed in the literal truth of the Bible, but he wanted to arrive at it independently, not under the firm and relentlessly constant direction of Dr. Bob. When he came down with bronchitis his doctor told him he needed sunshine. In Temple Terrace, a suburb of Tampa, there was a college with a "homelike, restful Christian atmosphere." Billy Frank's mother was enthusiastic when she saw it, and so was Billy Frank, who was put into college service on his first day as a Tampa tour guide for visiting Baptist dignitaries. He didn't know much about Tampa, but his eagerness to please was winning. It was the beginning of what he later called "three and one half glorious, happy, character-building, life-changing years." To his mother he wrote:

> Words can't express Florida Bible Institute . . . I never felt so close to God in my life. This is the first time I have enjoyed studying the word of God . . . I love it here. I am stronger and feel so much better.

He got a job caddying on an adjacent golf course, and for his favorite sports of swimming and canoeing there was the Hillsborough. He loved the river. He also loved clowning in boats, and one afternoon when he stood up in his canoe and shouted to a fellow paddler, "I see an Indian— bang!" both of them went pitching into the water. Billy Graham had thus a baptism, of sorts, in the river on whose banks he also practiced his first halting sermons. For an audience he had mockingbirds, cooter turtles, squirrels, and rabbits. His first public sermon was given at the Tampa Gospel Tabernacle. He thought he was terrible, but the congregation found him "dramatic."

One of the youth workers at the Tabernacle was Emily Cavanaugh. She was pretty, musical, and also a fundamentalist. She and Billy got engaged; they spent most of their time with "Tabernacle Youth" and afterwards would repair to her parents' house "for Billy's favorite fruit Jell-o."

Billy was a salesman. In North Carolina he had been a Fuller Brush Man. According to his official biographer, "on business rounds Billy learned before each call to pray for sales success and, if he could make opportunity, would at each call unfold the thrills of knowing Christ." It must have been a little disconcerting to housewives who only wanted implements with which to scrub dishes and clean upright radiators. Dr. Bob Jones had recognized him for a potential salesman as well as the Fuller Brush Company had, and when Billy was departing for Florida, Dr. Bob had told him, "Billy, if you leave and throw your life away at a little country Bible school, the chances are you'll never be heard of. At best all you could amount to would be a poor country Baptist preacher somewhere out in the sticks." Dr. Bob thought his own institution a veritable Oxford. Billy hadn't been distressed, but at Temple Terrace he began to be troubled by a new burden. He was still undecided about what to do with his religious education. Was it true, as a visiting evangelist told him, that America needed a man to call it back to God? Was he, Billy,

that man? There was a Sunday full of the intoxicating delight of hearing
no less a person than Homer Rodeheaver, "song leader to Billy Sunday."
Billy Sunday! So Billy Graham went out to the river again and preached
"even to the alligators." On a night in March 1938, he went walking by
the Hillsborough's banks. "The trees were loaded with Spanish moss," he
said afterwards, "and in the moonlight it was like a fairyland." Soon he
was on his knees. "Oh, God," he prayed tensely, "if you want me to preach
I will do it." The river water lapped gently against palm trunks and
cornels, and tears began streaming down Billy's face. On later walks he
began having visions of "big stadiums, big meetings." But if the river
was the scene of his surrender and his dreams, it was also the scene
of a disappointment. Emily broke to him the news one night, as they sat
on a swing of the Florida Bible College porch, that she had fallen in love
with another student. Billy took it philosophically. Afterwards he began
trying to get preaching jobs in local churches. None wanted him, so he
took to Tampa streets. Finally, because his reputation for eloquence was
growing, the Tampa City Mission offered him a job, and he was made
chaplain to the trailer parks where remaining Tin Can Tourists began
flocking to hear him. He never wrote out his sermons, only a framework
of notes, but he found that even rehearsing them in Hillsborough cypress
swamps was polishing him. "I didn't have a passion to be a great
preacher," he said later. "I had a passion to win souls." The Tin-Canners
understood his earthiness as they could never understand the refined prose
of Episcopalians. Tramps and alcoholics understood him too, and the
prisoners in Tampa's city jail, still a stockade. "Billy," noted a Tampa
colleague, "can walk into a crowd and within a few seconds it seems
that every eye is on him. I can walk through the crowd and step on their
toes or kick their shins and no one ever notices me!" Billy stayed at the
Florida Bible College until the spring of 1940, when he was immersed in
a lake near Palatka where one of his teachers was conducting a revival
and received formally as a Southern Baptist. In May, he left Tampa forever for Wheaton College in Illinois, midwestern pastorates, rocketing
fame, and final celebrity. "I've heard him live in Times Square," a friend
of mine once told me. "If you can imagine such a thing as a good Hitler,
that is Billy Graham. He has the same magnetism, and his commands
hypnotize." The magnetism, if not the hypnosis, was first formed on the
Hillsborough among shoestring ferns, orchids, and great blue herons nest-
ing high in the pines while squirrels chattered in the maples and bull
'gators slid down slopes rich with leaf mold.

In St. Petersburg, during the thirties, the Great Depression was a universe away from Tampa's Depression. Communist organizers didn't want to bother with pensioners. Their idol was Dr. Francis Everett Townsend of California, in his sixties himself and the author of a miracle of misty finance, the Townsend Plan. The Townsend Plan was simple in the extreme. Every oldster in the United States was to receive two hundred dollars a month on condition that he spend it in the country within a month after he got it. A two percent federal sales tax would provide the initial funds, and then the freewheeling aged would save the nation by their largesse. St. Petersburg abounded in Townsendites who held vociferous meetings in churches and public halls.

St. Petersburg had had its bank failures and its bank runs in 1930. Merchants went under and their clerks were laid off. Unemployment in the city was nothing like the agony in Tampa, for age had already retired a substantial share of the population. But the tourists stayed north, and those on the scene wandered from cafeteria to cafeteria checking prices. People didn't buy clothes. The agony of St. Petersburg was in black slums like Methodist Town, where old women and toothless old men sat on shack porches among their morning glories and geraniums and waited for begging sons and daughters to return with a handful of grits, black-eyed peas, and collards. Women who had left Methodist Town as maids in the morning returned jobless at night. The white folks had begun doing their own work, and for Methodist Town it was a disaster. The few "relief jobs" offered by private agencies involved raking leaves and scooping out refuse from roadside ditches. Everybody prayed for February, when the live oaks shed. St. Petersburg, too, was saved by the WPA and other federal agencies like the Civilian Works Administration. The city got a tiny airport, new sewers on the north shore of the bay, a park, and a new junior college. A veterans' hospital was built at Bay Pines, with no thought in the minds of the builders that World War II would put it to an extensive and tragic use greater than anything the people of the bay had believed possible. Yet where World War II brought fresh life to Tampa, and once again its noisy streets bustled and Ybor City cigar workers came home from war plants with silver in their pockets— enough for Marques de Riscal wine and a dinner at Las Novedades now and then—St. Petersburg remained lifeless. Tin Can Tourists with A gas ration cards could not drive down from the north. St. Petersburg had to wait for its salvation until the war had ended. By then the St. Louis Cardinals were holding spring training in local baseball fields, their players cheered by crowds in which were mixed the old, school-age young, and their parents who were starting in the tourist business, and St. Petersburg Junior College students. Salvation, in St. Petersburg, also meant tragedy for the over-sixty-five crowd. After the war, young pilgrims commandeered lodgings that oldsters had had and paid higher prices for them. Immigrating merchants naturally wooed the age group which had money to spend. Established merchants also took note of the lively new winter folks, snowbirds, in search not only of the sun but of nightclubs. Sequin earrings suddenly became a hotter item in Webb's City than rupture trusses. St. Petersburg was moving into a new phase with a giant lurch, though even today the transition is far from complete. People still swam in Tampa Bay after the war, but most of the young vacationers preferred Gulf beaches. Motels began to proliferate there, and later high-rise apartments within sound of foamy waves, crying herring gulls, and the plop of proffered fish in brown pelicans' throats.

They had their scars, these cities on the river and the bay. Tampa had its memories of torture and fiery crosses and malnutrition; St. Petersburg had its memory of silence and empty hotels. But both knew they had what had been their treasure all along, through good times and lean: a river winding among bauhinias and jacarandas and cocos plumosas past a fairy-tale palace out to Hillsborough Bay, and the joining of Hillsborough and Old Tampa Bay that created Tampa Bay itself. Shrimp still bedded in its sand, spoonbills, though fewer of them, still nested in the mangroves of the little indentation called Mobbley Bay delighting the summer visitors, and the curving white wings of sailboats dotted a horizon where blue met blue in an explosion of radiance. When Johnny came marching home from Europe and the South Pacific, he came to the river and the bay to build not only a resort with enough diversions to make even rainy days fun but to build a permanent lifestyle of fulfillment: The Good Life, he called it unoriginally. On the Suncoast the sun was still the pot of gold at the end of the latest rainbow, but a new generation began providing supplements, alternatives, and such sophistications as galleries whose painters made eyes look like fried eggs and whose sculptors constructed futuristic riddles out of monkey wrenches, doorknobs, and electric fans. The reign of the Commercial Swamp Scene was over. So, at last, was the provincialism which had seen the heyday of the vigilantes.

PART V

Citizens

27

The Triumphal
Return of José Gaspar

Once a year the bay and the river are conquered by lunatics. Early every February Tampa celebrates its Gasparilla Festival, which has become for it what Mardi Gras has become for its sister port of New Orleans. Mardi Gras may be madder, but Gasparilla is certainly noisier. A gaudily costumed band of pirates sail in from the bay up the river in a flamboyant galleon which sports a nostalgic Jolly Roger. All the time the pirates are shooting blanks from pistols in no way silenced by harmlessness. The din is happily deafening. The annual spectacle draws more than half a million spectators, says the Tampa Chamber of Commerce. By now Ye Mystic Krewe of Gasparilla has learned carnival technique well. It has also learned how to make spectators suspend their collective disbelief that eighteenth century Tampa was periodically captured by a gang of desperadoes who left behind them a tradition of glamorous terror. Swords and diamond stickpins still flash on pirates in the spring sunlight as—you are soon persuaded—they flashed in the time of José Gaspar. Black eye patches, beards, and hairy forearms abound. Merrily mock-sinister laughter reverberates in broad pirate chests. The freebooters climb down from their sturdy rigging and race out into streetfuls of waiting and adoring throngs munching on pink and purple cotton candy, waving polychrome balloons, and displaying smile buttons on their lapels. City banks and libraries close. So does the Hillsborough County Clinic. Schools are dismissed. The hotels are frenetic. At night, in Tampa ballrooms, chandeliers sparkle, the champagne-loving pirates dance with their ladies, and beauty queens and their kings smile down from high daises festooned in flowers. The Tampa frolic goes on for four days until it reaches its climax in a torchlight parade of floats through Ybor City. Never mind that there was no Ybor City in the time of José Gaspar. Never mind, either, that there probably never was a José Gaspar. If you haven't the fortitude to turn fable into festival you don't belong at Gasparilla. Tampa is a place which, as one of its newspaper editors once observed, demands men and women with romance in their souls.

The Gasparilla Festival began humbly enough. On a damp afternoon in March 1904, Miss Louise Dodge, the Society Editor of the *Tampa Tribune*, was at her desk working on organizing a May Festival which, she and her committee hoped, would attract statewide attention to Tampa, pride of the Plant System. Miss Dodge was chewing her pencil in perplexity when a visitor, George Hardee by name, dropped in. How, she asked Hardee, could she stretch out the May Festival into several days and fill local hotels? Hardee pondered, and then returned a question: "Wouldn't it be possible to develop a spectacular and merrymaking feature in connection with your festival? Why not take the story of Gasparilla, who operated along this coast, as a nucleus for a fete? Gasparilla would give it a theme, a foundation." Convincingly, Hardee added that he was a native of New Orleans. In Tampa he knew about the Gasparilla tales of old John Gómez. By the end of the afternoon George Hardee was chivalrously promising Louise Dodge to help put on the biggest festival the Suncoast had ever seen.

It must all be a secret at first. Hardee and Miss Dodge assembled a committee of forty young men and organized them into a "Mystic Krewe" patterned after New Orleans Mardi Gras Krewes such as Comus and Proteus. The whole affair would be headed by a make-believe Gasparilla who would "capture" the city when the time came. The potential pirates would come from the bluest of Tampa blood—as blue blood was reckoned on Florida's youngest coast in 1904, heavily WASP. Cynical spectators of the 1970s remind you that not pirates but bankers, attorneys, and doctors are the desperadoes swinging in the rigging whooping rebel yells and shooting off their elegantly embossed weapons. But the WASPs in control don't prevent hordes of white and black youngsters from staring with shining eyes as they lick taffy apples along the riverfront.

The Gasparilla Festival has long since freed itself from its original links with New Orleans. At the festival's inception, however, the pirates were forced to rent their costumes from distant Bourbon Street outfitters. It was humiliating but understandable. The would-be conquerors worked in a clandestine fever with Miss Dodge and George Hardee until the morning of April 23, 1904, when the *Tampa Tribune* made an announcement:

> After a century of obscurity and retirement in this His Royal Majesty's dominion, it has been deemed expedient and desirable by His Royal Majesty that the Royal Court of Gasparilla shall visit the fair and prosperous city of Tampa. . . . Our royal party will appear in your midst at some hour during your coming May Festival. If our entrance be opposed and your reception hostile, the consequences be upon your own heads!

On Monday, May 2, the May Festival opened with a sedate lawn fete and a band concert in the park in front of Henry Plant's hotel. Adults and children began assembling along the city's main streets on the opposite shore to see the parade of rose-decked barouches. Soon the spectators saw bandanaed men on horseback who were turning up at various points along the route. They all rode dashingly into the Tampa Bay Hotel grounds where the order of march was being organized. Their multicolored silks and satins rivaled the gaud of the minarets, and people identified them as the newspaper had primed them to do. "Gasparilla!" they began yelling. "The pirates! Welcome to Tampa!" It was all a little confusing, because Miss Dodge's parade had started as a flower display. But the city fell so deeply in love with the pirates that the May Festival had to go. Carriages gave way to confetti-strewed automobiles driven by goggled men of admissible lineage, and by 1911 the pirates were arriving in a three-masted schooner which sailed up the Hillsborough followed by a flotilla of pleasure boats. Newspaper correspondents summoned from outside the city and the state realized an institution was establishing itself. Tampa now had a street carnival as well as an Alhambra to distract snowbirds from the cares of offices back home.

José Gaspar did not have an official biographer until 1936, when veteran Tampa newsman Edwin Lambright obliged. Lambright had a fertile imagination, and Gaspar emerged from its reaches far more imposing than the buccaneer so hazily, if tantalizingly, recalled by John Gómez. Gaspar, Lambright assured his readers, was born in the mid-eighteenth century and was originally in the Spanish navy. As a cadet in

Gasparilla

Barcelona he had decided to model his career on that of Richard the Lion-Hearted. At twenty-two he became a lieutenant, fierce browed and splendidly moustached. His closest friend was "the bloody Roderigo López," a Spanish colleague of less than stainless reputation.

In 1783 Gaspar and López, bored with officialdom and naval tedium, turned pirate. Their first vessel was a sloop-of-war called the *Florida Blanca* which they filched from the Spanish navy. If José, with his black brows, was terrifying, so was López who had bushy red ones. Between them they recruited a band of fifty villains. Gaspar was always busy plundering, sailing, and killing (he favored the plank) but not too busy to fall in love with one of his captives. "Three months, Lady Anne, you have been my prisoner. I have respected you, protected you from the advances of these devilish fellows, and held in check my own desire because I love you as a true man should love a true woman. Never until now have I, the desperate and bloodthirsty José Gasparilla, felt for a woman as I feel for you—never before have I thought of marriage. I beg you to become the wife of Gasparilla." Lady Anne, as became her purity, refused. Chronicler Lambright was a lot of fun, and he understood southern rhetoric well enough to parody it affectionately:

> Such was the tale that was told to me
> By that shattered and battered son of the sea . . .

Gasparilla, as befitted a proud criminal, never submitted to capture. When the U.S. Navy finally caught up with him on the Gulf, he shouted at them, "Gasparilla dies by his own hand, not the enemy's!" The last that was seen of him was his sword waving bravely silver above Gulf waves before it sank with its owner.

Gaspar, Lambright's saga informed an eager public, named Sanibel and Captiva islands off the lower west coast near Fort Myers, and also Gasparilla Inlet nearby. Sanibel had been a maid Gaspar had loved in Spain, and Captiva was where he kept his women. A historian has recently pointed out that when Don Francisco María Celi, on his way to El Río de San Julián de Arriaga, used the name Gasparilla, Gaspar was supposedly a one-year-old baby frolicking under Spanish olive trees. But everybody knows, too, that historians must stick to dry facts. In February the same historians are as susceptible as their fellow Suncoasters to the magic of Gasparilla's raid.

The first time I saw Gasparilla it was in the middle of a record freeze.

For years uncounted a hot sun had always shone down on the festival's opening day. This time black walls of clouds were leaping out of the bay and a bitter wind roared around the corners of city buildings. A driving rain began falling, but it didn't deter the small boys who were dancing near me along the riverfront in yellow slickers, nor did it faze the balloon men who continued hawking their hugely transparent wares. Police motorcycles roared importantly back and forth as we all sat shivering on the chairs in Water Street that Tampa had provided us as Gasparilla ticketholders. Cheerfully, in the moaning wind, ancient veterans of World War I limped past from time to time to collect coins for the American Legion.

At Gasparilla the real action begins when the Kennedy Boulevard bridge goes up; this time it was outlined against a line of menacing grey tornado clouds. Nobody cared. The fronds of Washington palms glistened with frigid droplets half-ice. "Testing 1, 2, 3, 4," groaned the mikes in the universal language of amateur preparation. The kids beside me sucked at soggy Baby Ruths while announcers began telling us, "These are very unusual weather conditions!" Some fearless sky divers from Zephyrhills performed while we all waited for Gaspar to land. Nobody was surprised that the sky divers were blown off schedule halfway across Tampa. The Tampa Seabees Water-Ski Thrill Show had to be called off. But a bent black man continued doggedly pushing his peanut cart until the first motorcycle clowns appeared; then he sank gratefully if illegally into an empty chair.

A hundred motorboats preceded the pirates, but the shots drowned out both outboards and inboards. The pirates were exercising their pistols. When the galleon lumbered up the last stretch of its journey toward its Hillsborough wharf, it began firing its broadside cannons in orange explosions. The pirates, in the rigging, were wearing raincoats, and their pirate band was playing from limp music sheets. But nobody seemed to mind the increasingly hostile elements. "You know something?" the man beside me asked, wiping water from his camera lens. "This is the third biggest festival in the south. We've only gotta beat the Orange Bowl and Mardi Gras. We got the Orange Bowl scared, you know." The pirates began striding down their plank. An interviewer appeared with a walkie-talkie. "What are your plans?" he asked a buccaneer in green and gold who was popping off his blanks with abandon.

"Suh," the pirate murmured politely, "we gon' take the city."

The faces were still mostly WASP, I noted, although some latins had managed to join the elect; by now there are Cuban cigar manufacturers in Ybor City who are Episcopalians. A hawker was walking by: "Kosher sausages!" Gasparilla is getting its cosmopolitan elements. The parade was a melee: Clydesdale horses, their massive bodies curried into shine, Bouzouki dancers from Tarpon Springs, Conquistadores from Bradenton and Franciscan monks from God knew where. More than fifty papier-mâché floats glided slowly past, and electric company beauty queens were shivering under strings of light bulbs from confettied perches. Tampans will risk pneumonia to watch it all and, if they are lucky, be a part of it. The kids only knew there was no school.

Usually, Gasparilla weather is benignly in the eighties. The parade is for all; not so the balls, which are still too selective for public identification. Ye Mystic Krewe of Gasparilla is not the only Krewe, though it remains the most prestigious. The Krewe of Venus is slightly more democratic and its roster includes more latin names. Both party for weeks before Gasparilla, and during it they hold dinners and stylish dances where women trail clouds of sequin-trimmed chiffon bought expensively from "in" stores like John Baldwin's and Lille Rubin's. The Tampa Yacht and Country Club echoes with clinking glasses and small talk. The Lykeses greet the Lesleys and the Farriors and the McKays, and listen to the Gasparilla Queen's description of how, in the elementary school classes she teaches, she "planned a lesson on the history of José Gaspar and really learned something." The pedantic can only wring their hands. "Aye, Matey!" run the advertisements. "Be in Tampa at Pirate Time!" Anybody who is anybody is, and tourists who cannot penetrate the sanctum of the Tampa Yacht and Country Club have distractions of their own: Busch Gardens, for instance, a gigantic fun park provided by the Anheuser-Busch Brewing Company and boasting tame orangutans, parrot shows, and a village full of hand-carved dwarfs. By monorail you can take a "jungle safari" into what Anheuser-Busch assures you is an African veldt; the giraffes and cheetahs and zebras and kudus roam not far from a permanent exhibit of antiques, and if the mood of spectators is mellow perhaps it is because the beer is free. The hippopotamuses and the rhinoceroses are no hallucinations. Schlitz, nearby, fights bravely back with brewery tours and a Schlitz Hospitality House with starched-white-coated waiters. Grayline Tours maintains a full Tampa schedule, and the cigar factories open their doors: Garcia y Vega, Grandiaz-Annis,

Busch Gardens

and Hav-a-Tampa, where in rooms that once echoed with the droning of *el lector* the cigar machines now clang, bang, clatter, stamp, thump, squeak, and rattle in Rube Goldberg profusion. Over everything hangs a marvelously nutty smell, though it is jarring to see the women machine operators stolidly smoking cigarettes. Treasureland, near Busch Gardens, touts a *son et lumière* pageant where the stage is a full scale pirate ship and you are taken "on an imaginary trip through the modern miracle of Electronimation, replete with threats of mutiny, storms so real you'll grip your seat and a frighteningly realistic battle." Rubber-faced pirates loll in the live oaks, dummies pray on planks over a lakelet where factory-constructed crocodiles gape, and for the young there are tours on the good ship Calico Jack. When Electronimation palls there is a fish house dispensing Florida seafood to the footsore. Things are honest these days; Tampa fishmongers can't dye channel catfish and call it Alaskan salmon, as they used to do. The only trouble with Electronimation is that since the opening of Disney World upstate, it looks budget-ridden and weary.

Tampa's tourist attractions are many: jai alai, for instance, in a *frontón* whose Basque players are viciously dedicated as they slam hard jai alai balls against court walls. The players bear exotic names like Jesus and María. Ernest Hemingway had bullfighting; his surviving brother Leicester, more tamely, writes squibs about jai alai in the local press and explains parimutuel betting to novices. Greyhounds race, the World's Largest Advertising Sign stands at Port Tampa for all to see, and Ybor City's restaurants are overflowing, their wrought-iron filigreed rooms quivering with the rhythms of flamenco guitars. The charm of Tourist Tampa and of Gasparilla is the charm of boom. Nobody talks much about the recent threat offered by Mickey, Donald, Pluto, and Goofy up in Orange County. It is, like periodic recessions, visibly though not emotionally ignored.

"Tampa is a young, able-to-buy market," brags the Committee of 100 whose task it is to lure more factories and businesses. The jibe at St. Petersburg is considered fair play. Tampa's population has a median age of a frolicsome mid-thirty. In Pinellas County the median age for women is fifty, for men forty-six. St. Petersburg may have the H.M.S. *Bounty* rocking in its part of Tampa Bay, but impressive numbers of its inhabitants have never heard of Grand Funk Railroad or the Grateful Dead. Tampa has, and books them in the city auditorium. José Gaspar may not be real, but he is essential. Out of a tenuous bit of hearsay Tampa built a civic atmosphere for its drive, the energy that has established two universities—most recently, the University of South Florida—and created the third largest seaport in the United States. Gaspar is bold and brash and so is Tampa. He is a lie, but he is true. Because he is loved, he is also immortal.

Tampa has exotica unconnected with buccaneers. The socially important Farrior family does not dwell on the subject of Cousin James Searcy Farrior who to Tampa is Jim Fair, proprietor of the A-1 Jim Fair Catalog Discount House Department Store Get It For You Wholesale Company and Swap Shop and Rent All. Jim Fair, until recently shorn in a run-in with officialdom (Florida police still don't like long hair), boasted a Renaissance pigtail and a luxuriant beard. He ran as a write-in candidate for the U.S. Senate not long ago; Republicans disdainfully branded him as a Yippie. (Fair is suing the original insulter; he loves litigation.) He wears Elizabethan doublet and hose, a velvet striped vest, and a hat with a gracefully curving ostrich feather in it. His emporium displays a poster:

> WE WANT
> Long Hair
> Jim Fair
> Steak Rare
> Car Fare
> Less Prayer
> More Care
> Peace There.

For the poor of Tampa Jim Fair runs the Salvation Navy; the local desperate have learned to come to him for help when red tape has failed them. "I am," says Fair, "in love with someone pure and unattainable, Lady Justice." Conventionally, he came out of World War II a Navy lieutenant commander, but the family brokerage business soon bored him and he forsook the counters of finance for those of a mail-order business. Because he saw Tampa's depression as a youngster, albeit from the vantage point of one of the Right Crowd, he never forgot its tragedies. For years he has loaned out money at no interest to people who need it. When he ran unsuccessfully for the State Public Utilities Commission, he made his opponent so mad the opponent physically attacked him twice during the campaign. "They get along," noted a reporter,

"like Eldridge Cleaver and Spiro Agnew." Fair was also, briefly, Hillsborough County Supervisor of Elections until Republican governor
Claude Kirk suspended him in 1970 for what the state's attorney called
"malfeasance, misfeasance, neglect of duty, and incompetency." The
attorney's name was Spicola; Jim Fair didn't court public opinion when
he called him, pointedly, *Spic*-ola. Friends of Fair's say his desire to purge
election rolls was not helpful to his career in office. When he took his
dismissal to the U.S. Supreme Court, the American Civil Liberties Union
agreed to help him—if he promised not to talk. The muzzling may be
unique in the history of the ACLU, not noted for censorship. A racist? A
Yippie? A man who hates the Mafia? Paranoid? "Maybe he won't be
elected again," says the *St. Petersburg Times,* "and maybe he shouldn't,
but he's good for us." He is a conscience, a ham, and "a marvelous
freak" alternately beloved and hated in the bay area. And meanwhile
the hungry and the sick line up at his door; his eyes crinkle at the corners,
and he sees nothing preposterous in going into court to defend the good
name of his Weimaraner Smoky who allegedly bit a man when no wit-
nesses were around. If José Gaspar is Tampa's staple, Jim Fair is its spice.

Gasparilla time is Florida State Fair time. At night dark skies are
the backdrop for the varying diameters of the Ferris Wheels, circled in
red and green and blue neon. Chains of red and gold and green lights
deck carnival booths. The smell of hot popcorn lingers in byways, kids
shout, and babies clutch the strings of balloons in the arms of their
parents. Country singers Roy Clark and Tammy Wynette are the fair's
Caruso and Flagstad. Booths offer the standard prizes: stuffed dolls,
teddy bears in psychedelic colors so atrocious they are beautiful, dis-
dainful-looking pandas, and bulb-nosed clowns with synthetic red hair
under rakishly tilted top hats. The black young swarm thickly everywhere; this is their Gasparilla even more than the pirate parade. "Hurry,
hurr-y!" they hear from the sideshows and they rush from one to the
other wondering where to spend precious half dollars. Tightly curled
black hair flies red and blue ribbons, worn minicoats are clutched around
sturdy black thighs, and when the boys smile with their white, white
teeth it is divine. Has everybody seen the Great Icelandic Giant and the
Two-Headed Dog? How about the shooting concessions with their
little processions of rusty ducks? Calliope music rises and falls while
Baptist matrons sell applesauce cake at Benefit Bake Sale Booths. And
all the time, even in the starkness of a freeze, there is that sky just pale
at the edge with lights reflected. Somewhere you hear the iron wheels

of a train singing cold on its tracks. Fainter, fainter—until the sound dies away at the phosphate terminals, or maybe in Ybor City where cigar boxes wait. You smell mustard and ketchup and sauerkraut now, and frozen orange juice. Across the river the Gasparilla ship rolls in a sudden ripple, and the kids race even faster from booth to booth because they are long since due home for dinner. The dirty shows are gone forever, to the relief of their parents, though the furtive fun that went with them has gone too. Tomorrow there will be horse trials and cattle shows and sheep-judging and displays of homemade marmalade made from homegrown oranges. There will also be the exhibitions of big business, the citrus and cattle and poultry industries, the phosphate companies with hymns to detergent and fertilizer printed boldly on placards decorated with Florida palms and pines. The fair will have time for serious things like Plant City strawberries, like hay and soybeans and gypsum exhibits. But tonight throbs with the Gasparilla life, and that is all that matters.

In 1956, the most sentimental event in Gasparilla's history came to Tampa. On the pirate galleon's deck, along with the buccaneers, stood Arthur Wills Percy Wellington Blundell Trumbull Sandys Hill, Marquess of Downshire and Earl of Hillsborough, and his Marchioness, Maureen. They had never before seen the river which bore the name of his ancestor Wills Hill's manor, but Tampa was claiming them as its own. Society editors got a little flustered as they explained that "Marchioness is the proper title for the wife of an Earl," but nobody brandished copies of *Burke's Peerage* in their faces to set them straight. To Tampa the Marquess of Downshire was Lord Hillsborough, and the fact that he was tweeded and handsome and his wife was regally beautiful added to the romance. Lady Hillsborough threw the city into ecstasy by appearing at the Gasparilla Ball in her jeweled tiara; it was a gracious gesture, and so was her admiration of "the lovely, lovely girls." Wills Hill, Colonial Secretary, had not lived in an era of Miss Sunflavors and Pirate Kings—the oranges were then too sour and the pirates too real for comfort—but his direct descendant admired and praised—lavishly. During the years which have passed since "the Gasparilla of Lord and Lady Hillsborough," their memories have remained vivid, not only to social Tampa and the Junior League but to thousands of children and cigar workers and pensioners from Pinellas and Yankee tourists who were seeing a live British peer for the first time, much as they had seen the Great Icelandic Giant at the Fairgrounds. Afterwards the couple presented the Hillsborough County Historical Commission with a valuable map of English Florida from Downshire archives. A Lesley, of course, thanked them. In Hillsborough, County Down, perhaps the shade of Wills Hill was smiling. His heir had captured "my favorite colony" not when it was a raw wilderness but a teeming American city whose phosphate each year turned the fields of the old world green.

"Nineteen fifty-six," a soft-voiced elderly Tampa hostess once said to me, "was the Gasparilla the Hills came home."

28

Biography
of a Banana

In 1892, one of the cargo boats entering Tampa Bay brought a novel fruit. It was crescent shaped and green; when allowed to ripen it turned a rich yellow, and the Tampans who tasted it found it delicious. Thus arrived the banana. It could be grown in Florida—if there were no freezes, if the soil were just right, if there were no dry spells, and such a multitude of other "ifs" that banana raising in the state is still, at best, problematical, since Florida gets cold, has sandy soil, and also has prolonged droughts. Cubans had tried it in Ybor City with discouraging results even before the first bananas came into the harbor nearby. But after 1892 there was a source of supply of the choicest banana variety of all, the rich and succulent *Gros Michel* of Central America and the Caribbean.

It is difficult to imagine the bay without its banana docks, an enduring tourist mecca, or indeed American grocery stores without bananas. Before 1870, however, the fruit was virtually unknown except to immigrants who hailed from the tropics. Today, each individual in America consumes more than twenty pounds of bananas per year. A goodly share of them comes from Tampa, where banana importing is big business, banana workers are courted by labor leaders, and spectators flock to bustling wharves where several times each week the green fruits are unloaded in plastic bags by "pocket elevators" which lift the cargo from the ships' decks and then deposit it on the docks to await loading

into long-distance trains and trucks, or Tampa "ripening rooms" if they
are to be marketed so near they will not have time to ripen en route.
Stevedores chant, latin expletives ring out in the din, and black workers
sing songs as old as slavery days as they stand at their counters inspecting and culling. The fragrance of the bananas is heavy, and is mixed
with the resiny pungency of raw crates. Pulleys clank and conveyor belts
hum. You are lost in a very wilderness of bananas which will eventually
end up in American lunch boxes and on dinner tables. They will be
mixed in dry cereals, served by the sophisticated in rum and sour cream,
thrown to chimps in big city zoos, and used as the sole staple of a freak
diet by a nation eager to reduce. They are mashed, boiled, fried, baked,
pureed, minced into cakes and coffeebreads and ice creams, and used as
garnishes by gourmet groups specializing in Indonesian and Malayan
extravaganzas. They are one of the oldest fruits in existence, yet they
are used in greatest quantity in a new world rich enough to import them
on a steady basis. Nearly a quarter of a million stems loaded with green
bananas arrive on the Tampa docks each week. Bananas are, too, musical
Americana to anyone over twenty. In the Jazz Age, the country was
singing:

> Yes, we have no bananas!
> We have no bananas today! . . .
> Take home for the wimmens
> Nice juicy persimmons . . .
> But yes, we have no bananas,
> We have no bananas today.

In 1944 the New York advertising firm of Batten, Barton, Durstine,
and Osborne composed for banana king Samuel Zemurray, head of the
United Fruit Company, a jingle intended to instruct his countrymen on
how to treat bananas once they got them home. The tune was a rumba,
and the singer was—on her posters—a cartoon Carmen Miranda in
towering headgear:

> I'm Chiquita Banana and I've come to say
> Bananas have to ripen in a certain way.
> When they are flecked with brown and have a golden hue,
> Bananas taste the best and are the best for you.
> You can put them in a salad,
> You can put them in a pie, aye!

Any way you want to eat them
It's impossible to beat them.
But bananas like the climate of the very, very tropical equator
So you should never put bananas in the refrigerator,
No, no, no, no!

Only on incoming ships are unripe bananas refrigerated at 57°. Soon after its inception the jingle reached the hit parade; comic Fred Allen took it up and parodied it; a midwestern university voted Chiquita "the girl we'd most like to get in a refrigerator with," and United Fruit was finding it necessary to compose patois versions for French Canada and Spanish ones for the southern hemisphere. Opera singers took it up as a joke; swing bands arranged it. The sales of bananas in America soared to new heights, and Tampans began garnering their share of the riches. At first Samuel Zemurray had privately thought the jingle embarrassingly ridiculous. He was taught a powerful lesson in public relations. Even today, the memory of Chiquita (the jingle has been discontinued) stays the hands of housewives at the icebox door. They know—and know very well—that they must never put bananas in the refrigerator, no, no, no, no!

The banana is ancient. Rumphius, a classical botanist, called the banana a venerable fruit even in his time. It was one of the first crops raised by Neolithic man. Hindu, Chinese, Greek, and Roman literature all extol it. The Hindu epics *Mahabharata,* by an anonymous author, and *Ramayana,* by the poet Valmiki, devote their share of attention to bananas as do sacred Buddhist texts which advise monks to distill banana juice and drink it. Pliny wrote about bananas in his *Natural History,* and so did Greek naturalist-philosopher Theophrastus. Archaeologists have found bananas depicted on sacred monuments in Java dating back to the birth of Christ. Modern adherents of the *Hare Krishna* discipline beloved by poet Allen Ginsberg and by adventurously mystical college students who shave their heads, vow celibacy, and don lemon-colored robes, feature bananas at their *prasadams,* or "love feasts," while they chant mantras and search for Yogic Reality. Their parents are doubtless thankful they are on bananas, not pot. Life in America without the banana is inconceivable, and the reality of that, Yogic or not, is what has filled many a Tampa bank account. New York, New Orleans, and Mobile are also principal banana ports; they too have gathered their share of the wealth. But in Tampa, somehow, the proceedings at the docks are more colorful, the kerchiefs of the stevedores gayer, the songs of the Spanish and black workers more melodious, and the rustle of tall palms more nearly constant. Banana Tampa is a tropical Tampa exotic enough to arrest the imagination of even the most jaded snowbird.

Bananas probably originated in the tropics of southern Asia; today they still grow wild in Asian jungles, though the plants may be escapees from cultivation. From Asia the banana was carried to Egypt and Africa by traders who moved, along vast and rippled beige deserts, with belled camels and voluminous white burnooses. When the conquistadores arrived in Santo Domingo they found *plátanos,* cooking bananas or plantains, growing there. Initiates describe plantains as tasty. Critics say they are, when cooked, like a cross between shoe leather and a dishrag. Spanish historian Oviedo credits the introduction of fruit bananas in the new world to Fray Tomás de Berlanga, a monk of the order of Predicadores who brought them from the Canary Islands to Hispaniola. Thence they spread "to all other islands peopled by Christians and they have even been carried to the mainland and in every port they have flourished." The pioneer who introduced the Gros Michel banana to world trade in 1836 was a French botanist named François Pouat.

The man, however, who captured the taste of America for it was a New England sea captain with a strident voice and poor hearing. The deafer he got the more he shouted. Lorenzo Dow Baker had been named by his parents after a prominent evangelist. Captain Baker was duly devout and led his crews in daily prayer. One day in 1870 he tasted a banana in Jamaica and liked it. Around him on the docks at Port Antonio he saw green bunches of bananas ready for shipment to nearby islands. Lorenzo Baker had an idea. What if he could buy the least ripe ones and set a course of breakneck speed for Massachusetts? Would bananas go in Boston? The log he kept was terse:

May 8. Finished taking in coconuts—whole number on board 35,200. Took in 400 bunches of bananas.
May 9. Clear and pleasant. Took in some bananas . . .
May 28. At 8 P.M. passed Boston Light. At 9 P.M. came to anchor at quarantine.
May 29. At 6 A.M. got underweigh and came to the City and hauled alongside Long Wharf. Pumps duly attended and so ends sea log.

Lorenzo Dow Baker was in business as a banana merchant. "It is monkey food!" protested a timid neighbor on Cape Cod where he made his home between voyages.

"Sir!" roared Baker, "it is a dadblamed silly fruit for which I have an *intense* and *personal* liking!" Because Baker was known to be canny, his word was influential.

Young Andy Preston, who worked for a Boston commission firm, was strolling on the Boston docks the morning Lorenzo Dow Baker's shipment of bananas arrived. On his own initiative, Andy recklessly bought them. He tried one and found it good. Back at the offices of Seaverns and Company, he explained to his boss with gleaming eyes his belief in the banana's future in America. His boss was startled, then amused, by his brashness. Soon Seaverns and Company was issuing discreet little posters for the red brick walls of Boston buildings: "Fine Tasteful Yellow Bananas Fruit on Direct Import from the Antilles." "I saw 'em, I bought 'em, and I sold 'em," was Andy Preston's laconic answer to reporters in later life when he had become a banana mogul. It was not long before Lorenzo Dow Baker had retired from Cape Cod to settle in Jamaica, because if America were going to want bananas at the rate it seemed to be wanting them, somebody knowledgeable "had to raise the dadblamed things." By 1876 Andy Preston was manager of Seaverns and Company. Years later Baker ended life as "Godfather of the Jamaican Banana Trade and Foremost Friend of Jamaica" (so said the silver loving cup the Jamaican government gave him) and he was gravely asserting that his success was "due to God and the people of Jamaica."

In Costa Rica, a Brooklynite in his twenties named Minor Cooper Keith was building railroads on borrowed money. For every rail laid down, a man died of malaria or yellow fever. But Minor Keith persisted. What could he find as a paying cargo for his trains? They were far from upland coffee farms. (Coffee, then as now, was "mountain grown." Everybody's coffee.) Keith tasted a banana and decided it was awful, but he also noted that some of his Jamaican and Costa Rican laborers liked the things. Maybe you had to get used to them. Then he heard rumors Americans were actually paying high prices for them. He began to have his workers plant them in the lowlands. His first bunches he shipped to New Orleans, where there were jobbers willing to gamble on them, and the first time he made the net profit of a dollar a bunch. He also determined to open an island store for his banana and railroad workers. In charge he placed a beachcomber who said he was reformed, Newcomb Brown. "My kidneys is gone," Brown told Keith, "my stummick is gone, my lungs and heart is gone, and all I got left is Christian principles." When the store opened Brown gave away Keith's liquor by the barrel. His drunken customers then explained that they had no money, but they could barter for supplies with turtles, alligators, tortoises, sarsaparilla, rubber, and monkeys. When Minor Keith came for a tour of inspection he found his emporium "alive with reptiles, the shelves and kegs empty of merchandise, and the entire premises pervaded with the appalling stench of dead turtles and raw rubber." Nearby stood a patiently waiting and half-naked group of Indians who wondered out loud why they had seen Mr. Newcomb Brown going off toward the beach with the last keg of rum and Mr. Keith's money bag. One of them had also, in Brown's shirt pocket, seen a book Brown had once said was the Christian Bible. Heartsick, Minor Keith realized that he would have to concentrate on bananas, not merchandising.

By now New York had its own banana merchants, the Frank Brothers. In New Orleans the formidable Oteri dynasty controlled the banana trade. Minor Keith knew that if he consolidated his interests with those of Baker, of whom he had heard, and Andy Preston, the boy wonder of Seaverns and Company in Boston, he could more than meet competition because he could control the raising of the bananas, their rail transportation, their shipment by sea in an age witnessing the conversion from sail to steam, and their marketing in the United States. The United Fruit Company came into being in 1899, with Andy Preston as President and Keith as First Vice-President; Lorenzo Dow Baker was a substantial shareholder. United Fruit was not only in the business of shipping bananas and building railroads and running plantations, *fincas,* but in financing shaky Latin-American governments. For three decades United Fruit was the undisputed leader of the trade. Tampa was its port of supply for the southeastern quarter of the United States. Long white United Fruit Company ships came and went in the bay, commanded by elegantly uniformed captains. When ventilation was introduced on the ships, the bananas stayed in better condition. United Fruit pioneered research into tropical agriculture and built hospitals for its workers. Its banana vessel *Venus* was refrigerated in 1903. A refrigeration engineer had talked to Andy Preston about a plan to cool cargo ships, and Preston had been impressed.

"My boy," he said, "I think your piano is all right but my banana boys don't know how to play it. You better go down and show them how."

The engineer did. The *Venus* became the brightest star in what was now known as The Great White Fleet. At first nobody paid serious attention to a Bessarabian named Samuel Zemurray who had come to America in 1892 at fifteen, had helped his aunt run a tiny country store in Selma, Alabama, and then run into a New Orleans banana jobber who persuaded him to market bananas in small southern towns. From this beginning came the Cuyamel Fruit Company of New Orleans, with the volatile, brilliant Zemurray at its head. Zemurray began trading with Honduras. In 1915 he got into a territorial dispute with United Fruit over Honduran concessions on the Guatemala border. Honduras and Guatemala sent toy-soldier armies into the area and fought comic opera battles. Weary at length of banana wars, United Fruit bought out Cuyamel; Zemurray sold out his interest in Cuyamel for three hundred shares of United Fruit stock. With the advent of the Depression, he took over active management of the company. Inevitably, jokers called him the Top Banana. By then Andy Preston was dead. He had refused his medicine one summer afternoon in 1924 when a zealous secretary had pressed it on him. "No, Lotty, the medicine I really need would be nice cold water from that fountain the Spanish gent Mister De León kept looking for." After a board meeting, Preston had gone home to his bed. He left it only for the grave. Keith and Baker had also passed into the shades. Samuel Zemurray *was* the banana business now, and fortunately Americans kept on demanding even during the Depression a fruit to which they had become thoroughly addicted. The Great White Fleet came and went on swelling blue seas. In palm-choked Central American ports conveyor belts rumbled and clattered as they loaded trim vessels, and in Tampa dock laborers whose business it was to unload, grade, load again, and store bananas thanked God that, unlike many cigar workers, they still had their jobs. The heavy perfume of bananas floated down Ybor City streets on humid mornings, and the echoes of stevedores' songs floated after them. Ybor City didn't much feel like singing. Americans were willing to give up cigars, but not bananas. Most of the music of the docks was black, and some of the singers had come to Tampa from West Indian plantations. Tampa knew and loved banana songs long before Harry Belafonte made them famous.

A banana begins life as an idea in the ambitious brain of a *finca* foreman. He directs gangs of woodsmen who slash with broadaxes at the dense growth of tropical jungles to create banana fields; fallen branches and leaves are left to rot into earth already black and rich. From the time a banana root bulb or *hijo* is planted it takes three months for the ensuing floppy-leaved plant to reach six feet, and a year before the first rosy green and yellow and purple blossom gives way to a bunch of palely shaded fruit. The trees are called "stools" and they are planted four hundred to the acre. In Jamaica the banana men maintain that on damp starry summer nights full of the faraway sounds of Caribbean waves they can hear the bananas growing taller. "You doubt this, Señor? Stand beneath the leaves and listen. You will hear a cracking noise; it is the pain the plant feels when it must grow so fast." Maybe, too, it is the dripping of the leaves, or an animal footfall. But bananas are material for fables to the people who grow them if not to the people who ultimately eat them. A foreman always listens respectfully to his *hombres,* who know their fruit and their soil. He listens, too, to engineers who build irrigation ditches by day and at night under weeping thatch eaves drink gin by the fifth diluted in quinine water. To engineers and railroad men, it is a lonely life. But when they leave it to retire back in the states to tidy clapboarded and bricked towns, they usually find themselves suffering pangs of homesickness for the broad, tense, tightly packed, and profuse jungles of banana stools, for the wide-faced Indians of Central America and sweating black men of the West Indies, and for the chattering of parrots and macaws and monkeys in tangles heavy with the smell of cestrums and the rankness of vines that wind high into nameless trees where bats flit and roost and tree frogs chirp, hoarse and tiny in the thick velvet of the night.

When the blossoms have given way to jade-colored bunches of bananas, the reapers begin working. A bunch must not be underripe when cut; if so, it will have poor flavor. But a bunch reaped two days late means bananas that will ripen prematurely on their way to market. Reapers carry flat machetes attached to long sticks. The first reaper reaches high with his machete to cut a notch in the pithy stem a few feet below the bunch he wants. The tree bends down gracefully, and a second reaper catches the falling bunch. The first then hacks off the plant stem, also the remnants of the blossom stem. Finally he cuts down the fruit-bearing stalk to the thick, milky base of the plant. The next largest shoot, or *plantilla,* will begin growing rapidly and in six months will produce another bunch of bananas. The crop is thus perpetual. A "shoulder man" brings his cut bunch of bananas to a mule fitted with three baskets on either side. (On the most modern *fincas* the mule has been replaced by a tractor.) When the mulepack or tractor is finally full, a driver guides it through the banana stools to a field railway.

Each division of a banana *finca* is in charge of an overseer, a *mandador*, who lives in a bungalow framed by riots of hibiscus and flame vines. Thrice daily a cook feeds him Caribbean delicacies, conch salad and filleted grouper and tender little limes and rum and coconut drinks. Yard boys tend his lawn. But in spite of amenities like servants and silver, all provided by his banana company, he has his worries. In 1920 bananas being grown in southeast Asia were attacked by a fungus disease called sigatoka. Green banana leaves became spotted with grey flecks, and finally they withered and turned black. Eventually entire plants died. From southeast Asia sigatoka spread to Fiji and New Guinea. By 1934 it was in the West Indies; hot air currents had carried its spores halfway around the globe. A year later, Samuel Zemurray knew he was fighting for the life of the United Fruit Company. Sigatoka was in Honduras and Ecuador. He hired rafts of pathologists; little research had been done on the blight. Asian and African growers had merely watched it turn their plantations to fungus-blackened wreckages. In Honduras, Dr. C. V. Dunlap finally reported success to Zemurray with a mixture of copper sulphate, lime powder, and water. The problem of devising spraying equipment was put in the hands of United Fruit engineers, who installed central pumping stations and networks of pipes fitted at intervals with petcocks to which hoses could be attached. The hoses in turn were fitted with spray guns. Nozzle men and hose carriers began proudly calling themselves *químicos* as they sprayed the crop. Airplanes dusted banana plantations too; Zemurray foresaw their agricultural utility. He began making loans to independent banana farmers; they were all fighting sigatoka together, he told them. Today the disease is considered conquered, providing the *mandador* knows exactly when and how to spray and dust his fiefdom with the chemical mixture which has been permanently christened Bordeaux and is now a staple of temperate suburban gardeners.

Each banana *finca* has its materials and supplies department, the "M. and S.," which cares for everything from locomotives to vats of rum. It provides coffins when they are necessary and also bathroom fixtures. The plantation's merchandise department is the "company store" which sells workers routine daily needs—food, shoes, tobacco, bolts of bright cloth, and rum so potent that one worker reported excitedly to his *man-*

dador that the night before he had seen "a gigantic shape with fire-lighted eyes" stalking him through the bananas. He had fired a charge of buckshot, whereupon the beast "gave a hideous unearthly yell." It looked like an ape and had the tail of a horse, he said, and finally it disappeared into a waiting lagoon. Possibly it was a tapir.

Bananas are loaded into company trains from their mulepacks or tractors, but first they must be sorted and washed. Cargo cars wait to carry the bunches to United Fruit docks where the banana ships lie at anchor. Stevedores lift the fruit up to conveyors which rapidly fill the ship's hold. The average banana boat today is fully refrigerated and weighs from three to seven thousand tons. For forays into northern climates the ships also have heating systems. Ventilation is crucial, for as they ripen the bananas give off carbon dioxide, ethylene, and other gases which must be dissipated if the fruit is not to become overripe. They must not become bruised, or they will spoil; movable, vertical bin boards protect them from shifting when ships toss in rough seas. If all is well, the fruit arrives just on the edge of ripeness at its destined port. The ship is anchored and its lines are tied. Then its hatches are opened. An elevator crane is rolled into position, and the banana bags begin coming down by conveyor belt to waiting banana graders. An electric eye tallies the fruit count. Bananas are separated into the varieties banana jobbers have ordered: Heavy Nines, for stems with more than nine fruits, Light Nines, Eights, and Sevens. Banana bunches are seldom smaller than Sevens. Substandard fruits are sold on the dock as "specials." All the while the giant elevators groan, snatches of song echo along the vast Tampa docks, and the pervading aroma is that of a heavy banana cordial. Some of the bunches will go to jobbers' trucks, some to freight cars of the Seaboard Coast Line Railroad, and some to ripening rooms like those operated by N. Geraci and the Banana Trading Company and the Gulf Southern Corporation.

Tampa is serviced by more than thirty banana vessels. The city grants banana shippers free use of its dock facilities. Gulf Southern was a pioneer in the mashing of too-ripe "special" bananas into baby foods and ice creams. Tampa is now the third largest banana port in the country; New York is first and New Orleans is second. It makes no secret of the fact that it means to be the first. Most of its bananas now come from Ecuador, which in the early 1950s took the lead from Honduras. The sigatoka fungus exists minimally in Ecuador, and so does the Panama disease which attacks plant roots, but both are well controlled. Banana jobbers in the south and in mid-America know they can rely on Tampa shipments. From jobbers the fruit goes to the central warehouses of grocery giants like Winn-Dixie and Piggly-Wiggly and Publix and the A & P; from there it is shipped to individual stores. Small groceries buy from independent warehouses. Every day, in supermarket parking lots, glaring chrome trucks arrive with crates full of bananas. Moments later, housewives pick them over, and if the life cycle of the bananas has gone according to plan the fruit will be firm and golden and still faintly touched with green. Americans are becoming even now increasingly fond of the "dadblamed silly fruit" for which they, as well as Captain Lorenzo Dow Baker, have "an *intense* and *personal* liking."

Banana giants such as the United Fruit Company are variously regarded as villains or angels. They run schools and stores and build infirmaries and enjoy mercantile monopolies in their back reaches. Not long after the first United Fruit surveyor arrives to plot a waiting jungle and tough laborers follow him with their machetes to begin the clearing operation, company stores and supply depots come. Diplomacy follows too; Central American republics are anxious to please the titans that give their people livelihood. Radical sociologists maintain that banana workers are "kept in a state of peonage;" conservative observers regard the industry as a tropical Santa Claus dispensing quinine, smallpox vaccine, and electricity and plumbing to people who have never before had them. Hostile critics maintain that United Fruit often acquires land not because it needs it but to push out competitors. Recessions bring large cuts in the banana work force; so does abandonment of land that has become exhausted. Laborers who have spent their banana wages are helpless as they return slowly to the poverty level prevailing in latin countries in pre-United Fruit (or competitors like modern Del Monte) condition. When the United Fruit Company is attacked for this, it replies that its former workers can move, and that it has done more for them than their own governments have done, both of which assertions are true. United Fruit has an active public relations department; it supplies free of charge to anthropology classes throughout America films dealing with the archaeology and cultural anthropology of the peoples among whom it operates. The beauty of these films is stunning as they reveal, say, the hidden wonders of abandoned Mayan shrines like Bonampak, where Lacandone Indians now brave jungles to worship

Banana Trading Company

the art of their ancestors in a once-sacred temple. United Fruit is a doctor, teacher, parent, counselor, recreation worker, merchant, governor, policeman, and farmer. So are other banana complexes like Del Monte. In Tampa, the lives of thousands of dockmen are as dependent on banana importers as are the lives of mestizos on Honduras and Ecuador *fincas*. Tampa dock strikes are disasters, particularly to the ghetto of Sulphur Springs where many banana workers live. There have been banana wars as well as cigar wars. But most of the time, the air is full of the eternal rhythm of rolling belts and human voices, of fermenting pulp, of phosphate dust and an occasional gamy waft of shrimp from docks nearby. The Great White Fleet goes in the deep channels of Tampa Bay, and from the mouth of the Hillsborough you can watch them as they move slowly in and out of the Gulf. The Great White Fleet which brings Tampa its bananas is as stately as it ever was; and it is from Tampa that more than a quarter of the United States takes the cargo that fills fruit bowls with the clear, vivid gold of the Gros Michel in a romance of production that began on a sunlit nineteenth century day when Captain Lorenzo Dow Baker picked up an unknown food, bit into it, munched, and made a decision to educate the tastes of his countrymen to the finer things his beloved dew-jeweled islands had to offer. He was also to educate commerce and to leave an indelible atmospheric stamp on a bay and a river in Florida he probably never saw.

29

Salads and
Pink Gold

The urban bay is always a spectacular. The gracefully arching white
span of the Sunshine Skyway crosses it in epic length to link St. Petersburg with the busy canning town of Palmetto, drowsily tranquil Bradenton, and well-heeled Republican Sarasota. St. Petersburg houses fronting
Tampa Bay boast graveled courtyards and expensively transplanted
areca palms. In Tampa the bay is rich with the port's music, the
clanging of railroad cars and the horns of ocean liners. Everywhere lies
the pallid dust of phosphate. But there is an entirely different bay south
of Tampa. Wolfean trains groan through dark rural countryside, their
yellow locomotive lights long and solitary. No passengers ride now, as
they did in Thomas Wolfe's time. Instead the trains are packed with
oranges, tractors, and salad ingredients. The salad ingredients come
from Ruskin, where all year the crops of garden vegetables are harvested which at one time or another feed the eastern half of the United
States. Grocers alternate California with Florida produce according to
price. At Ruskin you are surrounded by forests of staked tomatoes, seas
of peppers, jungles of beans, cities of lettuce, and prairies of carrots
and endive and escarole. The town is a paradox; through its heart roars
the traffic of U.S. Route 41, yet on either side of the road the scenery is
bucolic. Some of Ruskin's vegetable workers are migrants, with all the
attending ills that status assures in Florida. Children miss school and
exist on dried peas, cane syrup, cornmeal, and pork intestines. Missions

try to alleviate the misery; Florida pretends it isn't there. But a majority of the vegetable workers are settled. They are hardly prosperous; most of them live in little white frame shacks with peeling paint, gallantly fronted by hibiscus bushes. Beside migrant camps they are palaces, though occasional porches sag, and scattered screens have broken beneath the rain-shedding and rust-producing eaves of tin roofs also rusty. But all around the shacks meadowlarks are singing and fat calico cats blink in the sun. Red and white long johns dry in the wind. The shacks have cars and television antennas. Here and there a metal trailer truck is parked, and in front of larger white bungalows are parked new station wagons, property of farm foremen. Castor beans grow rampantly beside dusty little roads where barefoot children play. Ruskin is at once an idyll, a scandal, and a triumph of mechanization that nourishes farflung cities.

The town began in 1908, when Dr. George Miller decided that he had had enough of being president of Ruskin College in Glen Ellyn, Illinois, where snow piled up every winter and leafless trees were melancholy looking. Dr. Miller moved to Florida and settled on fields south of Tampa as a site for another Ruskin College, still a tribute to English essayist John Ruskin, this one Dixie-style. Mrs. Miller's three brothers, the Dickmans, financed Miller in the purchase of twelve thousand acres. Soon he had set up educational shop and was selling lots; the price was ten dollars an acre for farmland, and ten for a lot in town. The growers were all supposed to form a giant cooperative, financing each other and working for neighbors as neighbors returned the favor. Dr. Miller built unpretentious cottages for his student dormitories and a concrete classroom; the students were expected to attend classes for four hours a day, study another four, and during four more work on vegetable farms to help finance their education. But Dr. Miller didn't know a farmer when he saw one. Most of the people who bought his land came to Ruskin with a halcyon dream of living on soil they had no idea how to care for. Ruskin crops repeatedly failed, and when World War I arrived Ruskin College failed too. During the Florida Boom the town slept; its cultivated fields were reduced to seventy-two acres, and the owner of twenty-five hundred of them, Mrs. Miller's nephew Paul Dickman, was busy selling land in Tampa. He knew nothing about farming. When the crash came he found himself heavily in debt. His Ruskin land was all he had left, and he began trying to sell it off to people with guaranteed incomes—ex-doughboys, for instance, with pensions. Dickman was a persuasive talker. He also persuaded the Manatee County Growers' Association to locate a plant in Ruskin to handle the ex-doughboys' produce. Unfortunately the produce did not materialize. The secrets of success in Florida's sandy soil eluded Ruskin's latest wave of farmers as hopelessly as they had the first. There was nothing for Paul Dickman to do but try farming himself. He was broke, and the Manatee County Growers' Association refused to lend him money because he was a novice. Unfazed by the rebuff, he began reading everything he could lay his hands on about the raising of vegetables. A fertilizer company took pity on him and let him buy its wares on credit. Otherwise, he had only his belief that Ruskin, protected by Tampa Bay, would continue to be frost free, that the soil was loamy enough to bring good yields under proper management, and that artesian water would continue to be abundant.

Paul Dickman was nothing if not resourceful. He invented machines with spidery arms that could cultivate, spray, and enrich. The first year he showed a profit; it was enough to enable him to plant a few more acres. Every year after that he put more and more of his fields under cultivation and as he prospered he hired men to work them. By the mid-1930s the Manatee County Growers' Association did an about-face and made him their president; afterwards he founded the Ruskin Vegetable Cooperative, developed a sales organization he christened the Ruskin Vegetable Distributors, and then had a brainstorm. Why not wash cabbage and lettuce and escarole and put them in sealed cellophane bags? Would housewives appreciate table-ready greens? Their national affirmative was resounding. Route 41 began to carry giant lemon-yellow refrigerated trucks (Dickman was fond of yellow) to the north where grocers marveled that the vegetables they got in transparent bags were harvest-fresh. Dickman also began planting citrus and again proved a Midas with scientific knowledge. He developed a hybrid between Hereford cattle and Brahmans and set them to grazing in thickly grassy Ruskin fields. Soon schoolchildren by the thousands were being transported to Ruskin to see the miracle of his salad bowl for themselves, and many of the rest of Florida's farmers arrived, pondered, and then converted to Dickman's fertilizing and cultivating methods. On the packages Dickman put recipes; he left nothing to chance.

Today, in spite of the complex of mammoth tomato cooperatives and

Dickman's Ruskin Pre-Pack industry, the town is rural enough to offer on Saturday nights a "giant horrathon" at the movies where *Dinosaurus* packs in the populace. *I Was A Teenage Werewolf* is also in demand. On Sundays Holiness churches ring with Unknown Tongues while more sedate Methodists pledge total abstinence. Everywhere truckers ogle pretty teen-agers whose pink hair rollers are covered with lace scarves as their wearers giggle in local restaurant booths. STOP ASSAULT INSTANTLY WITH SHERIFF 50! hawks a restaurant sign. SAFE! NON-TOXIC! EFFECTIVE PROTECTION $2.98. Nearby are stacked oversized postcards manufactured by a punster from Naples, south of Fort Myers, who calls them "the Hysteria of Flour-Dough." "Warning!" he urges. "The Flour-Dough postcard is banned in Miami. Stock up before you get there." St. Petersburg is Bench Sittersburg, Tampa is Temper, and Ruskin is Rough Skin. Southward lies the Razorblades National Park. Miami apparently forbade the cards because it was angry at emerging Mammy. Ruskin's truckers buy Flour-Dough cards for their friends and they drink bitter black coffee while they rest between loads of cabbage and tomatoes and peppers. And as you watch them, you become conscious that they are a raw America that keeps things moving. In Ruskin there is no suburban isolation which consumes but does not produce. The rough, tough men who haul salads risk their lives in unwieldy Fruehaufs, living on No-Doz and the lonesome wail of Tammy Wynette and a few laughs during Drive-In breaks. Ruskin is the richer for their humor and their zest for life.

Quiet, accordioned roads are bordered by red-blooming Turk'scap and white sea myrtle. In grassy creeks the red-winged blackbirds sing. Mockingbirds pick at the red berries of Brazilian pepper trees gone wild. Cardinals chip on hay-fresh mornings and bluebirds perch on telephone wires. Peace ends abruptly at the Ruskin Pre-Pack Plant. There the conveyor belts move greens and carrots and bell peppers. Girls turn up their transistor radios, the better to hear Glen Campbell and Loretta Lynn while they keep the machinery moving. In the plant's center stand skyscrapers of crates waiting to be loaded with sweet corn and spinach. Because Ruskin Pre-Pack feeds millions, it needs all the space it can get. In its offices a woman's steady voice drones repeatedly the same message as she calls the warehouses of supermarkets: "This is Ruskin. Your order, please." On a November morning the offerings were cole slaw, salad mix, spinach, turnips, mustard greens, collards, kale, mixed greens, French slaw with red cabbage, cucumber salad, bulk cole slaw and salad mix, carrots, celery, peppers, and onions. The tomatoes have castles of their own up the road, where transistors wail out the same soulful country ballads: "Don't Take Your Love to Town, Ruby." For the Rubies of Ruskin, there are always the temptations of Tampa. Forklifts move up and down near yellow Dickman trucks and the cars of the Santa Fe Railroad, which carries Ruskin tomatoes north and west along with Ruskin oranges and lemons. At the Bullfrog Creek Tavern a new batch of truckers is congregating, elsewhere the sheriff (who shares his building with the Chamber of Commerce) is catching up on "Wanted" lists, and in farmyards pied mother tabbies nurse kittens. AMERICA'S SALAD BOWL: Ruskinites use the label on everything from trucks to tavern fronts to tourist billboards. The town's other atraction is The Largest Rexall Drug Store in Florida. Because Ruskin is so near the bay, Rexall deals less in liniments and decongestants than in sun hats, beach towels, round balloons printed "Your Orange From Florida," Solarcaine for Sunburn Pain, and flipflop Japanese rubber sandals for the beach.

But not only land is farmed on the Suncoast. The bay and the Gulf are farmed too. Florida has begun experimenting with commercial aquiculture of pompano off Mullet Key. Electronic techniques have been developed which make it possible to herd the fish toward waiting nets, and also the type of fish wanted—third-year alewives, for example, a popular ingredient in commercial cat food. In St. Petersburg the Florida Board of Conservation has established a marine laboratory at which the feasibility of shrimp aquiculture is being researched. Shrimp is a Florida bonanza; the industry employs seventeen thousand people and its harvest is worth nearly a quarter of a million dollars. Eighty percent of America's domestic shrimp comes from Florida or from Mexican beds nearby. In 1949 shrimp flats were discovered off the Dry Tortugas Islands southwest of Key West. During the following year rich beds were also charted off Campeche, Mexico. Tampa got into shrimping with a vengeance then. Today Tampa boats fish mostly the Campeche beds; trips last over a month on vessels worth anywhere from thirty to forty thousand dollars. The shrimpers are nothing if not emotional; when the Board of Conservation finds it necessary to close off a portion of American shrimp beds because of undersized shrimp, fishing boats have been known to charge in and start shooting wars with patrolling wardens. Shrimp cocktail has replaced gold bullion as material for naval engagements. The shrimpers are a race as fierce as Gasparilla's band. Some of them are swarthy latins with formidable beards, ready switchblades, and a rich array of profanity. Others are crackers and gaunt Scandinavians, their leathery faces permanently reddened from years of killing sunlight and salt waves. Fights on board are common; men live closely on a shrimp boat and the work is tedious. When some of them are involved with the same women back home, catastrophes can emerge from the briny as well as the "pink gold" which graces national tables from the splendor of the Forum of the Twelve Caesars in Manhattan to Joe's Diner on the outskirts of Andytown, Florida: ALL PATRONS REQUIRED TO WEAR SHOES, NO FIREARMS ALLOWED, NO DANCING ON TABLES.

Shrimp voyages begin calmly, though. In Tampa Bay's dusk, under ruddy-amber stars, the fleet of thick-masted trawlers begins sailing out toward open sea with the sun's last light reflected in the freshly scrubbed windows of their pilothouses. Lights festoon black nets and rigging like crystal chains. Slowly, slowly, the trawlers go into the last light, muted horns blow, and then they round the bay's last bend and are gone in a final chorus of whistles.

Shrimp must be caught at night. By day they are buried deep within the sandy ocean floor; as darkness falls they begin rising to feed on plankton. The trawlers cast conical nets—trawls—bordered by a fringe of chaff to prevent tearing. Doorlike boards are rigged with chains at the trawls' mouths and plow through the deep water like gigantic oars. Back and forth the trawl goes, keeping just over ten knots an hour, while on board the captain shouts his commands. When he is satisfied he has a catch, the trawl is winched up from the bottom, its drawstrings pulled, and its sea life plopped out on deck while crewmen draw up low stools beneath high floodlights and begin sorting shrimp from trash—starfish, squid, sea cucumbers, sponges no one wants, globefish and tonguefish and pilotfish and needlefish and sea toads and manta rays and catfish and sea urchins, the latter armed with quills that can stab painfully into human flesh. "Oh, it don't hurt long," a rugged shrimper once told me on the Tampa docks, "but you know my hand was swole up for a year and I couldn't get no rubber glove on it?" Other hazards are gulls waiting to steal the sorted shrimps. Sawfish and sharks below can tear trawls so badly the catch is lost before it ever gets on deck. Red scorpion fish are armed with spines that deliver infection-prone wounds to hands that touch them. Such chances are all in a night's work, however. Unless a collector from a marine specimen house is aboard the trawler to claim trash he wants to sell to research organizations, the trash is thrown overboard to schooling sand and hammerhead and nurse sharks. Then the shrimps are shoveled into wire baskets and the baskets are emptied onto packed ice. If the trawler is to be out for more than a few days, the heads of the shrimps are removed to retard spoilage. A competent header can fill a sixty-pound basket in an hour. By the time the sun rises the gear has been secured, the cook is busy in the galley, and the crew are ready for a hearty breakfast of bacon, eggs, grits, and flapjacks with cane syrup. Then they will sleep, while the trawler rocks at anchor in the blue Gulf and frigate birds fly over its masts and occasional sailfish leap in sapphire arches. The smells are salt and pieces of fish carcass then. Yellow green dolphins will be swimming by in sinuous schools; in summer the rains will come, thunder will roar, lightning will stab deep into the horizon, and fresh torrents will rinse the rigging of its saltwater film. But by twilight the storm will have passed; once more the men are up and ready to begin their work, their hands blistered from the night before. Night after night, and day after day, the trawler's life goes on in its monotonous rhythm until the hold is filled with shrimp and ice and the captain announces that they are putting in for the Tampa docks.

Commercially important Gulf shrimp belong to three species. The white shrimp *Penaeus fluvialitis* is the most tolerant of low-salt conditions and has even been found in the Hillsborough River miles from its entrance into the bay. *Penaeus aztecus,* the delicately flavored brown shrimp, abounds in the Campeche beds and the pink shrimp *Penaeus duerarum* is found everywhere off the southwest Florida coast. There are many other kinds of shrimp, but the big three account for the money crop. No one wants tiny sea bobs or rock shrimps or the royal reds that are a risk to expensive nets because they favor only the deepest water. Shrimp lay their eggs offshore, hatch in twenty-four hours, and undergo a prolonged series of larval stages during which they slowly inch their way toward shore. Inshore, the young shrimp rest on grass flats; while they are in this nursery area they grow rapidly. Then they begin moving into deeper water once more; when they are about four inches long they make a return migration to offshore waters where they reach maturity and, finally, spawn. The cycle is completed in about a year. Around it are built the intricacies of conservation legislation. Spring is spawning time for the white shrimp, late winter for the brown. The spawning time of the pink shrimp varies widely because it is found in a variety of latitudes. In winter the shrimp docks on the bay are thick with trawlers which work not only waters to the south but the bay itself. At night the trawlers rock offshore, their lights weaving and bobbing as they reflect in the phosphorescent waves below. They are surrounded by tall buildings, but the buildings are dark by midnight. The boats and the stars have their lights to themselves, while underwater the trawl's boards sweep in and out, the chaff scrapes bottom, and finally the winches begin turning in clanks and squeaks and wrenches to bring up the haul. Suddenly the air is thick with the odor of fish, and with the scraping of stools on deck and the muttering of oaths and laughter and the continuous plop! plop! plop! of the sorting. Bay shrimpers are lucky; they can sleep on shore by day oblivious of storms or scorching sun.

When the trawler arrives at the shrimp docks it is fitted with a conveyor belt that begins unloading the shrimp from the hold. In Tampa packing houses the shrimps are washed and weighed and packed in crates for shipment to market in refrigerated trucks. By the time they reach the housewife, she pays from a dollar to more than three per pound; she is paying for shrimp nets and crew wages and winches, but also for middlemen and vehicles. Increasingly, in most of America, shrimps are sold frozen and canned; some are even prebreaded for quick frying. But Florida families still like their shrimps fresh. Sometimes they smoke them, and shrimps steamed in beer are a gastronome's Utopia.

Tampa's shrimp docks are close beside gigantic oil storage depots; the odor of petroleum is as heavy as that of seafood. At the wharves rock the boats, some elaborate, some primitive, the *Southern Belle, Proud Mary, Little Joseph* and *Deborah Lu* and *Miss Yo Yo.* Nearby are clustered the packing companies; more than fifty brands of shrimp are marketed from Tampa, which has its shrimp brokers and receivers and importers as well as fishermen. There are also shrimp inspectors; the largest shrimps go to institutions like hospitals and hotels, the smallest to supermarkets. Ocean Products Corporation, on the shrimp docks, deals in prebreaded shrimp, shrimp patties, and cocktail shrimps which it freezes with modern Freon gas equipment. The company has even developed a bride's boon, a shrimp that may be overcooked by ten minutes and remain tender.

At noon the docks echo the laughter and salutes of workers in white aprons. The women wear tiny white caps and hairnets, and their hands are red and scaly. They munch bag sandwiches in company commissaries and wash them down with icy Cokes; then they repair to rocking chairs on company porches until it is time to report for work once more. One enterprising private restaurant advertises western steaks, which must be a pleasant change to a shrimp sorter. In front of small galleried cafes are parked the trucks that will haul the shrimp north. It is a pastel world of white, green, grey, the sky's pale blue if there is a haze, red berries on the wild Brazilian peppers and the beige of dusty, spent weeds. "Get Right With God," warns a sign nearby. Occasionally a red-faced shrimper stops to muse over it, or a black woman whose head is wrapped with an African bandana. They glance at the ship *Gypsum Duchess* one dock over, at distant grain elevators and nearby oil vats. Radio music plays—surprisingly, softly. Nor is it the country music most of Florida cherishes. Shrimp people play sweet Sinatra and soulful Streisand over a background of boat whistles and crying gulls and far-off pumps and gushing hoses and the grind of machinery in Superior Seafoods and Tringali Shrimp. Nearby loom the storage columns of Illinois Grain and Portland Cement. Over everything, mixed with cement and cereal and oil and seafood, hangs a mysteriously sweet smell that pervades all the others subtly but surely. It is the odor of tenacious wild flowers in dockside ditches where redwing blackbirds are perched in spindly bushes to watch the passing parade of the seafood industry. At the Standard Marine Supply Company, the *Bill H.* is in, its rollers wound with cables, its nets stowed among tanks and chains and rope racks. In the store, walls are lined with nets and deck mops and lengths of chain, with rain gear and knives and gloves and motors and screws and wrenches and fire extinguishers and radio parts. EVERYTHING FOR THE SHRIMP FLEET, a sign proclaims. On the *Bill H.* a tall man in blue jeans and a crew hat is hosing down the stern deck while his transistor plays Bob Dylan.

Several of the trawlers are in drydock to have freezing equipment installed; soon ice in the hold will be a thing of the past. But not yet. And always the captains complain about the scarcity of experienced crews, even though the U.S. Department of Labor's program is training crews at Tampa's National Fisheries Center and adventurous youngsters with a will to learn turn up regularly as runaways from the biblical austerities of families in inland Florida cities. Shrimping also runs in families, and it is still called "following the sea."

Sometimes there are large profits, sometimes only torn nets, storms, disappointments, and mounting debts for marine equipment. When shrimp crews work offshore their girls are free to occupy themselves with other men. Tampa waters have known mutinies and stabbings and razor cuttings and shootings, and ghost ships from which crews have mysteriously disappeared. But the bay has known, too, the graceful geometry which is the network of the lighted shrimp fleet at dusk as it prepares its nets and winches and pulleys. In Ruskin, the tomato and salad warehouses are closing and the forklifts have grown silent until another dawn. On the shores of the bay, Ruskin works by day to feed America. In the bay itself the shrimp fleet works by night, and every conservationist's unspoken prayer is that it will continue, that the plankton will live and the shrimps bed and the gulls sweep and the terns arch downward for the seafood the bay has yielded since time's beginning.

"Them *damn* ee-cologists!" shrimpers swear with feeling. "Pot smokers in long hair and raised in cities, trying to tell *me* how to look after Tampa Bay. By God, I got to. It ain't no fad for me, its groceries." Shrimpers mean to stay in Tampa; because their staying means millions of dollars they have so far not been ignored. They guard the water by necessity, as Ruskin guards its land. For there are many kinds of farmers in Tampa Bay country.

30

Idyll of a King

November is always warm in Tampa. The allamandas and flame vines bloom, and pink corallitas spill over their trellises. The day the President came was radiant. City streets were lined on both sides twenty miles from the heart of town with shirt-sleeved and straw-hatted crowds waving small American flags. No President had ever come to Tampa before while in office. Even Republicans confessed a few festive feelings. Veteran Florida politicians called the sunshine "Democratic weather" and smiled knowingly. When Tampa was exposed to the magnetism of John Fitzgerald Kennedy there would be a few less Republicans than there had been in the city. Fathers were holding sunsuited toddlers high on their shoulders. The President was going to ride along Lafayette Street in an open convertible, as was his custom. Along the thoroughfare the crowds were four and five deep. On the river, the flag-decked Gasparilla ship leaned in the wakes of motorboats cruising back and forth. Ice cream vendors pushed their carts through the masses; you couldn't get near a hot dog stand. The President and his party were to land at MacDill Air Force Base between Old Tampa and Hillsborough bays in the giant four-engine presidential plane. From there the party would proceed to Al Lopez field, where the Cincinnati Reds held their spring training every year. Jacqueline Kennedy had not been able to come—housewives mourned—because she was scheduled to join her husband on a more strenuous trip later in the week.

Late that morning the temperature in Tampa reached eighty degrees. The crowds were stirring, because some people had been waiting three and four hours. Barkers were hawking souvenir buttons under the paper WELCOME, KENNEDY! banners stretched quiveringly across city streets. When the crowd first heard the roar of the President's jet, flag and star proudly blazoned on its side, they thrilled to silence. Moments later the plane touched down on the MacDill runways in a burst of final cacophony. General Paul Adams was waiting on the flight line with an honor guard. Kennedy looked suntanned and hearty as he descended the ramp with George Smathers, Florida's junior senator. When Kennedy was on the ground MacDill crowds surged past police lines; hundreds of hands were suddenly outstretched, and Kennedy smiled as he began to shake them. It was a winsome gesture. If people wanted him to, why not? Here he was, in the problem South which so desperately needed a Civil Rights Law and was so desperately fighting it—and yet people were welcoming him after all. His trip hadn't been announced as political; officially, he was here to celebrate Tony Jannus Day, the fiftieth anniversary of the country's first commercial flight, and to speak to the Florida State Chamber of Commerce convention and to some of Tampa's labor leaders. But, naturally, every trip was political. Here and there he could see Goldwater banners held aloft—Au H2o. But most of the crowd were cheering him all the way. Three years before, Democratic Governor Farris Bryant had been cool in the national campaign. Today Bryant was on hand applauding and smiling with the rest. Reporter Hayward Brady of the *Tampa Sentinel*, at the MacDill Officers' Club, congratulated himself on his good luck in managing to be hired as a waiter. A special heavy leather chair had been flown in for the President from Palm Beach. Brady got inches from it and the President with little effort, and he knew he would get a good story. He did. After Kennedy had lunched with Tampa civic leaders and military brass he made a special point of greeting each waiter, and outside, after he had retired to change his suit, he "led his Secret Service men another chase," reaching out to shake hands with a party of squealing high school girls. Cynics called his expression an "election-poster smile," but who could fail to be touched at all the enthusiasm? Kennedy was especially warm to his black supporters. When he started to get into a long pale convertible he spied a group of mothers and children standing in a nearby parking lot. He simply kept going through the car, walked out the other door, and began mingling with them while muttering Secret Service men clambered down from the back of their black Lincoln to keep up with him. Kennedy shook hands a dozen times with members of the base's enlisted men's families; then he was prevailed upon to return to his car, and the Secret Service sighed with relief. Two-month-old Brenda Lee Lindgren's mother hugged her; Brenda Lee would probably be the youngest person to shake the President's hand all day.

In Tampa, the highways were jammed with overheating cars as well as people. All the approaches from St. Petersburg were blocked as were roads leading northeast along the Hillsborough and due east to Cape Canaveral. Hillsborough bridges were groaning under their burden of vehicles. The police barked instructions to each other from patrol cars and walkie-talkies. Kennedy was now somewhat behind schedule; his advance aides explained he had arrived in a too-heavy grey suit but at MacDill had taken time to put on a lightweight blue one with a plain matching tie. Waiting Mrs. Eda Eisenberg was especially impatient; her great-great-great-grandfather had been a clerk in President Lincoln's office.

When the President's green helicopter began churning over Lopez field, the arena was packed. Normally it could seat 9,400 people but today there were many more than that, including a contingent busily distributing "Draft Barry" pamphlets which soon littered the ground. Most people hoped the President wouldn't notice. Several spectators had gotten into the park after the gate had closed; they had simply climbed the fence without interference. When Kennedy reached center field at 1:20 P.M. Cincinnati Reds Business Manager Al Stevens began joking that the Reds might have better attendance "if JFK will sign as short-stop." Stevens had rescheduled a game so that Lopez Field might be available. Most of his players had had to go to Clearwater that day to play in a game there; it was too bad, because the moment was obviously historic. Tampa was doing right by her first incumbent President. The police were publicly marveling that so far there had not been a single traffic accident; but then, when you could go only a few miles an hour, how could you hurt yourself? The business office clerks at Lopez Field said they wished the New York Yankees could draw crowds like Kennedy's when they came to play in Tampa. Sometimes the Grapefruit League was sparsely attended.

Moments of shouting acclamation passed before the Kennedy party were allowed to sit down on their Lopez Field platform. U.S. Congressman Sam Gibbons was grinning; his Hillsborough County district was behaving splendidly. When Kennedy stepped forward to begin speaking, the silence was swift. He was here, he said, to honor Tony Jannus, a "man who had taken the long chance" on his flight from St. Petersburg to Tampa fifty years before. He, Kennedy, hoped that "from Canaveral to Hawaii to Vietnam in this hemisphere and around the world" Americans would be willing to take the long chance in giving leadership and security. "I hope we will still be Number One in aviation a hundred years after Tony Jannus's first flight," he shouted authoritatively. Only sticklers for accuracy brought up *sotto voce* the fact that Tony Jannus had gone bankrupt four months after his jaunt across the bay. The balance of power in the world, Kennedy told his hearers, must be maintained on the side of freedom. The Communist World had suffered recent reverses; was it not common knowledge that in Cuba there had "been a steady deterioration in the standard of living under a regime that promised so much"? Tampa knew what the trouble in Cuba was all about; how many cigar workers had lost their jobs because of the embargo on Cuban leaf? Three thousand; yet the embargo was tragically necessary to "keep people free." The crowd—most of them on the young side, the reporters present noted for future stories—cheered even louder at this. Miami Congressman Claude Pepper, a veteran New Dealer, was beaming in the roped enclosure. So was Tampa Mayor Nick Nuccio and even the Republican Mayor of St. Petersburg, Herman Goldner. Cheers were deafening when Kennedy announced that by 1970 at Cape Canaveral there would be developed a supersonic plane which would carry passengers with three times the speed of sound. And before another year it would be going faster than that! In tremendous waves of love and pride, the crowd kept echoing their affirmation. When the speech was over, Kennedy broke away from his Secret Service men once more to mingle with everybody and shake their outstretched hands. He walked in a huge arc to home plate before he was ready to turn back and get into his convertible for a motorcade to the National Guard Armory on Cass Street, Fort Homer Hesterly, where he was going to speak to the Chamber of Commerce about the prosperity his proposed tax cut would bring. "There he is! There he is!" squealing girls chorused in falsettos as the convertible pulled away from them.

The Kennedy motorcade would proceed to within nine blocks of the Tampa Bay Hotel west of the river. Cass Street, which the armory faced, was thick with spectators. Inside, the armory was jammed with more than four thousand guests of the Florida State Chamber of Commerce. Governor Bryant nodded graciously to the business leaders in the audience when he arrived to introduce the President. Then Kennedy was saying to the businessmen that he "wasn't out to soak the rich," contrary to impressions they may have had, and that a tax cut was essential to boost the economy. After his speech—it dealt mostly with fiscal technicalities—there was an interval for questions. What about the Civil Rights Bill he was pushing in Congress, someone shouted?

"My job is different from yours here," Kennedy answered. He knew Floridians didn't agree with him, but it was his duty as President of the United States to ensure the equal rights guaranteed all citizens by the Constitution. If he didn't enforce the Constitution it would "begin to unwind." He was simply doing what he had to do.

What, he was asked next, was his Cuba policy? Well, he admitted, it "hadn't been too successful so far, but the United States is trying to band together with the rest of the free world to isolate the virus of Communism in Cuba." Canny political advisers had warned him not to appear Soft on Communism in Tampa. Too many conservatives there remembered the television debate in which Richard Nixon had insistently urged American defense of the nationalist Chinese islands of Quemoy and Matsu against Red shells, and Kennedy had proclaimed them not worth the risk of war. Memories still rankled at that. Floridians admired Richard Nixon for his stalwart opposition to Communist China and feared Kennedy's radicalism. It was why he had lost in Florida in the 1960 election. Now Nixon was a political cipher, but Democrats knew the reconquest of Florida would be difficult even so.

But Florida's businessmen predictably enjoyed hearing about the Virus of Communism from Kennedy. "I don't think there is any doubt," he confided, "that Castro as a symbol in Cuba is fading fast." Again, applause. Governor Bryant was still smiling. The Kennedy flair was having its effect. Things looked good for Democrats in Florida now. The governor, in his introductory remarks, had also praised Kennedy as a friend because of government help with the Cuban refugee problem in Miami, federal investment in space research at Cape Canaveral, and above all support of the Cross-Florida Barge Canal, a gigantic gash from shore to shore which would bring an unprecedented economic bonanza—when it was finished, that is. If it killed a few rivers like the Ocklawaha here and there, who cared?

Kennedy's conclusion was rousing. (Reporters were making notes that he was acting every inch the candidate—reelection was, after all, not that far away.) Modern life was complex, Kennedy said. The country expected more help from the government and needed it. "Whether we work in the White House or in the State House, or in the house of industry or commerce, mankind is our business. And if we can work in harmony, if we can understand each other's problems and position, if we can respect each other's roles and responsibilities, then, surely, the business of mankind will prosper and we will move ahead in a secure world, one where there is opportunity for all."

The President of the Tampa Chamber of Commerce was handed a note. He unfolded it and rose. "Mr. President, one more question if you will. It is from a little girl who asks simply, Why didn't you bring Caroline?"

Kennedy turned his contagious smile on his interrogator. "Because she likes the White House. I've got to get her used to Florida." Afterwards he filed off the stage with his entourage, and by now Florida industry was giving him an ovation.

There was one more speech to make. Labor leaders had gathered at the International Inn, a rather seedy low-slung motel near the city airport. The International Inn was an airport motel like thousands of others in the country—a lot of glass and chrome, fading curtains, and a cuisine that offered the three stalwart salad dressings of French, Thousand Island and Blue Cheese. But the Inn, if inelegant, was convenient to MacDill Field. The meeting there was being sponsored by the U.S. Steelworkers of America, AFL-CIO. Kennedy had promised to address them briefly; he needed a labor mandate. On the way over he stood up in his automobile to acknowledge more cheers and wave at the crowds still lining the streets. Senator Smathers and Congressman Gibbons sat in the car with him, smiling and waving too. Perhaps the two were mulling over in their minds the apparent about-face of Governor Bryant, who had been frigidly unenthusiastic about Kennedy in 1960. Now Governor Bryant said expansively, "The great force of change at work in Florida today should be used to further the progress of the state as sailors use the wind to get them to their destination." The simile had been appropriate for the Gasparilla City whose river was graced by a pirate ship. "The cross-state barge canal is now assured," the governor had added. Already industrial leaders were touring the state looking for factory sites. "This trickle of tours should become a torrent!" he declaimed; so maybe it wouldn't matter that he had tacitly agreed to letting a black man have a glass of water and eat a hamburger in the center of the town he was in and not on its outskirts. The President of Sarasota's experimental New College was reassured by Bryant's optimism as much as Kennedy's. That year he had a guest historian on the faculty, Arnold Toynbee from England, who had been going around saying democracies only lasted about two hundred years. Why couldn't the United States be the exception? (Earlier in the season Professor Toynbee had obligingly posed for New College public relations staffers face to face with a puzzled Dromedary camel; Sarasota had associations with the Ringling Brothers Barnum and Bailey Circus.)

The International Inn was packed. Kennedy was joined on his dais by union officials who nodded approvingly when he told them he could create ten million new jobs in the next two years if his tax cut were implemented. Moreover, the old needed medical care. The progressive legislation of the New Deal hadn't just happened in the 1930s; Franklin Roosevelt had made it happen, and he, John Kennedy, meant to show the same determination. The proceedings at the International Inn were not without lighter moments. Marcelo Maseda, titular *Alcalde* or Mayor of Ybor City, rose to proclaim Kennedy "the Commonwealth of Ybor City's Prime Minister."

"I accept the nomination," Kennedy answered straightfaced. "I understand you have no Congress." The audience broke into loud whoops of laughter. Marlene Maseda, six, was raised in her father's arms so that she could present Kennedy with a doll which had been specially imported from Spain for the occasion.

"Mr. President," she announced in her high, musical voice, "this doll is for your daughter Caroline." Maseda himself offered a box of Tampa cigars. The audience continued clapping and cheering in the loudest demonstration of the day so far. F.B.I. men from the Tampa office were mingling among them, they knew, "easy but alert." They didn't mind. They went on applauding until Kennedy and his party had left to begin the final motorcade back to MacDill. The sun was dropping lower over Old Tampa Bay now; darkness came early to Florida in November. Already the temperature had begun falling.

At MacDill, Kennedy delayed his departure nearly fifteen minutes. He wanted personally to "thank members of the U.S. Armed Forces and their families for their contribution to the country." The pilot of his C-137 jet started up one of its engines but he quickly ordered the engine to be shut off. "It won't damage anything," he laughed. Then he turned to the troops: "I am indebted to all of you. On behalf of the people I express thanks to you." It was twenty-five minutes after four by now, but he insisted on shaking hands with thirty-three Tampa motorcycle policemen who had helped to clear his route in the crowded metropolis. Then he announced his thanks to the sheriff's department and the mayor of Tampa for their help. Spectators marveled that he positively "bounced" with unabated energy up the plane's ramp. Who said he had back trouble or something called Addison's Disease? He had a speech to deliver in Miami that night but he showed no fatigue, and he was "smiling like a movie idol."

The next day the *Tampa Tribune* was full of photographs. Its lead editorial was headed "Mr. Sunshine":

> Tampa put on its best weather and manners for the President yesterday and Mr. Kennedy responded with a quick preview of the 1964 campaign. Both seemed to enjoy the meeting.
>
> The Democrats' main selling points next year, it appears, will be Peace, Prosperity, and Personality (Mr. Kennedy's) . . . Watching this relaxed, bright-eyed young man distributing cheer with an expert hand, it was easy for a Tampan to forget such disagreeable matters as Berlin, and Soviet troops in Cuba, and racial conflict and the Federal reach into new areas of private life. He had to keep reminding himself that the national weather wasn't really as sunny as Tampa's yesterday.
>
> This is a measure of the Republicans' problem for 1964. Sunshine, as reflected from Peace, Prosperity and Personality, is a tough product to compete against.

The *Tampa Tribune*, like Florida, was conservative.

Mayor Nuccio was still basking in Kennedy's personal thanks. George Hambaugh, the bell captain of the Hillsborough Hotel downtown, wondered how he himself had been able to get so close to the President on the street so easily; he had even been in the background of one of the news pictures. Shirley Wilson and Joann Sabo, both waitresses at Whitey's White Tower Cafe on Florida and Madison streets, happily remembered their first view of Kennedy at close range. Candy González,

who worked at the Hillsborough County Courthouse, boasted to her
fellow worker Conchita Jorge that her own niece, thirteen-year-old Lorraine Llana, had actually managed to shake the President's hand as he
leaned out of his automobile. Lorraine would never forget it. At El
Centro Español, the old men went on playing dominoes as they had played
them since the time of Vicente Martínez Ybor, but they took time out
to agree that the nation's leader was a man of much heart, he wanted to
help the Cubans, and he would not forget the workers of America. Soon,
doubtless, there would be more jobs in the cigar factories, those tall
buildings whose slatted windows were an Ybor City trademark. In the
restaurants along Ybor City's main boulevard, Cuervo's and Las Novedades and La Columbia, lunchers sipped their bean soup with satisfaction and went over the events of John Kennedy's Tampa pilgrimage in
happily reminiscent detail. The men all thought everything had been perfect, but their wives were disappointed even though one of them had
stretched out to touch the President and nobody had stopped her. If only
Jacqueline had come! Then the women could have seen her before them
with her couturier sleeveless dresses and bouffant dark hair. Maybe they
could have touched her, too, and it would have been fascinating to see
face-to-face if she really was as beautiful as the newspapers and Jackie
magazines said she was.

But Jacqueline Kennedy was preparing for her husband's next trip
and the first motorcade after the one from which he had seen the Hills-
borough River and had crossed blue green Tampa Bay. At MacDill Air
Force Base the band had played *Hail to the Chief* so stirringly; White
House servants were reading all about it. Texas had good bands too. On
Friday the Kennedys were due in Dallas.

31

Strangers
in a Strange Land

Most people who live on the Suncoast are passionately devoted to it. The star of the show, of course, is nature, whether it means arching porpoises in the bay or gaudily transient goldfinches up the river near the Hillsborough River State Park. But there are, too, people for whom nature is not enough. You cannot wake up and decide, on impulse, to spend the day seeing Picassos and Monets. The concerts of the Florida Gulf Coast Symphony are thriftily rationed. Culture is a road show, not a constant.

On Saturday, August 12, 1967, an item was buried deep in the back pages of the *St. Petersburg Times:*

> Death of Composer Blamed on Overdose
>
> An autopsy has revealed that Czechoslovak composer Jaromir Weinberger, 71, who resided at 32 45th Street South, died of an overdose of several kinds of sleeping pills and tranquilizing drugs, according to Assistant Medical Examiner Dr. John J. Shinner. He estimated the time of death to be 8:30 P.M. Tuesday.

The *New York Times* obituary column was even briefer:

> WEINBERGER, JAROMIR. We record with deep sorrow our beloved member and colleague Jaromir Weinberger on August 8 in Florida.
>
> Stanley Adams, President
> ASCAP

There was also a painfully short editorial paragraph. Jaromir Weinberger had long since ceased to be news.

Yet once he had been the toast of musical Europe. His first opera, *Schwanda the Bagpiper,* premiered in 1927, had been a record-setting international success. Jaromir Weinberger's world then had been one of stately grey cities, sculptured stone theaters in which crystal chandeliers had glittered indoors over the heads of music lovers in chiffons and evening dress, warm cafés, temperamental singers to be placated and praising conductors. Weinberger had loved that world. *Schwanda* made him rich and famous overnight. He was a small man, balding at thirty-one, diffident in manner, who had approached the great Viennese music publishing house of Universal Edition. They hadn't thought much of *Svanda Dudák,* as the opera was originally called in Czech. Then *Svanda* was given in Prague. A critic wired Universal post haste that here was a "world success." Universal promptly sent its agent, Dr. Hans Heinsheimer, down to Czecholovakia where he installed himself with Weinberger and his wife, "little Hansi from Baden-bei-Wien," in a corner of Piscacek's Restaurant "turning the very Czech Svanda into an international palatable Schwanda" with judicious changes in the libretto. The year 1927 was prosperous in Europe; music lovers could afford to buy plenty of tickets, and also the sheet music for *Schwanda*'s Polka and Fugue that were soon being heard in New York at the Metropolitan, in Chicago and Berlin and Copenhagen and Amsterdam and Athens and Stockholm and London and wherever people clamored for a tuneful drama that combined lively counterpoint with vigorous, Dvorak-like folk melodies. Lucky Weinberger! Many a struggling composer was rueful. He was being toasted with Pilsen in the bistros, sung by students, feted by state operas and followed by reporters.

Weinberger had already been to America. Briefly he had taught composition at the Ithaca Conservatory in New York State, but he had been homesick. He was haunted by the traditions of Czech composer Bedřich Smetana, by the fields and onion-domed castles of his native Bohemia, by the dazzle of Prague and neighboring cosmopolitan capitals like Vienna, Buda, and Pest. He returned to Europe and wrote *Schwanda* in the nationalist idiom he knew best. Between 1927 and 1931 more than two thousand performances of *Schwanda* were given on the continent alone. "Schwanda is a thoroughly pleasant fellow," explained a critic:

It is quite an unproblematic work and takes no shame in working with the established means which opera has recognized since the time of *The Magic Flute* . . . The author of the text and the composer have given to the theater what belongs to the theater . . . There is the general admixture of the realistic and the fantastic which seldom fails to have its effect on the wide public. Even the grotesque and the burlesque elements have their place, without descending to caricature. Thus the taste of the time is catered to and yet the work is not burdened with features of only temporary value.

The words read very wisely. The critic thought he knew exactly what made *Schwanda* a hit. The opera was the tale of the bandit Babinsky, who tries to win pretty Dorota away from her husband Schwanda. He does not succeed. To Jaromir Weinberger the future seemed assured; he would go on writing *Schwandas* and the world would cheer them all.

But he never found the formula again. Disastrously he tried setting Schiller to music, then American Bret Harte. Experimentally he used leitmotivs not as Wagner had, to introduce a character, but to portray an emotional state. Audiences were baffled and cold. Reviews were disasters. Soon Weinberger was being performed less and less. In the late 1930s he was living in Czech Sudetenland, and when Hitler invaded it he fled first to Britain and then to America. Would there be new life for American opera, since the composers of European opera were flocking to American shores? Weinberger now preposterously saw his future as a composer in the American idiom. It was a tragic mistake. He sought inspiration in Washington Irving, Lincoln, and Whitman, but he was too Czech to assimilate them. He even cast *Dixie* into "an orchestral prelude and fugue." But he soon realized that in American mass culture classical music had an insignificant place. "I cannot," he wrote an American musicologist, "be too optimistic about anything concerning America, and particularly about its music." Some variations and a fugue on an old English folksong were performed by John Barbirolli (not yet Sir John) in New York, but their vogue was brief. Weinberger lapsed into silence and retired to St. Petersburg with Hansi to brood. She became, simply, Jane. Weinberger was not a nature enthusiast. Day after day he sat in his study falling deeper into melancholia. The "terrible goddess of luck" had permanently failed him. "Poor Weinberger!" New York musicians began gossiping. "Exiled among the pensioners of a Florida pensionopolis!"

Other European composers had lived in Florida. English Frederick

Delius had found there in the 1880s the richness of black music and had taken it back to Europe with him, all his life remembering Florida rivers and gardens with poignant love. Hungarian Ernst von Dohnanyi was until 1960, the year of his death, a professor of music at Florida State University and was enchanted with so unlikely a base of cultural operations as Tallahassee, where his students were apt to greet him with "Hey, Maestro, you got on sharp socks today!" "Learn to play in the dark," he admonished them. "Florida has frequent power failures." But Jaromir Weinberger could not adjust. His defeat after the magic of *Schwanda*'s early triumph had brought him nothing but frustration and a sense of isolation no distraction could break. Where Delius would have shrugged and gone fishing, where Dohnanyi would have cheerfully given meticulous concerts in Florida's panhandle backwoods, Weinberger pined. No conductor wanted to perform him. He had become a relic, and at last he found his oblivion virtually unnoticed by a country in which he had always remained an alien. It is strange to hear the exuberant gaiety of the Polka from *Schwanda,* which Florida radio stations frequently play in his memory, and know how much at variance it is with the bitter pessimist its creator had been. Yet it was not Florida which failed him; it was the twentieth century. Nationalistic music had given way to a purer absolute music, and nobody wanted composers to sound like Dvorak any more. The success of *Schwanda* had been due to a temporary impatience on the part of the public with intellectualism. *Schwanda* was fun and undemanding. Looking back to the Victorian Age, 1927 adored him; 1967 simply didn't care. It was either addicted to acid rock or manfully ready to grapple with modern classical atonality.

Weinberger was not the only artist of international stature to seek a haven on the shores of Tampa Bay. Another knew not only the bay, along whose margins he often tramped head down with his hands in his jacket pockets, but also the river and its forests upstream. Once, in a student-frequented bar on the edge of the sprawling University of Florida campus near Temple Terrace, Jack Kerouac began declaiming redeyed over beer and bourbon at a group of youngsters who were amused. The character with the boilermaker was obviously very drunk and also very noisy. When they left they told their friends what had happened: there had been a middle-aged guy in there wearing a checkered shirt who claimed to be the inventor of the Beat Generation. What would the creator of *On the Road* and *The Dharma Bums* be doing on the fringes of the University of South Florida? Kerouac it was, though; he had moved in 1967 to St. Petersburg with his third wife, Stella, and his invalid mother, the French-Canadian *Memere* he had celebrated in his books. Whenever he got lonesome in his high-walled St. Petersburg house he crossed the bay to Tampa, where there was young life at the university. He knew every bar nearby because he was an alcoholic. In 1967 he was also, as Jaromir Weinberger had been, passé.

Kerouac, the *London Daily Mail* had once pontificated, "is one of the most vicious characters in America." *On the Road* had by then been translated into eighteen languages (according to Kerouac in his cups, forty-seven) and it had seized the fancy of a generation weary of the austerities of World War II. It had brought into currency a new language —hipster, bop, cool, dumbsaint:

> The only people for me are the mad ones, the ones who are mad to live, mad to talk, mad to be saved, desirous of everything at the same time, the ones who never yawn or say a commonplace thing, but burn, burn, burn like fabulous yellow roman candles exploding like spiders across the stars and in the middle you see the blue centerlight pop and everybody goes "Awww!"

For Kerouac the flame burned until it was quenched by whiskey and cognac and his body was taken back from the Suncoast by Stella to his native city of Lowell, Massachusetts. There he now lies in a cemetery he wrote about as early as 1950 in *The Town and the City,* his conventional first novel:

> . . . where the old cemetery sleeps, something in the soft swishing tree-leaves over the fields and stone walls tells . . . a story . . . The rosy sun slants in through the elm leaves, a fresh breeze blows through the soft grass, the stones gleam in the morning light, there's the odor of loam and grass—and it's a joy to know that life is life and death is death.

In *The Town and the City,* too, appeared Memere: "Nothing has escaped the vast motherly wisdom of this woman; she has foreseen it all, sensed everything." But had she foreseen St. Petersburg? "Oui, Jean, I do want a lil' home of my own," she often told him after she had been widowed and was living with a married daughter while he wandered from coast to coast. It was to get her "lil' home" for her that "one of the most vicious characters in America" came to a winterless bay which became, for him, the wintriest of defeats. Whenever he showed up at Haslam's Bookstore on Central Avenue—Haslam's is Florida's largest and a meeting-place of writers and readers and miscellaneous bookmen—he smelled of brandy, shouted and gesticulated, and embarrassed customers who moved gingerly away to avoid him. Even at Haslam's, where it is difficult not to make friends, he could not face the world without previously anesthetiz-ing himself into a callouness he did not fundamentally possess.

He was born in 1927, the year of *Schwanda*'s debut, in frigid Lowell and until he entered grammar school he spoke English with a French-Canadian accent. His long alienation from middle-class American society had already begun. As he grew up he found he could play football. His talent earned him attendance at the stylish Horace Mann School for Boys in New York, and subsequently a scholarship to Columbia Univer-sity, whose football coach was then the redoubtable Lou Little. During a stormy practice session Little accused Kerouac of malingering. The malingering turned out to be a broken leg. Disgusted, he abandoned Little and the team forever, flunked chemistry, and got an A in Mark Van Doren's Shakespeare class. Yet in spite of Shakespeare he was drifting spiritually, and then he dropped out of school altogether, but not before he had met an aspiring poet from Paterson, New Jersey, whose name was Allen Ginsberg, "a freshman with his ears sticking out all the time." When Kerouac ran out of rent money Ginsberg put him up in his Colum-bia dormitory, where Kerouac was discovered just before Ginsberg was expelled ("the first time") for "insubordinate behavior." Kerouac was barred from the Columbia campus, in days when such things were pos-sible, as "an unwholesome influence on the students," and the university's psychiatric pundits proceeded to diagnose gentle Ginsberg as schizo-phrenic. When Ginsberg began writing a sprawling diatribe, Kerouac suggested its title: *Howl*. Later he also suggested a title for the novel of his friend William Burroughs, renegade scion of an adding machine dynasty: *Naked Lunch*. Kerouac was good at labels. During World War II he served a brief hitch in the navy, from which he was discharged Ginsberg-like as a "schizoid personality." The schizophrenia didn't inter-fere with him in the Merchant Marine, which showed him the world. After the war he was successively a gas station attendant, railroad brake-man, ship scullion, Lowell sportswriter, script synopsizer for 20th Cen-tury-Fox in New York, soda jerk, railroad baggagehandler, "assistant furniture mover," and U.S. Forest Service fire lookout. In his railroad days he met a wild-eyed hobo named Neal Cassady who took to writing

him autobiographical letters. Kerouac began *The Town and the City.*
When it was published he was briefly hailed as a minor Hemingway and
continued to be broke. In one of Neal Cassady's letters came a forty-page
sentence which inspired him to sit down to his typewriter with a teletype
roll and begin typing *On the Road.* It was "go, go, go!" "I was a young
writer and I wanted to take off," he said later. In three weeks he finished
his saga, undeterred by a temporary delay when a dog ate the last part of
the manuscript. *On the Road*, publishers said, was awful. For seven years
the teletype wandered from editorial office to editorial office; its edges
got frayed and its margins got smudged. Finally the influence of Allen
Ginsberg, whom by now *Howl* had made famous, secured a stake from
a publisher who thought he could manage to advance Kerouac a thousand
dollars. "Don't despair, Ma! I'll take care of you whenever you need me
—just yell . . . I'm right there, swimming the river of hardships but I
know how to swim. Don't ever think for one minute that you are left
alone."

For Kerouac, the hipsters of the forties had turned into "beatsters,"
varieties hot and cool, of the fifties. "Beat" was a rural southern word
which meant tired. He had traveled in the Carolinas. "We are the Beat
Generation," he began saying. *Life* ran columns of adulation, *On the
Road* reached best-sellerdom, and the tag swept the country. In the comfortable world of Ike, Adlai, Jo Stafford, and Rosemary Clooney, Kerouac
the adventurer became a hero. "He has come in off the road," said a
friend, "and I hope he has a good set of snow tires." He was a public
personality, and it scared him. "Man, I can't make it," he complained,
"I'm cutting out. They don't know it, but I'm cutting out. I'm going to
my mother's. Always go back to my mother, always." The books he had
written while *On the Road* had been passed from hand to hand were
now published in rapid succession. Memere was in all of them, a con-
fidante, humorist, and family prophet. "You and your Buddha," she
teased him. "Why don't you stick to the religion you were born with?"
He was a Catholic, but such commercially agile gurus as California-based
Alan Watts were now writing pamplets: *Beat Zen, Square Zen, and Zen.*

Kerouac was always a Catholic, in spite of his dalliance with the
mysterious east. Writers should, he said, be "crazy dumbsaints of the
mind," but saints. One afternoon as he was praying in the Church of St.
Joan of Arc in Lowell "with tears in my eyes," he had a vision of what he
had really meant by Beat—beatific. "There's the priest preaching on

Sunday morning, all of a sudden through a side door of the church comes a group of Beat Generation characters in strapped raincoats like the I.R.A. coming in silently to dig the religion." Memere had moved to Orlando with his sister; he began shuttling between Lowell and Florida, always more terrified by his inability to find privacy yet appearing to the world as a swaggering vagabond. The crisis came when he was riding in a rail coach compartment to California. "All over America, high school and college kids thinking Jack is on the road all the time hitchhiking while there I am almost 40 years old, bored and jaded in a roomette bunk crashing across that Salt Flat." He had waited too long for a recognition that had unbalanced him by its violence. His novel *Big Sur* became the story of his breakdown, an alternation between delirium tremens and visions of the cross until he was shouting "I'm with you, Jesus, for always, thank you!" and praying that a waiting pack of devils would not seize his soul. *Big Sur* was a descent into hell; when he emerged, it was in quest of a Christian God. He had always been a political conservative, but nobody realized it when he began to mutter about the Atheistic Communist Conspiracy. People thought he had changed. "*Wanting* to vote for Eisenhower!" they exclaimed. The danger, he warned them, was "the Communist—the Jew." All of which sounded strange in the mouth of a friend of Allen Ginsberg. When royalties began to fall off, Kerouac decided publishing was controlled by "the Jewish literary mafia."

By the 1960s, Timothy Leary was stealing Kerouac's thunder. "The Beat revolution is over," said Ginsberg, soon the idol of inheriting hippies. What were hippies to think of Kerouac when he praised William F. Buckley, Jr., and wrote about the "red menace"? His "spontaneous bop prosody" was as speedily forgotten as jazz was. Kerouac, who had smoked "tons" of marijuana in his time, was horrified by acid. He decided to buy Memere her house in St. Petersburg, Florida, where she could grow flowers and relax with people her own age. He also got married a third time. ("I left one, and one left me.") Stella Sampis, whose accent and ancestry were Greek, had been a high school sweetheart. Her brother Nick operated a Lowell tavern. Kerouac took her to St. Petersburg, where he spent sun-filled days brooding about the upcoming young—"their awful 'likes' and 'like you know' and 'wow crazy' and 'a wig, man' and 'a real gas'—all this sprouting out all over America even down to high school level and attributed in part to my doing!" When he felt like it, he worked on an oil painting of the Pope. And then

Memere had a massive stroke, and he knew he and Stella couldn't leave her no matter how homesick they were for Lowell.

It was—and is—small, Memere's white concrete block house with an old-brick front, slender white columns supporting its eaves. Its awning windows were always heavily curtained. A young magnolia tree grew in the front yard, and also a few pink-starred abelia bushes. In winter the red hibiscus flowered. There was a palm tree. Kerouac had the backyard walled in with a high basket fence, and here Memere could be taken unobserved in her paralysis by passers-by. She lay still, staring up at the pines. In front of the house an Antique Shoppe streetlamp was conventional enough and so was a picture window. Only the garden wall was unusual for immaculate residential Florida, which seldom fences. Kerouac spent his days watching television with the sound turned down; on his record player blared Handel's *Messiah*. His well-manicured dwelling gave no hint to neighbors of the tragedy within. Unfortunately it was only a block from a discount liquor store; also it was near the John S. Rhodes Funeral Chapel, the Tyrone Boulevard shopping center, the Shear Delite Beauty Salon, and a Publix supermarket. The people in the markets, an Italian delicatessen, and the liquor store all got to know the chunky greying man in the checked shirt whose wife had eyes that were "sad—so awful sad, you know, so worried."

In his haunts he is remembered. "To be frank," a merchant recalls, "I didn't know who they were at all, except he looked like such a bum and she such a nice housewifey type. Not stout, you understand, but a little dumpy. He was always red-eyed and his hands shook. And at the end when I read the newspapers I went to my wife shouting 'Effie, Effie, that was no bum. My God! That was a famous man.'"

In 1968 Neal Cassady was found dead in a Mexican ditch. "I don't believe it," said Kerouac. To a reporter who stormed him in his den he shouted, "Don't try to take a picture or I'll kick your ass." Then he said, "Come on in. I'm awful lonesome." He didn't go out much; he had a "goddam hernia" and had to wear comfortable old clothes. But that was O.K. He had no place to go. He shaved when he felt like it—every couple of days. Most of the time he just sat with the curtains drawn while Stella glided noiselessly in and out as she cared for Memere, cleaned house, and cooked. "Call me Mr. Boilermaker," he told the reporter, intrepid young Jack McClintock of the *St. Petersburg Times*. "You know what I made this year? Between January and July 1? $1,770." He had been on Bill

Buckley's TV show, though—unaware, McClintock noted, that Buckley had made him look silly. "The Communist is the main enemy—the Jew." He was writing an article, *After Me the Deluge*; McClintock hadn't "the faintest notion of what it was about" when Kerouac declaimed it. There was also, of course, the anticommunist writing he planned for Sunday supplements.

After a while he no longer went to the liquor store himself. Stella went for him, and its employees began to forget the ragged-jowled man who had trembled when he reached for his wallet. On the evening of October 21, 1969, he was sitting in his darkened living room worrying about Memere, who was in St. Anthony's Hospital for treatments. The house was soundless. Hurricane Laurie was expected to hit St. Petersburg from the Gulf, the Chilean army was revolting far away, and the attorneys of Edward Kennedy were negotiating an autopsy with the family of Mary Jo Kopechne. Man had conquered the moon, Florida Shriners were convening in downtown St. Petersburg complete with tin whistles and fezzes, eight nursing homes had just failed a health inspection, and Jeane Dixon was coming to the Bayfront Center on November 5 to prophesy. Also, police motorcycles were being phased out. Perhaps Jack Kerouac was thinking of these things, perhaps of others like the words of Black Panther Eldridge Cleaver, who had just said that Kerouac was "the cultural turning point in American history" because he had written of himself

> . . . wishing I were a Negro, feeling that the best the white world had offered was not enough ecstasy for me, not enough life, not enough joy, kicks, darkness, music, not enough life.

And then Kerouac was engulfed in blinding pain. He cried out. Stella came, and knew she must take him to St. Anthony's. Outside it was very dark; Laurie's clouds had begun to roll in, hiding the stars. The road to St. Anthony's from the house on Tenth Avenue led to Ninth, past the liquor store, past the brightly lit St. Petersburg Public Library which he had never visited, past Allen's Wholesale Drugs and a pie factory and the Born Again Believers' Fellowship Sanctuary and a sleazy tourist court with pink shingles. St. Anthony's portico was studded with glaring lights. Inside were expanses of chrome and polished glass and pale green walls and fluorescence. Kerouac was in shock; he was rushed into surgery. Until midnight doctors fought for him while blood streamed from ruptured veins in his abdomen. Fifteen quarts were transfused into him and the depleted hospital blood bank began issuing radio calls for donors. When the surgery and transfusions were over, he was wheeled into the recovery room, a glucose bottle draining into him from a bracket above his stretcher. Stella was not allowed inside. Jack Kerouac died alone.

"We never really got him out of shock," a doctor explained when the reporters started coming. Stella told them, "He was a very lonely guy. He was drinking heavily the past few days." Then, with a friend who had come to be with her, she left the lobby. Memere had to be told. Outside, across the street, the lights in the Eborn School of the Dance had long since gone out. The night was complete.

"Jack Kerouac was a Catholic," Jack McClintock wrote simply. "Jack Kerouac was a writer." At the Rhodes Funeral Chapel, Stella made arrangements for a wake. Hurricane Laurie veered away from Tampa Bay. The *New York Times* composed its verdict: "Mr. Kerouac's admirers regarded him as a major literary innovator and something of a religious seer, but this estimate of his achievement never gained wide acceptance among literary tastemakers." Had not Truman Capote said Kerouac's work was "typing, not writing"? When Allen Ginsberg heard the news he went walking in the woods with fellow poet Gregory Corso and they carved Kerouac's initials into a tree.

After the wake in St. Petersburg—nobody much came—Kerouac's body was taken back to Lowell. Three hundred people attended the funeral mass, including Ginsberg and Corso. "Our hope and prayer is that Jack has now found complete liberation," said Father Armand Mousette, an old friend. "In his exquisite honesty he had the guts to live his ideas." In death he was news again; perhaps some of the people who loved him remembered the letter from Memere he had quoted in one of his novels; it went a long way toward explaining both people. It was about a cat named Tyke:

> Dear son, I'm afraid you won't like my letter because I only have sad news for you right now. I really don't know how to tell you this but Brace Up Honey, I'm going through hell myself. Little Tyke is *gone*. Saturday all day he was fine and seemed to pick up strength, but late at night I was watching TV a late movie. Just about 1:30 A.M. when he started belching and throwing up I went to him and tried to fix him up but to no *availe*. He was shivering like he was cold so I rapped him up in

a Blanket then he started to throw up all over me. And that was the last of him. Needless to say how I feel and what I went through. I stayed up til' day *break* and did all I could to revive him but it was useless. I realized at 4 A.M. he was gone so at 6 I rapped him up good in a clean blanket—and at 7 A.M. went out to dig his grave. I never did anything in my whole life so heart breaking as to bury my beloved little Tyke who was as human as you and I. I buried him under the Honeysuckle vines, the corner of the fence. I just can't sleep or eat. I keep looking and hoping to see him come through the cellar door calling MA WOW, I'm just plain sick and the weirdest thing happened when I buried Tyke, all the black Birds I fed all winter seemed to have known what was going on. Honest Son this is no lies. There was lots and lots of em flying over my head and chirping, and settling on the fence, for a whole hour after Tyke was laid to rest—that's something I'll never forget—I wish I had a camera at the Time but God and Me knows it and saw it. Now Honey I know this is going to hurt you but I had to tell you somehow. I'm so sick not physically but heart sick . . . I just can't believe or realize that my Beautiful little Tyke is no more—and that I won't be seeing him come through his little "Shanty" or Walking through the green grass. . . . P.S. I've got to dismantle Tyke's shanty, I just can't go out there and see it empty—as is. Well, Honey, write soon again and be kind to yourself. Pray the real "God."

Your old Mom.

Mawkish, over a cat? Possibly; probably. But the grief of the woman who wrote the letter and of the son who received it reveals their vulnerability. The world, even those parts of it labeled earthly paradises, is seldom kind to the vulnerable. In paradise they are strangers in a strange land.

Gregory Corso wrote a Kerouac elegy:

> Yours the eyes that saw, the heart that felt, the voice that sang
>   and cried; and as long as America shall live, though ye
>   old Kerouac body hath died, yet shall you live . . .

> The Archangel Raphael was I to you
> And I put the Cross of the Lord of Angels
> upon you . . . there
> on the eve of a new world to explore
> And you were flashed upon the old and darkling day
> A Beat Christ-Boy . . . bearing the gentle roundness of things
> insisting the soul was round not square

And soon . . . behind thee
there came a following,
the children of flowers.

Who have tried, whatever else they have done, to love. Literary tastemakers are not apt to be "crazy dumbsaints" nor ultimately, perhaps, do they make taste. The human heart is better at that. The shade of Catholic Fray Luis Cancer de Barbastro, as that of Catholic Jack Kerouac joined him on the shores of Tampa Bay, must surely have understood.

32

Operation
Birdwash

The morning of Friday, February 15, 1970, was swathed in a spiraling fog. Mournful horns blew muffled in the bay. The river looked as if it were steaming. Gulls were crying invisibly. A formless velvet softness hung over a groping world, and cars whose headlight beams dissolved inches ahead in the floating blue smoke were crawling along the arch of the Sunshine Skyway, its soaring outline unrevealed by a single beam of a sun hidden in the heights above the vastness of a dank cloud which smelled of fish and pines. Into this cloud slowly moved the bow of the S. S. *Delian Apollon*, a Greek tanker bound for the Florida Power Company plant on Weedon Island with a cargo of fuel oil almost as thick as crude. The fog showed no sign of lifting by midmorning. Skipper Demetrios Tsapelos paced his deck and then made a decision. He radioed for a pilot familiar with Tampa Bay channels as he was not. When the pilot came, he began steering warily into the Weedon Island ship channel until the ship's crew heard a harsh grating and felt an agonizing lurch that meant the *Delian Apollon* had gone aground. Sharply jagged rocks on the channel's bottom tore gaping holes in the hull, and out of it began flowing a deadly black fluid that would eventually cover more than a hundred square miles of bay and Gulf, destroying shellfish, killing marine life, and coating the feathers of birds until they died smothered by their tarry burden.

Five hundred barrels of oil flowed from the *Delian Apollon* before tugs managed to free her and help her, at noon, into a slip at the power plant where she was surrounded by styrofoam barriers to contain the still-oozing fuel. The birds began trying to ingest what weighted them down, and then their intestines burned until they died in racking convulsions. Grebes, scaup ducks, pelicans, gulls, and terns struggled in agony. As word of the spill spread, officials began hurrying to the bay's shore and wringing their hands as the black stuff widened and widened, more than one million gallons of it. Sometime during the day word got out that the Belcher Oil Company of Miami had refused the *Delian Apollon* permission to land at its own docks; the ship had had an oil spill in the West Indies, the company had learned, and its sides were still coated with sludge when it reached Miami, was rejected, and then set course for Tampa Bay. Word also began circulating that the "experienced pilot" provided for Skipper Tsapelos had never brought a ship through the Weedon Channel before, in fog or in sunlight.

During the night of the thirteenth, wind and tides spread the black film. By the morning of Saturday the fourteenth, Valentine's Day, it coated beaches, seawalls, boats, and birds all the way from Weedon Island to Point Pinellas. Hundreds of loons and ducks and mergansers began flapping desperately to reach shore only to find themselves stopped by slick barriers. At eight thirty that Saturday morning the St. Petersburg Audubon Society had scheduled a bird walk. When they met, a detachment was sent to the affected area to report on the situation. At ten o'clock the delegation reached Coquina Key, one of the areas hardest hit. What they saw had its impact in a tidal wave of pity. Everywhere people were catching oily birds. Some of the birds were docilely letting themselves be taken, as if they knew that someone wanted to help. Other birds were being scooped in dip nets from the seawalls' bases. Boy Scouts were braving the ebony water to capture more. But on Coquina Key, the volunteers who wanted to help did not know how. Some were using gasoline, some kerosene, some harsh detergents to try to free matted feathers. As the birds began dying the Audubon delegation made a swift return to report back to their Board of Directors. All Saturday night the Society began organizing what by universal consent was christened Operation Birdwash, to be started at St. Petersburg's Lake Maggiore in the morning. A woman was found who had nursed oily birds before. She suggested a bath of vegetable oil and water, then a drying with white cornmeal.

The Audubon Society notified radio and television stations of the project and by morning had received pledges of money which bought all the vegetable oil and white cornmeal locally available. By Sunday morning a tired Audubon member had arrived at Lake Maggiore with fourteen gallons of vegetable oil and fifty pounds of cornmeal in one-pound sacks. He was greeted by five other people and three dirty birds. Within an hour, however, the crowds began streaming in with willingly captive victims. The first oil and meal ran out by nine thirty, and throughout the day he made trips for more in distant towns. Everyone began washing birds: kids in beads, police, college students, plumbers, employees of the Florida Power Company who provided portable electricity by which to work at night. Oiled birds were kept in net enclosures until their turn for cleaning came. Housewives gently rubbed birds beside secretaries, Benedictine monks, veterinarians, newspaper reporters, social workers, tavern operators, society matrons, and retirees. Restaurants donated food and drink to the volunteers; truck after truck arrived laden with coffee, cola, and sandwiches. By midnight a thousand birds had been washed and sent to foster homes where they would be watched for a week. Through the damp, foggy night the operation doggedly went on. Monday was more hectic than Sunday had been. Citizens' Band radio ham operators had by then set up a communications network. Yachtsmen offered their ships and crews to pick up stranded birds. On Monday night the fog turned to rain. Someone sent in camping tents to save the supplies. Fires, a gold and orange tapestry at the lake's edge, were lit to warm the cleaned birds. Some of the birds were taken to Florida Presbyterian College laboratories away from the wet and chill. On Tuesday the Florida Game and Freshwater Fish Commission sent a tent incongruously reminiscent of Ringling Brothers Barnum and Bailey. The workers moved under it, impervious now to rain or sun. The Salvation Army arrived with a food kitchen truck which served hot meals. Snatches of conversation drifted everywhere. "What kind of a bird is this? A red-breasted merganser? God, you mean it's *red* when you get through with it?" "This is Richard Romeo from Bradenton and he's taking home seventy birds. Isn't that fantastic?" "Don't die, ducky, don't die!"

The hot meals were needed. On Tuesday a cold front moved in, and many of the weakened birds died in spite of efforts to protect them. Skippers went in search of others. By the following Sunday nearly four thousand birds had been treated. The St. Petersburg Rod and Gun Club had cleaned a thousand more. Hardest hit were the lesser scaup ducks; the Audubon Society estimated it had cleaned twenty-five hundred of this species alone.

Would the birds survive? Many would eventually succumb to liver damage and cancer, for oil on the *Delian Apollon* contained cancer-producing agents. But first, perhaps, the recovered birds would breed, and so ensure perpetuation of their kind in significant numbers on the bay. It is more than two years now since the nightmare. No one knows how successful, ultimately, Operation Birdwash was or will be, but the Audubon Society is compiling a manual of procedure for similar programs when and wherever oil spills occur as, inevitably in an industrial society, they must. Heated seal oil and coconut-oil-based soap, the Society has since discovered, are more effective and cheaper than vegetable oil.

The most moving part of Operation Birdwash, perhaps, was the array of signs left behind, falling live-oak leaves swirling by them like miniature ghosts as Lake Maggiore's trees prepared for new spring growth.

DUCK FEEDING:
Force-feed baby food vegetables or mixed greens blended in water. Ducks will eat any of the following: thick mash, dry crumbs, crackers, dog food, canned raw liver, canned fish cat food . . .

FEEDING LOONS, MERGANSERS, GREBES AND CORMORANTS:
Force-feed with finely chopped liver or raw fish. Note—feed loons *in* water! After they start regular feeding use raw shrimp, fish scraps cut in strips, and try to get live freshwater minnows if you can.

ALL BIRDS NEED PLENTY OF FRESH WATER. DON'T TRY FORCE-FEEDING WATER! KEEP YOUR BIRD OILED:
Use mineral oil or baby oil to keep feathers soft until natural oils are produced by the bird (up to five days).

EYE CARE ALL BIRDS:
We will put ointment in eyes before you take them home.

HOME CARE:
Use a drop of cod liver oil daily in eyes, or use veterinary ophthalmic ointment.

Below the last admonition appeared a cartoon duck with a speech balloon: "Murine is not for us." And who had Richard Romeo been, who had taken home seventy birds to nurse in Bradenton? Another Joe, perhaps, another lover of wild things who was determined that one individual could stem a tide of destruction?

The oil eventually disappeared from the bay's surface, though it continued its terrible work beneath. Ten million dollars' worth of damages were estimated minimal. Lawsuits proliferated: the Attorney General of Florida sued the *Delian Apollon's* owners for two million, the Humble Oil Company wanted reimbursement for loss of cargo and for cleaning up. The Florida Department of Commerce brought a two hundred and fifty million dollar suit against both the ship's owners and Humble for "damages to tourism and image." And after a year, when the oil had disappeared at last, stained seawalls kept its memory alive. So did the fallen count of birds in the bay and the waning of plants. It will be years before the ultimate damage is reckoned. Tampa Bay, say conservationists, is dying more rapidly since the catastrophe. Seventy percent of the bay's oysters perished. Probably eighty-five percent of the saved birds will go too, if they have not gone already.

Statistics are cold, even those which record the death of the first diver who tried to patch the chasm in the *Delian Apollon's* hull. Finally the ship left for Texas and embittered bay-dwellers watched it grimly as it steamed away. Only later did they realize that out of the ordeal something positive had come: man had had the courage to stand against himself. The *Delian Apollon* and Operation Birdwash had been an end and a beginning: the last of human innocence about the peril of creatures always taken for granted as a serene part of bay life, and the start of vigilance and an emotional resolve for reversal. Now, too, the people of Tampa Bay turned to the Hillsborough River. What of that? Was it, too, doomed unless new answers were found to the dilemma of man in nature? Suncoasters who had never bothered began driving to the edges of the Green Swamp and breathing with relief at its thickness, its pools, and its shadows. Here Tampa Bay had been begun because its maker the river had begun. At the back door of cities, a wilderness remained. What, exactly, did the Southwest Water Management District want to do in the Green Swamp? Even now the answers are unclear, but the question is being repeated louder. Has the upper Hillsborough a chance of being declared a Wild River? There are people on the Suncoast who have begun to move to a music which is the slow flapping of golden ibis wings in river maples and tupelos. An ibis was the sacred bird of Egypt—

Thoth, the Recorder of Human Deeds. The ibises have seen their share of deeds. Once they nested closer to the bay than they do now. Men have pushed them steadily back: Timucuans with arrows, Narváez bellowing theology on an empty wind, de Soto and Maria Celi whose men had waded in river rapids, Theodore Roosevelt on his charger, and Vicente Martínez Ybor who built a city and José Martí who sang of new pines. The bay and most of the river belong to men because they must, but still the ibises have their kingdom and men have begun turning not to devastate but to watch, perhaps to pray. In the Green Swamp where the sun rides high and five rivers begin, two of them flowing in opposite directions in the same pool humanity has been excluded. What the swamp has excluded it may also, spiritually, save.

And so the Hillsborough River and Tampa Bay flow on, bearing the Elysium dreams of a yearning America. But it is not the cargo which is fragile. Now it is the waters themselves.

Bibliography

Abel, Ruth E. *One Hundred Years in Palmetto.* Palmetto, Fla.: Palmetto Centennial Association, 1967.

Allen, John H. "Some Facts Respecting the Geology of Tampa Bay, Florida." *American Journal of Science,* Series 2., 1 (1846): 38–42.

Annual Report, Narrative Section, 1932. Dania, Fla.: Seminole Agency. Prepared by J. L. Glenn, Special Commissioner. MS.

Annual Report, Narrative Section, 1933. Dania, Fla.: Seminole Agency. Prepared by J. L. Glenn, Officer in Charge.

Arnade, Charles W. "Cattle Raising in Spanish Florida 1513–1763." *Agricultural History* 35 (1961) No. 3. Reprinted by the St. Augustine Historical Society, St. Augustine, Fla. 1965.

Atlantic and Gulf Coast Canal and Okeechobee Land Co. of Florida. *Prospectus.* Jacksonville, Fla., 1881.

Austin, Elizabeth S., ed. *Frank M. Chapman in Florida: His Journals and Letters.* Gainesville, Fla.: University of Florida Press, 1967.

Bader, Robert S. *Two Pleistocene Mammalian Faunas from Alachua County, Fla.* Bulletin, Flodida State Museum of Biological Science, v. 2. Gainesville, Fla.: University of Florida, 1957–58: 53–76.

Baily, David. *A Study of Hillsborough County's History, Legend, and Folklore, with Implication for the Curriculum.* M. A. Thesis. University of Florida, 1949.

Bain, John, Jr., ed. *Tobacco in Song and Story.* New York: H. M. Caldwell Co., 1896.

Barbour, Thomas. *That Vanishing Eden.* Boston: Little, Brown, Inc., 1944.

Barcia Carballido y Zuñiga, André Gonzalez de. *Barcid's Chronological History of the Continent of Florida.* Translated by Anthony Kerrigan. Gainesville, Fla.: University of Florida Press, 1951.

Barry, John. *Hillsborough: a Parish in the Ulster Plantation.* Belfast, Ireland: William Mullan & Son, 1965.

Basanier, Martin, ed. *L'Histoire Notable de la Floride.* Paris, 1586. Reprinted by Conseil Historique et Heraldic de France. Lyon: Les Presses de Crudan, n.d.

Beater, Jack. *Islands of the Florida Coast.* Fort Myers, Fla.: The Author, 1956.

————. *Pirates and Buried Treasure on Florida Islands.* St. Petersburg, Fla.: Great Outdoors Publishing Co., 1964.

————. *True Tales of the Florida West Coast.* Fort Myers: Workshop House, n.d.

Bellwood, Ralph. *Tales of West Pasco.* Hudson, Fla.: Albert J. Makovic, 1962.

Bennett, Charles E., ed. *Settlement of Florida.* Gainesville, Fla.: University of Florida Press, 1968.

Berner, Lewis. *The Mayflies of Florida.* University of Florida Studies, Biological Science Series, v. lv, no. 4. Gainesville, Fla., 1950.

Bethell, John A. *History of Point Pinellas.* St. Petersburg, Fla.: Great Outdoors Publishing Co., 1962.

Bishop, Ernest W., and Dee, Laurence. *Rocks and Minerals of Florida.* Florida Geological Survey, Special Publication no. 8. Tallahassee, 1961.

Bishop, Morris. *The Odyssey of Cabeza de Vaca.* New York: Century Co., 1933.

Bradford, Myrtle Taylor. *U-Le-Lah, Princess of Hir-ri-hi-gua of South Tampa Bay.* Tampa. Fla.: Tampa Women's Club, n.d.

Brinton, Daniel G. *Notes on the Floridian Peninsula.* Philadelphia: Joseph Sabin Co., 1859.

Brodkorb, Pierce. *Catalogue of Fossil Birds, Part 2-Anseriformes through Galliformes.* Bulletin of the Florida State Museum, Biological Sciences, v. 8, no. 3. Gainesville, Fla.: University of Florida, 1964.

Brooks, Jerome. *The Mighty Leaf.* Boston: Little, Brown, Inc., 1952.

Bryan, O. C. *The Soils of Florida.* State Department of Agriculture, Bulletin 42, Tallahassee, 1960.

Bullen, Ripley P. *Eleven Archaeological Sites in Hillsborough County, Florida.* Florida Geological Survey, Report of Investigations, no. 8., Tallahassee, 1952.

Butler, Pierce. *Judah P. Benjamin.* Philadelphia: G. W. Jacobs and Co., 1907.

Cálderon, Gabriel Diáz Vára. *A Seventeenth Century Letter of Gabriel Diáz Vára Cálderon, Bishop of Cuba, Describing the Indians and Indian Missions of Florida.* Translated by Lucy Wenhold. Smithsonian Miscellaneous Collections, v. 95, no. 16. Washington, D.C.: Smithsonian Institution, 1936.

Campbell, A. Stuart. *The Cigar Industry of Tampa, Fla.* n.p., 1939.

Casas, Bartolomé de Las. *The Tears of the Indians.* Translated by John Phillips. Stanford, Cal.: Stanford University Press, 1954.

Centro Español de Tampa. *Bodas de Ore.* Tampa, Fla.: Tampa Tribune Press, n.d.

Chapple, Joe Mitchell, ed. *Heart Songs Dear to the American People.* Cleveland and New York: World Publishing Co., 1950.

Charleston Courier, Jan. 3, 1838. "Arrival of the Indian Chiefs and Warriors." Jan. 6, 1838, Editorial.

Cohen, M. M. *Notices of Florida and the Campaigns.* New York: B. B. Hussey, 1836.

Collins, W. D., and Howard, C. S. *Chemical Characters of the Waters of Florida.* U.S. Geological Survey, Water Supply Paper 596, (1928): 177–233.

Committee for the Defense of Civil Rights in Tampa. *Tampa—Tar and Terror.* New York: The Committee, n.d.

Connor, Jeannette Thurber, ed. *Colonial Records of Spanish Florida.* 2 vols. De Land, Fla.: Florida Historical Society, 1925.

Conrad, T. A. "Catalogue of Shells Inhabiting Tampa Bay and Other Parts of the Florida Coast." *American Journal of Science and the Arts,* 2nd series, 2 (1846): 393–400.

Conrad, T. A. "Observations on the Geology of a Part of East Florida, with a Catalogue of

Recent Shells of the Coast." *American Journal of Science and the Arts,* 2nd series, 2 (1846): 36–48.

Cook, Bruce. *The Beat Generation.* New York: Charles Scribner's Sons, 1971.

Cooke, Wythe. "Fossil Man and Pleistocene Vertebrates in Florida." *American Journal of Science,* 5th series, 12 (1926): 441–52.

———. *The Scenery of Florida Interpreted by a Geologist.* State Department of Conservation, Geological Bulletin no. 17. Tallahassee: State Geological Survey, 1939.

Corso, Gregory. *Elegiac Feelings American.* New York: New Directions, 1970.

Covington, James W., ed. "Pirates, Indians and Spaniards: Father Escobedo's *La Florida.*" Translated by A. F. Falcones. St. Petersburg, Fla.: Great Outdoors Publishing Co., 1963.

Covington, James W. *The Story of Southwest Florida.* New York: Lewis Historical Publishing Co., 1957.

Cubberley, Frederick. *The Dade Massacre.* Washington, D.C.: Government Printing Office, 1921. 67th Congress, Department #33.

Cumming, William P. *The Southeast in Early Maps.* Princeton, N.J.: Princeton University Press, 1958.

Cushing, Frank H. "Explorations of Ancient Key-dwellers' Remains on the Gulf Coast of Florida." *Proceedings of the American Philosophical Society* 35 (1897): 329–448.

Dall, William Healey. *Contributions to the Tertiary Fauna of Florida with Especial Reference to the Miocene Silex Beds of Tampa.* Transactions of the Wagner Free Institute, v. 3, 1890.

———. *A Monograph of the Molluscan Fauna of the Orthaulax Pugnax Zone of the Oligocene of Tampa, Florida.* Smithsonian Institution Bulletin no. 90, Washington, D.C.: Smithsonian Institution, 1915.

Davis, John H. Jr. *The Ecology and Geologic Role of Mangroves in Florida.* Carnegie Institute of Washington, Publication no. 517 (1940) Papers from Tortugas Laboratory v. 32.

———. *The Natural Features of Southern Florida.* Florida Geological Survey, Bulletin no. 25, Tallahassee, n.d.

———. *The Peat Deposits of Florida.* Florida Geological Survey, Bulletin no. 30, Tallahassee, 1946.

Davis, T. Frederick. *MacGregor's Invasion of Florida.* Jacksonville, Fla.: Florida Historical Society, 1928.

Dean, Susie Kelly. *The Tampa of My Childhood.* Tampa: n.p., 1966.

Del Río, Emilio. *Yo Fui Uno de los Fundadores de Ybor City,* n.p., n.d., Tampa, Tampa Public Library.

Delanglez, Jean. *"El Río Espíritu Santo."* Edited by Thomas J. McMahon, S.T.D. New York: Catholic Historical Society, 1945.

Densmore, Frances. *Seminole Music.* Bureau of American Ethnology, Bulletin no. 161. Washington, D.C.: Smithsonian Institution, 1956.

de Soto, Hernando. "Letter Written to the Secular Cabildo of Santiago de Cuba from Espíritu Santo, Florida, July 9, 1539." *Florida Historical Quarterly* 16 (1938): 174–178.

Dictionary of National Biography 28 (1917) 1158–60 "John Lindley."

Douglas, Marjory Stoneman. *The Everglades: River of Grass.* New York: Rinehart and Co., 1947.

———. *Florida: The Long Frontier.* New York: Harper and Row, 1967.

Eldred, Bonnie; Williams, John; Martin, George T.; and Joyce, Edward. *Seasonal Distribution of Penaid Larvae-Postlarvae of the Tampa Bay Area, Florida.* State Department of Conservation, Technical Section 44. St. Petersburg Marine Laboratory, 1965.

Escalante Fontaneda, Do. *Memoir.* Translated by Buckingham Smith. Miami, Fla.: University of Miami Press, 1944.

Ewen, David. *The Complete Book of Twentieth Century Music.* New York: Prentice-Hall, 1952.

Federal Writers' Project, Florida. *Florida: a Guide to the Southernmost State.* New York: Oxford University Press, 1939.

Ferguson, G. E.; Lingham, C. W.; Love, S. K.; and Vernon, R. O. *Springs of Florida.* Florida Geological Survey, Geological Bulletin no. 31, Tallahassee, 1947.

Fewkes, J. Walter. *Preliminary Archaeological Exploration of Weedon Island, Fla.* Smithsonian Miscellaneous Collections 76, no. 13 (1924) Washington, D.C.

Florida Anthropologist, passim.

Florida Historical Quarterly, passim.

Florida Speaks Magazine, passim.

Florida Trend Magazine, passim.

Floridian Magazine, *St. Petersburg Times,* passim.

Forbes, James Grant. *Sketches, Historical and Topographical, of the Floridas.* New York: C. S. Van Winkle, 1821.

Ford, J. A., and Willey, G. R. "An Interpretation of the Prehistory of the Eastern United States." *American Anthropologist* 43 (1941): 325–63.

Frantzis, George Th. *Strangers at Ithaca.* St. Petersburg, Fla.: Great Outdoors Publishing Co., 1962.

Fuller, Herbert Bruce. *The Purchase of Florida: Its History and Diplomacy.* Cleveland: Burrows Bros. Co., 1906.

Fuller, Walter. *This Was Florida's Boom.* St. Petersburg: Times Printing Co., 1954.

Galtsoff, Paul R., ed. *The Gulf of Mexico: Its Origin, Waters, and Marine Life.* Fishery Bulletin 89, Fishery Bulletin of the Fish and Wildlife Service, v. 55. Washington, D.C.: U.S. Government Printing Office, 1954.

Gannon, Rev. Michael. *The Cross in the Sand.* Gainesville, Fla.: University of Florida Press, 1965.

Giddings, Joshua R. *The Exiles of Florida.* Columbus, Ohio: Follett Foster and Co., 1858.

Goggin, John M. "The Calusa. A Stratified Non-agricultural Society (with Notes on Sibling Marriage)" in Goodenough, Ward H., ed., *Explorations in Cultural Anthropology.* New York: McGraw-Hill, 1964: 179–220.

———. "Florida Archaeology and Recent Ecological Changes." *Journal of the Washington Academy of Sciences* 38 (1948): 225–33.

———. *Indian and Spanish—Selected Writings.* Coral Gables, Fla.: University of Miami Press, 1964.

———. "Manifestations of a South Florida Cult in Northwest Florida." *American Antiquity* 12 (1947): 273–76.

González, Mánuel Pedro. *José Martí, Epic Chronicler of the United States in the Eighties.* Chapel Hill: University of North Carolina Press, 1953.

Gray, Asa. *Scientific Papers,* vol. 2, "John Lindley." Boston: Houghton Mifflin Co., 1889.

Griffin, J. B. "The De Luna Expedition and the Buzzard Cult in the Southeast." *Journal of the Washington Academy of Sciences* 34 (1944): 299–303.

Grismer, Karl H. *The Story of St. Petersburg.* St. Petersburg, Fla.: P. K. Smith Co., n.d.

———. *Tampa.* St. Petersburg, Fla.: St. Petersburg Printing Co., 1950.

Gunter, Herman. "Ground Water Resources of Florida." *Proceedings of the Florida State Horticultural Society,* October-November 1950: 17–25.

Hackley, Richard S. *Petition to President Tyler by Richard S. Hackley Regarding his Claim to Certain Lands in Florida.* n.p., n.d.

Harcourt, Helen. *Home Life in Florida.* Louisville, Ky.: John F. Morton Co., 1899.

Harper, Roland M. *Geography of Central Florida.* From the 13th Annual Report of the Florida Geological Survey, April, 1921, Tallahassee.

Hay, Oliver P. "Descriptions of Some Mammalian and Fish Remains from Florida of Probable Pleistocene Age." *Proceedings,* U.S. National Museum, vol. 56. 1920. Washington, D.C.: Government Printing Office.

Heath, Ralph C., and Smith, Peter C. *Ground Water Resources of Pinellas County, Florida.* Florida Geological Survey Report of Investigations #12. Tallahassee, 1954.

Heilprin, Angelo. *Explorations on the West Coast of Florida.* Philadelphia: Wagner Free Institute of Science, 1887.

Heinsheimer, Hans W. *Best Regards to Aida.* New York: Alfred Knopf, 1968.

Hendley, J. A. *History of Pasco County.* n.p., n.d.

Herrero y Tordesillas, Antonio de. *The General History of the Vast Continent and Islands of America.* Translated by Captain John Stevens. London: J. Batley, 1725–26.

Hewitt, J. N. B. *Notes on the Creek Indians.* Smithsonian Institution, Bureau of American Ethnology, Bulletin 123 (1939). Washington, D.C.: Government Printing Office.

High, Stanley. *Billy Graham.* New York: McGraw-Hill, 1956.

Hrdlička, Ales. *Anthropology of Florida.* De Land: Florida Historical Society, 1922.

Ingram, Helen K. *Florida: Beauties of the East Coast.* St. Augustine and Jacksonville, St. Augustine and Indian River Railway, 1893.

Jackson, Page. *An Informal History of St. Petersburg.* St. Petersburg: Great Outdoors Publishing Co., 1962.

Jacobstein, Meyer. *The Tobacco Industry in the United States.* Columbia University Studies 26, #3, New York, 1907.

Joyce, Edwin A., and Eldred, Bonnie. *The Florida Shrimping Industry.* Board of Conservation, Florida Education Series #5, Marine Laboratory, St. Petersburg, 1966.

Kaufman, Matthew. *Color of Water in Florida Streams and Canals.* U.S. Department of the Interior, Geological Survey, Map Series #35, 1969.

Kenny, Michael, S. J. *The Romance of the Floridas.* Milwaukee: Bruce Publishing Co., 1934.

Kenworthy, Charles J. *Ancient Canals in Florida.* Smithsonian Institution, Annual Report, 1881. Washington, D.C. 1883, 105–9.

Kepner, Charles David, Jr. *Social Aspects of the Banana Industry.* New York: AMS Press, 1967.

Kerouac, Jack. *Big Sur.* New York: Farrar, Straus and Cudahy, 1962.

———. *The Dharma Bums.* New York: Viking Press, 1959.

———. *Lonesome Traveler.* New York: McGraw-Hill, 1960.

———. *On the Road.* New York: Viking Press, 1957.

———. *The Town and the City.* New York: Harcourt Brace, 1950.

Kramer, Jane. *Allen Ginsberg in America.* New York: Random House, 1969.

Krieger, Alex D. "An Inquiry into the Supposed Mexican Influences on a Prehistoric Cult in the Southern United States." *American Anthropologist* 47 (1945): 483–515.

———. "Recent Developments in the Problem of Relationships Between the Mexican Gulf Coast and Eastern United States." In Bernal, I., and Davalos, E., eds. *Los Huastecas, Los Totonacs, y Sus Vecinos.* Mexico, D.F.: Sociedad Mexicana de Antropologia, 1953.

Kunz, George F. "Gold and Silver Ornaments from Mounds of Florida." *American Antiquarian,* July, 1887. Reprint.

La Grasserie, Raoul de "Esquisse d'une Grammaire Timucua, Langue de la Floride." *Revue de Linguistique* 21 (1888): 209–34, 295–313.

Lambright, Edwin D. *Life and Exploits of Gasparilla, Last of the Buccaneers.* Tampa: Hillsborough Printing Co., 1936.

Lanier, Sidney. *Florida: Its Scenery, Climate, and History.* Philadelphia: J. B. Lippincott, 1876.

Laumer, Frank J. *Massacre!* Gainesville: University of Florida Press, 1968.

Leon, Joseph M. *The Cigar Industry and Cigar Leaf Tobacco in Florida During the 19th Century.* MA Thesis, Florida State University, 1962.

Lewton, Frederick L. "Notes on Some Wild Flowers of Central Florida." *Florida Naturalist* 23 (1950): 114–18.

Long, Durward. *Tampa During the Thirties.* Paper read for the Florida Historical Society, May 9, 1970, MS, courtesy of the author.

Lorant, Stefan, ed. *The New World: The First Pictures of America, made by John White and Jacques LeMoyne and engraved by Theodore de Bry.* New York: Duell, Sloan and Pearce, 1946.

Lowery, Woodbury. *The Spanish Settlements Within the Present Limits of the United States.* 2 vols. New York: Russell and Russell, 1959.

MacGregor, Sir Gregor. *Narrative of a Voyage to the Spanish Main in the Ship "Two Friends."* London: John Miller, 1819.

Magly, Milton Paul. *The Bell(e)s of St. Petersburg.* New York: Exposition Press, 1963.

Mahon, John K. *History of the Second Seminole War.* Gainesville: University of Florida Press, 1967.

Manach, Jorge. *Martí, Apostle of Freedom.* New York: Devin Adair, 1950.

Maria Celi, Don Francisco. *From Havana to the Port of Tampa, Year of 1757: A Journal of Surveys.* Translated by John D. Ware. MS, Museo Naval, Madrid, copy courtesy University of South Florida.

May, Stacy, and Plaza, Galo. *The United Fruit Company in Latin America.* New York: National Planning Association, 1958.

McDuffee, Lillie B. *The Lures of Manatee.* Bradenton, Fla.: B. McDuffee Fletcher, 1961. 2nd ed.

McKay, D. B. "Pioneer Florida" Series, *Tampa Tribune,* passim.

McReynolds, Edwin. *The Seminoles.* Norman: University of Oklahoma Press.

Meade, Robert Douthat. *Judah P. Benjamin: Confederate Statesman.* New York: Oxford University Press, 1943.

Menke, C. G.; Meredith, E. W.; and Wetterhall, W. S. *Water Resources of Hillsborough County, Florida.* Florida Geological Survey, Report of Investigations #25. Tallahassee, 1961.

Ministerio de Educacion, Direcion General de Cultura. Revista Cubana *Homenaje a José Martí en el Centenario de su Nacimento.* Cuba: La Habana, 1953.

Moore, Clarence B. "Certain Aboriginal Mounds of the Florida Central West Coast." Philadelphia Academy of Natural Sciences *Journal* 12 (1903).

Neill, Wilfred T. *Florida's Seminole Indians.* St. Petersburg: Great Outdoors Publishing Co., n.d.

———. "Historical Biography of Present-Day Florida." *Bulletin,* Florida State Museum, Biological Sciences, vol. 2, 175–222. Gainesville: University of Florida, 1957–58.

Núñez Cabeza de Vaca, Alvar. *The Journey of Alvar Núñez Cabeza de Vaca.* Translated by Fanny Bandelier. Chicago: Rio Grande Press, 1964.

Olsen, Stanley J. *Fossil Mammals of Florida.* Florida Geological Survey, Special Publication #6. Tallahassee, 1959.

Oviedo y Valdes, G. Fernandez de. "The Expedition of Pánfilo de Narváez." Translated and edited by Herbert Davenport. *Southwestern Historical Quarterly* 27, 28 (1923–1924).

Pent, R. F. *History of Tarpon Springs.* St. Petersburg: Great Outdoors Publishing Co., 1964.

Phillipps, P. Lee. *Notes on the Life and Works of Bernard Romans.* De Land, Fla.: Florida Historical Society, 1924.

Pizzo, Anthony P. *Tampa Town 1824–1886: The Cracker Village with a Latin Accent.* Miami: Hurricane House, 1968.

Pollock, John. *Billy Graham.* New York: McGraw-Hill, 1966.

Post, Charles Johnson. *The Little War of Private Post.* Boston: Little, Brown, 1960.

Pride, R. W.; Meyer, F. W.; and Cherry, R. H. *Interim Report on the Hydrologic Features of the Green Swamp Area in Central Florida.* Florida Geological Survey, Information Circular #26. Tallahassee, 1961.

Puri, Harbans S., and Vernon, Robert O. *A Summary of the Geology of Florida and a Guidebook to the Classic Exposures.* Florida Geological Survey, Special Publication #5 (Revised). Tallahassee, 1964.

Raisz, Erwin, and Dunkle, John R. *Atlas of Florida.* Gainesville: University of Florida Press, 1944.

Ribaut, Jean. *True Relation of the Discovery of Terra Florida.* Edited by Jeannette Thurber Connor. De Land, Fla.: Florida Historical Society, 1923.

Robbins, Thomas L. *Hillsborough River State Park Area and the Second Seminole War.* MS, n.d.

Roberts, Kenneth L. *Sun Hunting.* Indianapolis: Bobbs-Merrill, 1922.

Roberts, William. *An Account of the First Discovery and Natural History of Florida.* London: T. Jefferys, 1763.

Romans, Bernard. *A Concise Natural History of East and West Florida.* New Orleans: Pelican Publishing Co. Reprint, 1961.

Roosevelt, Theodore. *The Rough Riders.* New York: Signet Books, 1961.

Rose, R. *The Swamp and Overflowed Lands of Florida: the Disston Drainage Company and the Disston Purchase—A Reminiscence.* Tallahassee: T. J. Appleyard, 1916.

St. Petersburg Evening Independent, passim.

St. Petersburg Times, passim.

Sanger, Marjory Bartlett. *Mangrove Island.* Cleveland and New York: World Publishing Co., 1963.

Sheean, Vincent. *Oscar Hammerstein I: the Life and Exploits of an Impresario.* New York: Simon and Schuster, 1956.

Simpson, Charles Torrey. *In Lower Florida Wilds.* New York: G. P. Putnam's Sons, 1920.

———. *Out-of-Doors in Florida.* Miami, Fla.: E. B. Douglas Co., 1923.

Simpson, J. Clarence. "Report on Activities in Hillsborough County." *Second Biennial Report,* Florida State Board of Conservation: 109–16. Tallahassee, 1936.

Small, John Kunkel. *From Eden to Sahara: Florida's Tragedy.* Lancaster, Pa.: Science Press Printing Co., 1929.

———. "Plant Explorations in Florida." Reprints from *Journal of the New York Botanical Garden* 1916–1938. Florida State University Library, Special Collections.

Smith, Buckingham, ed. *Narratives of the Career of Hernando de Soto.* 2 vols. New York: Allerton Book Co., 1922.

———. "The Timuquana Language." *Historical Magazine* 2 (1858) 1–3.

Smyth, G. Hutchinson. *The Life of Henry Bradley Plant.* New York: G. P. Putnam's Sons, 1898.

Solís de Méras, Gonzálo. *Pedro Menéndez de Avilés.* Translated by Jeannette Thurber Connor. De Land, Fla.: Florida Historical Society, 1923.

Stirling, Matthew W. *Mounds of the Vanished Calusa Indians of Florida.* Explorations and Field Work of the Smithsonian Institution for 1930. Washington, D.C.: Smithsonian Institution, 1931.

Stuart, W. L. *History of Pinellas County,* Florida. St. Augustine: Record Co. Printers, 1929.

Sunshine, Sylvia (Abbie M. Brooks). *Petals Plucked from Sunny Climes.* Nashville: Southern Methodist Publishing House, 1886. 2nd edition.

Swanton, John R. *Indian Tribes of the Lower Mississippi Valley.* Bureau of American Ethnology Bulletin 43 (1911). Washington, D.C.

————. *The Indians of the Southeastern United States.* Bureau of American Ethnology Bulletin 132 (1946). Washington, D.C.

————. *Religious Beliefs and Medical Practices of the Creek Indians.* Bureau of American Ethnology Annual Report #42. Washington, D.C.: Smithsonian Institution, 1928.

————. *Social Organization and Social Usages of the Indians of the Creek Confederacy.* Bureau of American Ethnology, Annual Report #42. Washington, D.C.: Smithsonian Institution, 1928.

Tampa Magazine, passim.

Tampa Bay Planner. Tampa Bay Regional Planning Council Bulletin.

Tampa Times, passim.

Tampa Tribune, passim.

Titles and Legal Opinions Thereon of Lands in East Florida Belonging to Richard S. Hackley, Esq. Brooklyn: G. L. Birch, 1822.

Van Doren, Mark, ed. *Travels of William Bartram.* New York: Dover Publications, n.d.

Veitia Linaje, Don José. *Pasajeros a Indias.* Madrid, Compania Ibero-Americana de Publicaciones, S.A. 1930.

Vignoles, Charles. *Observations Upon the Floridas.* New York: E. Bliss and E. White, 1823.

Walker, E. T. *Report on the Shell Heaps of Tampa Bay.* Smithsonian Institution Annual Report, 1879. Washington, D.C.: Smithsonian Institution, 1880.

Ware, Captain John D. *A View of Celi's Journal of Surveys and Chart of 1757.* MS, University of South Florida, Tampa.

Wetterhall, W. S. *Reconnaissance of Sinks and Springs in West Central Florida.* Florida Geological Survey, Report of Investigations #39. Tallahassee, 1965.

Willey, Gordon R. *Archaeology of the Florida Gulf Coast.* Smithsonian Miscellaneous Collections #113. Washington, D.C.: Smithsonian Institution, 1949.

————. "A Prototype for the Southern Cult." *American Antiquity* 13 (1948) 328–30.

Williams, John Lee. *The Territory of Florida.* Gainesville: University of Florida Press, 1962.

Wilson, Charles Morrow. *Empire in Green and Gold: The Story of the American Banana Trade.* New York: Henry Holt, 1947.

Wolf, Daniel, and Fancher, Edwin, ed. *The Village Voice Reader.* New York: Doubleday, 1962.

Young, J. L., and Odum, H. T. *Productivity of Florida Shrimps.* 2nd Annual Report to Biology Branch, Office of Naval Research, Washington, D.C., 1955.

Index

399